WHILE THEY'RE
AT WAR

BOOKS BY
KRISTIN HENDERSON

DRIVING BY MOONLIGHT:
A JOURNEY THROUGH LOVE, WAR,
AND INFERTILITY

WHILE THEY'RE AT WAR:
THE TRUE STORY OF AMERICAN
FAMILIES ON THE HOMEFRONT

KRISTIN
HENDERSON

WHILE THEY'RE
AT WAR

....

THE TRUE STORY

OF AMERICAN FAMILIES

ON THE

HOMEFRONT

HOUGHTON MIFFLIN COMPANY

BOSTON · NEW YORK   2006

For information about permission to reproduce selections
from this book, write to Permissions, Houghton Mifflin Company,
215 Park Avenue South, New York, New York 10003.

Visit our Web site: www.houghtonmifflinbooks.com.

Library of Congress Cataloging-in-Publication Data
Henderson, Kristin.
While they're at war : the true story of American families
on the homefront / Kristin Henderson.
p. cm.
ISBN-13: 978-0-618-55875-9
ISBN-10: 0-618-55875-6
1. Iraq War, 2003. 2. Military spouses — United States.
3. Families of military personnel — United States. I. Title.
DS79.76.H46 2006
956.7044'3'08655 — dc22   2005013578

Printed in the United States of America

Book design by Robert Overholtzer

QUM 10 9 7 6 5 4 3 2 1

Portions of this book first appeared in different form in the *Washington Post
Magazine*: "Maneuvers," October 5, 2003; "Love & War," October 10, 2004;
"How to Write a Love Letter," February 13, 2005. Excerpts from "10 Commandments
for Homecoming for Married Marines & Sailors" are used here with the generous
permission of Commander Bryan J. Weaver, CHC, USN, and Lieutenant
Commander Richard Saul, CHC, USN.

FOR THOSE WHO SERVE OTHERS

ACKNOWLEDGMENTS

WHEN I WROTE AN ESSAY for the *Washington Post Magazine* about my husband's homecoming from the Iraq War, my agent, Sam Stoloff, asked me if I'd consider expanding it into a book.

"No way," I said. "I've had enough of staring at my own navel." I'd just finished writing a memoir about my personal journey during my husband's earlier deployment to Afghanistan following September 11.

"Actually," said Sam, "I was thinking more along the lines of something that would focus on the other military wives you mentioned in the essay." That brief glimpse of their lives was what interested him. And then I thought about the civilian neighbor who, when she found out my husband was in a war zone, exclaimed, "Wow, what is that like? Having him in harm's way?" I was the only person she knew with someone in the fight. It hit me then that most Americans no longer personally know what it's like to send someone you love to war. Since civilians are the ones who send us to war, that could be a dangerous development.

So thanks, Sam, for getting me started on this mostly untold war story. I decided to write it as an article first and began to gather research material and set up a few interviews. Then it kind of snowballed: In the end, more than a hundred people shared their experiences with me. I was aided by a dozen hardworking military public affairs officers from New York City to Fort Bragg, most especially Ellen Hart of the XVIII Airborne Corps, a military spouse herself, who never prevented me from asking a question and answered more than her fair share of my stupider ones. Public affairs officers John Gilbert, of Womack Army Medical Center, and Sergeant Joseph Healy, of the 82nd Airborne Division, also were helpful time and again, not to mention good company.

While I worked on this project, my family and friends encouraged me and put up with my long absences. In particular, my friends Kathy Moakler, with the National Military Family Association, and Marion Sakowitz, formerly with the Army Well-Being Liaison Office, patiently allowed me to pick their brains; Kathy was my human Rolodex. For the same reasons, I am also grateful to Meg Falk, Lillie Cannon, Lynn Ferguson, John and Julie Hamre, Marcelle Leahy, and Daniel Ginsburg, while Nancy Lessin, Charley Richardson, and Chuck Fager helped me connect with military spouses I might not otherwise have met.

I wound up with a lot of material. So much material that, as I began writing the article, I couldn't get a handle on it. Thanks to the patience and persistence of David Rowell, my wonderful editor at the *Washington Post Magazine*, I finally figured out how to tell the story. He continued to believe in this project when few others did. Thank you, David, for your faith in me.

By then, I could see that the full scope of this story could only be told in a book. I'll always be grateful to Deanne Urmy at Houghton Mifflin for seeing that, too, and for her thoughtful editorial guidance. But most of all, Deanne, I'm grateful to you for growing to care so much about military families. My thanks go to the whole Houghton Mifflin team for helping me tell the story of these families to the best of my ability. Thanks, too, to my writers group — Randi Einbinder, Leslie Kostrich, Rochelle Hollander Schwab, and Catherine Petrini — for their feedback and support. Many experts, such as those in the Army's office of Casualty and Memorial Affairs, devoted extra time to reviewing parts of this book for accuracy. Everything that's right about it is thanks to them; any mistakes are mine.

As I said, I began this project with a few interviews. One by one, my fellow military spouses and the people who serve military families began to entrust their parts of the story to me. Then they'd introduce me to others. They all generously gave me the gift of their experiences — many of the spouses offering up experiences filled with pain, saying, "If I can help someone else, it's worth it" — and then they'd thank *me*. Well, thank *you*, every single one of you who added to this story, those I quoted and those who provided background, everyone listed at the end of this book. It would not exist without you. Most especially, thank you, Marissa Bootes and Beth Pratt, for opening your lives to me. Thank you for your trust, your courage, your hardwon wisdom, and your unselfish hearts. I'm proud to know you both. I'm proud to know you all.

And finally, to my husband, whom I can't even begin to thank enough: Thank you for answering the call to serve. It has changed my life.

CONTENTS

WHILE THEY'RE AT WAR

CHAPTER 1

Welcome to the Sisterhood

DOES IT GET EASIER?" asked Beth Pratt.
She had a voice that was flat as the Midwestern Plains state she came from. She had a long, fragile neck and a willowy dancer's body that drooped with sadness. She had a husband in a war zone. She was asking me because, twice already, I too had waited for my husband to come home from a war — first Afghanistan, then Iraq.

I was visiting Fayetteville, North Carolina, home of the Army's Fort Bragg, when a friend said he knew a woman who needed to talk to me. He introduced me to Beth.

"This is our first deployment," she said.

Her eyes were wide and blue green and shadowed by her straight, dark hair. She gave me a level look before withdrawing her gaze and adding, "They say it's supposed to get easier but it's been four months and so far it's just been hard. When does it get easier?"

"Oh," I said, and the *oh* dragged itself into a sigh while I decided whether or not to lie. I wanted to fix it for her; I wanted to make it all right. But I knew the only thing that would make everything right would be for her husband to walk through the door right now, safe and whole in body and mind, the same man he was when he left. So in the end, I couldn't. I couldn't lie to her. When does it get easier?

"It doesn't," I said. "Wartime deployments are always hard."

"Don't tell me that," she said.

But they are, they're just so hard. Eventually you figure out ways to cope — or not. But they never get easy. A wartime deployment is always a mountain, no matter how you climb it. All I could do was tell her some of the climbing techniques I'd relied on to help manage the fear and the loneliness, and listen to her anger and bewilderment as she climbed it now herself. When Beth left, she hugged me. And I thought, *Welcome to the sisterhood.*

Over the course of her husband's deployment, while she was worrying about his survival, Beth Pratt's own survival was hanging in the balance. Though I didn't realize it at the time — no one did — Beth had begun to think about killing herself. This is her story.

I came across Marissa Bootes on the Internet. She belonged to a group of Fort Bragg wives who had formed their own private support group on-line. The first time I met Marissa in person, she had tied her long, dark hair in a ponytail. She was broad-shouldered and narrow-hipped in a black tanktop and black pants with a racing stripe down each leg. She looked faintly exotic and streamlined; she was moving fast.

She talked fast, too. "When my husband deployed, I was working sixty-plus hours a week and suddenly taking care of our five-year-old daughter by myself, and this house, and the bills, and volunteering with the Family Readiness Group for my husband's unit —" She paused long enough to light a cigarette. "I'm an overachiever." She exhaled smoke. "I was doing the Superwoman thing, I felt awesome."

I was forty-two, nearly twice her age. I saw right through that smoke she was blowing, spotted a part of my younger self through the haze. I used to get busy like that, too. When the feelings got to be too much, I'd just get too busy to feel.

The first half of the deployment, that's what Marissa did. Gave herself four hours each night to sleep, the other twenty hours devoted to constant motion, because when she took the time to think about her husband she couldn't breathe. But before this deployment ended, because of this deployment, Marissa Bootes would find herself crashing head-on into the memories of a painful past she was trying to outrun. Not only that, she would be forced to give up one dream — the career she had hoped for since she was a child — but she would make another dream come true. This is her story, too.

Anyone who watches TV has seen the familiar images from the warfront: military men and women in desert camouflage uniforms riding in Humvees, patrolling dusty streets, firing their weapons.

The homefront gets a lot less screen time — the camera swings around to focus on military families just long enough to peek through the window at the tearful goodbye and the joyful homecoming and, in between, the occasional yellow-ribbon moment. The rest of the homefront experience is hidden behind a closed door. Out of pride, or perhaps from a feeling of vulnerability, those of us who live the homefront life often feel the need to protect ourselves from anyone who has never been left behind during a deployment.

"They don't have any idea what it's like," I complained to an Army chaplain. "They just can't understand."

He looked thoughtful for a moment. Then he said, "Maybe they don't understand because we don't tell them."

So this is the story of Beth and Marissa's friends and fellow military spouses, and the chaplains, social workers, teachers, and support staff with whom they crossed paths. It's the story of the Beths and Marissas scattered across America and on military installations around the world, who, like them, hurry through their days listening for the distant sound of guns.

Both Marissa Bootes and Beth Pratt are married to junior enlisted men in the 82nd Airborne Division. Beth's husband, Private E-2 Luigi Pratt, drove Army trucks on convoys through Iraq's Sunni Triangle. On other convoys along those same roads, Marissa's husband, Specialist Charlie Bootes, manned a Mark-19 fully automatic grenade launcher.

Marissa and Beth never met while their husbands were deployed. Marissa was twenty-three when the deployment began. She grew up in foster homes, had a two-year degree under her belt, and was married to her high-school sweetheart. On the subject of the war, she had no patience for Americans protesting in the streets; it killed morale, she said, made life harder for soldiers and their families. Beth was thirty-three. She had a happy childhood, held multiple postgraduate degrees, and was newly married for the second time, with no children. As for the war, she believed it was wrong from the start. The UN weapons inspectors, it seemed to her, had been doing just fine.

Beth and Marissa didn't have much in common except for this: In the fall of 2003 they both faced the frightening challenge of their husbands' first deployments. And they knew it wasn't likely to be their last, either. Given America's increasing military commitments around the world, even if their husbands came home, they wouldn't be home to stay.

This shared experience creates a bond like sisterhood. Those of us who are married to the military may be female, or may be male — our honorary sisters. We may be white, black, or brown, young, old, Republican, Democrat, or independent. We may worship different gods or no god at all. We may be high-school dropouts or holders of advanced degrees. We may not even be officially married, may be engaged or living together or seriously dating. But at one time or another, we have all been left behind while the one we love has gone off to train for battle, or keep the peace, or wage war. Particularly for those of us who have waited for our loved ones to return from a combat zone, it's like joining a secret society — when you encounter another member of that society, not much needs to be said.

"Is your husband home?" I asked a woman I had just met at a conference of military spouses. She looked like a southern belle and talked like a trucker.

Her macho voice suddenly shrank. "No, he left two months ago. Iraq."

Tears suddenly welled in our eyes. We both ran a careful finger along the lower edge of each eye, to wipe the tears without smearing the makeup. We were at a cocktail party. You don't burst into tears at cocktail parties. For a moment, she blinked at the far distance, swallowing hard. Then she suddenly turned to me and told a deliciously dirty joke about southern belles that saved us both.

A civilian reporter once asked me, "Does it ever bother your husband that you're . . ." He fumbled for the right words. "That you're writing about the wives instead of the real story?"

The question itself speaks volumes. Despite the fact that America is once again engaged in major combat operations overseas, most Americans have only a limited grasp of what it means to go to war, and no wonder. The Persian Gulf War and the Iraq and Afghan Wars a decade later are the first major wars in America's history that have been fought without broad-based conscription to mobilize all levels of American society. Going forward, this is a potentially ominous development for our democracy. In a country of nearly three hundred million people, only two and a half million serve in the active-duty armed forces, the Reserves, and the National Guard. Only these warriors and their families are experiencing the day-to-day sacrifices, small and large, that war requires.

Yet in our American democracy, the warriors themselves don't get to decide when those sacrifices are to be made. Civilians make that decision. It's up to our civilian Congress to declare war. It's up to our civilian president to send the troops into battle. And it's up to the civilians who elect those leaders to pay attention, to make sure that the cause of the hour is worth the sacrifices being made on their behalf.

The sacrifices start as soon as a person signs an enlistment contract or accepts an officer's commission. Those who join the United States Armed Forces give up many of their constitutional rights in order to ensure that other people can continue to enjoy them. They give up their freedom of speech. Sometimes, they give up their right to live. No other institution in America wields so much power over the lives of its members. And even though their families haven't joined the military, it controls the families' lives, too.

Of course, *it* isn't really an "it." The military is more of a "them." Though we say the Army did this, or the Marine Corps did that, as if a military institution is a monolithic giant operating under the control of a single brain, in reality it's a big, messy collection of individual human beings. Some of them are military service members and some of them are civilian employees. Many of the people who provide services to military families, for instance, may work on a base but in fact work for private companies that have won contracts from the Pentagon. All these individuals — whether they wear a uniform or are a private contractor, a federal employee, or a political appointee — are the military. Some of them are very good at what they do. Some are not. All have the power to affect the lives of the military families who cross their paths.

Is my husband bothered that I don't train the spotlight on him and his combat experiences, or on the experiences of the Marines he serves, or the soldiers, sailors, and airmen who serve alongside them? Of course not. Because the men and women who go to war will tell you that the loved ones they leave behind have a profound effect on their ability to hold up under fire. These days, this reality is recognized even in official Pentagon policy. A Department of Defense philosophy statement reads:

> . . . families as well as the service member contribute immeasurably to the readiness and strength of the American military. Efforts toward improved quality of life, while made out of genuine respect and concern for service members and families' needs, also have a pragmatic goal: a United States that is militarily strong.

Military readiness is like a three-legged stool. The first leg is training, the second, equipment. The third leg is the family. If any of these three legs snaps, the stool tips over and America is unprepared to defend herself.

When our nation decides to wage war, we women and men who love America's war-fighters comfort them when they call home sounding hollow, we manage their lives while they're gone — we pay their bills, service their cars, care for their children. We're told: "If there's a problem, don't cry to your spouses, there's nothing they can do about it, it will only distract them, and where they are, distractions can be fatal." So we solve the problems ourselves. And while we're doing all that, we're waking up every morning knowing today could be the day the staff car pulls up in front of our house and two or three people in dress uniforms walk up to our door. Today could be the day our life as we know it disappears into a black hole of grief. As a result, when our warriors return, they're not coming home to the same person they left behind.

This is the war story you never hear. This is the story of what happens while they're at war.

PART I

LEAVING HOME

CHAPTER 2

The Waiting

THE BUSES WERE LINED UP at the curb and brightly lit in the rainy dark, the kind of big, gleaming, air-conditioned motor coaches that usually carry passengers in shorts with cameras around their necks for a day of sightseeing. But the passengers waiting in line to climb aboard at 2:00 A.M. here on the coast of North Carolina were in desert camouflage uniforms. They were on their way to a war.

Officially, they were headed to Kuwait. Unofficially, they were headed to Kuwait to invade Iraq. They all wore body armor and loaded gear belts and carried lumpy backpacks and gas masks, and most had slung M-16s over their shoulders — most except for my husband. He's a chaplain; he carries no weapon.

I shivered against the side of the barracks, trying and failing to stay warm and dry, my German shepherd's leash in my hand. It was early February and forty degrees and the steady rain had been falling for hours. I watched Frank, loaded down with a backpack and an equipment case in each hand, shuffle heavily forward in a line alongside one of the buses. He paused and turned toward me, his face pale in the darkness. He gave me a long look. I pushed off from the wall and hurried over, Rosie straining at the leash, tail wagging.

"Thank you for everything," he said softly.

"You're welcome," I said.

"I'm coming back."

"Yes, you are." And I held his face and kissed him. Then I backed away with Rosie and he moved on in the line, shuffling farther and farther away from me as the Marines ahead of him slowly climbed up into the bus. The rain ran off the floppy desert cover on his head. Then it was his turn. He was forty-five, more than twenty years older than most of the men around him. He huffed himself and his load up the steps. The bus's lighted windows framed him as if he were on a stage, moving down the aisle, stowing his gear, sitting down, peering out through the rain-spattered glass in my direction. I waved. I wasn't sure he could see me.

I never wanted to be a military wife. My father's family is Quaker, all the men conscientious objectors, so when I was growing up the only member of my family who'd ever served in the military was my grandfather on my mother's side, and that was way back in World War I, and then not even in the right army — he'd fought *against* America, on the German side. In my teen years, my stepfather was an Air Force reservist, but all that meant to me were the occasional weekends when he was gone to MacDill Air Force Base a couple hours away in Tampa, and two treks of my own to MacDill — once with my mother to stock up on underwear at the base's department store, called the exchange, and once to see the Thunderbirds go roaring overhead. This does not prepare one for a life married to the military.

My husband was a civilian when I married him. Thirteen years later, early in 1998, he was still a civilian, an ordained Lutheran pastor who'd taken a break from the parish to go back to school to study psychology. We were living in Washington, D.C., and I was doing freelance writing and also copyediting for a shipping magazine, which basically required me to read the entire magazine three times every week, with the result that I now knew more than I ever wanted to know about how to move anything — frozen fries, body parts, office furniture — from point A to point B. I was trying to stay awake while correcting the grammar on the finer points of logistics software when the phone rang in my cubicle.

"This is Kristin," I said.

On the other end of the line, Frank's voice began to sing, "Anchors aweigh, my boys, anchors aweigh . . ."

Long before I met him in college, Frank had been in Naval ROTC. He'd planned to be an artillery officer in the Marine Corps, which is part of the Department of the Navy. But right after he'd sweated and grunted his way through Officer Candidates School, he wound up in the hospital. Eventually he recovered, but by then he'd been given a medical discharge. He became a minister. He liked helping people. But he missed the Marines. He missed the tight-knit feeling of family, the sense that what he was doing made a tangible difference to his country. A couple of times, he explored going back in as a chaplain, but for one reason or another it never worked out.

Until now. "Oh my God," I gasped.

He'd always supported me in the pursuit of my dreams, and I did the same for him. I just hadn't expected this particular dream of his to actually come true. It didn't feel real. He didn't know yet when he'd have to report for chaplains school, nor where he'd be assigned when he was done, and I had no idea what it all meant for me, nor how I felt about it. With one exception. For the rest of that day in my cubicle, through stories about railroad backups and trucking regulations, one thought kept popping into my head: *Soon I get to quit.*

Five years after he sang "Anchors Aweigh" over the phone, and not quite forty-eight hours before he boarded that bus in the middle of the night, I came home from my morning walk with our dog, Rosie, to a message on the voicemail. It was Frank, calling from his office on board Marine Corps Base Camp Lejeune — his new unit would be leaving before dawn in less than two days. We'd been waiting for this for three weeks, ever since he'd been told another chaplain who was supposed to deploy had had a family emergency and Frank was going to Iraq in his place. Frank had just returned from Afghanistan nine months earlier, and even though he had volunteered to go to Iraq if a need came up, everyone, including us, had figured he'd get a pass on this one. He didn't, but this was what he'd signed up for: to serve the men and women who serve America.

After being in limbo for three weeks, it was strange to finally have a specific time and day when the waiting would be over. For three weeks I had been drinking up every minute together, but at the same time I had felt my chest constricting from not knowing how many minutes were left. I had thought it would be a relief to have a date. It was. But the disbelief that it was really happening was breathtaking.

I turned on the TV and watched Secretary of State Colin Powell, live at the United Nations, make the case for war. As I watched, I packed. I'd been packing up the house ever since we first got word Frank was going. I didn't know very many people here in North Carolina; I knew none of the wives in Frank's new unit. While Secretary Powell talked about Iraq's weapons of mass destruction, while I fought tears and the realization that my husband would soon be over there within range of it all, I prepared to flee to my sister's in Richmond.

I taped the Powell presentation for Frank. He came home in the afternoon, wanted me to sit with him while he watched it. I didn't really want to watch it again, but I did, his head in my lap, my fingers working the creases from his forehead. Secretary Powell's report was just as disturbing the second time around and now tedious to boot. The still room, the two of us barely moving, the TV's static talking heads, the stifling diplomatic language — I started to think, *I can't take this, I can't take this.* I wanted to get up and move, *needed* to move. Motion was always how I coped.

Then I noticed Frank's eyes were closed. "Are you falling asleep?" I asked. I was damned if I was going to sit here and watch something I didn't want to watch while he slept through it.

"Wake me up in twenty minutes," he mumbled, which really annoyed me because he always sets an alarm for twenty more minutes or asks me to wake him up and then all he does is groan and reset the alarm or ask me to come back later. Two decades ago, when I first started waking up with him, I woke up to four different alarms going off at five-minute intervals all around the room, which he'd set the night before to ensure that he got up.

Now I snapped, "Why don't you just set the alarm for an hour or two and be done with it? That way at least you'd get a nice long uninterrupted stretch of sleep instead of torturing yourself and me along with you." I got moving, loading boxes into his truck, and when I woke him twenty minutes later, sure enough, he groaned and set his alarm and I stomped out the door, off to hurl the boxes into a rented storage unit.

Two hours later we were fighting over who'd get to write the final draft of a letter we had to provide to our landlady.

"I'm writing it," I insisted.

"But you got to write the last draft."

"Because you got to write the first *and* second drafts." My voice was cold and hard. "I should get to write this one, too."

I was typing furiously when he touched my arm and said, "I'm sorry."

I melted. I was sorry, too; it was so petty, to fight over a stupid letter when we had so little time left. "I guess," I confessed, "I just want to control . . . *some*thing."

I'd just gone through most of the classic emotional phases of predeployment — disbelief, grief, and irritability, which keeps your spouse at arm's length and makes it easier to say goodbye — but instead of spreading out the phases over a couple of months, I'd compressed them all into six hours.

Now I felt close to him again, the way I'd felt for the past three weeks, except not quite. There was an edge that hadn't been there before, and for the rest of that day we swayed our way along that edge, Frank tipping between sweetly funny and distractedly abrupt, I between loving understanding and self-pitying irritation.

The next day, our last day together, I went with him to the office in the morning, where he was jolly with the Marines. We stopped in at the exchange and bought a new chain for the locket I wore the whole time he was in Afghanistan. Inside was a lock of his hair. I put it on again now. We drove to an International House of Pancakes for one of his favorite comfort foods, pigs-in-a-blanket. We went home. He repacked the same gear he'd been packing and repacking for three weeks now. We made love. We crawled under the covers to take a nap. Half an hour later, we were both still wide awake. We turned on the TV and puttered around the house to the evening news. The space shuttle Columbia had been lost the week before. After its tumbling, crumbling reentry, pieces of it were being found all over Texas. Frank lay down to try again to sleep. Instead, he started talking.

He talked about how he was still excited about going, and yet he didn't want to go. He didn't know anyone in this new unit. He didn't want to be separated from me. He didn't want to leave the dog. "For the first time," he said, "I'm starting to feel a little scared."

I was lying beside him. He turned his head on the pillow to look at me, and he said, "I think I'm afraid of the gas."

Never once, in all the years I'd known him, had he ever before admitted fear to me, not even when he left for Afghanistan after September 11, when any horror seemed possible. Once when he walked in on a burglar in a church office, he tackled the guy. Self-preservation is not his first instinct. Listening to him admit now that he was afraid scared me, made me want to cocoon him in my arms, soothe him like a child. I took his hand, as if that could keep him from leaving the imaginary safety zone of home.

After a while, he broke the silence again. "I used to think if I had become an astronaut I'd go up without hesitation. But now I don't think I would."

That surprised me, too. He'd been born the same year NASA was born. He'd grown up dreaming of space, yet now he was saying, "I used to think it was safe. But it's pretty dangerous."

He was quiet again, his thoughts far away from me. He watched the ceiling. I watched his profile. "When I was young," he said, "I thought I was immortal. I always thought I wasn't afraid of death, but maybe I am. Maybe I'm getting old, feeling my mortality. Or maybe I'm just afraid of the pain of the transition, even though I know I'm going to something better."

His religious faith has always comforted me, the doubter. "And maybe you just value this life, too," I said. "It's the only one you get."

"Yeah." He squeezed my hand.

We carried his gear out into the rain and loaded it into his truck. Rosie knew something was up; she circled us and whined, tail tucked, followed us closely as we went back in for the last load. Inside, Frank knelt to stroke her head. He sank his fingers into the fur of her ruff and looked up at me, his eyes suddenly red with tears. He said, "I don't want to leave you."

I got down and wrapped my arms around him. "You'll come back."

He took a shaky breath. "You're right. That's what I needed to hear. This won't last forever. I'll come back."

He did a final check of the house. I picked up my purse and Rosie's leash and followed him to the door. He stopped and turned to me. "Hug me," he said.

I did. Here, where it was safe, hanging onto each other, alone together, we crumbled together. When he let me go, I got myself a tissue and handed him one. We both took a steadying breath and shored ourselves up. And then Rosie and I followed him out the door.

Most families aren't there for the final departure. It doesn't matter whether the date is long-planned, like Frank's first deployment, or on short notice like this one. A lot of spouses and lovers and parents drop off the one in uniform and leave right away; many, many more don't come at all. I never understood why until that night at the barracks, while we waited in the rain for the buses. Around midnight, I overheard a young Marine ask an officer, hopefully, "Can we send our wives home now?" He was looking for a direct order so he wouldn't have to be the bad guy. For him, for most in fact, being surrounded by what you're leaving behind makes walking away from it that much harder.

The waiting is hardest if you try to talk. By now, either everything's been said, or nothing's been said; either way, now is not the time to say it. Now is the time to just *be*. If they can't simply be with the ones they love, some people want to be by themselves. Others want to be distracted by small talk with someone with whom they have nothing at stake, no past hurts, no deep longings. Someone safe — a weightlifting buddy. A smoking companion. A chaplain. Frank moved among the waiting Marines, stopping here and there to talk.

Then the buses pulled in. The waiting, the tension, it all went *pop*, and suddenly the Marines were moving around, hoisting gear, shouting, "Ooo-rah!" But as the buses muttered at the curb, as the rain pattered the pavement, as the Marines, dressed in their warmaking costumes, carrying their warmaking equipment, climbed up out of the darkness and into the lighted buses, their faces were revealed in the stark overhead light, and they were very somber and very young.

Frank peered out the window. I waved. I waved till he finally saw me and lifted his hand.

When they pulled out, just a handful of us still stood there, waving. One by one the buses roared past into the night, and we whooped, and cheered, and someone shouted, "God bless America!" The buses would take them from Camp Lejeune to Cherry Point Marine Air Station, a little over an hour up the coast, where a plane would take them to the other side of the world. The last bus roared by and turned the corner out of the parking lot. The night was quiet with the shushing beat of rain. A short, plump, middle-aged woman had been waving a farewell sign over her head with a bright smile — someone's mother, ferociously waving her sign. Now the sign sagged down by her side. She turned to the middle-aged man standing beside her, buried her face in his chest, and sobbed.

CHAPTER 3

Uncle Sam Wants You

ON MARCH 20, 2003, the forces of the U.S. Army and Marine Corps poured over the line from Kuwait into Iraq, supported by the Navy and Air Force. On April 9, American tanks rolled into Baghdad. Over the summer and into the fall, as the Marines redeployed back home, more and more units from the Army's 82nd Airborne headed to Iraq to support the occupation and fight a violent, shadowy enemy. The scenes of families saying goodbye played out over and over again, and the planes filled with men and women in desert camouflage uniforms regularly rose into the air, carrying them to the other side of the world.

Early in September, the husbands of Marissa Bootes and Beth Pratt were among those boarding the planes. Beth's husband had been in the Army a year. Marissa's husband had enlisted a year earlier than that, in 2001. She and Charlie were living together at the time, and when he came home and told Marissa he was thinking about joining the Army, she said the same thing I'd said.

"Oh my God," she said.

It was a few days after September 11. She asked him, "Why would you join *now?*" They were watching TV in the living room of their trailer in Erie, Pennsylvania. The jumbled remains of the twin towers, still hazy with smoke, weren't that far to the east. The wounded earth in the Pennsylvania field where the fourth hijacked plane had crashed was even closer, to the south. Charlie joining the Army right at the moment when the nation seemed to be under attack brought the terror into their home and plunked it right there in front of her on the coffee table.

They'd met four years earlier in eleventh-grade history, a class Charlie slept through and Marissa made A's in but rarely showed up for — it was first period and, between working and partying, first period usually came way too early for her. She fell in love with Charlie's all-American, blond good looks. He fell in love with her style. Once, he happened to wake up and open his eyes just as she walked past his desk wearing an amazingly tight pair of spandex bell-bottoms in black-and-white camouflage. The next day, she was wearing a prim sweater vest with a collar shirt. Carefree, no-rules Marissa.

He waited for her before school, leaning tough against the Coke machine. She walked over and looked up through his tough mask into his eyes, and they were unguarded and tender and blue. All of a sudden she had the strangest feeling. Her knees felt as if they'd gone liquid; the world went silent except for his breathing. She'd been with a lot of boys, cute boys like Charlie, but she'd never felt like this before. She was speechless. She was seventeen. She was hopelessly in love.

Charlie was the son of a mechanic, the son of a man whose hands were permanently stained by a life of broken-down engines. He grew up helping out at his parents' gas station garage, and he'd shower that life off his skin two and three times a day. The only good car was one that could take you, *zoom*, on a road out of Erie, a colonial lumber town that had grown into a twentieth-century industrial machine that by the century's close was grinding down. It still belched steam and soot, ships moving in and out of its docks, but the good money jobs in manufacturing were heading to Mexico and India. The paper mill was shutting down. GE was downsizing. Charlie and Marissa agreed: Erie was a dismal place to live.

Marissa was the daughter of divorced newcomers, her mother a first-generation flower child of British and German immigrants, her father a Vietnamese refugee. But the past wasn't something Marissa ever talked about much. She was already living on her own, working at the mall and modeling and competing in Hawaiian Tropic and Venus swimwear pageants. Her teachers, her aunt and uncle who kicked her out — everybody told her she was living too wild, that she was either going to wind up pregnant or dead, but she was going to show them. She was making plans to go to college. She'd been reading college-level books since the fourth grade.

"I read *Black's Law Dictionary* when I was a kid," she told Charlie. People had laughed at her — she'd been seven or eight — but she didn't care. The only constant in her life was books. Her library card was her best friend. She wanted to learn, she loved knowledge, had to know everything; knowledge was power, she firmly believed. Her mother taught her to read before kindergarten. It was one of the things her mother got right, and by the time Marissa was eight, she was reading that law dictionary. She was going to be a lawyer one day because she wanted to change a lot of laws, she wanted to change the way the child welfare system worked. "Because I have seen," she told Charlie, "time after time, personally, what it was like and where it was failing."

Charlie just looked at her with a little smile on his face and that made her nervous, so she said, laughing, "You know, I want to save the world." And he said, "I never met anybody like you."

Four months later, she was pregnant. She hated herself for proving everyone right, but in a way, she was glad it happened, because otherwise she might have wound up dead. Instead, she had to slow down and think about life, and she realized it was time to grow up.

So Marissa shifted gears. She gave birth to a girl, named her Alexis Rae Ann, and called her Lexie. She gave up on her dream of becoming a lawyer and settled for becoming a paralegal instead. She and Charlie agreed to take turns putting each other through college. He went first, studied accounting while she worked at his parents' gas station. But school had never fit him and college was just more of the same.

After a couple of semesters, he passed his turn to Marissa and went to work at a plastic assembly shop. He'd work nights and during the day Marissa's mother, who had turned out to be better at grandmothering than she ever was at mothering, would watch Lexie till Charlie woke up. Marissa kept on at the gas station while she threw herself into business college, working toward her associate's degree, studying to become a paralegal.

For a while, they crammed into a small apartment with Marissa's mother. When Lexie was two, Charlie's parents helped them buy a trailer and move out on their own. You walked into the trailer and through a door off to the right was a kitchen bright with windows and big enough to dance around in. In the living room, three of the walls were regular ugly trailer paneling, but one was a mural of etched glass. A hallway led past Lexie's bedroom, then a bathroom with an oversized tub, and then their bedroom on the end.

The trailer was twenty years old but it was quiet, except for the trains that passed nearby, in a trailer park with a few actual trees, a place where the neighbors minded their own business. Saturday nights, Marissa and Charlie would leave Lexie with Charlie's mother or sister and go clubbing with their friends at the Kingsrook Club. They'd pack in like sardines to dance and shoot pool, or get trashed and play volleyball out back. The seven-dollar annual membership and seventy-five-cent drinks fit their budget.

The rest of the week, they hung out with their neighbors in the trailer park, single guys who'd had more than one Big Mac too many, guys who'd come over, *shoosh* open a beer, and sit around laying out schemes for how they were going to make it big. One guy was going to be a professional wrestler one day, he had it all worked out. Sometimes Marissa would roll her eyes and laugh. Other times she'd worry about Charlie, that they might be rubbing off on him, and she'd remind him, "Those guys have all got Peter Pan syndrome."

By September 2001, Marissa and Charlie were saving money for a wedding the following summer. Marissa had gone shopping for a wedding dress and found the one she'd always wanted — beaded bodice, dainty straps, and a big poofy skirt like a princess, eight hundred dollars on sale. She put it on layaway. When she was little and had been passed off to yet another family, she would curl up in the dark in a strange bed in a strange house and squeeze her eyes shut and wish for a family that was hers. She imagined the mother and father and the children all playing together like in a fairy tale, her imaginary family she dreamed of having one day.

The morning of September 11, Marissa was three hundred dollars closer to owning her princess wedding dress and a couple of weeks into her second year at business school. As news of the terror attacks spread through the classrooms, the professor turned on the TV and in stunned silence they all watched the twin towers burn until the loud speaker boomed and sent everyone home.

She found Charlie awake in the back bedroom of the trailer, watching the towers fall down on TV. Over and over, the towers fell down. She and Charlie turned off the TV and went out to the living room where Lexie was playing. They hunkered down with her, the three of them cuddled together. The blue, vinyl-sided shell that sheltered Marissa and her tiny family had never felt so fragile.

A couple of days later, the TV was on again in the trailer. As Marissa and Charlie watched, firemen dug through the hazy, apocalyptic rubble in Manhattan. Men and women in uniform hugged their families goodbye, and along with other units, a Navy battle group began pushing off from ports up and down the East Coast, headed for a storm on the other side of the world — a massive aircraft carrier, a fast combat support ship, destroyers, cruisers, submarines, and three amphibious assault ships. My husband was on one of those assault ships, on his way to Afghanistan. As his ship sailed out of the port near Camp Lejeune, with camouflage-painted trucks lined up on the flight deck and young Marines leaning on the rails, a crowd of civilians about the same age as the Marines stood on the pier and waved American flags.

In the trailer in Erie, watching TV, Charlie said, "I'm thinking about joining the Army."

Marissa asked why, but really, she knew. They hadn't bought a flag, but they'd been talking about how patriotic they felt, like the whole country was in this together. She muted the TV. "Is that really what you want to do?"

"I don't know what I want to do," he said. "All I know is I'm killing myself working third shift. I'm working seventy hours a week and we're still living paycheck to paycheck." His shift started in a couple of hours and he was already dressed for work, in T-shirt and jeans. He slouched deeper into the couch. "We're not going anywhere, Marissa."

Somewhere out in the trailer park, wrestler guy was tossing another beer in the general direction of the trash and droning on about his road to fame and fortune. Beneath the chassis of their own trailer, the wheels were blocked in place. Marissa looked at Charlie and she knew he was right. She nodded. "We need to get out of this town and never come back."

They drove down to the recruiting office together. Charlie grilled the recruiter, and then while he took the placement test, Marissa grilled the recruiter some more — What would his pay be? What would he be doing? How much would he be gone? The recruiter told her every four-year tour included six months of hardship duty overseas, but the truth is recruiters can't know the answers to any of those questions. They have no crystal ball. One thing the recruiter did know: Soldiers with legal dependents receive more money for housing than soldiers without dependents. Charlie and Marissa thought about the big June wedding they had planned and decided to elope right away instead.

Charlie's mother talked them out of it. Instead they took out a loan to pay off Marissa's dress and buy a flower-girl dress for Lexie and a cake and some flowers. That November, Marissa walked herself down the aisle through the crowd in Charlie's parents' living room, because she figured she'd always done everything on her own all her life and she'd earned the right to give herself away, too.

Charlie left in February. For eight weeks, he was at Fort Jackson in

South Carolina for basic training. From there he went to Aberdeen Proving Grounds in Maryland for thirteen weeks of advanced individual training in his chosen military specialty, heating and air. The recruiter had tried to get him to opt for motor pool, but that was the last thing Charlie wanted to do. He went for heating and air, a marketable skill, even though the signing bonus was $4,000 less than the motor pool bonus. Later, once he got to Fort Bragg, the manpower decision-makers would stick him in the motor pool anyway, because that was where the Army needed him, and there he'd be, stuck with the trucks, and half the signing bonus to show for it.

But at Aberdeen, he was still a heating and air specialist, and after completing his specialty training, he headed south again, this time to airborne jump school. That was at Fort Benning in southeastern Georgia, three weeks of learning how to parachute out of airplanes. Between basic training, advanced individual training, and jump school, he was gone for most of eight months.

During that period, Lexie saw him only twice, the first time when he graduated from basic training down in South Carolina. On graduation day, Lexie orbited Charlie like he was the sun, her pale, round little face shining. As twilight came on, as she realized he was leaving her again, she wailed and clung to him, and Marissa had to peel her body from his and carry her back to the car.

Late that summer of 2002, as Charlie threw himself out of a plane into the Georgia sky, he could see the eastern horizon rolling toward the Atlantic.

Over on the coast, moss-draped live oaks brooded along marshes and lazy rivers that sheltered behind barrier islands. Moving south along the edge of the Florida peninsula, live oaks gave way to Spanish palms and dune-hugging sea grape and condo towers that crowded the beaches where surfers paddled out astride their boards.

After the sun had set, three people walked along the sand, ambling easily in shorts and T-shirts, two men and a woman, just talking — Beth Pratt and her friend David and a big-boned guy with dark hair down to his shoulders, David's friend Luigi. Beth had just met Luigi. He looked like maybe he could be the drummer in a rock band of Native Americans, or at least the roadie. But actually he was a surfer, couldn't drum a lick, and the America he'd been born in was South America, not North. When he smiled, which he did a lot, his cheeks dimpled deeply. He was thirty years old, a couple of years younger than Beth. He had lived in the

United States since he was twelve. He had a rollicking Spanish accent. He had just enlisted in the Army. He dropped Beth and David off at David's condo and drove away.

That fall Beth bought a house, her first house all her own. She practiced her drum licks, danced with her community dance troupe, and on Sundays floated in her new house's curvaceous pool instead of going to church, because ever since her divorce two years before, she hadn't been very happy with God. She worked as a nurse at the clinic in the jail. Whenever she had to wait for an inmate in the control room, and the deputies' talk turned to the war in Afghanistan and the possible war in Iraq, she would say, "Now Pearl Harbor, that was a perfect example of defending our country, I thought that was what war was for." She believed that was why America had gone into Afghanistan after September 11. But Iraq she couldn't understand.

One of the deputies was an Air Force reservist, and that got her thinking. She'd done flight nursing once to earn some extra money and she liked it — the hum of the engines as they flew through the night sky with the patient. In the help wanted pages, the Air Force was advertising for nurses. The recruiter met her for coffee when he was in the area, and he told her, "We don't get extra money or anything if we recruit you, so it's really your choice, no pressure." He gave her some pamphlets. He told her she'd go in as a first lieutenant due to her level of education, a registered nurse with multiple degrees. She figured the extra money would be nice. David's surfer friend Luigi, she recalled, had enlisted in the Army for similar reasons. He was hoping to help out his immigrant family with some steady money.

Patriotism is the second biggest reason people join the military. But it's a distant second. The number one reason is money. In 2003, the year the Iraq War began, the average brand-new private, airman, or seaman made about $15,500 a year, plus either some form of military housing or an allowance to put toward rent or a mortgage off base. Such a paycheck was small enough to qualify many junior enlisted families for the Women, Infants, and Children welfare program, or WIC. Military benefits included health care, and if they served out their enlistment period (usually four years of active duty), a little money for college as well. They'd have to serve at least twenty years to earn the right to any pension benefits; there is no such thing as vesting in the military.

People who join for that kind of money tend to come from places that lack other economic opportunities. The same also tends to be true for those who join the National Guard. Still, today's enlisted ranks do not include the extremely disadvantaged people who were occasionally pressed into service during the Vietnam conflict. Instead, the ranks are filled with the upwardly mobile working class: 96 percent graduated from high school, compared to only 84 percent of the rest of Americans.

They're more likely to describe themselves as conservative but, like civilians, they're relatively evenly divided among Republicans, Democrats, and independents. That's no longer true in the officer corps, however, where trends over the last thirty years have resulted in Republicans outnumbering Democrats eight to one.

Compared to the average American, those in the military are more likely to be following in the footsteps of a close relative who also served. They're more likely to have been raised in a hierarchical religion such as Catholicism, by a single parent, in the Old South — nearly half of all service members hail from the South, the rest from the other regions and even other countries.

A year after the Iraq War started, if you looked at the people who were laying down their lives for their country, if you looked at where they came from, you found yourself looking across America at small rural towns, at decaying urban cores and close-in suburbs past their prime, and at minority and immigrant communities. Two years into the war, the state with the most war zone deaths per capita was rural Vermont. The state with the highest rate of National Guard mobilization was multiethnic Hawaii.

In some ways, the United States military is thrillingly American — since President Truman ordered its integration in 1948, the military is the one institution in America that has come the closest to achieving Martin Luther King Jr.'s dream of rewarding people for the content of their characters, not the color of their skin. More and more people of all colors and both genders, speaking in a Babel of accents, are rising through the ranks to positions of leadership, and at a higher rate than in the civilian world. In this way, today's all-volunteer, professional military is a uniquely modern tribute to the egalitarian ideal of the American melting pot.

However, if you look at the U.S. military from a slightly different angle, it suddenly becomes as monochromatic as the armies of Europe's nineteenth-century empires. Virtually none of those who serve come from America's elite classes: business executives, politicians, academics, and celebrities — their children do not join the military. The few who do don't add up to even a statistical blip. Which makes our military even more monochromatic than imperial Europe's, because at least Europe's elite classes had a tradition of filling the ranks of the officer corps.

This wasn't always the case. Until the 1960s, America's elite saw military service as a duty of citizenship for themselves and their children. Among recent presidents, John Kennedy and George H. W. Bush both came from wealthy families and both volunteered for active-duty military service during World War II.

Vietnam changed all that. After President Johnson pushed the country much deeper into the Vietnamese conflict based on intelligence that was at best inconclusive, at worst a lie, and as General Westmoreland widened the credibility gap with inflated enemy body counts and sunny predictions that never came true, opposition to such a war grew among those in a position to know — the elite classes. College deferments enabled their children and the children of the educated middle class to escape the draft. Vietnam created an entire generation among the privileged that still mistrusts anything to do with the military.

It's true that recruiters actively target those with fewer options. But it's human nature to go where you're wanted, and today's recruiters are not wanted in America's privileged neighborhoods. There, parents who were in college during the Vietnam War now fight to evict recruiters and junior ROTC programs from their children's schools. At the college level, Reserve Officer Training Corps (ROTC) programs on the nation's elite campuses were closed down late in the Vietnam era and never restarted. In many college political science and history departments, national security specialists and military historians who want to join the faculty need not apply.

At the same time, the military's on-the-job training and educational opportunities are appealing to those who can't afford to go to college. And the military's nondiscriminatory promotion practices make minorities feel welcome — while minorities are only 20 to 25 percent of the general population, they make up 36 percent of the military. However, during the wars in Afghanistan and Iraq, African American enlistment began a dramatic drop, from nearly a quarter of new enlistees to less than 14 percent — probably because the wars were unpopular in the black community, while at the same time more opportunities were opening up in civilian society.

Traditionally, African Americans have been more likely to see the military as a job opportunity. So they often gravitate toward military specialties such as communications, the medical corps, and administration, which equip them with marketable skills. In fact, they go into administration and support two and a half times more often than do Caucasians. By contrast, young white men, who more often view a stint in the military as an adventure, are 50 percent more likely to choose the infantry and other frontline combat units. The most elite combat units — such as Air Force Pararescuemen, Navy SEALs, Marine Reconnaissance, and Army Rangers, Green Berets, and Deltas — have historically been almost all-white.

All the services have Delayed Entry Programs (DEP) that make it possible for recruits to enlist up to a year before they actually leave for basic training, which gives them time to acccomplish goals such as finishing high school. Between the day DEP recruits enlist and the day they report for training, they meet regularly with their recruiter to get in physical shape and learn such skills as saluting, marching, identifying rank, telling military time, and reciting the alpha-bravo-charlie phonetic alphabet (which the military uses to prevent confusion over sound-alike letters such as *b* and *d*, known as *bravo* and *delta*, respectively, in military-speak).

After all that studying ahead, DEP recruits enter basic training already knowing some of what they need to know. This earns them a promotion in rank, which means a small increase in pay. They also get to reserve a seat in the advanced military training program for their chosen military specialty — an advantage in jobs that have limited openings. And if a DEP recruit convinces a friend to join up, too, the recruit receives another promotion on top of the first.

In return, DEP provides the military services with more recruits. More people can join on impulse even if they're not in a position to leave for basic training right away. But until they do leave, they can still back out, though the pressure not to can be intense. Generally, all the recruit has to do is write a letter explaining why he no longer wants to join the military, send it to the recruiting station commander, and then stand his ground. To prevent that from happening, recruiters regularly bring all their DEP recruits together, not only for physical training but also for recreational activities that bond them emotionally to each other, the recruiter, and the military.

Luigi Pratt, however, wasn't interested in DEP. As soon as he signed the enlistment contract, he was ready to go.

One night just after Christmas, Beth's doorbell rang. Her sheltie, Danny, yipped a couple of times till he caught a whiff of who was on the other side of the door, and then Danny shut his mouth and his black plume of a tail waved like a flag. Beth flicked on the outside light and looked through the peephole. It was her friend David and some other guy, their heads embryonically large. She opened the door. "Hi," said David. "We were just driving around and Luigi wondered if he could see your new house."

It was David's surfer friend, except his hair was gone. Or most of it anyway. "I just got back from basic training," Luigi said, smiling. The dimples, at least, were still there.

Coming out of the blue like that, late at night, the visit was a little weird, but Beth gave them the tour. She liked having her own house, her own space. The walls had become an extension of her own skin. Sinking into the curving pool was like sinking into herself. Danny led them past the pool. She asked Luigi, "So now that you're done with basic, what happens next?"

"After the New Year, I go to AIT," he said. She asked what AIT was, and he explained it was short for "advanced individual training." "I'll be at Fort Leonard Wood in Missouri learning about trucks, maintaining them and driving them. Then jump school. After that, the recruiter said I'll get to go to Italy and drive trucks."

"Italy!" Beth said. "That sounds good."

"Sounds good to me, too!" said Luigi, and the dimples flashed. His accent gave ordinary words a sinuous rhythm. The pool's electrified, turquoise glow lit their faces from below. David was an afterthought. She and Luigi talked for an hour. Luigi loved the ocean. He'd wanted to join the Coast Guard, but the cut-off age was twenty-seven. The Navy was no good because they packed you into confined spaces with too many people for too long. He was thinking if it turned out that he liked what he was doing in the Army, he might stay in for the long term. Otherwise, after the Army he hoped to have a little money to finally go to college and become a paramedic or a firefighter. Beth had finished up her master's in forensic science. She'd graduated in nursing from Johns Hopkins, had degrees in biology and Spanish, too. She'd lived in the Dominican Republic for nearly a year to work on her Spanish. English was the language she and Luigi spoke that night, but the Spanish lay between them like the discovery of a shared past.

"Well, that was nice," she said to Danny when Luigi and David left. "Kind of strange, but nice. Too bad we'll never see him again." Luigi was in town for only a week.

The next night the doorbell rang again, and again Danny pranced at the door with his tail waving. This time it was Luigi, alone, and he was saying, "I just wanted to invite you to a New Year's Eve party tomorrow night."

Twenty-four hours later, as the party was winding down, Beth took Luigi home with her and he didn't leave again for three days, when he set out for Fort Leonard Wood. He said he'd call. She didn't believe him, but she told herself she didn't care. She told herself that three days with him had been worth it.

He called her that night from the Greyhound bus station. He sent her a love letter in Spanish, all blooming adjectives and twining, tendriled verbs and nouns. From Missouri, he called her every evening after waiting in line at an outdoor pay phone near his barracks, hunched over the receiver in the wintry night air. When Beth flew out for a weekend visit, he slipped off post without a pass. He told her he had never wanted to get married until he met her. Now he realized he couldn't live without her, wanted to be with her forever, have a family with her. Beth had never wanted to have children before, not until Luigi, but walking hand in hand with him, she found herself imagining a smaller hand in hers, a tiny person skipping between them, swinging from her hand on one side and Luigi's on the other, linking the two of them together for the rest of their lives. Sunday evening, Luigi reported back to the post, where he was yelled at and put to work cleaning things that were already clean, and Beth flew back to Florida.

Beth's parents came down from Minnesota for a visit. "Don't be surprised if I'm married the next time you see me," she told them.

A deputy she worked with at the jail said, "You know he's going to get sent off at some point, right?" The deputy was prior military.

"Yeah," she said, "I know."

"It's not an easy life." He shook his head. "I don't know that you're going to like it that much."

She wasn't sure she would either. But she was thirty-two. Her first marriage had brought her to South Florida and lasted three years. Three long years during which she'd grown smaller and smaller, curled as far away as she could get from the man she'd married, deep within herself on the couch while he stood over her yelling and blaming, or pressed away from him in the front seat of their car while he slammed on the brakes at seventy miles an hour, still yelling and blaming. She knew from experience how hard it was to find somebody you love who actually loves you back. She wasn't willing to give that up.

"You know what?" she said to the deputy. "I love him. And I got to do it. I got to marry him. I have to. Besides, he's got less than four years left on his enlistment. Anything can be gotten through for less than four years."

The following month, as Luigi was nearing the end of AIT, American cruise missiles and precision-guided bombs pounded Baghdad. It was March 2003. American television broadcast the terrible, strangely beautiful explosions live.

The next night, bulldozers with desert-camouflage paint jobs pushed through the sand berm on the Kuwaiti side of the border, filling the tank trap ditches on the other side with sand. Hundreds of U.S. Army tanks and Bradley fighting vehicles and Marine amphibious assault vehicles roared through the new gaps, crossing over the line into Iraq. Along with them went Humvees and trucks loaded with supplies, convoys that stretched for miles, long plumes of dust racing north across the desert past startled camels and herds of goats. Embedded journalists beamed the invasion to America as it happened.

Sitting in front of the TV at my sister's house in Richmond, I peered at the dust plumes and wondered which one was being kicked up by the Humvee carrying my husband.

Beth caught glimpses of the invasion on the big TV in the lobby as she entered the jail every morning. Suddenly the question of war in Iraq was much more than just an intellectual exercise. "Why can't we work with the UN?" she asked the deputies, her voice rising. "And have people go in and look for more weapons? I don't think six more months would have been all that much to ask."

A female deputy had a picture on her desk, her husband in his Marine uniform. He was already over there. They had young children. "How do you deal with it?" Beth wanted to know. The deputy shrugged. She'd done it before, was all she said. She figured she could do it again.

Beth was in the Florida room when Luigi called from jump school. "Baby, I got great news. After I finish here, I got ten days before I report to Fort Bragg." Beth silently said goodbye to her tropical paradise, opened the phone book, and dialed up an outfit by the name of "Weddings by the Sea."

Two days later, she and Luigi were married on a public deck overlooking his favorite surfing beach in front of all their friends and family who lived close enough to get there on short notice. Beth's father hadn't been able to get away, but her mother had grabbed a flight down from

Minnesota. After the minister pronounced them husband and wife, everyone spent the rest of the day sitting around Beth's pool, eating grocery-store party platters, drinking, and laughing. A FOR SALE sign would soon stand in the front yard. Beth would sell the house she loved in Florida after marrying the man she loved more. She would follow him to Fayetteville, North Carolina. She would leave behind her drum teacher and her community dance troupe and her friends. She would leave behind her life.

Fayetteville is a city of a little over one hundred thousand in the pine-studded sandhills of central North Carolina. Downtown was once infamous for its strip clubs and prostitutes and throngs of GIs. When Beth arrived, downtown was quaint and one-half renovated, one-third vacant, and always seemed like Sunday morning. The real action lies on its western edge, where the mall is, and two Wal-Marts, and chain restaurants and auto dealers and installers of auto accessories, and — as you get closer to Fort Bragg — tattoo parlors, pawn shops, gun dealers, and the relocated strip clubs. It is not a town with a community dance troupe.

What it does have is the Army's Fort Bragg ("Home of the Airborne"), which butts up against Pope Air Force Base ("We put the air in Airborne"); together they make up one of the world's largest military complexes and the area's largest employer. Bragg alone sprawls across 160,000 acres and bustles with more than 45,000 soldiers in the airborne and special forces, including the 82nd Airborne Division. That number shrinks as the post's full-time active-duty soldiers deploy and swells as some of the members of the National Guard, called up to active duty, pass through on their way overseas. Guard units may come from as close as neighboring Sampson County or as far away as Pennsylvania. They come to Bragg to train and prepare for deployment. Sometimes they stay for months, sometimes for only days.

In the piney woods west of town, there's a prefab starter home that's one of many in a neighborhood built right up against Fort Bragg. Some days, when you walk out on the back deck, the sky is polka-dotted with parachutes, airborne troopers drifting silently down to the drop zone beyond the pine trees. When they jump at night, they're invisible against the stars.

This was Marissa and Charlie's house. Inside, Marissa hung prints of lions and tigers and leopards on the walls. She placed her wedding bouquet on one of the knickknack cabinets, along with Charlie's model cars, and rows of novels, and photographs — Lexie wearing red, white, and blue in front of an American flag; and many pictures of the wedding, Marissa with her hair up, which made her look older, and Charlie with a goatee and mustache, which made him look younger than he looked now that he was clean-shaven and crewcut. He was twenty-two. Marissa was twenty-three.

Charlie wasn't making much more in the Army than he did at the plastics shop, but the benefits were better and he wasn't working seventy hours a week either. When Marissa followed him to Fayetteville, she landed her first paralegal job. It was at a small local law firm, not great money but better than the gas station. With two newly steady incomes, they bought the house. They bought a dining set on which Marissa served three-course, sit-down dinners every night. They bought a rott-weiler named Razor, a new TV, and two pillowy, mocha-colored couches, though they only used a small portion of all that couch space when the three of them snuggled together to watch cartoons.

Crowds of young soldiers like Charlie with newly steady incomes stream in and out of Fayetteville's strip malls and big chain stores. The military community pumps nearly three billion dollars into the Fayette-ville economy every year. Some retailers respond like Sears, which do-nates millions to help children with a deployed military parent go to summer camp.

Others are not so benign. Young soldiers can always find plenty of businesses happy to take their money, and when that runs out, just as happy to extend credit, lots of credit, at fat interest rates. Dozens of pay-day lenders near the post supply one- and two-week loans to soldiers liv-ing paycheck to paycheck. The typical $30 fee for a short-term $200 loan doesn't sound so bad till you calculate the annual percentage rate — a staggering 400 percent. Businesses are happy to extend credit of all kinds because they know if the service member tries to default, military reg-ulations will let them garnish the service member's nice steady wages. For the sharkier operators that cruise every military town, it's a no-lose proposition.

In a sunny office in the Center for Family Life and Religious Education on Fort Bragg, a middle-aged man wears a woodland green battle dress uniform with a black cross on the lapel, both soldier and chaplain. He has a pleasant, angular face and light brown hair, shorn very short on the sides, longish in front. You'd miss him in a crowd. He was one of the crowd once. Before Chaplain (Major) James Hartz became an Army of-ficer and chaplain, before the time even when he was a parish pastor at a church in Kentucky and a youth and education minister in Illinois, before any of that, he was an enlisted man, a military police officer here on Fort Bragg.

"I know what goes on in town," Chaplain Hartz says dryly. "Lots of people will want to connect with you — strippers, business people, who will want to connect with your paycheck. If you want to survive here you must get connected." He raises his eyebrows. "With the right people." If you ask the chaplain, he'll recommend women's groups for Protestants and Catholics, Bible studies, and youth programs. Not the strip clubs and not the strip malls.

Across the street from Hartz's office, the staff at Army Community Services teaches money management to any soldier or spouse who takes the time to walk through the door. All the military services try to arm their young men and women through such financial literacy programs and through mass briefings about the predators circling outside the gates. Some listen. Some don't. Throughout the Army, about 10 percent of soldiers wind up seeking help every year from Army Emergency Relief, a private charitable organization. In 2003, noting that the Navy had begun mandatory classes in personal financial management for all new enlisted sailors, Army Emergency Relief began working with the Army to develop a similar course for soldiers during their advanced individual training.

After retiring from active duty, Colonel Dennis Spiegel became a deputy director at Army Emergency Relief. He's a spare man with a dry sense of humor and a clear-eyed view of the financial challenges a soldier can face. "The biggest cause of trouble," he says, "is how they handle their money. Although soldiers don't make a lot of money, if you spread it around properly, you can get by." But, he adds, "When the transmission falls out of the car, or there's a death or serious illness in the family and they need to buy plane tickets home, or when they get to a new duty station and there are no quarters available so they have to live off-post and that means two months' rent in advance and a security deposit . . . they don't have that kind of cash."

For those on active duty, deployments bring extra pay. But they can also add extra expenses, especially if the spouse who's gone is the handy type — all of a sudden the one left behind has to pay someone else to repair the car or the plumbing and at the end of the month, there's no money for food.

So Army Emergency Relief provides interest-free loans or grants. Similar charities help out members of the Air Force, Navy and Marine Corps, Coast Guard, and their families.

Marissa and Charlie avoided financial trouble because, aside from a few initial shopping trips, they left the house only to work. Charlie trained and jumped out of airplanes. Marissa carried a briefcase to an office each morning. For entertainment, the three of them piled into their big old gold Grand Prix and drove to the exchange on post. They ate pizza in the food court while Charlie emceed their own private military trivia quiz show, which consisted of Marissa squinting at the collars and shoulders of nearby soldiers and guessing their rank and specialty. She figured if Charlie made a career of this — if she was going to be an Army wife — she was going to have to know this stuff.

The rest of the time, all they did was sit at home and watch TV together. They dropped no money in clubs. For the first time in their lives, they had no grandparents to leave Lexie with on a Saturday night, no friends to go out with, and no idea where to go out *to*. Fayetteville was a foreign country. The whole steamy, cicada-shrilling, grits-eating southeastern end of the continent was an alien universe.

Four-year-old Lexie was miserable. She cried every day, "I'm going back home and live with Nanna!" She had always had an imaginary friend, the Magic Deer. Back in Erie, she would walk around with her fist out as if she were leading her imaginary deer friend by its leash. She'd struggle to get into the car with only one hand because the other hand was holding an invisible leash. She'd say, "Mom, you can't sit there, the little Magic Deer's there."

When they moved to Fayetteville, Lexie's imaginary friend's name changed to Izzy, the name of her real friend back in Erie, the daughter of Marissa's best friend. Now, whenever Marissa buckled Lexie into the car, she said, "Mom, you have to buckle Izzy up, too." Marissa would do it. And she would worry.

Among the spouses of officers, isolation tends to be less of a problem. Not long after I followed my husband to his latest duty station, the wife of his commanding officer called to take me to lunch and invited me to the next monthly gathering of the coffee group for the battalion's spouses. I also received a visit from a representative of the much larger Officers' Spouses' Club, which was open to all the officers' spouses on the entire base — officers' wives have a long tradition of organizing themselves. The club representative came to my door bearing a box of chocolates, a handful of newcomer's guides to the local area, and an application to join the club.

On the surface these clubs and groups seem to be all about eating and drinking, and occasionally conducting business meetings, raising money for military charities, or hosting bunko parties (a popular dice game I'd never heard of until my husband joined the military). But really they're all about making connections. This is how you meet people who can give you advice or step in when you need help.

There are clubs for enlisted spouses, too, but we officers' spouses benefit from the fact that there are a lot fewer of us — the service branches vary, but on average, there's one officer for every five enlisted service members, and a corresponding difference in the number of spouses. So a new officer's spouse is more difficult for her fellow officers' spouses to overlook; it's a small, tightly knit community. And it's a community with more resources — officers' spouses are likely to have more education and more income. They also benefit from greater life experience — among officers' spouses, the biggest single age group is over age forty-one, whereas the biggest age group among enlisted spouses is under twenty-five. If the officers' spouses don't mingle with the enlisted spouses, the novices among the enlisted will vastly outnumber the mentors.

Officers' spouses and enlisted spouses don't *have* to socially segregate themselves. But frequently they do. There are differences in background, perhaps a lack of common interests. And then there are old habits. In the hierarchical world of the military, officers are not supposed to form close friendships with their enlisted subordinates. There are many reasons for this, but they all boil down to the unhappy reality that, as an officer, one day you may have to order your subordinates to go die. You have to be able to make a decision like that based on the needs of the mission, not friendship. In the past, officers' wives followed suit, refusing to socialize with the wives of enlisted men. There was no life or death reason. For the most part, it was just the human need for a pecking order back in the days when a woman's social status depended on her husband.

Military spouses are free to live their own lives now. When I attended orientation classes for Navy and Marine Corps spouses, sort of a Military 101, we were told not to use our last names in class and not to discuss what positions our sailors and Marines held. You had no idea if you were talking to the spouse of an E-5 or an O-5. (Among the enlisted, the ranks range from E-1, such as a private, seaman recruit, or airman basic, to E-9, such as a sergeant major, master chief, or chief master sergeant. Among officers, the ranks range from O-1, a second lieutenant or an ensign, to O-10, a four-star general or an admiral.) The leaders of those Military 101 orientations were making a deliberate point: We spouses are not in the military, we have no rank, therefore rank is irrelevant.

So socializing between spouses in the senior and junior ranks is no longer frowned upon. When I hit it off with a young enlisted wife, I told my husband I was meeting her for dinner.

"Just don't invite me and her husband along on a regular basis," he said. Even as a chaplain, he couldn't make a habit of it with any one enlisted person. "But there's nothing wrong with you and her getting together."

And yet, not long after Marissa became the wife of an enlisted soldier, she met a junior officer's wife through an online discussion board. The officer's wife posted a question about Fort Bragg — she and her husband were moving there. Marissa's own move was still pretty fresh, so she posted an answer and shared everything she'd learned. Soon the two of them were posting back and forth.

Then the officer's wife found out Marissa was married to a mere E-3. She posted a scolding rebuke, claimed it was inappropriate for enlisted and officers' spouses to socialize, told Marissa she was out of line. Marissa was taken aback. She'd only been trying to help, but for all she knew she *had* screwed up. Yet the discussion board was open to everyone, and no other member had ever treated her that way. Just the opposite — senior wives had gone out of their way to mentor her.

Before Marissa could figure out how to respond, one of those much more senior wives on the discussion board who saw the exchange posted a rebuke of her own. *That sort of snobbery is a thing of the past,* she wrote to the junior officer's wife. *Take it somewhere else.*

Bustling between the cubicles at Army Community Services, Martha Brown has been at this business of being an Army wife for a while, though it's hard to peg her age. She has that fine-boned look that's pretty at any age, laugh lines around her mouth, dark hair swept back. She's wearing a peasant blouse and denim skirt and ornate, dangling earrings. She's easy to talk to, speaks with a slight lilt, as if her first language might be Spanish, but she reveals very little about herself. We're sitting in her office when our conversation is interrupted by a voice bursting out of her speaker phone, a staffer using the office intercom to talk to her. Martha sends her packing in a cheerful sing-song. She's kind, but she's no pushover. I've met a lot of senior wives like her. They know the ropes.

The new spouses often don't, and the learning curve is enormous. Since the early nineties, the military services have begun to try to help spouses and families adapt to military life in a more formal way with those Military 101 classes — called "Army Family Team Building" or AFTB in the Army, "LINKS" in the Marine Corps, "Compass" in the

Navy, and "Heartlink" in the Air Force. On Fort Bragg, AFTB classes are held at Army Community Services, which is housed inside what was once a sixties-era elementary school, the classrooms with their walls of jalousie windows now divided into offices and meeting rooms.

In addition to being a longtime Army wife, Martha Brown is also the manager of the deployment and mobilization program at Fort Bragg's Army Community Services. She explains that every company or battery — units of anywhere from sixty to two hundred soldiers — is supposed to have a volunteer network of spouses known as a Family Readiness Group. It includes both enlisted and officers' spouses, volunteering and socializing together. "Ideally," she says, "the Family Readiness Group would identify a new spouse and highly recommend Army Family Team Building."

AFTB and the other programs usually include guidance on how to manage the emotional phases of deployment, and teach, among other things, the history of the Army, Navy, Marines, or Air Force; what the chain of command is; and how to recognize rank insignia, read military paystubs, set up a household budget, and gain access to benefits. "But the best part," says Martha, "is the acronyms. So when that soldier comes home and starts talking about the BDUs, and the MREs, and the spouse is going whaaaa . . .?" She laughs. "AFTB can give them all the information they need to know."

Information such as: What's the difference between a brigade and a platoon? Answer: In the Army, several thousand people. The smallest element in the Army infantry is the squad, which generally consists of four to ten soldiers led by a staff sergeant. Three to four squads make a platoon, led by a lieutenant. There are three to four platoons in a company, which is led by a captain, and three to five companies in a battalion, all together five hundred to nine hundred soldiers, all led by a lieutenant colonel. Historically, a full colonel would lead a brigade of three or more combat battalions, and a major general would lead a division, usually made up of three brigades, or ten to eighteen thousand soldiers. However, during the Iraq War, the top brass at the Pentagon began reorganizing the Army, ditching its old-fashioned divisions and brigades in favor of more modern, vertically integrated "units of action."

Neither Beth nor Marissa had attended AFTB by the time their husbands deployed. Many spouses don't know such orientation programs exist; others just don't have time; and some don't see the point. I didn't. I'd heard about LINKS for a couple of years without bothering to attend because I figured the military was my husband's business, not mine, and besides I was too busy. I hadn't yet grasped that the military institution Frank had joined now controlled his life. And since my life was intimately bound up in his, it now controlled me, too, and it would be to my benefit to know a little something about it. Like Marissa said, knowledge is power.

The small, fair woman marched into the conference room for a meeting of the Family Readiness Group for Charlie Bootes's company. "All right," the woman said, "let's get this done." Her name was Jenn Marner and her husband was one of the more senior enlisted men in the company. Jenn was coleader of its Family Readiness Group.

Marissa, from her seat next to Charlie among the rows of soldiers and wives, sized her up. Marissa had been sizing people up since before she could remember; she did it without thinking. It was a survival skill. When Jenn Marner spoke, she rapped out her words then leaned back in her chair, but not a relaxed lean back, more like she was sparring, stepping in, stepping out, stepping back in again. You got the feeling she would never pull punches, that you would always know where you stood with Jenn. She seemed older and squared-away, an Army wife for years.

Marissa was right on all counts but the last: When they met, Jenn was just twenty-six, only three years older than Marissa, and she'd been an Army wife for little more than a year. Fayetteville was the first place she'd ever lived outside of Elkhart, Indiana, where she grew up eating Sunday dinner every week at her grandmother's house with the rest of her cousins and aunts and uncles. In the summer of 2001 she married for the second time, a civilian computer programmer who happened to be a reservist.

He got called up right after September 11. He made the switch to active duty, and all of a sudden Jenn was an Army wife living on the edge of Fort Bragg. She hated it. She was unexpectedly pregnant again. She was getting fat. Another Army couple they'd just met suggested they try wife-swapping, and Jenn erupted, "*Excuse* me?" For the first couple of months she escaped home to Indiana every other weekend, a fifteen-hour drive each way, back to the place where she knew who and what everyone was.

But gradually she began to notice that, living so far away, she wasn't getting caught up in her family's dramas anymore, and that was a real time- and energy saver. She realized she liked setting up a new house, meeting new people; she found herself looking forward to doing it again. Being a firm believer in mind over emotion, she gave herself an order:

Suck it up. And being a strong-willed woman who usually accomplished whatever she set out to do, she did.

Jenn moved the Family Readiness Group meeting briskly through the agenda, planning for the Christmas party, making various announcements. "I have information about other groups that you can participate in," she said. "If you're interested, talk to me after the meeting."

When the meeting was over, a young woman who looked Hispanic, or perhaps Asian, but mostly just young, walked up. Jenn was an oldest child, she'd been a working single mom, a professional. She'd always been in charge. Sometimes she'd meet these young wives and she'd feel like their mother and then she'd find out they were only a year younger. This one introduced herself, "Hi, I'm Marissa Bootes."

Marissa had never been a joiner. She'd never had the time or patience. But now she told Jenn she needed to meet other people with children. "My daughter needs some friends," she said. "We're new here and she's really homesick because she's more routine, she doesn't take change easily." She explained that Lexie was a very emotional child, very sensitive, a lot like Charlie. Marissa herself was emotional but she wasn't sensitive like they were. When bad things happened, she just let them roll off her.

Jenn rattled off a list of several groups, and looking at her up close as she laughed and talked, Marissa realized this woman wasn't as old as she had guessed. Among the list of groups Jenn mentioned was an informal support group of Fort Bragg wives who posted discussions online and got together for coffees and for play dates with the kids.

Marissa joined. At first, she'd just lurk online, but as she read what the other wives had posted on the discussion board about world events, she couldn't resist throwing her opinion out there on everything from capital punishment (for it) to religion in schools (against it). Then she tagged along with Jenn to a party the group hosted. The first thing she saw when she walked in the door was a man wearing sweatpants and no shirt, sitting on a beat-up couch. The house was on post in a neighborhood of rundown military housing that was still waiting to be renovated, with stained linoleum, stained carpet, grubby walls. She didn't know anyone except Jenn. Wrestler guy and the trailer park she thought she'd left behind were breathing down her neck. She didn't stay long.

In the end, she didn't go to any play dates either. After the party, she didn't want to and, in any case, weekdays she was at work and weekends Lexie just wanted to be with Charlie. The house began to feel like a cage, the big cats watching them from the walls.

Charlie started to hang out with some guys from his unit. He'd say, "I'm going out for a beer." In Erie it had been no big deal — sometimes they'd each go out with their own friends, give the other a few hours of breathing space. But in Fayetteville, Marissa had no friends of her own. She snapped, "What am I going to do while you're out having fun?" And then she launched herself into a fury of smoking and house cleaning till he came home.

Other times, like when he didn't jump at the opportunity to vacuum, she'd snarl at him, "Oh, you lazy bastard." She would do laundry, he would do dishes, but it seemed as if that was all he'd do, besides man the grill when they cooked out on the deck. He tried to fold the laundry because she hated folding laundry, but he didn't fold it right. What he was really good at was *making* laundry. He was the guy who couldn't drop his dirty clothes into even so much as a pile. He'd just drop them on the floor two and three times a day, still feeding his showering habit, which added up to a lot of clothes, all of them spread across the bedroom floor. Lexie was just like him. One little smudge and Lexie wanted to change clothes. A speck of dirt on her hands and she wanted to take a shower. Marissa called her "C.J.," for Charlie Junior.

At least all that new couch space meant the three of them could watch TV at the same time without having to actually touch each other. Above the TV, a grandmother clock ticked, pendulum swinging. Its hands always pointed to two o'clock, stuck, the way Marissa was starting to feel, stuck in this town with no friends and no escape, just Charlie in her face all the time.

A few miles away, Beth and Luigi rented a beige one-story, two-bedroom duplex and unloaded their Florida life into it. Luigi, bighearted and ·easygoing, made the rooms seem cozy and snug. He leaned his surfboard in a corner of the living room, between the two striped couches. Beth hung her pink toe shoes by their ribbons on the wall in the second bedroom, next to her drum kit. A print from *Lady and the Tramp*, the romantic spaghetti-eating scene, looked down on the table in the eat-in kitchen. Their compact cars sat side by side on the concrete pad out front. Out back, in a grassy no man's land that ran behind the long row of identical duplexes, Danny would joyfully chase imaginary sheep and make them both laugh.

Beth started knocking on doors, looking for a job in forensics. Nothing opened. A 2000 Rand study has found that women married to military men earn on average nearly a third less than women married to civilians. The more education the military wife has, the bigger the income gap; for those with post-graduate degrees, incomes drop by nearly half. This is undoubtedly also true for men.

According to a 2004 Rand study, frequent moves are only partly to blame. Frequent moves interrupt educations and careers. Some employers avoid hiring military spouses in the first place because they don't want to invest in someone who may soon move on. But deployments play a part, too. The demands on the time of the homefront spouse go up while the deployed spouse is away, especially if the couple has children. Even when the service member is home, military culture is not family friendly — if a child is sick at school, the service member is less likely to be allowed to leave work to pick up the child. All this makes it hard for the spouse to maintain a demanding career or pursue more education, assuming the base is located anywhere near higher educational institutions.

Wartime compounds the problem, as deployments happen more often and less predictably. While the service member is home, the spouse may have the time and energy to accept a promotion or start a new semester, but if there's a sudden deployment, she may find she can no longer juggle it all.

It's probably not possible to compensate spouses for the personal loss that goes with missed opportunities, but legislative efforts to compensate military families for the spouse income gap haven't gotten anywhere either.

Whenever the job hunt got Beth down, Luigi said, "Oh, you'll get a job, don't worry." Beth smiled, but she didn't share his optimism. In the end, she settled for a job in her original nursing specialty, labor and delivery, at Womack Army Medical Center on Fort Bragg. She came home and slumped against the kitchen counter, sighing, "I feel like I wasted the two and a half years I spent working on that forensic science degree."

"Am I going to have to tickle you?" Luigi asked. And then he did and she laughed and everything was better.

They started trying to have that baby they both wanted. They'd been married and trying to get pregnant for three months when his unit received new orders. In two months, in the beginning of September, Luigi was going to Iraq.

CHAPTER 4

Preparing for Goodbye

BEFORE SEPTEMBER 11, 2001, on any given day, four or five thousand soldiers were deployed out of Fort Bragg around the world. Two years later, that number had topped twenty-four thousand. Families say goodbye here all the time.

In fact, goodbyes are on the rise all across the services, including the Guard and Reserve.

The National Guard answers to two masters. A governor can call up the Guard units based in his or her state to respond to emergencies such as riots and natural disasters. The president of the United States can call up the Guard, too, and did during the first Gulf War in 1991. But other than that, large-scale federal mobilizations were rare between the end of World War II and September 11, 2001, both for the Guard and the Ready Reserve.

Each of the service branches have their own Ready Reserve, which consists of Individual Ready Reserve, Selected Reserve, and Inactive National Guard. At the time, reservists in the Individual Ready Reserve were on inactive status and never trained; it was easy for their families to forget they even had a connection to the military. Reservists in the Selected Reserve, on the other hand, served about as often as active National Guard members — the Guard drilled one weekend a month and two weeks a year, with the occasional call-up by their state's governor; only a few were deployed, mostly in Bosnia and Central and South America. The rest of the time, reservists and Guard members lived and worked in the civilian world.

The wars that followed September 11 brought big changes. With active-duty forces stretched thin by new commitments in Afghanistan and

Iraq, plus old commitments in Korea and elsewhere, members of the Guard and Ready Reserve began receiving orders to mobilize and deploy to fill in the gaps for as long as eighteen months. The small number of deployed Guard members quickly ballooned to 150,000, while the number of reservists on active duty tripled.

On Fort Bragg, Marissa had been hearing the deployment rumors for a while. You didn't have to be a genius to know it was coming. Every week, units were flying out of Green Ramp, the departure point over on Pope Air Force Base. Charlie and the rest of his company were coughing their way through extra training in the gas chamber, practicing land navigation, going up on more jumps. Then the possibility of a deployment hit the papers, but you can never believe the papers. Marissa focused on work. She'd just landed her dream job, high pressure but high paying, with a big law firm out of Charlotte. It wasn't *exactly* her dream job — she was still a paralegal, not a lawyer, and the job was all about real estate foreclosures, not neglected children. But she was bringing home a good salary; for the first time in her life she didn't have to worry about money. So she didn't let herself take any of the rumors to heart until the day Charlie came home and said, "We're getting deployed."

She'd watched other people experience this moment. Through Jenn and the online group, she'd met a woman named Tiffany, and Tiffany's husband was special forces. He was coming and going all the time. She had felt for Tiffany but she hadn't really been able to imagine what it was like, just that it would be sad and it would suck. And now it was happening to her and it was sad and it did suck, but it was more than that. It hurt like a punch to the gut.

"Well," Marissa said, and took a deep breath, "how long do we have?" And that was all she said, because it was going to happen whether she cried about it or not. Charlie was in the Army. She'd known this day would come. She just wanted to know what he had to take with him, what the two of them had to do, and how long they had to do it.

They had two months.

Even though they were both so busy that sex had become an afterthought, the remaining days that Charlie would be sleeping beside her suddenly seemed to Marissa rare and fragile and in need of her protection. All those petty things they'd been bickering about the last few months — none of that mattered anymore. They sat up late holding hands, trying to say all the things they needed to say before he left. They talked about their relationship and their mistakes and strong points.

They told each other, "We've always been there for each other, we've always been together on what we need for Lexie."

Honesty was everything to them. They'd had trouble trusting one another in the beginning. They had even broken up for a while. When Marissa had found out she was pregnant, she had cried alone at first. She had used birth control and on top of that she had a tilted uterus and wasn't even supposed to be able to get pregnant. She was supposed to go to college and law school because she just knew if her dreamy mother had had a good lawyer she wouldn't have wound up in prison when Marissa was nine. Marissa cried alone, because in her experience, it had never been safe to cry around other people. Crying was a sign of weakness and you couldn't trust people not to use your weakness to their advantage.

When she called and told Charlie she was pregnant, he took her to Toys-R-Us to cheer her up and they played with the bouncy balls and video games. They were at the checkout, they'd just bought something. They looked at each other. And he kissed her. It had been a long time since he'd last kissed her. Within a few days, she wouldn't be able to remember what they'd bought. But she never forgot that kiss. She never forgot, either, that when she finally let down and cried in front of him, he just held her. He held her while she cried.

"I have bad news," Luigi said quietly when he came home.

He told Beth his new unit was deploying in two months, and after that everything for her was a blur. "No," she heard herself say. "That can't be right." One thought stood out clearly in her mind: The unit of the 82nd Airborne that he'd been assigned to had only just come back from Afghanistan a couple of months before he joined it in April. She insisted, "They told you they wouldn't be going anywhere again for a while."

Maybe she paced around, maybe she didn't — she was trying to catch a glimpse of their future together, the one she'd been anticipating so happily as they'd begun trying to start a family, but that future had vanished. "The Army's so big," she said. "They shouldn't have to keep deploying the same people all the time." Maybe she was in the kitchen, or maybe it was the bedroom — the room was vague with tears. "We just got married," she said. "We just got married."

She sat down on the couch suddenly. Luigi sat beside her and took her in his arms.

"I can't believe it," she whispered.

"I can't believe it either. I mean, we knew it was going to happen."

He kissed her head on his shoulder. "I just didn't think it would be this soon."

In a handbook for Marine Corps spouses, I found a list of the standard emotional phases spouses typically go through during deployment. It's based on the work of Kathleen Vestal Logan, a marriage and family counselor and former naval officer. A textbook worst-case scenario for the predeployment period might look like this.

Spouse gets the word about deployment and enters the Anticipation of Loss Phase, during which spouse can't believe it's really going to happen. Spouse either ignores the news and goes on as if nothing has changed, or denies reality, imagining, for example, that the boat or plane will break and they'll call it all off, or that if spouse breaks her own leg and is unable to get around with the baby while on crutches, the military will say to their significant other, "Gee, why don't you stay home and help your gimpy spouse." This is a fantasy.

Spouse eventually accepts reality and decides garage reorganization project begun two years ago *absolutely must be finished* before departure date. Spouse also surprises self at least once by bursting into tears at some inappropriate moment, say, while standing in line at the credit union. Spouse is pissed off at the military for deploying people and pissed off at significant other for joining the military in the first place. Increased tension leads to increased arguing. Spouse doesn't feel like being in the same room with that asshole, much less like having sex with him or her.

As the deployment date looms, the Detachment and Withdrawal Phase begins. Spouse feels like the marriage is out of control. Spouse despairs, finds it hard to make decisions, and withdraws emotionally, which, not coincidentally, makes it easier to say goodbye when the significant other finally leaves.

This is usually not funny until you look back on it. Then you either laugh or cry, and laughing is a lot more bearable. Different people in different circumstances experience these phases to different degrees and not necessarily in the same order. A few, like Marissa, don't really experience them at all. But if a spouse knows that all of this may be coming, he or she is better able to deal with the turmoil if it does.

By the time the Iraq War began, spouses could learn about the typical emotional phases of deployment if they attended Military 101–type classes. They might also have learned about what to expect through their unit's family support group. In the Army, this was the Family Readiness

Group, which, in military fashion, was usually referred to by its acronym, the FRG. The Marines called it the Key Volunteer Network, or KVN. The Air Force called it the Key Spouse Program. The Navy and Coast Guard relied on two programs to do the same thing — what they called Family Support Groups and an appointed spouse liaison called an Ombudsman.

Each unit's family support program was usually run by the executive officer or the family readiness officer, but it was the responsibility of the commanding officer, a.k.a. the CO, because the CO was responsible for his or her unit's military readiness. If the family wasn't ready to go, neither was the service member. In the Army, the CO designated a spouse, often the CO's own spouse, to organize the unit's FRG — though, since rank is irrelevant among spouses, COs could ask any spouse if he or she would like to lead, in which case the CO's spouse might help out as a seasoned adviser. Sometimes, two spouses would share the job as coleaders, and together they would recruit a network of spouses who volunteered to pass information to and from the command, help other spouses adjust to the Army or a new post, prepare for deployment, and then get through it. Some became key callers on the phone tree, others handled fundraising, got out the newsletter, arranged for child care during meetings, or welcomed new service members and their families to the unit.

"The regulations say the FRGs have to meet on a regular basis," says Martha Brown, the deployment and mobilization manager at Army Community Services on Fort Bragg. "'Regular' is according to whatever tempo that unit is in. If they're between deployments, they might only meet every couple months. If they're in the very first weeks of the deployment, you have FRGs that are meeting on a weekly basis. After that initial weekly meeting period, they're probably going to meet on a monthly basis, just to make sure that information is getting out."

Like all volunteer efforts, some FRGs were squared away, with monthly get-togethers and energetic phone trees to pass on information from the unit and check on each other. Other FRGs withered and died. The spouses were too busy, or too alienated or shy, or just didn't want the Army in their personal business. Some soldiers would tell their spouses not to participate, because their relationship was built on control, or because they were afraid their spouses would say or do something that would embarrass them or get them in trouble. Soldiers also filled out an information form when they first joined a unit; among other things, they indicated whether or not they wanted to receive calls at home about unit activities. When one wife complained that her FRG never called her, a review of the information form revealed that her soldier had checked the box next to "Do not call."

So when Martha Brown says, "We will also come out and do some training for that FRG, about the ups and downs that they're going to be having in their emotions because of the deployment, the kinds of things that are going to be coming out of the kids," and when she says, "We give them coping-skills training," she's saying that's how it *could* be, assuming that the unit has a functioning group, assuming it occurs to someone in the group to invite such a speaker as Martha Brown, and assuming the spouses actually attend.

If spouses don't want to participate in a family support program, no one can make them. "Families didn't sign the contract, they aren't in the military," points out Jana Lord, another longtime Army wife who's also coordinator of Army Family Team Building and Army Family Action Plan programs in Europe. "They can't be ordered to do anything, even for their own good." They don't even have to go to the unit's predeployment briefing, though it's mandatory for service members.

And even if the spouses do go, there's no guarantee any of the speakers will mention the emotional phases they can expect to go through during a deployment. It's not necessarily a standard part of the briefing. As a result, many spouses stumble into their first deployment — or worse, their first *wartime* deployment — with no idea of what's coming or how to cope with it.

The room where Luigi's unit held its predeployment brief was long, harshly lit, crowded with rows of people sitting in chairs and leaning up against the walls, and hot. Beth and Luigi stood at the back near the door. It was open to the July evening outside, which was slightly less hot than inside. Two women with big hair whispered to each other. A plump woman in a T-shirt and capris bounced a sweaty, fussy toddler on her hip. A trio of small children poked at each other, their father hissing, "Cut that out!" Half the men in the room were in woodland green battle dress uniforms, or BDUs, half were in after-hours civvies — polo shirts, blue jeans, belted shorts with loafers. They all had severe haircuts.

Beth didn't know anybody in the room, not a soul. She wasn't sure she wanted to. None of the other wives looked to her like they were hurting as much as she was, none of them looked the way she felt, like she was about to come apart at the seams, which seemed literally possible in a world as surreal as the one she was living in right now. She figured maybe the other wives had gone through the previous, very recent deployment and by now were getting used to it, but she didn't want to get used to it. She armored herself in her misery and anger.

Way up front, some guy in a uniform was going on about the history of the 82nd, how it was such a great organization to be a part of. She muttered to Luigi, "This is such bullshit. Why can't they just tell us what we need to know and be done with it?"

After the pep talk, other uniforms got up and talked vaguely about deployment dates, more specifically about wills, and powers of attorney, and personal security for the wives being left behind — keep shrubs around your doors and windows trimmed, park as close to the mall entrance as you can, don't tell strangers your husband's deployed because then they'll know you're home alone. A woman in civilian clothes said something about Army Community Services and then another uniform got up and talked about pay — once Luigi arrived in Iraq, each month he could count on receiving extra money in hazardous duty and family separation pay, and he wouldn't have to pay any income tax. When Beth did the math later, all the extra money added up to $22 a day. "A little bit of extra money, so what," Beth fumed. "I'd rather have you home."

The CO talked about how his men were going to be extremely busy for the next two months, getting themselves and their equipment ready to deploy. "But we're going to try to get these guys home each day to see you as much as possible before they leave," he promised. Beth looked at Luigi, tears in her eyes. At least there would be that.

Attendance at these meetings varies between the Army, Air Force, Navy, and Marines.

Lillie Cannon has been an Army officer's wife for fifteen years. She's also an Air Force lieutenant colonel, now retired. She's a vivacious, businesslike African American woman who carries you along with her like a smiling freight train, and it doesn't even occur to you to ask where she's taking you. As we speak, the Iraq War is ongoing, and she estimates that these days 85 percent of the spouses in her husband's Army battalion come to at least a few FRG meetings.

Lieutenant Colonel Cannon states flatly, "Wartime, we get more spouses involved. We *could not* pull them together in peacetime. Whereas in the Air Force, the spouses came out during peacetime, too." In her experience, the Army's FRG meetings tend to be more social, while the Air Force's family readiness meetings provided readiness information at every event, including social ones. "The Air Force spouses saw it as getting connected, they saw the value." Then she adds, "And don't forget, frequent deployments are also a regular part of their lives in the Air Force, even in peacetime."

The Air Force, Navy, and Marine Corps all have this in common — they are expeditionary forces. Individual air wings, ships, and battalion landing teams are constantly going out and coming back. Even in peacetime, airmen patrol overseas air spaces and sailors crew ships at sea, some of which carry Marines, who are regularly deployed on standby.

The Army, on the other hand, deploys in large numbers only on an as-needed basis, such as whenever the United States invades and occupies another country. Until recently, that didn't happen all that often, so peacetime deployments were much less frequent in the Army than in the other services. (These are admittedly gross generalizations, and there are exceptions, especially in the Army's airborne divisions and special forces.)

As a result, the spouses in the expeditionary services get a lot more practice. When my husband was preparing for a peacetime deployment with the Marines, the predeployment briefing I attended was packed with the vast majority of the spouses in the battalion. The Key Volunteers, the Marines' version of a family support group, were active both during and between deployments. Later I became a Key Volunteer, or KV, in a Marine unit that never deployed, yet we were still active. We met with the CO every month, passed on information to the other spouses, planned the occasional social function, made sure families got the services they needed — the same tasks we would perform during a deployment, just less frequently.

To keep Navy and Coast Guard spouses connected, the Chief of Naval Operations established the Ombudsman program in 1970. Each naval command, such as a ship or an air squadron, has an Ombudsman, the volunteer spouse appointed by the CO. Like the KVs, the Ombudsman continues her liaison and referral work year-round, consulting with the support staff at one of the Fleet and Family Support Centers when she's faced with difficult issues. The Navy also has Family Support Groups, but usually only in deploying commands, such as the supply ship my husband was on, and mostly just for social support; they often disband between deployments. In the Navy and Coast Guard, which also deploys ships and crews to the Persian Gulf, it's the individual Ombudsmen who do the heavy lifting.

At the start of the Iraq War, the Army lacked anything like an Ombudsman to make up for low participation in many of its Family Readiness Groups. It's possible that low FRG participation was the result of the sheer size of the Army — nearly half a million soldiers in the active-duty Army shortly before the Iraq War, and nearly seven hundred thousand in the Reserves and National Guard. That's compared to fewer than 174,000 on active duty in the Marine Corps, fewer than 365,000 in the Air Force, and around 380,000 in the Navy.

My Navy experience hints that size may indeed be a factor. After the Army, the Navy is the next largest service. Before my husband left on a peacetime deployment aboard a Navy supply ship, the predeployment class for the families was held in a large theater on base that was capable of accommodating all the spouses — out of a crew of more than four hundred sailors, statistically close to half would have been married. I learned a lot at the class, and so did the couple dozen other women who bothered to show up, scattered around that big, empty theater. At least the others who didn't show up were able to turn to our Ombudsman when they had questions during the deployment.

In smaller, flatter organizations, both the service members and their families may feel more connected, both to each other and to the mission, as I saw at the Marine briefings, while the vastness of the Army may tend to encourage alienation. The families of newly activated reservists and National Guard members may face the added difficulty of just getting to a meeting, since most Guard members live more than fifty miles from a base or armory, and many reservists even farther.

But as Lieutenant Colonel Cannon pointed out, no matter what the rate of participation may be most of the time, war changes everything.

At the predeployment briefing for Charlie's unit, Marissa noticed there were a lot more wives there than usually attended the FRG meetings. She didn't know many of the faces, but she did know many of the voices from Charlie's company. She had been a key caller on the spouses' phone tree since that first FRG meeting she'd attended eight months before, when she'd volunteered. Whenever the CO had information he needed to get out to the families, or whenever there was a meeting or a social gathering, she and the other spouses who were key callers helped pass the word.

The briefing was long, and boring in places, some of the speakers droning on, some inaudible, but she made notes on the handouts because knowledge is power, and she was feeling like she could really use some power right about now. She was alone in a strange town, far from the family and friends who had helped her get through every other challenge she'd faced in her life. She was afraid she'd be a bad mother or be a bad wife to Charlie, that she wouldn't be able to handle it all. She was as scared as she'd ever been.

It was better not to think about it. Better to throw herself into her new job. Better to rush home and make dinner for Charlie, who was as busy as she was with the predeployment workup. Better to clean the house for him and do laundry for him and make sure they got their wills done.

At the briefing, the Army lawyer from the Fort Bragg legal office had told them they could all get wills drawn up on post for free, but no, honey, not Marissa. She knew any fill-in-the-blank form was full of shit, that was the first thing you learned in school, and that such a will could be overturned. Since graduating, her paralegal work had given her experience handling estates on a regular basis, so she wrote up a will for Charlie, as well as a general power of attorney. Then she wrote up a will for herself, too, because he was going to war and she would be here alone and traveling, and what if she got into a fatal car accident and he was killed in combat? Lexie had to be taken care of. Together, she and Charlie made sure the house, car, and personal loans were all on a death clause, so if he died they were paid for. Marissa was a detail person.

While Marissa was doing that, Charlie filled out a record of emergency data, or personal notification form. He wrote in Marissa's name as primary next of kin and his parents as secondary next of kin, the first and second people he wanted notified in the event of his injury or death. And then, without telling Marissa, he doubled up on his life insurance.

For Charlie, it was easy to decide which names to write in on the notification forms. Upstate from Fort Bragg, when a National Guard member who was planning a wedding got the word her unit was deploying, she called a friend saying, "We're supposed to get married in seven months! What am I going to do?"

Her friend was a practical woman. "Go to the courthouse now and wear the dress later when you get back" was her advice, and it was good advice, because in this case it wasn't some whirlwind, wartime romance — the couple had been living together for seven years already. "If, God forbid, something happens to you while you're deployed," her friend said, "they're not going to talk to your boyfriend."

She may have been right. Though boyfriends, girlfriends, and fiancées may experience the same anxiety and loneliness as their married sisters, they have no formal legal status. Therefore, depending on which service branch their significant other is in, they may not exist as far as the military is concerned. A young woman named Hannah, who was waiting in

Illinois while her Marine was in Baghdad, wrote in a wistful e-mail: *I hope with all my heart that he will come home for me, and I won't be one of the ones receiving that awful phone call.* But because their wedding plans fell through when Hannah's Marine abruptly deployed, that's not a call she'd be getting, at least not from the Marine Corps — not unless he listed her on his notification form and gave her some sort of legal status, such as a power of attorney. The other services have similar requirements.

Boyfriends, girlfriends, and fiancées don't receive much support from the family programs, either. The Marine Corps' Key Volunteers, in fact, are prohibited from passing information to anyone who's not listed on a Marine's emergency data or notification form. Across the services, if unmarried significant others are invited to participate in the family support groups at all, it tends to be on a haphazard, informal basis. They're frequently left out of the loop. "We're just kind of forgotten," Pam Heitz complained as she made plans to tie the knot with her soldier when he came home from Iraq for two weeks of R&R.

Before that could happen, though, his e-mails and phone calls grew more depressed and paranoid and angry, the result of his duty as a helicopter gunner in Iraq. Having no official status, Pam couldn't do much on his behalf. As she listened to him talk about how he was afraid to ask the doctor for an antidepressant, as she listened to him sound less and less like himself, when he called off the wedding, all she could do was helplessly watch from a distance.

There are two reasons for the tight rules: privacy and security. The military services have to have a consistent, legally defensible way of determining who's entitled to information about a service member and who's not. They'd be sued if they handed out information to anyone who called claiming they were a close friend, or to an estranged parent or lover the service member hadn't authorized and wanted nothing to do with. In addition, some of the information, especially homecoming dates, can be operationally sensitive. You don't necessarily want to publicly announce ahead of time the exact day and hour a ship will be entering a harbor, where it's difficult to maneuver. Still, some family support groups and readiness groups make an effort to reach out to their unofficial sisters, but only if they know them, and only if they have the time.

Upstairs in an old brick building on post, the Army lawyer laid out the documents for Luigi to sign: his last will and testament, a general power of attorney, and a special power of attorney that would allow Beth to get access to Luigi's frozen sperm.

When they had failed to get pregnant for the third month in a row, Beth hadn't wasted any time. She got a doctor she knew at the hospital to check them both for infertility. Her hormonal levels all tested normal. Luigi's sperm count, however, turned out to be low and the doctor had recommended artificial insemination, or AI. But then came the order to deploy. With Beth's biological clock ticking, Beth and Luigi decided to store some of his sperm so she could try AI while he was gone. She found a cryogenics lab in Minnesota and Luigi overnighted several samples, mixed with a special preservative that kept them viable until they arrived at the lab for freezing.

More and more military men are banking sperm before a deployment, not because they suffer from infertility now, but because they're afraid they might before the deployment's over. They're trying to bank a little control over the uncontrollable — land mines, roadside bombs, mortars, gunshot wounds, exposure to chemical, biological, or nuclear weapons — all of which, aside from maiming or killing you, can leave you unable to have children.

After the first Gulf War, a significant number of returning veterans complained about a mass of symptoms that came to be called Gulf War Syndrome. The symptoms ranged from chronic fatigue to abdominal pain to blurred vision to sterility to birth defects in children conceived after the war. The medical evidence on the sterility portion of the syndrome is conflicted. Duke University Medical Center studied a combination of substances used in the Gulf War — the insect repellent deet, an insecticide, and an anti-nerve-gas agent. The study, released in January 2003, concluded that together they caused extensive cell degeneration and cell death in the testes of laboratory rats. But a Department of Defense official told CNN that other medical studies indicated "male Gulf War veterans had a higher rate of birth compared to those who did not deploy."

Information about banking sperm is not part of official predeployment briefings. Service members brief each other. When a Gulf War veteran in one National Guard unit told a newer Guard member that he believed he had come back from the war sterile, the new soldier made an appointment to bank sperm before he deployed to Iraq.

He had company, but it wasn't a crowd. In the run-up to the Iraq War, the phone at a sperm bank in Augusta, Georgia, began ringing twice as much. The callers were mostly healthy young men, soldiers preparing to deploy from nearby Army posts. About a dozen actually came in to make a deposit. In Virginia, less than a hundred military men made appointments at the country's second-largest sperm storage facility. In California, the country's largest facility reported having on deposit the sperm of only thirty service members. So the numbers, while growing, are not great.

The trend raises a number of ethical questions. Should all service members, regardless of gender or income, be given the opportunity to ensure their future ability to have children if serving their country leaves them infertile? In 2003, it cost a man a few minutes and $600 to store his sperm for a year. For a woman, the cost was $10,000 for drugs to spur egg production and an invasive medical procedure to harvest them, plus she needed someone to provide sperm to inseminate the eggs before freezing them — eggs often don't survive freezing, but embryos do. Not surprisingly, there's no evidence that female service members were going to such lengths.

Charlie brought home a long list of all the things he might need while he was in Iraq. The whole family went shopping for everything from a portable chair to underwear — seven hundred bucks worth of stuff, paid for out of their own pockets. This is not unusual. Commanding officers give the service members in their units a list of the items they must have but won't be issued. The service members then have to find a way to make their small paychecks stretch to pay for it all, or get family members to chip in. One Marine mother claimed that her son's CO threatened to deny his Marines permission to travel home to visit family before deploying if they didn't buy everything on the list.

When it comes to receiving equipment, National Guard and Reserve units have a reputation for winding up at the back of the line, behind the active-duty forces. This is at least partly because when the state militias were organized into the National Guard, military planners anticipated that most of the fighting would be left to active-duty units. So Army leaders didn't see the point of investing much money in equipping and training the Guard to fight, with the result that one Guard advocate reports even ammunition has been in short supply for training exercises.

When it came time to deploy, a North Carolina Guard unit on its way overseas had to get by with hand-me-down rifles from the 82nd Airborne and outdated body armor. But just before another North Carolina Guard unit left for Iraq, a sergeant with connections scored a bonanza of coveted equipment for everyone in the unit — water-dispensing Camelbak backpacks that would keep the soldiers well-hydrated while they worked in the desert heat, and best of all, Kevlar vests.

At the time, the latest bulletproof vests cost a little over $1,500 and were made from Cordura and Kevlar fabric that could stop shrapnel fragments and 9mm rounds. These Interceptor vests were reinforced with removable composite ceramic plates coated with boron-carbon and silicon carbide tiles so hard that if you were wearing one and you got hit in the torso with a burst of AK-47 rounds traveling 2,750 feet per second, you'd walk away with bruises instead of dying of a fatal wound.

But as the Iraq War began, the Army decided to save money by equipping only dismounted combat soldiers with the high-tech vests. That meant many active-duty soldiers and most Guard members and reservists, including those on dangerous convoy duty, were unprotected. When one reservist was sent to Iraq with a flak jacket from the Vietnam era, his father took $660 out of his own pocket, bought a set of ceramic plates from one of the companies that manufactured them, and mailed them to his son. A deluge of complaints to Congress eventually led to a change in Army policy.

Meanwhile, down at Fort Bragg, Charlie and his single soldier friends also had their own lists of must-have items. Marissa looked at what they were packing and started laughing. She said, "You're going off to war and you're making sure to pack your Playstation?" She knew from her Vietnamese father what life in the Third World was like. These guys were going off to fight people who lived in dirt huts and they were packing microwaves and televisions. She couldn't help wondering how prepared Charlie and his friends were to travel light and fight.

They were her friends now, too. They'd started coming over on weekends for beer and barbecue and TV boxing matches. They hung out over the rails of the deck and draped themselves across the couches like a pack of orphaned puppies. Lexie was getting rich waiting on them.

She had come into the kitchen one day, asking, "Mommy, where's the chips?"

Marissa put her hands on her hips. "What do you need them for? We're about to eat dinner."

Lexie put her hands on her hips, too. "Simmons said he wants some chips."

Marissa gave her the bag of chips. A few minutes later, Lexie was back, opening the fridge with both hands and pulling out a beer. Marissa laughed, "Where do you think you're going with that beer?"

Said Lexie, "Simmons asked me to get it for him."

Marissa suggested that next time she tell Simmons she wanted a quarter. Lexie had had to get a piggy bank to hold all the quarters.

After midnight, a couple of the guys crashed on the couches. Marissa drove some of the other guys home, the ones who'd had too much to be able to drive but still had duty in the morning. She never drank when the guys came over. That way no windows got broken and no one wrapped his car around a tree.

Charlie drank. Some nights, with all his friends getting drunk around him, he drank too much. Then he'd say things to Marissa that hurt, especially with her heart already raw from the looming departure. He made confessions, things he normally never would have said, except he felt like he had to tell her before he left, "Because," he mumbled miserably, "I don't know if I'm coming home."

Back when Marissa had just found out she was pregnant and was at her most vulnerable, Charlie had simply held her and let her cry. After that, she had trusted him not to hurt her. And now here he was, about to leave and hurting her so badly with the things he was saying that for a while Marissa decided she was the one who was leaving. In the end, she told herself they had been through too much for too long to quit now. But the damage had been done.

She said coldly, "A best friend can't hurt you the way a lover can." She told him she had loved and trusted him even more than she trusted her best friend back in Erie. Now he listened as she said, "I'm not sure I can ever trust you not to hurt me again."

As Charlie's time ran down, he never said *trust me*. He just said, "I'll show you." He said, "I know you don't trust me, but I'll prove it to you."

With two weeks to go, Charlie was vaccinated for smallpox and a number of other Third World diseases. He brought home a backpack and a pile of gear and began packing it in the living room. He headed out on a convoy down to Charleston to deliver the unit's trucks to a ship. Marissa spent the morning auctioning off a foreclosed house on the coast and was headed north for a hearing in Johnston County at one o'clock when her cell phone rang.

It was the babysitter. "Lexie's got a rash I never seen before." It had started after Marissa dropped her off and was getting worse and worse. Said the sitter, "It's really terrible."

Marissa was two hours away. She wanted to turn the car right around and rush back, but she couldn't, she had to be at that hearing, so she went to the hearing and the whole time she was imagining her daughter covered in sores oozing pus. Afterward, she jumped in the car, blasting back toward Fayetteville, and on the way she called the advice nurse at the health clinic on post. The nurse quizzed her, but Lexie hadn't eaten anything different lately, hadn't been exposed to anything new, hadn't been in the woods or even played in the backyard; no, it wasn't poison ivy.

"The only thing she's been exposed to," said Marissa, "is my husband. He was vaccinated a week and a half ago to go overseas."

"Well, it wouldn't be that," said the nurse.

They hung up, but not long after that the phone rang again and this time it was someone from the department on post that handled the vaccinations. Marissa felt her heart beat faster. If it wasn't the vaccinations, like the nurse said, then why the hell was this expert on vaccinations calling her and asking, "Does your daughter have any skin conditions?"

"Yeah," said Marissa. "She has eczema, but she hasn't had an outbreak in two years."

The voice on the other end of the phone said something about how her husband should have stayed away from Lexie, something about she should take her daughter straight to the emergency room at Womack Army Medical Center and she should be quarantined, they'd call ahead, the ER would be expecting her. Marissa stared blindly at the road ahead.

She got to the sitter's at three-thirty. It was worse than she'd imagined. Lexie looked as if someone had slashed her face, her arms, her legs, the entire surface of her body. She was completely covered in raised welts and they were red, red, red. As Marissa rushed into Womack's ER carrying Lexie, people turned and stared. But the staff hardly looked up. "Just have a seat here in the waiting room," said the woman behind the desk.

Marissa carried Lexie over to the rows of chairs. She sat down. People were staring. Even Marissa was afraid to hold her daughter, not knowing what it was or if it was contagious. But she did hold her because, poor little kid, she was miserable and itchy and crying, and as she held her daughter close, she decided, *This is bullshit.*

Marissa got up. She carried Lexie back to the desk. "Did you *look* at my daughter when I came in?" she asked, loudly enough for all the staring people in the waiting room to hear. "*Look at her.* I don't know what she has. I was told she was supposed to be *quarantined.*"

The staff put her and Lexie in a specially pressurized quarantine room.

A doctor came in, a specialist. He examined Lexie. Then he just stared at her. Then he said he'd be right back. He returned with another specialist and they both stared at Lexie. They told her they had no idea what it was, they'd never seen anything like it before, it wasn't in any of the med-

ical dictionaries. It might have been the cowpox Charlie had been vaccinated with to protect him from smallpox, but they just didn't know. They
sent her home with steroids and an antihistamine and orders to stay
away from her father for two weeks.

Charlie was leaving in two weeks.

According to the pamphlet my husband brought home when he was vaccinated before going to Iraq, those who are vaccinated are supposed to
avoid contact with a number of people, including children under the age
of five, people with weakened immune systems such as those with cancer,
or anyone with a skin condition. Eczema, for example. Neither Charlie
nor Marissa received such a pamphlet. Maybe at the prevaccination brief
the soldiers were told to stay away from family members with autoim-
mune diseases, but if they were, Charlie didn't remember hearing it. Even
if he was told, he wouldn't have thought of Lexie because it had been so
long since her outbreak.

Marissa knew if she had been there, *she* would have remembered it
right away, because she was Lexie's mother, she was the one who always
took her to the doctor. But she wasn't there, and he got no brochure,
no nothing. Marissa concluded they needed better briefings. Later, she
would start working with the FRG to improve family notification on vaccination issues.

The first week in September, a couple of days before his departure
date, Charlie was allowed to hug his little girl again. He came home from
work and swung Lexie up into his arms and Lexie hugged him around
his neck. He was wearing his beige and brown and tan desert camouflage
uniform, known in the Army as DCUs. Marissa watched. Her husband
was about to go to war. She was half Vietnamese, a daughter of war from
the very beginning. Now she was married to war.

CHAPTER 5

Green Ramp

BETH WATCHED LUIGI get his gear together: rain poncho, canteens, gas mask. It was September and it was cold, just before dawn outside his unit's big brick headquarters. She was seeping tears. He was sweating. Another soldier, passing by, asked Beth, "He's not sick, is he?"

She shook her head. "He's OK. He just sweats when he's nervous." As the soldier moved on and Luigi continued to pack his gear, she wiped his face with her hand, then her own eyes. A minute later, it was as if she hadn't wiped either. Despite the CO's promise, Luigi had had to work late so often that Beth felt like she'd hardly seen him. And now he was leaving.

Luigi walked Beth out to her little white compact in the parking lot. "I hate this war," she said. Whenever she said that, her voice took on the tone of a child who'd been wronged. "I don't know why we had to go in there in the first place."

He nodded. "I know, baby." Then he tensed. "Uh oh, they called formation. I got to go." A quick hug and a kiss, as if he were just going down the street, and then he was gone.

While he and the other soldiers in his unit waited for the cattle car buses that would take them to the airfield, Beth drove home to the duplex. Pictures of her and Luigi were on the coffee table, the bookshelves, the refrigerator, the nightstand. Her dog, Danny, followed her from room to room. The blinds were still closed, the rooms twilit as the sun rose. She curled up on the bed with Danny and a box of tissues.

A couple of hours later, her cell phone rang. It was the FRG's key caller for Luigi's platoon, Camilla Maki. Camilla had first called Beth back when the word came down that the unit was deploying again.

Camilla Maki had come to Fort Bragg from Ireland by way of Tennessee, along the way exchanging her brogue for a twang. She'd heard horror stories about backstabbing Army wives, so for two years she avoided getting to know anybody in the military. But then in the weeks before her husband's first deployment, the one to Afghanistan, she met his platoon sergeant's wife. They hit it off. Most of the guys in the unit at the time weren't married, and later, she got to know the only other two wives in the platoon, and for the rest of the deployment, the four of them lived at each other's houses. They had sleepovers, quit cooking, and took all their kids out to eat. They celebrated Halloween and Thanksgiving together. They videotaped Christmas dinner and sent it to the guys. It was a support group of their own making. If their company had an FRG, they never heard from it.

On the phone from Afghanistan, her husband told her he liked how independent she was, taking care of things while he wasn't around. Even people she ran into around Fayetteville would comment on how great she was doing. Those were people who didn't know her very well. The three other wives in the platoon knew better. They were the ones who heard her say, "My husband and me, we can't be apart, we're one person now." They were the ones who knew they could call Camilla any time of the day or night, because she was always awake. They watched her lose eighty pounds she'd been carrying around since her last pregnancy. She called herself a worrywart, but it was much more than that. Her doctor sent her to see a counselor. The counselor told her she wasn't eating or sleeping because she was depressed, and put her on an antidepressant.

Six months after he left, her husband came back. He'd been home five months when they got the word about Iraq. This time around, Camilla volunteered to be the FRG key caller for her husband's platoon. The platoon had a lot of new guys who'd arrived since the Afghanistan deployment, and a lot more of them had wives. With the last deployment still fresh in her mind, Camilla called them all and said, "Let's go out to eat and get to know each other before the guys leave."

She and the wives gathered around a table in one of the chain restaurants on the western edge of town. Most of them were very young, nineteen or twenty, but Beth Pratt, the oldest of the wives, was the one

Camilla worried about most. She had seen Beth and Luigi together, and they reminded her of herself and her own husband. *They're just so cute,* she thought, *and so in love.* Beth especially reminded Camilla of herself, looking all through dinner as if she might break down right there, the skin around her eyes tinged pink and her smile brief and trembling. She had no family nearby, no friends. Camilla thought to herself, *It's going to be really rough up here for her.*

"Beth," Camilla said, "where are you?"

Curled up on the bed with her dog and her box of tissues, Beth said softly, "I'm at home."

"You need to come out here to Green Ramp to see him before he leaves."

Green Ramp was what passed for a waiting terminal at the airfield. Beth wiped her nose with a tissue. "I don't want to. I'm a mess."

"That doesn't matter."

"I'm not up to it, really. Anyway, I thought we're not allowed to go to Green Ramp."

"Screw 'em," said Camilla. "Come on."

By the time Beth and Camilla got to Green Ramp, it was nearly noon and the other wives had been shooed away. Beth peered in the door of the hulking concrete-block building. Men in beige DCUs stood and sat on rows and rows of bleachers like drifts of sand, talking, reading, sleeping, killing time. Someone yelled, "Pratt! Your wife's here!" and several rows over, a face turned toward the door.

Instantly, there were the familiar dimples. Luigi jumped up, a surf magazine flapping open in his hand, his grin getting bigger the closer he came. "Oh my God!" he said, and he wrapped her in a bear hug. "You came back!"

She'd given him the magazine while he was packing. She'd written something on every page. *I'm so lucky you showed up on my doorstep . . . Te amo,* which was Spanish for "I love you" . . . And what he always said to her: *Time, distance cannot keep us apart.*

He'd already read them all. Camilla hung back while they stood there grinning at each other, his hands resting on her hips, her arms resting on his shoulders, her red-rimmed eyes almost level with his. They stood that way a long time, until their grins finally faded. Then someone yelled, "Pratt! Get over here!" Beth hugged him, but he was wearing his Kevlar vest and to her he suddenly felt awkwardly hard and inhuman. She let go and he ran to pick up his rucksack. She turned away before he walked out the door to the plane.

A week later it was Marissa's turn. The alarm woke her at four A.M. She slid out of bed without turning on the light, a slim shadow in T-shirt and boxers, dark hair trailing down her back. She showered and dressed fast in her black power suit, shoved files into her briefcase as she combed out her wet hair, but before she left the house, she sat on the edge of the double bed and watched Charlie sleep.

He wasn't supposed to be here beside her in the bed, not this morning. He was supposed to be gone. She'd taken yesterday off so she and Lexie could go with him on post. They'd planned to stay with him until the buses came to take his unit to Green Ramp, where a plane waited. But at the last minute, the plane was canceled.

She'd called her supervisor at the law firm to ask if someone else could please cover her foreclosure hearings in the morning so she could be there to say goodbye. But she didn't get anywhere with her supervisor, and so here she was, stealing a few last minutes, watching Charlie breathe.

He didn't wake up when she kissed him. "I love you," she whispered.

She went down the hall to Lexie's room and kissed her, too, before slipping back through the long strands of pink and purple crystals that hung in Lexie's doorway. They were still swaying and clicking when the front door closed.

From the front page of the *Fayetteville Observer:*

> ## 1,000 FLY TO IRAQ
> By Matt Leclercq
> Staff writer
>
> Some soldiers stared blankly at the hangar walls. Others laughed, played games or closed their eyes in the heat.
>
> But no matter how hundreds of soldiers spent their final hours before deployment, few could avoid thinking about what lay ahead — at least six months of dangerous, uncertain work in Iraq . . .

Seven months earlier, I had waved goodbye to my own husband. Two thousand years before that, Claudia Marcia Capitolina did the same. Her husband's name was Fortunatus, he was a Roman centurion, and when he left Marcia behind, he was headed for a fight on the banks of the Tigris and Euphrates, in the part of the world we now call Iraq. I don't know what Marcia did after Fortunatus's legion marched away to that place. But after Frank's bus followed the other buses away into the rainy night, after the middle-aged mother lowered her sign and sobbed in her husband's arms, I put Rosie in Frank's truck, climbed into his seat, gripped the steering wheel he'd held, and cried.

He had deployed many times before, twice for more than half a year, once in a time of war. I never cried any of those times. Maybe this time it was the rain, or maybe the eerie fearfulness of the midnight hour. Maybe it was this particular war. Maybe it was because Frank had admitted he was afraid.

You'll come back. I had said it as if I could see through some secret feminine spyglass to the future. I had said it for him, not for me. *I* knew I was blind. He might never hold this steering wheel again. I might never sit beside him in this truck again. I'd been holding my heart in a clenched fist for three weeks, and when I finally loosened my grip, alone in his truck as rain grieved against the dark windshield, I was bewildered to discover my heart was broken.

PART II

THE HOMEFRONT

CHAPTER 6

The Knock at the Door

TWO DAYS AFTER MARISSA kissed Charlie goodbye, a week after Beth hugged Luigi at Green Ramp, on the front page of the *Fayetteville Observer*, there was this:

CASUALTIES OF WAR
By Allison Williams
Staff writer
. . . On Aug. 7, one piece of news shattered everything for Michelle Hellermann. That Thursday morning, she opened her front door in the Nijmegen neighborhood on Fort Bragg to three men in Army dress greens . . .

The night before those men appeared at the door had been a clear night in Baghdad, but dark once the moon dipped behind the buildings. On a shadowy street off Highway 8 on the city's southern edge, a squad on patrol in a Humvee and a confiscated Land Cruiser had just pulled over a car that was out after curfew. It was an hour before midnight. Seven American soldiers, an interpreter, and the two Iraqi policemen riding with them stepped out of their vehicles into the quiet night.

The quiet vanished in a stuttering roar — muzzle flashes of AK-47s spurted from the corner of a building only fifteen meters away, more flashes from a roof a little further up the road. Windshields shattered, the soldiers hit the pavement, the policemen dove into the ditch. Someone screamed in pain. Then the roar deepened as a streaming blast of neon tracers stitched the darkness from somewhere up ahead, tracers that could be coming only from other Americans, a weapons squad the patrol hadn't even known was out there.

Ten seconds after it began, it was over, all sound sucked into a deep, black silence. Then the soldiers began to scream to each other, "Where are you, you all right?" The interpreter had been shot in the legs. One soldier had been hit in the face with shrapnel and couldn't see, another lay dead, and a third was on his back, unconscious, each breath a gasp. This was Michelle Hellermann's husband.

His fellow soldiers loaded him and the others into the Land Cruiser, on top of spent ammunition rounds and broken glass, before realizing the engine and all four tires were shot to pieces. Desperate to get going, all their radios shot out, they hauled the dead man and the wounded from the Land Cruiser, shoved them into the already crowded Humvee in a tangle of bodies, and took off for the field hospital.

Later that night, one of the casualty reports — Staff Sergeant Brian Hellermann, shot in an ambush — made its way back to the headquarters of Company C, 2d Battalion of the 325th Airborne Infantry Regiment, 82nd Airborne Division, then on up through the theater of operations to Casualty Assistance Command (CAC) in Kuwait. CAC sent the report back across the Middle East and Europe, over the Atlantic to the Pentagon, to an office in the Department of the Army.

From Washington, D.C., the report made its way down to Fort Bragg in North Carolina, to the CAC of the XVIII Airborne Corps, of which the 82nd is a part. Company C's records were checked to see who Sergeant Hellermann had designated as his primary next of kin when he filled out the personal notification form, back before he deployed.

The casualty report and the name and address of the primary next of kin wound up in the hands of the three people who would put on their dress greens and make this particular casualty notification: a chaplain, a sergeant major from the brigade, and the lieutenant in charge of Charlie Company's rear detachment, a man who knew Brian. The rear detachment, or rear D, consists of the few members every unit leaves behind to act as the liaison between the base back home and the unit out in the theater of operations. They're the liaison for the families, too. However, usually they're not among the people knocking at the door. That's because some spouses deal with their grief by getting angry at the people who deliver the bad news. The rear D's job is to provide support immediately *after* the notification, and that can be hard to do if the spouse is already directing her anger and grief at them.

Now a phone rang in the home of the woman whose husband was in Iraq commanding the 2d Battalion. A phone rang, too, in the home of another Charlie Company wife who was active in the company's Family

Readiness Group. Both were told a notification would soon be made. They weren't told who. They weren't told where. They called themselves a "comfort team." According to Army policy, families that have just been notified must never be left alone. After the notification has been made, if no family or friends are available to come over, and if perhaps the bereaved family has had enough of people in military uniforms, comfort teams like these two women make themselves available. On Fort Bragg at that time, they waited outside. Today, they wait at home, on call, the same procedure followed by most of the rest of the military, which helps ensure that the family is the first to know.

The women's car fell in behind the car carrying the casualty notification team. Beneath a gloomy sky, the first car led the second across Fort Bragg. They passed barracks and office buildings and neighborhoods of military family housing named for battles of the past. They drove along streets named for more battles and streets and buildings named for some of the soldiers who had died fighting them. New construction was going up, some of the housing areas under renovation, others in need of it. The two cars turned in among the tired, moldering ranks of enlisted apartments that hunkered beneath the spread of oaks in a neighborhood named for the battle of Nijmegen.

Two thousand years ago, in the Dutch town of Nijmegen, along a branch of the Rhine, the Romans erected a monument to honor the victory of eight Roman legions over an army of Germanic warriors. The families of those who fought on both sides probably waited then, as families wait now, for their loved one to return, or at least for news of him, any news, brought back by the survivors who staggered home.

Half a century ago, another monument was erected in Nijmegen in honor of another victory over a German army. This time the victors were American paratroopers, members of the 82nd Airborne who came by parachute and glider down out of the sky and then, in broad daylight against well-defended German positions, crossed the river in twenty-six rowboats, seized the Nijmegen bridge, and liberated the town from the Nazis. Once again, the families of those who fought waited for news. Any news. By then, the worst news no longer came by way of survivors. It came by telegram. Every week of the Second World War, an average of three thousand American families received the news that someone they loved had been wounded, killed, or was missing in action.

After that war, for twenty years the U.S. military had relatively few casualties to report, with the brief exception, early on, of the Korean War.

Then, in 1965, a backburner conflict in a remote corner of Southeast Asia boiled over. American soldiers and Marines had been dying in Vietnam in twos and threes when a battle erupted in an isolated valley called Ia Drang. In a matter of days, more than 230 American soldiers were dead. The sudden avalanche of casualty reports overwhelmed the Army's notification system. Taxi drivers were enlisted to deliver telegrams that began, *The Secretary of the Army regrets to inform you . . .*

In the Georgia town where many of the wives lived near the Army post, word quickly spread about the taxi deliveries. The sight of a yellow cab pulling up in front of a house caused panic inside. Julia Compton Moore was the wife of then Lieutenant Colonel Harold Moore, one of the commanding officers who was at Ia Drang. In the days after the battle, she'd been hurrying to the homes of those visited by the taxis, trying to comfort the young widows left holding yellow telegrams. Even in Army towns, they were isolated compared to the World War II years, when all your neighbors had someone in the service and the family next door or down the street knew exactly what you were going through when you received one of those telegrams. Vietnam was different. When a taxi driver knocked at Julia Moore's own door, she hid at first, for a long time, before she finally forced herself to open the door and face the news that her husband, too, was dead.

The driver just wanted directions to another address.

Within two weeks, Julia Moore forced the Army to find a better way to notify families. No more taxi drivers, no more wives or parents left alone with a telegram. In fact, no more telegrams. Since that time, regulations have required that the news of every death must be delivered in person. Major injuries may also prompt a visit, but injuries are often reported to the family in a phone call. News of a death, however, is delivered in person by a member of the military, someone whose rank is equal to or higher than the rank of the casualty, preferably someone from the same overall unit or a similar one, or at least with a similar military background. They receive some training and, depending on the service (Army, Air Force, Navy, or Marines), they may be accompanied by a casualty assistance officer, whose job it will be during the days and weeks ahead to guide the bereaved family through a blizzard of military and government paperwork, insurance forms, legal hoops, and funeral arrangements. Casualty assistance officers do this job in addition to their regular duties. The casualty team also usually includes a chaplain. They all wear their dress uniforms.

Once they've located the home of the next of kin, walked up to the door, and knocked, the casualty notification officer delivers a memorized, Pentagon-approved, thirty-second script. Procedures vary slightly between the service branches. The version played out in a Navy training video reads almost like poetry.

CASUALTY ASSISTANCE OFFICER: Mrs. Keel? Good afternoon, I'm Lieutenant Fletcher. This is Chaplain Grayson. Mrs. Keel, we have some news for you. Unfortunately, it's not good news. It is about your daughter, Seaman Susan Keel. Susan was involved in an automobile accident while on liberty in Sigonella, Sicily. Susan was very seriously injured and I'm sorry to report, she died as a result of her injuries.

CHAPLAIN: Ma'am, may we come in?

After those first few lines, there is no script. The chaplain narrating the Navy video says:

The process is to break the news to them in increments and ensure they have someone with them after you leave. These visits do not always go smoothly . . .

There will of course be apprehension at the door, and once the notification is given, there will be shock. Each family and each individual in the family is unique. It's reasonable to expect each person may respond to the news differently.

Young children will often reflect the behavior of their mother. If she cries, the children are likely to cry. If she is restrained or unemotional, they're more likely to be, as well. If the father becomes emotional, the children may see you as a threat, and may be afraid of you. Avoid the temptation of reaching out to them at that time.

For this reason, it may be wise to make the initial notification away from the ears of children who are old enough to understand.

Sometimes family members express anger or denial. Often tears and mournful wails will punctuate the notification. The chaplain and the CACO [Casualty Assistance Calls Officer] must remain patient and composed.

Do not invalidate their grief by giving unrealistic assurances. Do not attempt to stop or truncate an emotional outburst. In such situations, simply allow the family members to express whatever they need to express without any interference from you, unless it begins to appear that someone might get hurt . . .

In the summer of 2004, an immigrant father in Florida opened his door to three Marines in dress blues who told him his twenty-year-old son had been killed in Iraq. He picked up a hammer, a can of gasoline, and a propane torch and brushed aside the Marines on his way to the government van they'd left parked at the curb. He smashed a window. He shook the Marines off again and climbed inside. Moments later, flames engulfed the van. The Marines pulled the father out, his arms and legs on fire. Television helicopters were soon hovering overhead, broadcasting images of the flaming van, the father strapped to a stretcher, his arms shaking uncontrollably. Nearby, the three Marines stood together, two of them quietly, one of them too agitated to stand still.

The training video advises:

> When the initial emotional wave passes . . . Always offer to call someone for them. Close family, or family members not at home, should be notified without delay.

This procedure was developed and fine-tuned during the Vietnam War. It was firmly in place by 1993. That year, on April 3, the husband of Trish Rierson's best friend was killed in a skydiving accident near Fort Bragg. Both women's husbands were members of Delta Force, the Army's most secretive special forces unit. Trish rushed to the hospital to be with Barb, who was twenty-seven years old, three months pregnant with her first child, and had never even been to a funeral. Barb wound up moving back home to Seattle so her mother could help her when the baby came.

In the weeks following the death of someone so close to them, Trish and her husband, Matt, talked a lot about things they hadn't really talked about before, the what-ifs, the what-are-your-wishes. They were only thirty-two. Trish wore her strawberry blond hair efficiently short, no makeup on her fresh face, her small, full mouth always ready to smile, even now. She joked that she wanted enough money in the bank to sit on the couch and eat bonbons and watch *General Hospital*. She teased him, "If something happens to me, you'll be married within six months because most soldiers can't make it without the backbones of their wives — you'd never be able to manage the household *and* maintain your job." Matt laughed, but he didn't disagree. They didn't disagree on most things — they'd grown up looking out at the world from the same tiny corner of Iowa, a farming community so small it didn't even have a McDonald's.

Four months after the skydiving accident, Matt's Delta Force unit deployed. He and Trish had just built a house, three bedrooms on either side of a high-ceilinged great room, two sunlit glass panels flanking the front door, a cute blue house with white trim. It looked down on a quiet street in a hilly, wooded neighborhood that was off-post but still full of military families. They'd been in their new house ten months, or rather Trish and their two little boys had been in it ten months. Matt had been gone for training so much that out of those ten months he'd been home for only three. That's how it is with special forces. The training is intense and continuous, and as you master skills few can master, it feeds your ego, makes it easy for you and everyone who loves you to deny how dangerous your job really is. And then Matt deployed, as usual on short notice, as usual without a whisper of where he was going. It was just the latest deployment of many.

The first week he was gone, Trish got a call to attend a family support group meeting. That's what Family Readiness Groups were called back then. At the meeting, she and the other wives were told their husbands were now on a forty-five-day mission in Mogadishu, Somalia, which CNN had actually reported three days before, but the wives dutifully sat there pretending it was news to them.

For the next month and a bit, Trish got into the single mom routine, getting two-year-old Kaleb and four-year-old Jacob to daycare and herself to work each day, getting together with friends when she could. There was no phone contact with Matt, no e-mail back then, just letters. Then came word that his trip had been extended a few weeks, and she and the other wives looked at each other and said, "OK, there's nothing we can do about it." And on they went, Trish's days busy with her own children and the children she worked with as a speech pathologist.

On the first Sunday night in October, the phone rang around 9:30. It was the family support group leader. "Trish," she said, "I'm calling to let you know our husbands were engaged in a fierce battle, and we've sustained casualties — deaths and injuries."

As a team leader's wife, Trish in turn was supposed to call the wives on her team. "Can you give me any details?" she asked.

"That's all they told me."

"No names? No nothing?"

"No," said the support group leader. "They're in the process of making notifications now."

Trish glanced involuntarily toward the front window and the steep, darkened slope down to the empty street. The support group leader told her to tell the other five wives on her team, "We'll be in touch. Remind them that no news is good news. We'll keep you posted."

Trish hung up the phone and turned on the TV. CNN was running footage of rockets and gunfire in the dark streets of Mogadishu, but it told her nothing, really, about what was happening over there. She left the TV on while she called the wives on her team. She told them exactly the same thing she had been told. She cried with a few of them, prayed with a couple, and said she'd get back with them as soon as she knew something. She sat down to wait.

About an hour later, the phone rang again, and again it was the family support group leader, calling to tell her all the notifications had been made for the evening and they would start again tomorrow.

"What are you really saying?" Trish asked.

The support group leader sighed. "I'm saying it's too late to contact anyone else, so they're done for the night."

And Trish said, "Can you tell me, have they notified all the wives whose husbands have been killed?"

And she said, "No."

So Trish called the women on her team and told them exactly that, and by the time she got off the phone she was falling apart, because she thought, *How can they know and not let us know?* She'd had no idea that the official casualty notification policy stated that notifications should not be made after ten o'clock at night or before six in the morning. The reasoning was well intentioned: This wasn't good information to receive, and receiving it in the middle of the night wasn't going to help. But in the age of the twenty-four-hour news cycle, sometimes this policy just prolonged the agony.

During the long, sleepless night, Trish bargained with God. "Please," she whispered, "whatever it takes, just let him live, and I'll owe you, I'll be in your debt." When the night finally neared an end, she showered and dressed. She knew they were going to notify her and she wanted to be prepared, wanted to at least look right because there wasn't anything else she could do. She sat down to wait again.

Nobody came. Then Jacob and Kaleb woke up, and she was changing diapers and laying out Eggos and Cheerios and still nobody came, and she began to think, with a blink of disbelief, *They're not here, I made it, I dodged a bullet.* She took the boys to daycare and went to work.

At ten-thirty she got the phone call that answered her prayers — Matt was alive. The word was that he wasn't even injured. In the seventeen-hour battle of Mogadishu, two Black Hawk helicopters had been shot down, eighty-four Americans injured and eighteen killed, the bodies of some of them dragged through the streets. Matt's Delta Force unit had lost three soldiers and two were missing in action, but Trish was so relieved Matt was alive that she didn't really hear the bad news. She shoved it to the back of her mind.

It wasn't until after she'd called the folks in Iowa with the good news about Matt that it hit her — she knew three women whose husbands were dead, two women whose husbands were missing. Trish's relief turned to guilt. *What do you pray for?* she wondered. Do you pray that the two missing men were OK, that they'd been able to use their training in E&E, escape and evasion, and that even now they might be in the process of making contact? Or do you fear the worst, that they'd been captured? In which case you prayed to God, *Please let them die quickly.*

Trish got busy. She organized the five wives on her team to make meals for the families of the dead and missing. It gave her a sense of control. But each time Trish knocked or rang a doorbell, her sense of control evaporated. She never knew what to expect, how the wife on the other side of the door was going to react. One wife, right after she was notified, had seen the car full of commanders' wives waiting outside, and said, "I don't want those women in my house. I'll call my friends." Other wives were glad to see those women. One wife didn't want to be alone at all. She wanted everyone there, even if they just sat together in silence. Trish sat next to her, thinking, *How can I say anything cheerful or supportive? I'm one of the lucky ones, Matt's OK, these women should be mad at me.*

When she got home from visiting that first night, she called her recently widowed friend Barb out in Seattle. "What can I say?" Trish asked. "What should I do? You've been there, you can help me. You know."

What Barb knew was that those wives were in shock. She knew they were exhausted with sudden responsibilities, that they couldn't even begin to express what they were feeling. Barb said, "I think I need to come."

Trish protested, "You have a three-week-old baby, what can you do?"

"I have a three-week-old baby," said Barb, "*and* I've survived widowhood for six months. Maybe I can help. Maybe I can be an example."

Barb and her baby landed in Fayetteville less than twenty-four hours later. Together, she and Trish went to the home of one of the new widows, twenty-two years old, her face brittle as she acted the part of the hostess, trying to make them feel comfortable. "Honey," Barb said, "we're here to help *you.*" They stayed with her late into the evening. The next day brought more of the same: Trish hurrying home from work, her head spinning, an evening of more visits ahead. Her little boys were already staying with another military family that lived across the street. Barb gathered up the baby and the diaper bag. Trish grabbed her purse, reached for the front door to lock it before heading through the house to the garage, and saw three men in dress greens coming up her walk.

She stared at them, her hand on the doorknob. She stared at them, those three men in their sharp green uniforms. *If I don't open the door,* she thought, *it won't be real. If I don't open the door, I won't have to deal with it. If I don't open the door, maybe it will just turn around and go away.*

The men climbed the front steps. They saw her there on the other side of the glass and knocked at the door. Then they stood there. And she stood there, her hand on the doorknob. And they stood there. And she knew that they knew that she knew. And time stopped. And time raced, both at the same time, one minute, or fifteen, she was outside time, outside the whole world, it was just her, standing there with her hand on the doorknob, and them, standing there waiting for her. Standing there. Just standing there. And then they knocked again.

She opened the door.

The men walked into her foyer, the world rematerializing around her as they did, Barb and the baby behind her, the great room, the house, the street outside, all the streets of Fayetteville sprawling across the Carolina sandhills, the continent stretching away to the west and to the east the ocean rolling all the way to Africa, and Somalia, where soldiers had been killed and injured, *injured,* there was still hope, and as one of the men started to say something, she interrupted. "I just want to know. Is he dead?"

And the man said, "Yes."

She'd been standing at the door but now she found herself next to the couch. She sat down. They sat with her, a chaplain, a major, and the sergeant major of the unit. Barb quietly went out the door and across the street to the neighbors. Trish said, "I want to hear everything. But I'm just not quite ready."

So they just sat there for a while. The house surrounded them in silence until she was ready. And when she was ready, they told her that today, two days after the battle ended, when it was already after dark in Somalia, Matt had been in the camp compound, standing outside with his company commander, the unit commander, and the unit surgeon. With two soldiers still missing, Matt was of the very strong opinion that things weren't being done right, and he was sharing that opinion with the commanders in no uncertain terms when a mortar round exploded behind him. Mortar attacks on the camp were common. The Somalis lobbed mortars at the airfield almost nightly in an effort to take out the Americans' aircraft. But this one fell short. Matt's body — the body that had raced down an Iowa football field, that had rolled on the living room floor with the boys, that had loved her completely — that body had absorbed most of the explosion. The three men he was standing with were badly injured.

Barb returned with the news that Jacob and Kaleb were going to spend the night with the neighbors. While the notification team waited, Trish called a friend back home in Iowa. She asked him to gather the family together, and right away the friend knew something was wrong. She said, "This is the hardest thing I've ever had to ask anybody to do. But you have to tell Matt's mom that he was killed in action today." Her friend just said, "Whatever you need."

The notification team would have done it differently. They would have let the local casualty assistance command in Iowa tell the family in person. But sometimes the real world refuses to operate according to regulations — a witness to a casualty sends an e-mail that's quickly forwarded . . . a press release is accidentally released to the media before the family is notified . . . notification teams in separate states mistime their arrivals and notify a secondary next of kin before a primary. The real world operates according to its own rules, and suddenly people are receiving the news by phone. Which isn't always bad. Trish knew her mother-in-law well enough to know she would take the news better from someone she knew. So the family was gathered, Matt's and Trish's, and the friend told them what little news Trish was able to pass on over the phone. Then Trish handed the receiver to the notification team, and they answered the questions being asked far away in that Iowa living room.

After the notification team left, it was just Trish and her best friend Barb and the shared black hole of their two dead husbands.

When Trish was off in college and Matt was back home working for her dad, trying to figure out what he wanted to do with his life, she had called his parents' house.

"He's not home," his mother said.

"Where's he at?" Trish asked.

His mom said he was at Camp Dodge, at the Army recruiting station. Trish couldn't believe it. To make such a major decision without including her when they were talking about spending the rest of their lives together? "You just tell him I called," she snapped.

"Hi," he said later when he called her back.

"Yeah," was all she said.

"So Mom told me you called. I was —"

"We're not having this conversation on the phone," she said. "I'll see you Friday."

That Friday she listened as he talked about the Army's elite units. Skydiving, scuba diving, survival training — he'd grown up in a little town in

Iowa. He'd never heard of such a life. He liked pistol shooting and being outdoors. The Army was the first career he'd ever come across that sounded good or felt right.

"OK," she said, but she was skeptical. Matt wasn't a yes-sir kind of guy. This was a man whose mother was still cutting up his meat for him so he could eat and get out the door faster. Matt had earned a two-year degree but his dad wanted him to go on and get a full four-year degree. Trish was just hoping Matt would get out there, start the training, and hate it — get this Army thing out of his system so that by the time she was done with college and grad school, he'd be done with his enlistment and they could get on with their lives.

But he came home from his first six months of training and he was fit, and thin, and humble. And happier than she'd ever seen him.

The next morning, the boys came back across the street. Trish hugged them, so happy and chattering, and she could not tell them. As the day went on, Jacob would come to her and say, "Mommy why are you sad?" And Trish would say, "Oh, Mom's just having a bad day, I'll tell you about it later."

Then the doorbell began to ring and sad-looking people arrived, and flowers, and big plants with sympathetic cards. And Jacob asked, "Mommy, why is all this stuff coming into our house?" Trish said, "Well, something's happened, and people are just coming over to share their concern."

He bought that for a little while longer, and then he came to her and asked, "So what happened?"

By then it was late in the afternoon. The chaplain and the unit psychologist were there. Trish led the boys to the couch and Jacob climbed up to sit next to her and Kaleb hopped on her lap. She told them, "There was an accident with Dad at work. He was hurt badly and Daddy died. He's not coming home again. And all these people here are sad because they love Daddy and they're going to miss him."

Jacob looked away. Then he bolted from the couch, tore away to his room, and crawled under the bed.

Kaleb watched his brother go. After a moment he looked up at his mother. "Can I go play now?"

Trish tried to smile. "Sure, honey, you go play." And he did.

She looked over at the psychologist and the chaplain. "Is this normal?" she asked. "What do I do now?"

It was perfectly appropriate, they assured her. Just go be with Jacob, they said.

So she crawled under the bed with her son, and together they cried. They stayed there a long time. They stayed until Jacob was ready to come out.

It was hard for the other wives in the family support group to make themselves go see Trish Rierson. They'd all thought it was over. By the time the notifications were completed on Monday, the guys weren't engaged in any more fighting, their wives had thought they were out of harm's way. A lot of the men in fact were packing up to come home, the injured already on the way, and their wives were looking forward to the reunions. To go visit Trish was to be reminded that nobody was safe, not until they were in each other's arms.

But they did go to her. They organized food for the people who crowded the house in those first days, the front door constantly opening and closing, the family arriving from Iowa, more florists, visitors offering condolences. Their small Delta unit was overwhelmed with widows, but still the other wives were there to answer Trish's phone for her, pick up people from the airport, watch Jacob and Kaleb so the boys could keep to their normal routines while Trish went with the casualty assistance officer to the funeral home to make arrangements. The wives handled the small daily details while Trish was in such a fog that she couldn't think clearly.

It was in that state that she was plunged down a rabbit hole of benefits changes, paperwork deadlines, legal issues, insurance payoffs, and financial decisions — a maze that left her dependent on the casualty assistance officer for information and guidance. Trish and many of her fellow survivors report that they were well served by the officer assigned to them. Others say that while their casualty assistance officers were compassionate and respectful, they weren't adequately trained and often didn't know the answers to their questions, and then sometimes deployed in the middle of everything, since they were, after all, regular military officers in addition to their duties in casualty assistance.

Part of the problem could be solved by turning the job over to fulltime, professionally trained, civilian government employees. In addition, a private company called Armed Forces Services Corporation, or AFSC, has developed a computer program that plows through the survivor benefits regulations of an alphabet soup of government agencies and programs, then spits out a personalized printout of all the benefits for which a surviving spouse and children are eligible — and does it within minutes. There's a membership fee for the service, but the military mutual aid and relief societies, like Army Emergency Relief, will pay the fee for any widow or widower of an active-duty death who requests it. After spitting out the initial printout, for the rest of the survivors' lives AFSC tracks the inevitable changes in laws and benefits and lets them know how those changes affect them personally. It's the sort of service that common sense says should be provided to every survivor automatically as part of the casualty affairs system.

In addition to working her way through the official benefits maze, Trish also had to make personal decisions, and quickly. She was grateful she and Matt had talked about what he wanted all those months ago when Barb's husband was killed; that was his gift to her now, knowing what Matt wanted. When the family said, "He should be buried in Iowa," she could say, "No, he wanted to be buried here in Fayetteville with other soldiers."

The day Matt was buried, Trish went that same night to another soldier's memorial service and more in the weeks that followed, as the wives closed in around her, getting her through each day. The neighborhood closed in around her, too. The media showed up outside in their news trucks and the neighbors said, "No comment." The men returned home and closed in around her, in spite of their survivor's guilt, or perhaps because of it. They wrote letters about Matt for her sons to read one day. One morning she woke up to the sound of a lawn mower, and thought, *Yeah, I need to do that, too.* She looked out and there in her yard was a guy from the unit who lived in the neighborhood, already doing it for her.

Two months flew by. Trish returned to work. Most of her coworkers were military spouses, and they opened their arms and welcomed her back. She and several of the other widows met together with a psychologist once a month for the first year or so, but Barb and another widow from the unit were the ones Trish called when she found herself completely unable to make a decision about, say, new tires. It was something Matt always used to take care of, but it was a simple decision really. And she was frozen. She would call one of them and ask, "Is this normal?" And they would say, "Yeah."

Experts say it takes two years to get over a death, longer if the death is traumatic. And if the death occurs during a deployment, sometimes the grief process doesn't actually start until the rest of the unit returns. After all, the service member was already gone, so when he died, nothing really changed. But when everybody else comes home, suddenly it hits the survivors — *he didn't come home like the rest.*

Whenever the grief process starts, it tends to follow the same path. A sudden death occurs, and the survivor feels like he or she is going crazy. Her life feels out of control, surreal. In quick succession, loss piles on top of loss: Her husband, gone . . . her role within the military community, gone . . . if she's living on post, she must move out within six months — her home, gone . . . her beliefs about the world and how it functions, gone: Bad things happen to good people for no apparent reason, prayers go unanswered, you cannot control what happens to you.

Often, in the initial days, she's numb. She's suffering from disbelief and shock. She's disoriented, apathetic. As the weeks turn into months, the intense numbness gives way to equally intense, overwhelming emotions: anxiety about the future, fear, irritability and anger, sadness and depression, a feeling of powerlessness. Gradually, as the months turn to years, the intense emotions overwhelm less often. But anniversaries, holidays, and special family occasions can bring them right back.

As the months went on, Trish stayed so busy she didn't have time to face how her life had changed. But then she'd go grocery shopping at the commissary on post and have to show her new ID card in the checkout line, and sometimes the clerk would squint at the status box — where most of the time there was printed either an "AD" for "active duty," or "RET" for "retired" — and the clerk would say, "'URW?' What's that?" And Trish would have to say, "Unremarried widow." The clerk would look at her, thirty-two years old with small children hanging on her cart, and the clerk's face would fall and so would Trish's heart.

Eventually it started to catch up with her, all the things she would never have. That first year, there were so many firsts to remind her, like Jacob's first day of kindergarten. Matt wasn't there to take him. The grief washed over her, and then the anger kicked in. She'd get so angry at the men who were alive, the men who were crappy husbands. *OK, God,* she'd demand, *why didn't you take one of them? His wife wouldn't mind!* And when she was angry, that was when she finally realized *she* was still alive and the numbness, at least, was gone.

At the end of the first year, she took off her rings. It just seemed like the right time. *I've survived a year,* she told herself. She had the oval diamond reset into a necklace. From here on in, she was sure, it was going to be easier. She went on with her life as supermom and superdad both. Her kids were going to be perfect. She was going to be perfect. Her house was perfect, clean and tidy.

Two years after taking off her rings, she found herself in bed for four days with the worst case of the flu she'd ever had, feverish and exhausted. At last she went to her doctor. He asked her a series of pointed questions, and then he said, "I think it's about time you deal with your depression."

"I'm not depressed," she said. "I'm sick, I've got the flu, I'm tired, I have two little kids."

That was all true, he agreed. "And you're masking your depression with all your activities. You really need to look at it."

Of course she called one of her fellow widows and told her what that crazy doctor had said, that she was depressed, and the other widow said, "Yeah, I think we all are."

By the time Trish reached the fourth year, she and her children were beginning what would become two years of counseling. Before she finally turned to a therapist, though, she told her widowed friend, "Maybe I need to get some help." And the friend said wryly, "Well, *we* all did."

As the years went on, eight, nine, ten new military widows sought Trish out. "Am I crazy?" they'd ask. "When does it get easier?" She was invited to speak to one group about her experience. Then another. She told them, "In the early years, it's Family Heritage Week at school, the children drawing their dad as an angel in the sky. As time goes on, it's the birthdays. It's when your kids come home really excited about something. Those are the times it hits you: *He's gone.*"

When Jacob told Trish he'd made the varsity football team, it hit her: His dad would be so proud. When Kaleb burst in the door from paintball and said, "Look at me, there's no paint on me!" because he was so good at evading and firing back, it hit her: That's his dad. Jacob would laugh like him. Kaleb, the son who couldn't remember him, would put his hand on his hip and cock his head like him. And it would hit her.

In the fall of 2003, as the husbands of Marissa Bootes and Beth Pratt traveled the roads of the Sunni Triangle, Luigi at the wheel in one convoy, Charlie manning the Mark-19 in another, Trish Rierson and her sons attended a memorial service with Matt's old unit. It had been ten years. They visited the memorial wall. They listened to the stories, heard about the sacrifices, and Trish watched helplessly as both her big boys sat there and cried as if they were hearing it all for the very first time.

In a way, they were. They were older now. They had a better under-standing of the world, and what it meant to die. They had a fuller appre-ciation for what their father had done and for what their friends' fathers were continuing to do. They said, "Wow, Johnny's dad's still doing that every day." They said, "He's awfully brave, 'cause my dad died doing that."

On the way home from the memorial service, and in the days that fol-lowed, Jacob and Kaleb had so many questions running through their heads that they were overwhelmed. Trish had to revisit the stories she thought they'd already heard and understood, such as why the command didn't move the Deltas and Rangers to a safer location when mortars were coming down every night. And it was true, they had already heard these stories, at age seven, or nine, but now they needed to hear them again, with the understanding of a twelve- and fourteen-year-old. They had listened to the men who were Matt's friends discussing him with re-spect and admiration. Now they talked about how watching those men grieve opened their own eyes. They discussed how it felt to hear about this man they didn't remember, this hero who helped save the lost con-voy, running from vehicle to vehicle through waves of bullets and rocket-propelled grenades, and the pressure they felt to live up to that same standard.

Looking ahead, Trish realized in two or three more years she would undoubtedly have to go through it with them yet again, and again when-ever she finally let them see *Black Hawk Down*, the movie based on the book about the battle of Mogadishu. She'd seen it, and she could already hear the questions they'd be asking afterward, the details they'd need to have explained to them in order to comprehend what had really happened.

That fall, whenever news about the war in Iraq flashed across the TV, Jacob and Kaleb would stop and watch in silence. When they heard about two Black Hawks crashing, Jacob asked, "Mom, do we know any of those people?" Trish had to admit it was possible. His voice, just starting to change, was cracked and somber. "I sure hope not." He and his brother knew Mitch Lane, who would be killed in another year while fast-roping down to check a cave in the mountains of Afghanistan. They knew Mitch's teammate, Peter Tycz, had been killed in Afghanistan the year be-fore, a plane crash. They lived in Fayetteville, after all. They were sur-rounded by soldiers. The 82nd's 2d and 3d Brigades were in Iraq; the 1st Brigade had returned from Afghanistan a few months before.

Over on Fort Bragg, 1st Brigade Chaplain (Major) Jeffrey Watters was in a morning staff meeting with the brigade commander. Just back from Afghanistan and his own first wartime deployment, Chaplain Watters had the face of a man you could picture leading other men into combat, all flat planes and strong jaw. But as a chaplain, of course, he was forbidden by the Geneva Conventions from even carrying a weapon.

So far in Iraq, the 82nd had absorbed sixteen KIAs, soldiers killed in action, all of them since May 1, when the president had declared an end to major combat operations. Lately, KIAs had been on the news day and night, and in that morning staff meeting, one of the brigade officers was talking about how a friend of his wife was crying when she stopped by the house over the weekend. She'd been at the funeral of a soldier who was KIA. "She was just devastated," the officer said. "She was thinking, you know, what would happen if that were my husband?"

Alarm bells went off in Chaplain Watter's head. He'd been seeing the same thing: wives coming into his office, crying. There were sixteen KIAs and a handful of grieving widows, but maybe thousands more women out there grieving for husbands who were still alive, grieving as if they were already dead. *My word,* he thought, *it's the elephant in the living room — what are we going to do for all these ladies?*

After the meeting, he started calling around to other chaplains, who agreed they'd been seeing it, too, spouses exhibiting all the same symptoms, even the same physical symptoms, as those who were grieving an actual death: tightness in the throat or chest like an anxiety attack, shortness of breath, sensitivity to loud noises, forgetfulness and difficulty concentrating, agitation and restlessness, extreme hunger or lack of appetite, crying jags, headaches, and insomnia. Some were resorting to drug use and excessive drinking.

He and the other chaplains of the 82nd, the ones who weren't in Iraq, did some digging. As the division lost a soldier a week, sometimes a soldier a day, as this mass mourning swept through the post, the chaplains discovered there was a name for it: anticipatory grief. They learned that if you recognized it for what it was, you could deal with it. Give yourself permission to turn off the TV news. Become part of a team — join in at church, jump in at the FRG — and discover you're not alone. Learn about the grief process. Think through what you'll need to do if The Worst That Could Happen happens to you, and what to say if it hits so close to home that it happens to someone you know: *I'm so sorry, I can't imagine how difficult this is for you . . . If it's OK, I'd like to stay with you for a while . . . Do you feel like talking about him? . . .* Make your offers of help concrete, unlike the vague, ever popular "Let me know if I can do anything," which just puts the burden back on a person already overburdened with grief and new responsibilities.

The chaplains decided to empower the spouses of the 82nd with this knowledge about the grief process and how to deal with it. They started planning a seminar for the leaders of the Family Readiness Groups, so those spouses could take the information back to their units. They developed PowerPoint presentations. They lined up speakers. One of the chaplains knew an Army widow in Fayetteville; they lined her up, too. Her name was Trish Rierson.

That winter, inside Fort Bragg's Center for Family Life and Religious Education, chaplains and other officers wearing the same green BDUs and jump boots they wore to work every day sat down with a roomful of commanders' wives and FRG leaders in sweater sets and turtlenecks. The group would have looked like an odd combination in any other setting, but it was normal on a military installation.

On that day, the overall toll of American casualties in Iraq included thousands of wounded and around three hundred KIAs. By then, the 82nd had contributed a total of eighteen KIAs to that toll, one of them killed the day before when suicide bombers attacked the division's headquarters west of Baghdad.

Among the men in uniform was a young chaplain who had served under Chaplain Watters in Afghanistan. Chaplain (Captain) Christopher Dickey was a lean Texan with a high-and-tight haircut and a mouth that slid into a boyishly crooked half-smile when he talked. Now that he was back at Bragg, Chaplain Dickey's days were filled with briefing Family Readiness Groups about deployments and counseling spouses whose soldiers were over there.

He was getting the fearful calls from wives, too, the calls that started out, "My husband's just deployed . . ." He knew what they were afraid of. Because since coming back from Afghanistan, more than once now, he'd had to carefully put on his dress greens, make sure all the ribbons and emblems were in place, creases sharp, and walk with another soldier or two up to a home, knowing that inside was a woman who had no idea she was already a widow. In that moment, as they walked up to the door, the life she knew still existed. As soon as the soldier beside him knocked and she opened the door, that life would be gone.

He'd listen as the officer delivered the news. He'd listen as the wife, or the parents if the soldier had been unmarried, tried to make sense of what they'd just been told. Watching the pain take hold of them, part of him was always thinking, *How can I take that away? How can I make it better?* But he couldn't. Their lives were never going to be the same. He never said, "Hey, it's going to be OK." Because it wasn't. She'd just lost her husband. They'd just lost their son. There isn't a lot you can say in a moment like that, but Dickey trusted that the Holy Spirit, the divine comforter he trusted and believed in, was present, so he just tried to let God's love pass through him to the family.

The question of *why* always came up. Sometimes the soldier had been in the Army for less than a year. "He was so young," they would struggle to say. "He had so much of his life ahead of him. Why would God take him?"

"That's a valid question," Dickey would answer in his soft drawl. "That's the kind of question we all ask. Unfortunately, sometimes there's no answer." Out loud, he'd tell them it was all right to be angry. Silently, he'd tell himself, *Wherever this family is on their walk through the valley, just meet them there, just be with them. Though I walk through the valley of the shadow of death, I will fear no evil.* "Whether you're active in your faith or not," he'd say, "God is going to be with you." *For thou art with me; thy rod and thy staff they comfort me.*

After a while, when the family seemed ready, Dickey or one of the other officers would ask if there was anyone they could call to come now and be with them. The officers would explain there was a comfort team waiting outside.

Starla Smith had sat in that waiting car twice.

Now she sat in the same seminar room as Chaplain Dickey, listening to the speakers talk about anticipatory grief, its symptoms and solutions, and she thought to herself, *Twenty years in the Army and this is eye opening.*

Her husband, Jeff, had been active duty for almost as long as they'd been married. They'd started out at Fort Bragg and now, twelve moves and two children later, they were back. She'd lost track of the number of deployments and training exercises that had taken him away from home over the years. These days Jeff was a colonel and he'd taken the 82nd's 3d Brigade to Iraq. This deployment didn't feel different from any of the others, till she heard from Jeff that they were in Fallujah. She'd heard a lot about Fallujah, none of it good. But no deployment, not even this one, was going to keep her up at night. She was a fast-moving woman with highlights in her hair and a dimpled smile on her face. "Until I ever get that knock," she'd say in her sweetly snappy Tennessee way, "I really don't sit and think about it."

But the kids worried about it — their son in college, their daughter in a new high school. So far on this Iraq deployment, Starla had really been going through it with her daughter, who was wiped out with worry about her father and hated her new school. At one point, Starla got so she was thinking, *I've been doing this for twenty years! And it's enough! And it's his fault that I'm having to deal with all this myself!* Starla's friends got her over it. A huge people person, that was how she described herself. She knew she was lucky that way — it was a personality trait that had equipped her with a wide safety net of friends, most of them fellow Army wives.

The first time Starla sat in that waiting car, she was a battalion commander's wife, back when Jeff was in Kosovo. It was a notification of a serious injury. The second time had come during this Iraq deployment, a fatality. Ordinarily, the battalion commander's wife would have gone with the comfort team, but she was out of town, so Starla went in her place. The notification team went inside, and Starla and the other women waited in the car for about forty-five minutes.

One of the officers came out. Inside, when the chaplain had said, "There's some ladies from the FRG outside, would you like them to come in?" the wife had looked surprised and said yes. She was not involved in her FRG. She admitted she wouldn't have thought they would come like that, for someone they didn't really know.

She wanted to talk. She told Starla and the others what a great soldier her husband was. She showed them his medals. She had just packed a care package that she had planned to close up the next morning to send to him. She wondered what she should do with it now. She made several phone calls. They stayed with her until her best friend rushed in the door an hour later. For Starla, it felt like the most worthwhile hour she could have spent; she felt a sense of gratefulness that she could be there.

She felt grateful to be at the anticipatory grief seminar, too. The sorrow, the anger — she'd felt it all at one time or another, and now, after twenty years, she finally knew why.

Nearby in that same seminar room, a chaplain's wife who'd never told anybody she'd been making plans in her head in case her husband was killed finally had a name for it. A lieutenant colonel's wife was just wishing the seminar had happened sooner.

One of the 82nd's brigadier generals got up and said he'd probably seen more grief in the last three months than he'd ever seen in his life. A chaplain said, "These wives are watching CNN and they've had it up to here, they want more information and what they want to know is that their husband will come home now, they want to know he's coming home alive." Which of course was information no one could give them. Trish Rierson said, "This is just one situation we're not prepared for, no matter how it happens, how you get the news, you think you're ready but you're not." And then she described, step by step, exactly what happened when three men in dress greens walked up to her door and told her that her lover, her best friend, the father of her children, was dead. Ten years later, her voice was strong and sometimes funny, and when she smiled it seemed as natural as the tears that leaked steadily down her face.

After making a notification, Chaplain Dickey always left with a knot in his gut. Usually, he didn't feel like talking about it with anybody. He was glad he was so busy. He'd make the notification and then he'd be right back in it, briefing FRGs, counseling soldiers and their families. The needs were so great. When he could just focus on helping other people and their issues, it was paradoxical, but he found that his needs got met, too.

He had notification officers tell him, "That's the hardest thing I've ever done in my life, Chaplain." He never felt as if he quite had a handle on it either. It wasn't something he ever wanted to get a handle on. He was honored and humbled to serve the families in that role; it was a privilege he was thankful for. And he wished he'd never had that opportunity.

On a gloomy August day, the car carrying the casualty notification team and the news that Staff Sergeant Brian Hellermann had been shot in an ambush in Baghdad pulled into the parking lot in front of one of those moldering apartment buildings in the Nijmegen neighborhood on Fort Bragg. The comfort team's car pulled in behind it. The news about Sergeant Hellermann had traveled from his company's headquarters in Baghdad all the way around the world to the Pentagon and from there down the coast to the Casualty Assistance Command on Fort Bragg. Now it came to a stop in this parking lot. While the women waited, three men in dress greens got out of the first car, walked up to the battered door of apartment 12B, and knocked.

It was midmorning. Michelle Hellermann had already taken her son to summer camp. Her daughter was still asleep in bed when Michelle opened the door.

She knew it was bad news the instant she saw them. She was the acting leader of her FRG. She saw the car with the comfort team waiting in the parking lot and knew FRG leaders like herself usually were part of the team. She said, "Wait, I need to change clothes."

"Michelle," one of the men said, "we need to talk." She told them she'd be quick.

"Michelle," he said. She was dressed for a summer morning around the house, in shorts and a T-shirt. "We need to talk," he said. She couldn't get in that car and go try to comfort somebody looking like this, it wasn't right.

"Michelle," he said, "we need to talk," and as if she'd been bewitched and the third time broke the spell, she realized the bad news was for her.

Brian had been shot in the ankle in that ambush, but he'd also been shot in the head. It was a large caliber round, and it went straight through his Kevlar helmet. Not long after he arrived at the field hospital, the soldiers who'd picked him up from that shadowy street, his friends, gathered around him again as the doctor turned off the life support.

His wife, Michelle, was thirty-one. Their son was fourteen, their daughter nine. Brian Hellermann was thirty-five when he became the fifth 82nd paratrooper to die in Iraq. He had grown up in Freeport, Minnesota, about a ninety-minute drive from where Beth Pratt was growing up in Hutchinson.

One month later, as Beth was saying goodbye to her husband Luigi, and Marissa and Lexie Bootes were saying goodbye to Charlie, that interview with Michelle Hellermann appeared on the front page of the *Fayetteville Observer*. The article painted a portrait of a strong Army wife determined to make a new life for herself and her children while stoically grieving the loss of her husband. "Brian died doing what he loved doing," she was quoted as saying. "I can't be angry at anybody. There's nobody to be angry with."

What she was, was numb. In the months ahead, she would have to uproot her children and move off-post. She would feel herself rejected by her FRG. Only one member of her husband's unit would continue to reach out to her. After the unit returned from Iraq, the family therapist recommended that the children be allowed to visit the unit's headquarters, see the place where their father had worked one last time and the soldiers with whom he had worked. The commanding officer said absolutely not. Perhaps he was trying to protect his soldiers from what would undoubtedly be an emotionally wrenching visit. But a unit that fails to close ranks around the survivors increases their sense of dislocation, making it especially hard for the children to find closure and begin healing.

As one rejection followed another, Michelle's daughter came apart. Within a year, her daughter, her son, and Michelle herself were all diagnosed with post-traumatic stress disorder. When Michelle Hellermann sat down for that interview, she had no idea she was only one month down a road that would stretch ahead for years, through a valley where the shadows only seemed to grow longer.

Across town, every time Trish hears about another loss on the news, her gut tightens and she thinks, *Oh no*. The thought is automatic. She can't help it. Tap that spot and it's like tapping a knee: *Oh no*, she thinks, *there is one more wife who is walking this road that she just should not be walking.*

CHAPTER 7

Connections

THAT KNOCK AT THE DOOR is what the rest of us are afraid of.
Late one evening, an FRG leader on Fort Bragg got a phone call
from one of the young wives in her group. She was distraught.
Someone had called her to report that her husband had been seriously
injured and she should go immediately to the unit's headquarters on
post, but she was scared and confused and couldn't drive herself and she
wanted to know: Could the FRG leader please help her get over there tonight? That didn't sound right to the FRG leader, and she was correct.
The young wife was lucky she and her leader had established enough of a
relationship that she felt comfortable about checking with her leader, because it turned out the call was a hoax. Either someone's idea of a joke, or
a setup for a crime.

Many of the military spouses I know have no idea how a casualty
notification is actually made. They tend to have only a vague image in
their minds of receiving a phone call. Spouses who don't know how the
system works are doubly vulnerable; our fear alone makes us vulnerable
enough. Take me, for instance. I was on the road a lot during my husband's deployments. The rear party (as the rear detachment was known
in his Marine Corps unit) and the Key Volunteers always had both my
cell phone number and my sister's number so they could track me down
if they needed to. I was in Florida at my mother's, lying awake in bed
early one morning when I heard my mom's phone ring. Frank was somewhere in Iraq. My mother cracked the door. "Kristin?" she said. "It's for
you. It's a sergeant somebody."

The distance from my bedroom door to the kitchen phone is nineteen
feet. It takes four seconds to cover it. Plenty of time to bury my husband

and resurrect him by the time I picked up the receiver, because maybe, maybe he was just injured. I managed to say, "This is Kristin," and Gunnery Sergeant Crim cheerfully informed me he was responding to the message I had left with the rear party the week before; he now had an answer for my question about Frank's combat pay.

When I hung up a few minutes later, my mother was already back in bed, blissfully unaware of my tragedy that didn't happen. Me, I was wide awake — me, who had already been through a previous wartime deployment, a chaplain's wife who knew good and well how the system worked. Say it really *had* happened, say Frank had been severely wounded or killed. Once my sister told the CACO team where I was, the way she had apparently told Gunny Crim, two or three men in Marine or Navy dress blues would have simply showed up at my mother's door. They wouldn't have called ahead. I knew that. And I still panicked.

Beth Pratt would imagine them showing up at her door. She imagined them telling her, "Your husband died." And in her fantasy, she yelled at them, "My husband died because of something that wasn't supposed to be going on in the first place!" And then she'd beat the crap out of them.

Beth thought about that the day Camilla Maki, her key caller, telephoned her because Camilla herself had had a panic experience. She'd been on the phone with another friend when she heard a knock. Her young son peeked out the window next to the door and came running to her, eyes wide and anxious, saying there were two Army men out there. Camilla said to her friend, "What do I do! What do I do!" They kept knocking, probably because they'd seen her son peek out, until at last her friend persuaded her to put down the phone and go open the door. And there, on her front stoop, were two dogcatchers. Uniformed animal control officers.

They said, "Ma'am, your gate was open, your two dogs were running around the neighborhood."

Camilla burst into tears. "My husband's deployed!" she cried. "You can't just go around knocking on doors — you can't do this to people."

The dogcatchers were stricken. "Ma'am, we're your friends."

It took her all day to get over it.

The possibility of that knock at the door creates the toughest challenge of a wartime deployment: uncertainty and lack of control. You don't know if it's coming and if it is, there's nothing you can do to prevent it. Spouses are advised to cope by staying busy while also making time to take care of themselves. Marissa Bootes took only the first half of that advice.

Marissa accelerated through the yellow light and glanced at her watch. Work had taken her through three counties, but if she kept hitting the green lights, she could spare Lexie extra minutes at the babysitter's.

As soon as Charlie left, everything started to go wrong. The heater at the house broke, then the air conditioning, and now the babysitter was giving her the creeps. Right after Charlie left, the sitter started taking on more and more kids and then Lexie peed her pants and was still wearing them when Marissa picked her up at the end of the day. She wound up sick with a urinary tract infection. She cried when Marissa left her at the sitter's in the mornings. She was still taking her invisible friend, Izzy, with her everywhere she went.

Outside the sitter's, Marissa checked her face in the rearview mirror. She didn't cry at all the first two weeks after Charlie left. She just smoked and chewed her lip, peeling off the skin with her teeth, and blasted music as she raced between county courthouses, funky R&B and loud pop with the kind of beat that made it hard to think too much. Then one day, she started to cry, as lonely as she'd been before she met Charlie, as lonely as she would be again if he died and left her by herself. She had helped him study when he was learning to be a soldier. Along with him, she'd learned that the first person you shoot is the guy on the gun, so she knew damn well that the other guys were aiming for the same thing: Her husband. On the gun.

The deployment was completely different from when he was gone during training. During training, although he wasn't there and she missed him, she could look forward to him coming home. Now she didn't know if he was ever coming home. Now she cried all the time, but never in front of Lexie, just alone in the car, or at night after Lexie was asleep, so as not to scare her.

The tears weren't visible in the rearview mirror. She bounded up the steps to the babysitter's door. Inside, Lexie ran to her and as soon as she was in her arms Marissa felt it. She hugged Lexie tight and yelled at the sitter, because how could the poor kid have been left in peed pants *again?* The sitter protested that she didn't have to be so rude, but Marissa didn't care if the sitter was offended, this was her daughter and she'd been sitting in her own urine since before lunch. Marissa swore they were never coming back.

She swept Lexie home, bathed her, fed her, and cuddled her to sleep, as if that solved everything. But she was alone in Fayetteville. No husband. No mother. No mother-in-law or sister-in-law. No one she could ask to take Lexie till she figured out what to do.

She could have called Military OneSource, a twenty-four-hour, toll-free help desk that service members and their families could call or e-mail any time day or night for information or referrals on everything from how to find a job to where to find accredited child-care providers. She could have called her FRG leader, who would have referred her to Fort Bragg's Army Community Services center, which also kept a list of approved child-care providers. Or she could have called the only woman in town she halfway knew, Jenn Marner, who used to be her FRG's co-leader but no longer was, in fact was no longer even in the same FRG, because Jenn's husband's unit was no longer attached to Charlie's.

Jenn was whom she called. Marissa knew Jenn, she could vent to her. "What the hell do I do now? I still have to go to work tomorrow."

"I'm home all day," said Jenn. "Bring Lexie here. I'll watch her with my kids."

Actually, Marissa's house was close to a clean, bright, well-equipped daycare center. But she had to put Lexie on a waiting list. It would be months before an opening came up.

More than 60 percent of military spouses work outside the home, and 6 percent of service members are single parents. They all face the problem of finding child care, and whether you're civilian or military, it's catch-as-catch-can, working your contacts until you find a solution. This problem isn't unique to military families. However, for them, every time they move to a new assignment they're starting from zero in terms of who and what they know.

The military services have moved in to help meet the need. At the time of Marissa's crisis, they were providing child care to military families through nine hundred Child Development Centers on three hundred military installations. The families paid for the care, but at least they didn't have to hunt for it. But there were more children than the centers could accommodate, so the military services had also developed a network of nine thousand in-home child-care providers. Even so, the centers and in-home providers met the child-care needs of only about two thirds of active-duty families, and that number did not include National Guard and Reserve members who'd been suddenly mobilized for active duty. They, like Marissa, scrambled to make do.

At Womack, the Army hospital, Beth worked the overnight shift. In the morning, she'd drive out through the checkpoint at the gate and on toward home, where Danny waited in the quiet. She'd watch, unsmiling, as he ran in circles out back. She'd eat a breakfast bar while she checked her e-mail — more often than not there was nothing from Luigi.

His first call had come soon after he arrived in Kuwait, on his way to Iraq. "It's so beautiful here," he said. He spent most of the call telling her about the desert birds he'd seen. She was crushed. She cried to Camilla, "He doesn't miss me. Are they always like this?"

"Honey," said Camilla, "just give them a couple months and then they want to come home so bad."

There were many days when Beth would push a videotape into the VCR and sit down to watch. It always took ten minutes. That's how long the tape was: ten minutes of Luigi surfing, goofing around on the beach, playing with Danny here in the living room, taking a shower. "Show me your butt," her voice laughed from behind the camera. Now she couldn't watch without reaching for a tissue.

Alone in the duplex, she wished she were the type of person who could just call someone up and say, "Hey, let's get together." But she wasn't. She was the type of person who believed if you opened yourself up to people, people you didn't know very well, you made it possible for them to hurt you. She'd seen it happen over and over again to friends of hers, nice people who were also a little naive. So she kept to herself.

Before going to bed for the day, Beth performed her new bedtime ritual. Place the cell phone on the nightstand next to the framed photo of Luigi in his desert tan DCUs and maroon beret. Pick up his picture. Kiss it. Then lie down with Danny curled next to her feet.

She rolled one way. She rolled the other. Danny got up and moved out of reach of her legs. Whatever random thoughts paraded through her mind, lurking behind them was always Luigi getting shot, Luigi getting blown up, Luigi careening down an embankment in his truck and drowning in a river. There were always a few hours each day when Luigi wasn't on her mind — that would be when she was asleep. But in the weeks since Luigi left, she'd been lucky to get four good hours of sleep out of the many she lay in bed each day.

Then it was hard to get up and do it all over again. Shower. Walk Danny. Feed Danny. Mix up instant mac and cheese for dinner. Eat some of it. Drive back to Womack for the overnight shift. Take the elevator to Labor and Delivery. Help deliver babies.

Upstairs from Labor and Delivery, there's an office stacked with piles of paper that would seem orderly if there weren't so many of them. Each day a slight man in BDUs and jump boots rolls his office chair back and forth between the stacks and his computer. For eighteen years, Lieutenant Colonel Joseph Pecko has been practicing social work in the Army. The day he meets with me, he's the chief of the department of social work at Womack Army Medical Center on Fort Bragg. His tough camouflage and harsh haircut are undermined by his eyes, which have seen a lot of other people's pain.

As he describes the initial phases of deployment for me, his voice is gentle. "Well, ma'am," he says, "typically the spouses suffering from more acute difficulties are dealing with the adjustment, such as becoming, full-time, *both* parents. Having to take care of the family finances, having to take care of things that the soldier had taken care of." He sees a lot of anxiety and depression.

From a handbook for Marine Corps spouses, on the way spouses typically react right after the Marine deploys:

Emotional Disorganization

a) Relief that the "goodbye" part is over, but feeling guilty for the relief
b) New routines develop, but overwhelmed by all the new responsibilities
c) Sleeping is difficult due to loss of security and the spouse

Over the years, Lieutenant Colonel Pecko has learned that while the initial reaction is acute, most spouses seem to adjust to it and move on. He sees them realizing, *Hey, I can take care of this, I can perform these roles, and I'm not doing that bad at them.* They develop a new routine. This is what the Marine spouse handbook calls the "Recovery & Stabilization" phase.

After the initial acute period of Emotional Disorganization, much of the trouble he sees is the result of the spouse never getting a breather. He knows that if spouses get involved in the programs within the units, they establish connections and support systems and do quite well.

Problems arise when spouses come to Fayetteville from somewhere else, when they move away from their families and friends, and they choose not to participate in support programs and services or don't know how. "And those folks are at greater risk for having problems," he says. "When the Family Readiness Groups try to reach out to their people, it makes a dramatic difference."

Across the post, the shelves in the old school that houses Army Community Services are stocked with materials for FRG leaders. One handout suggests ways to reach out, aside from simply phoning and e-mailing and meeting. Under a graphic of a shining light bulb and the title "Event Ideas," on three pages printed front and back, is a long list of suggested events. A random sampling: bridge tournaments, origami classes, pet shows and turtle derbies, home video contests ("G-rated only!" the handout admonishes). Behind all the frivolous activity is the deadly serious business of getting through a time when a simple knock on the door can change your life forever. Staying busy is good, yes, but staying busy making connections with other human beings is even better.

Given how busy most of the volunteers' lives already are, however, most FRGs are doing well to simply meet.

Beth stepped gingerly into the big, white, windowless room at the unit headquarters where the FRG held its meetings. The room was filled with rows of metal chairs and women she didn't know. Most of them looked like they were just out of high school. She hung back, craning to see over heads. When she finally spotted Camilla's familiar dark hair and fair-skinned face, like Snow White, she smiled for the first time in a long while. Beth sat with her and the rest of the support and transportation wives, exchanging hellos and waiting for the meeting to start, listening to the young women around her compare notes.

"My husband calls me every day, just about . . ."

"Oh, yeah, mine too . . ."

Someone asked Beth how often she heard from her husband, as if it were some sort of contest.

"Well," she said, knowing she'd already lost, "I heard from him last week — for two minutes. Because the damn satellite telephone didn't work. You know, all the static — how're you doing *shhhhhhhh,* yesterday I *shhhhhhhh,* missing you *shhhhhhhh. Click!*"

The other women laughed because they knew exactly what she was talking about, and she laughed, too, though her eyes drilled right into whoever she was looking at. The conversation went on, but after that Beth didn't say much. When the meeting was over, she went home and had another cry.

Less than two hours north from where Beth lived in Fayetteville, Lynn Sinclair had lived in the little hamlet of Stem most of her life.

The members of Pleasant Grove Baptist Church knew her husband Danny was deployed with the National Guard and often asked after him. Danny drove a dump truck for a paving company in civilian life, and the folks he worked with sent her e-mails about how much they missed him. One neighbor had started cutting her grass and another came over and fixed her hot water heater when it broke, didn't charge her a penny. The Family Readiness Group that met at the armory in Oxford wasn't far away. Lynn was a stay-at-home mom, and if she felt too alone in the house, she could just call her mother and say, "Let's go shopping." One day she came out of the grocery store, put the bags in the trunk and the kids in the back seat, and then, just as she was climbing in behind the wheel, she saw a single yellow rose under her windshield wiper.

No note, just a rose. But she guessed whoever had put it there must have noticed the stickers on her car — on the rear bumper: HALF MY HEART IS IN IRAQ with half a broken heart, KEEP MY HUSBAND SAFE, KEEP MY DADDY SAFE, SUPPORT OUR TROOPS; on the side, the Blue Star Service Flag, a red-bordered rectangle with a single blue star on a white background symbolizing the deployment of a family member; and on the windshield: HAVE YOU HUGGED A SOLDIER TO-DAY? Passing truckers would give her a big thumbs-up. On military installations, safety briefings recommend against advertising that your soldier's away and you're home alone, but in Stem, everyone knew it anyway.

Many of the families of activated National Guard members and reservists have a particular advantage over full-time active-duty families: Most of them haven't been uprooted, moved to a military town far from anyone they know, and left isolated when their service member deploys. They're still home, surrounded by family and friends, with all their support networks in place. They may be the only military family in their circle, they may be one of only a few in their neighborhood or town, and while this can isolate them in a different way, it can also make them feel special if their community acknowledges what they're going through. A simple thank you, like Lynn's yellow rose, can go a long way.

In Illinois, when it became known that during deployment a number of Guard and Reserve families were barely getting by, the state began providing emergency grants of $500 to help pay for rent, utilities, and child care, all of it from money donated by Illinois residents. In Minnesota, the governor's wife spearheaded a program to connect military families in need with civilian volunteer services. Through a program that started in Maryland, travelers donated frequent-flyer miles to help the families of the wounded visit their loved ones in hospitals. And in Vermont, lawyers donated free legal services to families with a deployed service member.

When civilian communities say thank you to military families and service members, or when they offer them practical support, they're acknowledging that in a democracy like America, soldiers don't declare war. Our civilian leaders do, and they're elected by all Americans. Communities that support military families are acknowledging their own responsibility for the sacrifices those families have to make.

However, there is a downside to living in a civilian community far from a military installation.

Four months into her husband's deployment, Lynn Sinclair was one of only about fifty National Guard spouses who showed up for a regional spouse-appreciation dinner put on by the military at a high school cafeteria in Raleigh. After they'd all gone through the line and served themselves spaghetti and salad, officers in casual civvies got up one after another and talked about how much they appreciated the sacrifices they knew the spouses were making. The invitation had come in the mail, and Lynn sat at a table with a few of the spouses from her National Guard FRG who'd been able to make the trip down. When the speeches were over, the lights dimmed and a video tribute began — slow-motion scenes of husbands in tan DCUs hugging their wives goodbye, their small children hanging on them, crying, while the guitar wailed and a man's voice sang that he was an American soldier, proudly taking a stand and doing what was right.

It was a replay of one of the hardest days of Lynn's life, and watching it she felt as if she were cracking open. All the emotions she'd carefully managed for four months came pouring out, and suddenly she heard herself sobbing. She heard the woman across the table sobbing, too, and the woman next to her. She saw tears well up in the eyes of the lone husband in their group. Everyone at their table was crying, and at the next table, too, and the next, and the next. All across the cafeteria, everyone was in tears. Then the lights came up and the family readiness officer boomed cheerfully into the microphone, "Well, that's it for tonight, have a safe trip home!"

In all the time that her husband had been gone, Lynn hadn't let herself get more than a little teary-eyed, because she had known if she let herself go, she would be a long time stopping. A general came over and apologized to their table of weeping spouses, but his apology couldn't stop the tears. That night, Lynn and another woman she rode with cried the whole way home. She cried for three days. She cried till she threw up. She could see she was scaring her children and she couldn't do a thing about it, not till she'd cried it all out. The video just kept replaying in her head, over and over, scenes of sacrifice that she didn't need to see because she knew them already, she lived those sacrifices every day. *Show it to civilians,* she thought bitterly, *not us.* And she knew that if she ever needed help, no way would she ever call the military family readiness officer who understood so little as to show that video.

Lynn had come up against one of the disadvantages of being a National Guard spouse: many fewer points of contact with the military. Through its armories, temporary family assistance centers, and guard family.org Web site, the Guard supports all geographically dispersed families, whether they're Guard, Reserve, or active duty. But if one connection goes sour, many spouses wouldn't know where else to turn should they ever require official help. Lynn was lucky to have an active FRG and doubly lucky to live close to the place where the FRG met. She also lived less than two hours from Fort Bragg, but if she had a problem, there's no reason why it would have occurred to her to go there for help — her husband's North Carolina National Guard unit wound up deploying out of a base farther away, up in Virginia. And the two hours to Bragg still meant she had no practical daily access to any of the benefits of a large military installation.

In addition, as far as Lynn lived from Bragg, many Guard and Reserve families lived just as far or farther from their Guard armories, much less a fully equipped military installation. Some even lived in different states. Those families were sometimes at a loss when even minor problems came up. In Iraq, one of the American Red Cross workers there delivered five hundred emergency messages to service members every week, usually about seriously ill family members. But often she'd see messages from National Guard wives about relatively minor problems, such as child care. She would mutter to herself, "I cannot believe this message is being sent all the way to Iraq." It wasn't really an emergency, and what could the Guard member do about it in any case? But gradually it dawned on her that these women simply didn't know where else to turn.

Such families, isolated and far-flung, worried Martha Brown in the deployment and mobilization office on Fort Bragg. "It's really hard for that FRG leader to get her arms around all those people," she says. "Those far-away families are the ones that are having the most difficulty getting accurate and timely information."

Denise lived in South Florida, a very long day's drive from the base in Georgia from which her husband, Luis, deployed to Iraq for a year. He'd been an officer on inactive status in the Individual Ready Reserves for nearly ten years. She was shocked when he was suddenly called up just six months short of the end of his commitment, and for a war she opposed. She had three young children and no experience with military life. There were no military facilities near her; she knew no military families.

At night, she'd lie with her back to Luis's side of the bed, eyes closed, imagining him there beside her. Sometimes the fantasy was so vivid she could smell him, could almost believe she felt him warm against her back, except she knew that wasn't logical. He was in Baghdad. When she finally fell asleep, Luis's mother came to her in her dreams to comfort her, though she had been dead for years. In her nightmares, she opened her door and gasped at the three officers in dress greens who waited there, staring at her with sad eyes.

Even when Denise was awake, she still felt as if she were stumbling through a dream. In the grocery store, she moved among the other people pushing their carts. She wore her despair over the news from Iraq like a brand, yet they pushed past her as if she were invisible. She watched the other women check off the items on their lists, the same lists as the week before, still full of their husbands' favorite items, too absorbed in their everyday lives to see her, a walking ghost. She wanted to stop in the middle of the aisle and scream.

"We all live in civilian communities surrounded by people who have no clue how hard our days are" is how Rebecca Wilkins describes it. Her husband is an officer with a full-time career in the North Carolina National Guard. He was a major when he received a mobilization order for eighteen months. "They don't intend to be mean, but they say things that are hurtful, like, 'I don't think my husband could leave me for a year,' as if to say I'm married to the world's biggest jerk because he can."

Rebecca lived in Rocky Mount. Her husband's unit trained at Fort Bragg for six months before deploying. As long as he was there, Rebecca strapped their toddler into the car after working all week as an investigator for the state of North Carolina, and drove ninety minutes down the interstate to Bragg to see him for the weekend.

She and the other wives would gather with their children in the hotel for breakfast and they would ask each other, "Is it really going to be as long as they say? How are we going to get through this?" Rebecca was stunned at the number of women, even sophisticated officers' wives, who didn't know what their husbands did in the Guard. But it was understandable — when their husbands finally left for their yearlong deployment, it was the first time the brigade had deployed as a unit since World War II.

The brigade's families were scattered all over the state of North Carolina. Even at the company level, geography limited what the FRGs could do. So Rebecca invited the women around Rocky Mount whose husbands worked with her husband to get together each month. They were informal gatherings; no official information was passed. Just a group of women and children meeting up for a pool party, or a picnic in the park, or an outing to a portrait studio, photos they then sent to their husbands. No more than 10 percent showed up, but that 10 percent came to depend on each other. Rebecca watched as they empowered themselves with information, sharing news articles about the brigade, poring over maps of Southwest Asia. She could see why their husbands married these women. She became close friends with many of them.

As the deployment dragged on, they all seemed to hit the wall at the same time. When Rebecca was feeling down, she'd call one of the other wives and they'd be feeling the same. They assured each other, "It's just a natural reaction to an unreal situation."

They were right, but they were guessing. Like most of the Guard, Reserve, and active-duty Army spouses I met, they were never briefed about all those emotional phases they could expect to go through during a deployment. They just helped each other deal with it as it happened.

Back in Fayetteville, Beth had decided not to go to any more FRG meetings. She didn't see the point.

At night, the headlights humming up the highway from Beth's house flashed past a club called Broadstreet Café and Billiards. It didn't look like much from the outside, flat and nondescript in the middle of a strip mall so old and funky and unimproved the original Jetsons-era sign still towered over the parking lot like a flying saucer coming in for a landing. But behind the flat facade, Broadstreet's was thumping — it was Nickel Night. The really good music started around midnight, the badass hip-hop, and people were packed onto the dance floor and around the pool tables and in front of the bars ordering drinks for a nickel.

Marissa was in the dance pack with her club gear on — shiny silver zippers up and down the legs of her shiny black pants, silver multichain belt, zipper-edged top with one long sleeve and one bare shoulder, and on her feet, her platform dancing shoes. Charlie had told her to go out and have fun, so she was, full-bore de-stressing. She'd been dancing all night and she always had plenty of partners, all of them women. Marissa and her dance partners met through the online group that Jenn Marner had introduced Marissa to back in the spring. Now they were founding a group of their own and calling it the "Hooah Wives." "Hoo-*ah!*" That's what soldiers shout in the Army when they want to say, "Good to go!" or "Way to go!"

Spouses form their own informal groups outside the FRGs for a number of reasons. Some have nothing in common with the other spouses in their FRGs besides the fact that their soldiers work and fight together. Some are afraid that if they bare their souls to someone in their FRG, the next day all their soldier's buddies will be talking about it. Some have had a bad FRG experience in the past and want nothing to do with it. And some, such as Marissa, like their FRG just fine but get to know spouses from other units whose company they simply enjoy.

At Broadstreet's that night, a month after Charlie deployed, there were about a dozen Hooah Wives. Within a few months, they'd number nearly forty, with husbands in units all over Fort Bragg. They were every color, of different religions, some with children, some without, but mostly young, as young as eighteen. The group's two den mothers, hard-charging Jenn Marner and a warm black Englishwoman named Angela, were twenty-seven and thirty-three. About a third of their husbands, including Angela's, were overseas.

Angela's husband, Reggie, was in Afghanistan, a maps man. Though he was senior enlisted, they'd only been together a few years; it was Angela's first deployment. She had cried the day she got the news Reggie was leaving and most days since then. A sad song would come on the radio, and she'd cry. Or she'd be grocery shopping in the commissary and reach for his favorite food before remembering he wasn't home to eat it, and she'd cry. Or it would be evening, the kids in bed, the house silent, and she would miss not the sex but the cuddling, and she'd cry. Or their three-year-old son, Regan, would see planes go over, and remembering a photo Reggie had e-mailed from Afghanistan of himself standing next to the tail of a plane, Regan would point at the sky and call, "Daddy, Daddy!" Or Angela's mum would ring her up from England and ask how Reggie was, or an e-mail from him would pop up on her computer screen. And she would cry.

Only a few members of Reggie's company had deployed, so the other spouses in the FRG hadn't reached out to Angela, maybe because they didn't need to reach out for themselves. She felt forgotten. She gave her time to the Hooah Wives because she didn't want anyone else to feel that way. To the Hooah Wives, she was as soft as Jenn was tough, the good cop to Jenn's bad cop. She never had much advice to offer, but she could listen and share a hug and a glass of wine.

A few months later, I joined a gaggle of them in Jenn's kitchen, eating leftover cookies and chips and drinking Pepsi and dodging kids. Beside me, the woman named Tiffany whom Marissa had met online long before the deployment, cracked her knuckles, *crack, crack, crack.* Tiffany, she of the oft-deploying special forces husband, was half-Haitian, half–Puerto Rican, and all-girl, with the exception of the knuckle-cracking, in her flowered, bell-sleeved blouse that revealed a lot of cleavage, her hair back in a fall of ringlets, her nails and makeup perfect.

"Who's cracking?" demanded Angela, sounding, with her British accent, like someone's stern governess.

"Sorry," Tiffany said meekly. "Won't do it again." Then: *crack!* with an impish smile, and Angela just groaned.

Behind me, Christine Perry introduced herself as she emptied Jenn's dishwasher without having to ask where things went. "I'm half-Korean," she said, "like Marissa's half-Vietnamese. So basically she could do my nails and I could do her dry cleaning."

The Hooah Wives all e-mailed each other obsessively, talked for hours on the phone, to the point that one of their husbands called it "the cult." Once, when they couldn't reach one wife, Jenn and Tiffany went to her house to check on her. Her youngest was sick, so Tiffany took mother and child to the ER at Womack while Jenn watched the other children and cleaned the house and Marissa and Lexie brought over sodas and moral support. Even though Marissa was active in her FRG, these were the women she would come to depend on, sitting around laughing and bullshitting in each other's kitchens, and at Broadstreet's, their favorite hangout, where they'd dance with each other.

Back at Broadstreet's, Marissa worked her way through the crowd to the two tables they'd pushed together. They were celebrating Christine's birthday — opening presents, blinding each other with flash photos, talking about push-up bras. Christine pointed out, matter-of-factly, that she and Marissa didn't need push-up bras.

Tiffany shouted over the music, "Well, *some* of us *do!*" Tiffany was the kind of person who, when she talked, you could almost *see* the italics and exclamation points. Her husband was in Afghanistan for the second time. She shouted, "But I don't *buy* those damn bras, they're too *expensive!* I use tube socks! They give that added *boost!*"

All the Hooah Wives laughed. They laughed harder as Tiffany made a big show of digging around in her décolletage, as if she really were going to pull out a tube sock. When she actually did, they screamed. She waved it over her head: a real live tube sock. The guys at the next table were so impressed they sent over a round of drinks.

A month into it, with a little help from those same women, Marissa had sucked it up. She had it all figured out, starting with when and where to cry. Crying in the car and crying at night hadn't worked. In the car, she arrived at her destination puffy-eyed and red-nosed; at night, it left her stuffy and headachy and unable to sleep, and sleep was important — it was the only time her fear for Charlie wasn't scratching somewhere at her brain. But in the shower, she had discovered you could bawl as long and as hard as you wanted and no one would hear you. You could get all the fear out of your system while the steam kept your nose open and your eyes from getting puffy, and when the hot water ran out, the cold water woke you up.

So she'd roll out of bed after the second alarm. Since she was only allotting herself four hours of sleep a night, she'd learned it took two alarms to set herself in motion. She'd leave Lexie asleep in the double bed and step into the shower for her morning cry. Then she got on with her day. Later on at work, if the fear started to get to her again, she told herself that Charlie was doing work that had to be done, helping America fulfill its promise to the Iraqi people and making the world a better place. She found comfort in that.

On her way out of town, Marissa would stop off at Jenn's house and unbuckle Lexie, and only Lexie, because Invisible Izzy had disappeared completely ever since Lexie started spending her days with Jenn's kids. Marissa and Jenn would share a smoke before Marissa hit the road with her cell phone headset on in case Charlie called. She had set up the home phone so she could forward it to the cell, in order to miss as few calls as possible. He called or got on the Internet almost every day except convoy days. He wasn't allowed to talk about operational details over the phone, so since Marissa wasn't a churchgoer, he would say, "Are you going to church?" to let her know he was heading out. When he got back, he would go straight to the phone and as soon as she heard his voice, she'd know he was all right.

One night after picking up Lexie, Marissa got back to her house around nine. She loved her new paralegal job, loved the challenge of ferreting out titles on foreclosed properties and then managing the auctions on her own. She just wished the hours weren't so long. She felt guilty about being away from Lexie so much. Her own mother hadn't been

there for her, and it was her example that had taught Marissa how to parent — she just looked back at everything her mother did and made a
point of doing the opposite. Marissa grabbed Lexie and her briefcase out
of the car and the mail out of the mailbox. She threw the bills onto the
pile on the coffee table and charged around to feed Razor, scoop up an
armload of dirty clothes from the bathroom floor, and crank on the fau-
cet for Lexie's shower.

Nothing happened. She tried the sink. Nothing.

She ran out into the cold and circled the house. The yard around the
foundation was bone dry, no sign of a burst pipe. It was a mystery, but
there was nothing she could do about it till morning. She tucked Lexie
into the double bed and sat down at the computer in the dining room,
one foot tucked under her, a cigarette and a Pepsi beside her. She worked
till midnight before she let herself stretch out on the couch and escape
into a book. Since Charlie had been gone, she had learned to read only
while Lexie was asleep. It wasn't safe to read without Charlie there to
watch Lexie, because Marissa escaped into books the way other people
escaped into drugs, always had: checked out, no one home, gone to her
own private world where there were no memories of foster parents who
had tried to exorcise demons out of her when she was a little girl, no husband manning a gun on convoys, no houses without water.

The next morning, she called the water company from the car. "I don't
know why my water's shut off. Is there a problem in the area?"

The voice on the phone put her on hold to check. Then he came back
on the line. "Uh, you know you didn't pay your bill?"

She started to say, "But we always pay our bills —" Except it wasn't *we*
who'd always paid them. It was Charlie. She chewed her lip. Since he left,
she'd figured out how to mow the lawn, whacked bushes with a hedge
trimmer for the first time in her life. "Baby, I'm amazing!" she told him
once when he called, and he agreed. She thought she'd figured out his
system for paying the bills, too.

It was a $25 bill. It cost her $60 to get the water reconnected. It was so
humiliating, after hanging up she called Jenn to tell her all about it. That
way, when Charlie called and asked how things were going, she'd be over
it and could honestly say, "Just fine." And then he'd tell her about the
mortar attack that had hit their camp the night before.

Every day, tens of thousands of voices raced over cables and bounced off
satellites, making connections between Southwest Asia and America.
Tens of thousands of e-mails flashed back and forth through cyberspace

at the speed of light and mail servers. If all the connections between the war zone and the homefront left comet trails, some would be clear and solid, some broken like a dotted line, all of them binding the two parts of the world together in a tangled web of words.

"Hello?" said Beth.

"Hey, baby, it's me."

"Luigi? Oh my God, I love you so much!"

"I can't stand being away from you, baby."

And then there were always many *I-miss-you*s and more *I-love-you*s and then the *how-are-you*s. Over the weeks, Beth had told him work kept her busy and that she'd gone out with Camilla and the other wives a couple of times, and also about the burglary next door, and how Danny the dog got pancreatitis and almost died but pulled through. Luigi told her about camels and sunsets over the desert, because seeing the beauty in things was how he dealt with being over there; she'd finally figured that out. He told her funny stories about the locals trying to sell the soldiers cigarettes and CDs and porn, but then one time he mentioned something about how little sleep he was getting and how lately there wasn't enough food but maybe that was a good thing because it was so nasty.

"Are you OK?" she wanted to know. "Is everything OK?"

"Oh, yeah. It's just so good to hear your — *shhhhhhh*." *Click*.

On the other side of the strip malls and shopping centers, Marissa's friend Christine Perry, the half-Korean Hooah Wife, found herself constantly waiting for the phone, like Beth. She and Beth didn't know each other and an absent husband was the only thing they had in common. Sometimes, when Christine's husband was off training, she didn't want to hear from him too much, because then she couldn't help waiting for a call and if it didn't come it ruined her day. At gatherings of the Hooah Wives, it was easy to spot the women with deployed husbands and husbands off training, because their cell phones were always out where they could see them, to make sure they had a signal.

Across town, Jennifer Gaines walked into her mother's house while her fiancé was deployed. She was checking her cell phone, and her mother teased, "That cell phone is like your third arm." Jennifer was a surgical technician; the only time her phone wasn't within reach was when she was in the operating room. She announced it to her friends, "This is my new appendage!"

Up in Stem, North Carolina, National Guard wife Lynn Sinclair began to worry when she didn't hear from her husband, Danny, for a week, two weeks, three. It seemed as though all the spouses in his unit were getting calls from their husbands, all except her. The silence grew into an ominous, agonizing eternity and just when she didn't think she could take it any more, there he was on the other end of the line.

"Why haven't you called?" she asked in her no-nonsense way.

He was quiet for a moment. "Well, how much can I tell you?"

"I have support here," she assured him. "I'm fine, you can tell me anything."

Danny, it turned out, hadn't called because he'd been upset and didn't want to upset her, but she told him he might as well tell her because she'd eventually hear it from the other wives anyway, but only after it had been twisted out of shape from being passed from their husbands to them to her. So he told her that while on convoy, a sniper had hit his vehicle in the fuel tank. Being diesel, it didn't blow, but it was spouting fuel and he and the other man in the truck had worried the tank would run dry and strand them before they could get back to the safety of the camp.

One state to the north, I was in Richmond, Virginia, at my sister's house early in the war. While my husband's convoy was dodging bullets on the way from An Nasiriyah to Baghdad, I didn't receive so much as a postcard for a month, but then I didn't expect to. "We won't have connectivity," Frank had warned me in military-speak before he left, and since it's all about expectations, I could handle not hearing from him. I figured no news was good news.

Across the ocean on a U.S. Army post in Germany, when the phone rang Halloween night in Patricia Bahl's apartment, it was the rear detachment commander. "Patricia," she said, "your husband's OK, but he's been in an accident." The rear D commander had to repeat herself three times because Patricia's husband was downrange in Iraq, and all she kept hearing was, "He's been in an accident" — all trick, no treat, and she couldn't cry, couldn't breathe, just stood there until suddenly, as if someone had finally turned up the volume, she heard, "He's OK." After that she wasn't nervous or scared. She just felt as if she weren't quite all there.

Then the phone rang again and it was him, weak sounding, but still him. He had been on a convoy when a roadside bomb blew up, though he didn't remember any of it. He'd been hit in the head in the explosion. He insisted it was minor. "All they had to do was patch me up," he said. "I'm going right back to my unit."

The colonel's wife came over, and she and Patricia talked for an hour. It was only later, alone in the quiet, that Patricia closed her eyes and let herself see her husband lying on a road in Iraq, his head covered in blood. Trick. Or treat. It could have been so much worse. It could have been The Worst That Could Happen, but it wasn't, he was all right. He was all right. One day he'd be coming home to her. He was all right. That was when she finally cried.

And in another part of Iraq, another phone was dialed. In a matter of seconds, connections were made across thousands of miles and in Southern California, Kimberly Huff's phone rang. Whenever she heard the voice of her husband, Roger, who'd been in Kuwait since leaving home, she was always relieved. "I'm so glad you called," she said. "I've been really worried."

But the satellite connection was so bad, all Roger heard on his end was *shhhhhh* "I've been really worried." And he said, "How did you know?"

"How did I know what?" she asked.

It was one of those "Oh, shit" moments. He had to admit to her he wasn't in nice, safe Kuwait anymore. He was now in Iraq, but he hadn't planned on telling her that because he didn't want her to worry.

He had good reason to be concerned. Within two weeks, Kim worried herself into an asthma attack. Her best friend rushed her to an emergency room, where she struggled to pull in enough air to stay alive. The next time Roger happened to call, she told him about it.

"Keep your chin up!" he said lightly. "We'll be home soon!"

Kim frowned at the phone in her hand, thinking, *That is not the man I married.*

The man she had married a year and a half before was so sensitive she had thought at first he was gay; his sensitivity was what she loved about him. He was a reservist, a medic, and ever since his Southern California unit had been called up and shipped out for a yearlong deployment, with each call home he had begun to sound more militarized, as if he was constructing a cold, hard, protective shell around himself.

The deployment was having the opposite effect on Kim. She was Mexican American, an actress, a self-described ice queen with a sarcastic sense of humor, but these days she was feeling more like a drama queen: crying, losing her temper, delivering long, impassioned soliloquies against the war. Roger was almost at the end of his enlistment contract, and even though he had accumulated fourteen years, with only six years to go before he was eligible for retirement benefits when he reached sixty-five, she did not want him to reenlist.

A month later, in another call, he admitted that he wanted to. *Really* wanted to. "I don't care how many bonuses the reenlistment guys are offering," she said, her voice rising. "I don't care if they said they'd pay for you to go to physician's assistant school, I don't care if they promised you the whole pot of gold. Have you ever heard of 'too good to be true'?"

He said the other guys were calling him a pussy for not standing up to her.

"Well, maybe those other wives don't care if their husbands don't come back," Kim said. "But I don't want to be separated and I don't want to lose you."

They left it at that. Until another month later, when it came up again.

"I don't know what it's like to be a wife anymore," she told him.

Roger just said, "I really want to do this." He had always wanted to be a physician's assistant, and he believed reenlisting would get him there.

Kim's new reservoir of emotions welled up in her eyes, but she managed to say, "If you sign up, I will leave right now."

Roger was quiet for a long moment. When he finally spoke, his voice was cold. "That sounds like an ultimatum."

She tried to explain, as her emotions overflowed into weeping, that she just wanted him to know how she felt, what she was planning. She didn't want him to be blindsided if he went through with reenlisting. "I don't want this marriage to end," she said, "but I cannot be married to a full-time military man, I will leave."

"OK," he said at last. "I won't reenlist."

Kim was relieved, but she didn't feel victorious. She felt terrible for forcing him to give up something he wanted. But she told herself she had no choice. The long-term deployments and the danger that went with them — she just couldn't do it anymore.

A month later, after Roger redeployed back to an Army post in Colorado in preparation for his return to civilian life, while they were on the phone again, he admitted he had never had any intention of not reenlisting. He told her he was just afraid that if she left him while he was still in Iraq, she might take everything, including everything that was his.

"You lied to me?" Kim gasped. "You deliberately *lied*?"

Later he contradicted himself, said their marriage was too important to him, but he wanted to reenlist, too. Kim felt the same contradictory way, half of her wanting to stay with him no matter what, half of her wanting out of this life. She didn't know what to believe about anything anymore.

"E-mail and telephone," says Chaplain Hartz, "can be helpful if you're wise about how you use it. If you use it for sharing events, staying connected, the immediacy of sharing while it's fresh, that's good. But if you're unwise, if you use it to fight and complain about who's got it worse — that is not reconcilable, who has it worse. Then you have to say you're sorry, and you can't see them to know if they really mean it."

E-mail is convenient; it can give you quick answers to everyday questions. It also tends to be written in a hurry. In addition to transmitting no facial expression, it provides no tone of voice. If it's not an obvious love letter, it can be as cold and impersonal as the computer it's written on. Take something the wrong way, get your feelings hurt, whether by e-mail or phone, and it's easy for a fight to drag on because you're not confronted by the other's unhappy physical presence. With six thousand miles or more between you, you can't just reach across the cold space in the middle of the bed and take the other's hand.

E-mail and regular, frequent telephone access while on deployment didn't become common until the late nineties, about the same time Sylvia Kidd's husband retired from his post at the Pentagon as the Army's top enlisted man, Sergeant Major of the Army. That's when she became director of family programs for the Association of the United States Army, a private, nonprofit educational organization. "Back during the Vietnam War," remembers Sylvia, "all you knew was what you saw on the news and what your husband told you in letters home."

Toward the end of the war, Sylvia was in her late teens and a new mother living on Fort Bragg. In the days before her husband left for another tour in Vietnam, she watched him stand over their baby's crib as if he were memorizing his daughter. Long after he left, she received a letter from him that was a single, strange sentence, scrawled diagonally across the page: *Babe, I'll write you when I get settled.* She knew something was very wrong — he was long since "settled." But there was nowhere she could go for information, no one she could ask for help. She could only wait for his next letter, which was when she finally found out that when he wrote that sentence, he was being medevaced to Japan, delirious with malaria.

Sylvia Kidd, a quietly forceful redhead, joined other wives over the years in working to convince the Army's leadership that supporting the families could improve military readiness. By the early eighties, a family liaison office was established up in the Pentagon and a few years later, down at the small unit level, company and battery commanders were organizing their soldiers' spouses into what are now known as the Family Readiness Groups. Thanks to those wives, the flow of information back to the families is much better now.

Sometimes it's a little too good. "Some families are getting information before the rear detachment or anybody else," says Martha Brown, the deployment and mobilization manager on Fort Bragg.

With the exception of casualty notifications, information from the unit is supposed to be passed back like water in a bucket brigade: In-theater contacts rear D, rear D contacts FRG leader, FRG leader calls key callers, key callers disseminate information to unit families. "But there were some cases of people getting on the satellite phones in theater," Martha Brown says. "Soldiers calling back here and letting their spouse know, 'I'm OK, but so and so has just been killed.'" It's easy for a soldier with a phone or a computer to get out ahead of the bucket brigade.

The amount of contact between deployed service members and their families back home depends on the service member's location and personality. The ships Frank was on had commercial phones that the sailors and Marines could line up to use, but the phones were frequently down, and even when they were working, the connection at sea was unreliable and cost a dollar a minute. Frank was cheap. During his first major deployment, he called home exactly once in six months. His second major deployment, he called home twice, the first time for a minute, the second time for five minutes, both times because it happened to be free. As long as he was on the ship, though, he could e-mail me for free all day long, assuming he had time and the ship's outdated computer system hadn't crashed.

During the early months of the Iraq War, however, when he was either on the move in that Humvee or camped in the desert, he had no e-mail, no phone, just a pen and the little brown paperboard boxes that held his MREs, or Meals, Ready to Eat. After he ate what was inside, he'd cut the paperboard into pieces with his knife and write on them as if they were postcards, except instead of featuring famous landmarks or resort beaches like real postcards do, they boasted the nutritional data of, say, beef strips in teriyaki sauce. On the back of one, he wrote, *Hey Babe! Starting to miss you, although it is not a heart ache. Looking forward to the first mail drop.* Then because postage is free when you're mailing from a war zone, he'd draw a squiggly stamp in the upper right corner above my sister's address, label it *FREE!* and hand it off to be mailed.

He numbered them so I'd know the order in which they'd been written, which helped because some apparently came by plane, the quickest arriving after about two weeks, and some came by lame donkey and rowboat, washing up on my sister's front stoop after a couple of months. But eventually each one would wend its way around the globe back to me, and I'd sit on the stoop in the sunshine and read it, and reread it, and then add it to the rubber-banded stack I carried with me everywhere.

While he was waiting in the Kuwaiti desert for the invasion to begin, I wrote to him: *I've been thinking about how we sometimes talk about what we would do if one of us survived the other . . . And it used to be that I would fantasize about how, if I had to start over with someone else, I might have a shot at having children . . . It's a fantasy that I don't ever want to become real. I don't want to start over with someone else, even if it would mean having children. I want you. You're the only one I want or need and I can't wait for you to come home to me. I love you more than I ever thought possible.*

He wrote me back: *Many people are leaving "dead letters" in their sea bags — I am not. You already know all that is in my heart for you . . . If anything happens, just read my old mail — I will be there for you all over again . . . I will no longer be trapped in time — you will be with me again. There will be no passage of time for me as I am lifted out of it. But you will have to wait. So as you read my letters, know that I am still real, still exist, and will have better, clearer, deeper thoughts and feelings for you than I ever could have expressed in any letter.*

Love you forever — Frank

I came to love each of those slow-motion postcards more than I ever liked e-mail or the occasional phone call. Whenever I felt lonely for him, especially during the first month after the invasion began, when I had no word from him at all, I pulled out that fat stack of cards — mixed fruit, beef with mushrooms, wild and yellow rice pilaf — and ran my fingers over his familiar cramped handwriting. I couldn't hold him, but I could hold these cards that he had held.

CHAPTER 8

Live from Fallujah

O N THE EVENING of Sunday, March 23, 2003, three days into the invasion of Iraq, I received a phone call from Jennifer Lewton, my Key Volunteer. She was the wife of the operations officer in the same assault amphibian battalion as my husband, and she had volunteered to keep out-of-town wives like me in the loop. She asked me if I'd seen a report on CNN about the battalion being involved in some fighting in a town called An Nasiriyah.

"I heard there was a battle going on there," I said. I walked out of my sister's busy kitchen with the phone. "But I didn't realize it was us."

Jennifer hadn't seen it. She'd been out all day with her kids, and when she got home her answering machine was full of anxious messages from the Key Volunteer chain of command — the KVs had a serious message to pass. I heard later from other wives at Camp Lejeune that rumors were flying. The CNN report had shown a burned-out amphibious assault vehicle and implied that all the deaths were from our amphibian battalion. By evening, the rumor mill had half the battalion wiped out.

"Well, some guys have been killed, haven't they?" I asked Jennifer. I sat down on the bottom step of the staircase in the quiet front hall. "Like a couple dozen soldiers and Marines, I think."

All Jennifer could tell me was that an amphibious assault vehicle had been hit in An Nasiriyah, and that the battalion was investigating. "Do you want me to call you back as soon as I have more news?" she asked. "It might not be till late tonight."

I knew the only news that really mattered would come from a knock at the door, not from her, and besides, Frank was probably safely in the rear and Jennifer still had a lot of calls to make. "You can just let me know tomorrow," I said, and then I added, "I guess I'm lucky Frank's with your husband in headquarters and service company."

"Why?"

"Isn't their company always at the rear of the action?"

"No . . .?" She drew the word out, as if she couldn't quite believe she'd just heard me say that. "Not necessarily."

"Oh," I said. "OK. I'll wait to hear from you." We hung up. And then I muttered to the empty hall, "Well. I could have done without knowing *that*." And yet I was glad to know the truth.

The next day, Jennifer called back and read me a written statement from the battalion's rear party. According to the statement, the incident on CNN *was* related to our battalion. The family notifications had been made. We were asked to respect the privacy of the families and not to speculate on who they might be.

Eventually, I learned that the news media had gotten it only partly right. Of the eighteen Marines who died at An Nasiriyah, two were from our battalion.

On the front page of the *Fayetteville Observer* on Wednesday, September 3, 2003, the day Luigi Pratt climbed aboard a plane at Green Ramp:

> SOLDIER FROM 325TH KILLED
> By Kevin Maurer
> Staff writer
> BAGHDAD, Iraq — An 82nd Airborne Division soldier died and 10 were injured early Tuesday in a helicopter training accident south of Baghdad . . .

Below it, was another headline.

> GREEN BERET DIES OF INJURIES

And next to that one:

> TROOPS UNDER FIRE

The live, twenty-four-hour news cycle has changed the way we experience war, both as a society and — for those of us with someone in the fight — as friends and family.

In the converted school on Fort Bragg, deployment and mobilization manager Martha Brown tells her FRG leaders to advise the spouses in their units to limit their time watching the news. "Because initially," she says, "everybody was glued to the news, and anytime anything happened with the 82nd, or even just the mention of a soldier, the phones started ringing." *Do you know anything? What kind of information do you have?* Martha believes the media have begun "pinpointing a little better," as she puts it. "The media have changed."

When the Iraq War started, most of the members of the news media were as ignorant about the military as most Americans. In the first few days of the invasion, I watched a young CNN reporter in a small southern Iraqi port town breathlessly announce that the Marine unit with which he was embedded was being reinforced by another division of Marines. Now, I was about as civilian-minded a military spouse as you could be, but even I knew the small cluster of Marines that could be seen arriving in the background was no division — the Corps' 174,000 active-duty Marines are divided into three units, three *very large* units. They're called *divisions*. In all of Iraq, there was one, single *division*. I heard him claim that puny little platoon of Marines was a division, and I thought, *I'm supposed to trust the observations of some kid who doesn't even know what he's looking at?*

Since then, the journalists who cover the wars in southwest Asia have been more or less educated along with the rest of us, sometimes in spite of ourselves, just by being exposed to military operations to a degree we hadn't been since Vietnam.

From the front page of the *Fayetteville Observer*, Thursday, October 2, 2003:

> ## GI WHO DIED IN IRAQ NAMED
> By Rebecca Logan
> Staff writer
>
> The 82nd Airborne paratrooper who died trying to rescue another soldier has been identified as Sgt. Andrew Joseph Baddick of Jim Thorpe, Pa. . . .
>
> The Defense Department said Baddick was trying to rescue a soldier whose vehicle went into a canal Monday near Abu Ghraib prison in Iraq . . .

Some spouses avoid the news. TV, radio, newspaper, Internet — they want nothing to do with any of it, but not because they don't want to be reminded of the danger their loved ones are in. You can't be reminded of what you can never forget. Every single moment you're awake, that primal voice is whispering at the back of your mind, *danger, danger, danger.*

It's just that if the TV and the people around you start echoing that primal voice, it can escalate into an overwhelming shout.

From the front page of the *Fayetteville Observer*, Tuesday, October 21,
2003:

> BRAGG SOLDIER IS KILLED IN ATTACK
> By Tarek Al-Issawi
> The Associated Press
>   FALLUJAH, Iraq — Iraq's hit-and-run resistance struck
> U.S. forces in this tense city west of Baghdad for a sec-
> ond day Monday, killing one 82nd Airborne Division para-
> trooper and wounding six other American soldiers, the U.S.
> command reported . . .

Day after day. It just starts to get to you.

Beth walked into a delivery room to check on a patient. The TV was on,
the overnight news muttering. She kept her back to it while she checked
the fetal heart-rate monitor and entered data in the chart. She managed
to get out of there before the newscast got around to the latest on the war
in Iraq.

She was in the nurse's station filling out paperwork when one nurse
said to another, "Oh, did you hear about that convoy, all the people that
died?"

Beth picked up her paperwork and moved out of earshot.

From the front page of the *Fayetteville Observer*, Saturday, October 25,
2003:

> ANSWERS NOT EASY FOR U.S. IN IRAQ
> The number and severity of attacks on American troops on the
> upswing. The 82nd Airborne is in the thick of the fighting.
> By Charles J. Hanley
> The Associated Press
>   BAGHDAD, Iraq — The "long, hard slog" foreseen by Don-
> ald Rumsfeld is already playing out in Iraq — in the tallies of
> attacks, in the toll of American dead, in the cold eyes of
> many Iraqis . . .

Before dawn, the car rolled slowly through the neighborhood with its
windows down. Every couple of houses, a rolled-up newspaper flew out

and smacked onto a driveway. There was no smack as the car rolled past Marissa's house. She didn't take the *Fayetteville Observer* or any other paper. Inside, the big television was never tuned to a news channel. Charlie's calls and e-mails told her all the news she needed to know: that he was all right.

Most of the time when Marissa got up these days, she felt as if she were wearing a big Superwoman *S* on her chest. She was driving all over the eastern half of North Carolina in a company car, always working against the clock, because when she was searching titles for a foreclosure, she didn't know what was going to happen with a house, it could have been a house owned by the same person going thirty, forty, fifty years back, and she had to search through every single mortgage they had taken out. The foreclosure business didn't tolerate mistakes, and she liked the constant striving for perfection and working against the clock, though sometimes the clock seemed to run too fast. She'd be thinking, *Oh, I almost have it done, I almost have it done!* And by the time she had it done, she was running late, jumping in the car and slapping on her cell phone headset, talking a mile a minute and speeding to get to the next location, over on the coast maybe, because she had to be there for a sale. "That property," she might be telling Hooah Wives managers Jenn or Angela on the phone, "sells like hotcakes — a foreclosed property on the coast? That's beachfront property, top-of-the-line property that's going for dirt cheap." It kept her from thinking about the war.

Then, when she got home she always had paperwork to do, and her volunteer work with the FRG, which lately had grown more time-consuming. The FRG leader had left when her husband rotated to another unit. Marissa and another wife had filled in to pick up the slack and wound up as coleaders. It was a little unusual for someone as young as Marissa was, married to a specialist, a junior enlisted soldier, to be coleader of an FRG. But there wasn't exactly a long line of people stepping forward, and it made sense because she already knew all the wives. She'd been a key caller for the FRG for about a year now, calling and e-mailing the wives and girlfriends and parents of the guys in Charlie's unit. She was on the company's comfort team, too, though so far she hadn't had to perform that duty.

As an FRG leader, Marissa learned on the job. In the Air Force, Navy, and Marine Corps, training was required for spouses who volunteer to serve in the family readiness programs. In the Army at that time, such training was voluntary. The professional staff who lead the FRG training classes at Army Community Services on Fort Bragg put on a whole series of programs, all of which were very educational, some even downright inspiring, but they were optional.

Some spouse volunteers didn't get the training because they simply did not have the time. Marissa, for instance, took on the job of FRG co-leader after the deployment was already in progress, when she no longer had any free Saturdays or several free nights in a row to sit through an exhaustive — and exhausting — training class. She had all she could do just keeping up with her responsibilities as the coleader, staying in touch with the family members, and planning and attending monthly meetings. As a working single mother, she was proud of her ability to make time to volunteer. She just didn't have time to eat.

The husband of one Hooah Wife asked, "Marissa, are you eating?"

She'd lost thirty pounds in less than two months. She was small to begin with. Now when she stepped on the scale, it flashed barely over a hundred.

From the front page of the *Fayetteville Observer*, Saturday, November 1, 2003:

> AMBUSH KILLS SOLDIER FROM SPECIAL FORCES
> A staff report
> A Special Forces soldier assigned to Fort Bragg was killed
> Thursday in an ambush in Afghanistan . . .

The Hooah Wives were at Jenn's. The subject of war news came up. Marissa said emphatically, "I don't watch the news, I don't ever watch the news."

One of the younger wives, a girl named Erin, said, "One time I was watching the news while I was eating dinner and all of a sudden I had to run out and throw up."

"You got to turn that TV *off*, baby," said Tiffany. Tiffany wasn't just an expert in unusual uses for tube socks. She had become an expert as well in maintaining her sanity during deployment. She herself had been obsessed with the news online until she finally figured out she was one of those people who had to do just that, turn it off.

"I couldn't," said Erin. "The TV was right there in the mess hall. It was *always* on."

Erin Ukleja, married to a soldier, was a soldier herself. She didn't look like a soldier. She looked like a girl the Dutch artist Vermeer might have painted with a shy smile carrying a pitcher of cream. Back in Cleveland,

Ohio, her parents had made it clear they were going to kick her out on her own as soon as she turned eighteen. She considered her options, and there weren't many, so she signed up to join the Army, even though she was only seventeen and still in high school. Like Marissa, she was a study-the-night-before kind of student and yet made very good grades. She joined the Army to get money for college through the Army's Delayed Entry Program. It was during all those physical training sessions and social gatherings with her recruiter that she fell in love with another DEP recruit. They got married while Erin was still in training, just before Bryan reported to Fort Bragg, so the Army would be more likely to station them in the same place. A month later, Bryan was in Iraq.

He was gone by the time Erin arrived at Bragg. She'd sit in the mess hall and watch the news on the mess hall TV. Even when it upset her, she couldn't stop watching. So she changed the order in which she did things. Instead of eating, watching, and throwing up, she'd watch, then get her food and take it up to her barracks room to eat in peace.

She started looking for an apartment for herself and this new husband of hers with whom she'd never actually lived. She looked in rental magazines and called to get prices. She didn't have a car or even a driver's license, but she got a friend from her unit to drive her to look at one place. It was just past the ghetto, but it was what she had figured out she and Bryan could afford. She took the bus back to Cleveland and picked up his car, taught herself how to drive it. She found an unwanted couch in the barracks, and a bed the Army was throwing away, and a hundred-dollar table at Wal-Mart, and a used dresser set for fifty dollars. Once, when Bryan called from Iraq and she said something about "my apartment," it freaked him out. She didn't say it again.

She set up her very small TV in the living room. She didn't bother to get cable for it. She rented movies instead, comedies and action flicks and thrillers. Her favorite movie of all time was *The Princess Bride.* She'd hear her friends talk and she'd realize she no longer knew anything about current events, which she thought was probably a bad way to live, but it was better than being sick to her stomach.

Inside the *Fayetteville Observer,* on Wednesday, November 5, 2003, a large headline:

MORTARS SLAM INTO U.S. COMPOUND

Next to it, a small, related article:

82ND SOLDIER KILLED BY ROADSIDE BOMB

A staff and wire report

A Fort Bragg soldier died Tuesday when a roadside bomb hit his vehicle, an Army spokesman said.

The soldier, Sgt. Francisco Martinez, was a native of Humacao, Puerto Rico, said Jose Pagan, a spokesman for Fort Buchanan in Puerto Rico.

Martinez was a member of the 82nd Soldier Support Battalion, 82nd Airborne Division.

Martinez was 28 and single.

On TV, I saw a soldier being interviewed in Iraq. "I think our families have it worse than us," he said. "We're out here doing our jobs. All they can do is watch and wait and wonder what's going on."

That pretty much sums it up. The one you love is in harm's way, and you're powerless to do anything to protect him or her. One National Guard spouse tried her best not to watch the news, but she couldn't escape all of it. If she heard something that unnerved her, she'd hit the floor, get down on her knees, and pray, "Heavenly Father, comfort my husband and keep him safe."

Overexposure or addiction to media coverage takes that sense of helplessness and multiplies it by a hundred. During a war, media coverage is like a drug. At any hour of the day or night, you can get your fix of news on cable TV, radio, or the Internet. Whenever you stumble across a little hit of information that might tell you something about where your loved one's unit is, what he or she is doing, it's like a high.

On Christmas Eve 2001, I turned on the evening news and there was a two-second shot of my husband leading a group of Marines at a candlelit worship service inside the cavernous terminal at Kandahar International Airport in Afghanistan. I leaped around the living room whooping like a kid. I spent the rest of the night on the couch with the remote, clicking from channel to channel, hoping for another glimpse of him. I never saw him again like that, but I did see lots of shots of Marines dug in at the airport sending greetings home, which made me feel all warm and fuzzy, because my husband probably knew these kids, might even have been somewhere nearby when these greetings were being videotaped. On Christmas Day, I searched again, but I saw nothing else of Frank.

You get so you're hungry for hits like that. But since you never know when the next hit might come, you keep watching hour after hour, prone in front of the TV, hunched in front of the computer, staring at the urgent, irrelevant headlines and the dismally repetitive images that hustle across the screen. For some people, this obsessive viewing doesn't just go on for a few hours or days. It goes on for weeks. Months. Eventually, like all out-of-control addictions, too much media will leave you paralyzed and wasted.

While Frank was in Iraq, I rationed my daily dose of news. I couldn't cut myself off cold turkey because I was one of those people who needed *some* news. Although too much information was overwhelming, for me zero information made the fear and uncertainty worse. A little bit of news gave me the illusion that I was in the know, and therefore in control. I'd turn the TV on only once or twice during the day, for no more than a few minutes at a time. I'd check the newspaper headlines. Then just before bed, I'd watch an hour of *Newsnight* on CNN, which took me live to Iraq as the day began over there. I got the summary, the analysis, and then once it was over, I forced myself to turn it off just as the live feeds began to roll in from the embedded journalists racing across the morning desert with American soldiers and Marines. I took an over-the-counter pill to help me sleep.

By the time I woke up at dawn, the Iraqi day was drawing to a close. I would reach for the TV next to the bed and turn it back on to see what I'd missed while I slept. This was always the worst moment, because I was waiting to hear that Saddam Hussein had finally dug up all those stockpiles of chemical and biological weapons he had supposedly been hiding and unleashed them on my husband. I'd watch for a few minutes, just long enough to reassure myself that nothing too awful had happened, and then I'd turn it off. *Click.*

CHAPTER 9

Different Planets

URING THOSE EARLY DAYS of the war, with the action still live on all the news channels, I was hovering behind an electrician in our house in Washington, D.C., which we had rented out to a couple of tenants while we were at Lejeune. He poked around. He asked me a question about the wiring to the washer and dryer. I told him my husband wired it.

"Can we call him?" he asked.

"Uh, no, he's —" I hesitated, because a husband in a war zone wasn't my idea of casual conversation. "Not in town."

He frowned at the wiring. "Maybe we should wait and do this when he gets back."

"I don't think we can wait that long," I said, knowing Frank could be gone for up to a year.

The electrician poked around some more. He was a very nice man who really wanted to fix my problem. He sighed. "It would sure make things simpler if I could just talk to him for a minute."

"I'm sorry, there's no phone where he is." And then I confessed, "He's in Iraq."

His face lit up. "Your husband is in Iraq? Oh, wow! That is so cool!" Every day after work, he was rushing home, he told me, turning on MSNBC, and watching all night as the reporters embedded with the Marines and soldiers beamed their day's adventures into his living room, live and in color. He asked eagerly, "You've been watching it, haven't you?"

"No, just a little," I said with a nervous laugh, trying to keep up with his jolliness, but I couldn't, because, aw man, he couldn't get enough of it, last night he'd watched a firefight right as it happened. The best part about it was he didn't know how it would end; he never knew how any of it was going to end.

"And the technology!" he raved. "It's amazing! I can't wait to tell my wife I met someone whose husband gets to be over there doing all that stuff! It's just so cool!"

I think I was smiling. Behind my smile, I just wanted this nice man out of my house. To me, it was a matter of life and death. To him, it was a video game. We were living on different planets.

Alienation comes in many forms during a wartime deployment — alienation from civilian society, from the military, from the people closest to us, and from God.

Beth got a letter from Luigi. He mentioned again that they didn't always have enough time to eat or sleep. The next time she talked to Camilla Maki, Beth told her she wished she could get her husband out of the Army, or at least make sure he was getting enough food and water.

Camilla had so far spent most of the deployment fighting the Army. Just before her husband left for Iraq, the docs over in medical thought he might have colon cancer. His unit shipped him over anyway, and by the time he got off the plane in Kuwait, he'd lost so much blood he passed out. Camilla contacted her congressman and got an investigation started, and eventually the medical personnel over there ruled out cancer and got to work trying to diagnose what it was he *did* have.

Camilla told Beth she knew someone who might be able to help her help Luigi — the woman who had helped Camilla when she was trying to figure out how to help her own husband. She seemed to know all the right people to talk to, Camilla said. Her name was Marena.

It had been a busy deployment. In the seven months Marena Groll's husband had been in Iraq, with what would turn out to be four more months to go, Marena had been serving as the key caller for all of the out-of-town families in her FRG. She had battled health problems, and she had moved herself and their fifteen-year-old son, Josh, from one house to another alone. She hadn't been online in a couple of days. When she finally logged on, two e-mails from her husband were waiting for her. The first was a sweet, nonchalant note: *I'm here . . . are you there?* The second was a wistful little follow-up: *I guess the system must be down, since I haven't heard from you.*

Marena pounded at the keys, rushing to send her love back to him. By the time she hit send, she was gasping as if she'd just run a mile. In seven months, she had learned how finite time was. Arguments, misunderstandings, even disappointments — they were devastating now, because he could be dead tomorrow, he could be dead right now, before she had gotten around to reminding him that he was loved.

Years before, they'd been dating when he called her from a pay phone to tell her he had to say goodbye. He was on his way to the miniature war on the Caribbean island of Grenada. She rushed over to Green Ramp. Back then, deploying units were herded inside a chain link fence, often with little notice. The soldiers stood at the fence, wives and girlfriends pressed up against the other side, fingers curled together through the chain link. Marena was a small woman, and she leaned into the fence on tiptoes, trying to see around the soldier who was walking up right in front of her and making it hard to look for her boyfriend. She was wishing him out of her way, when all of a sudden she realized this soldier wearing green camouflage and carrying a weapon *was* her boyfriend. She'd never seen him in uniform before. And she thought, *What have I gotten myself into?* Her next thought was that she needed to marry him right away, because they might not have much time together.

Twenty years later, he'd earned the rank of staff sergeant and she'd earned a master's degree in education supervision. Her hair, thick and wavy, had turned prematurely, strikingly gray. Ask her and she'd tell you the Army opened up opportunities to travel and serve your country. She'd met a lot of leaders she admired in the Army, and she believed in the readiness role of Army families. She was a member of the National Military Family Association. Her father was retired Air Force. And she'd been opposed to the Iraq War before it even began.

Soon after September 11, she said to her husband, "Mark my words, the president's going to invade Iraq." And then, as was her habit when she wanted to underscore what she'd just said, she paused and gave him an emphatic, wide-eyed, purse-lipped look. Not quite a year and a half later, the invasion began.

A week after Marena's husband left for Iraq, the bombs began to drop on Baghdad. Watching the explosions live on TV, listening to the booms, she was surprised at the overwhelming fear and grief she was feeling. She soaked up all the news she could get, surfing from Web site to Web site, cable TV newscasts trumpeting in the background. She read in the newspaper about a peace vigil in the middle of Fayetteville's sleepy downtown.

She drove over there, not to do something, like protest — she had never protested anything in her life — but rather to *be* something, to be not alone. She didn't know anybody on post who felt the way she did, and she just wanted to be with people like herself, people who would hear her when she said, her eyes welling with tears, "The way my country is using the military is in conflict with my values." *What do you do,* she sometimes wondered, *when your nation breaks your heart?*

As the deployment wore on, she continued to attend the vigils and even began holding up a sign, PEACE THROUGH JUSTICE, though passing motorists gave the small group the finger, and one driver threw a bottle at her. When a reporter came around asking questions, she stepped behind the others and kept her mouth shut. On the Internet, she'd seen the Army wives at Fort Stewart, Georgia, protesting when their husbands' deployments were extended. She'd heard how they were pressured by the senior wives to shut up. And when she got out of her car in front of her house on post late one night after shopping with Josh, the soldier next door was suddenly standing there on the other side of the driveway, cursing at her, yelling that what she was doing was shameful. She had no idea how this soldier had even found out that she opposed the war, much less attended the vigils downtown, where most people never set foot. She pushed Josh ahead of her to the door. The next day, an official with some authority spoke with that soldier, and he didn't bother her again.

On the phone, her husband reassured her that *he* didn't think what she was doing was shameful. "Look," he said, "I'm a professional soldier. I follow orders so that you have the freedom to speak." But still, she worried that because of her he might face the same sort of freelance harassment, only in a dangerous place with fewer rules.

She winced when one of the family members on her out-of-town FRG key caller list sent out a couple of mass e-mails demonizing other countries. She knew he was sending them to bolster himself and the others during a difficult time, assuming everyone felt the same way, but each time she received one she was reminded she didn't fit in. When she talked with her FRG leaders, though, they said they respected her feelings; they insisted she was entitled to her viewpoint.

Then one night, she was at an FRG meeting when the speaker said, "We *know* we're doing the right thing over there." And the woman sitting next to Marena muttered under her breath, "We *know?*" Which was exactly what Marena was thinking. She whispered back, "I understand." As the meeting broke up, their whispering continued with a few more words in the parking lot, but they were nervous about being overheard. They picked it up again later on the phone.

At another FRG meeting, the same thing happened again with a different wife. Then yet another wife called her with a nuts-and-bolts question about deployment that led to a conversation full of questions about how well the Army and the country were being led. Women started to call Marena to pass on the names of other Army wives who needed to talk. At the Wal-Mart, Marena heard a woman cry out, "My husband's over there and I have children!" Marena turned to see a young woman leaning back from an older man in a Wal-Mart smock. The young woman was saying, "We have no business being over there." When the man told her she was wrong, Marena said to her, "Actually, you're right." Soon, she and the young woman were exchanging phone numbers.

Marena and four or five other Army wives began to educate themselves on the war in Iraq. They'd research on the Internet, read the reports of the International Atomic Energy Agency, then get together at Marena's house to discuss what they'd learned. She listened as Pam, a blond woman in a silky blouse, said, "I voted for the president, but when my hairdresser muttered —" and Pam's bracelets jangled as she cupped her hand next to her mouth in imitation of the hairdresser — "'It's all about the oil,' I had to agree with her. If this is a game about oil, my husband is not just some pawn. He's the father of my four children."

Marena listened, too, when Beth Pratt called one day saying her husband was in Iraq and she was worried about him. Beth said, "I'm concerned that he's not getting enough food or water, and we're both opposed to this war."

Marena gave her the phone number for Quaker House.

A short walk up the hill from downtown Fayetteville, near the dead end of a quiet neighborhood street, there's a sign in a front yard. It's a small white wooden sign, with the words QUAKER HOUSE and a dove's silhouette. Quaker House, which consists of two or three professional counselors and staffers and about that many volunteers, had been one of the sponsors of the ongoing peace vigils downtown.

Since the Vietnam era, Quaker House has helped GIs who believe they've been discriminated against because of race, gender, sexual orientation, or religion. They've helped others who took off without authorization, what's popularly known as "going AWOL," advising them on how to come back and seek a legal discharge. And they've helped military personnel who become conscientious objectors either get out of the military or shift to noncombatant service.

The year that Beth Pratt turned to Quaker House, the first year of the

Iraq War, its staff had fielded more than six thousand calls to their portion of the GI Rights Hotline, which is a network of nonprofit, nongovernmental organizations that provide the same kinds of services as Quaker House. That number of calls was double the number two years earlier. Nationwide, the entire GI Rights Hotline received nearly thirty thousand calls.

The scruffy blue bungalow that houses Quaker House sits back from the street, behind a deep front porch equipped with cheap white plastic chairs and a rust-speckled café table and chair set. The tall windows that line the porch look in on a humble living room of mismatched sofas. Through a broad entryway, in the dining room, a homemade display of posters of old newspaper articles and mimeographed broadsides tells the history of the peace movement in Fayetteville, which was driven by GIs on Fort Bragg. There, in the fall of 2003, Beth perched on the edge of a chair across the dining room table from Chuck Fager, the director of Quaker House.

With Luigi in a war zone, Beth had been forced to think about war more than ever. Talking about it with him on the phone, they both agreed Saddam was bad but the world had a lot of bad dictators, and America couldn't go fight all of them. The more she analyzed it, the angrier she got. She had decided on her own to go to Quaker House, hopeful that afterward she'd be able to tell Luigi she'd found a way for both of them to act on what they believed.

Sitting at the table, she told Chuck, "My husband and I are both opposed to this war. Can you help him get out of the Army?"

Chuck, gray-bearded and wearing khaki shorts and a T-shirt, slouched at the other end of the table like a melancholy, off-duty Santa. "It's not easy," he said.

It's not. Successful conscientious objector applicants who are already in the military have to be able to prove they've changed and now believe the use of violence is always wrong. The process involves a lengthy application and interviews with a psychiatrist, a chaplain, and an investigating officer. It's all designed to weed out those who want out for political reasons, or are afraid of combat, or have a new spouse who wants them out. Despite the flood of calls to peace organizations such as Quaker House, in 2004 only sixty-seven soldiers actually went through with applying for conscientious objector status, and that was triple the number that applied in 2001. Of all those, the Army approved about half. "Chances of success are not good," Chuck Fager tells would-be applicants. "People who take this route need to be prepared to take a stand and suffer."

As Chuck described the application process, Beth sat slumped in her chair. "I don't think that's going to fit my husband," she said. She knew Luigi wasn't the type to rock the boat. Besides, it was only this war he was opposed to. He said all along he would have been proud to serve in Afghanistan.

As they continued to talk, Chuck watched Beth blink back tears, as if sternly forbidding herself to cry. He had the sense that what she really wanted him to say was that her husband was going to come home safely. But that wasn't something he could tell her, and they both knew it.

Beth picked glumly at the skin around her fingernails. "I love my husband, with my whole heart, I love him. But I don't love the Army." The Army, she was sure, was fine for a lot of people. She could see it was fine for many of the other wives in her FRG, women younger than she was, women with whom she didn't have much in common. But not her.

By the time Beth left Quaker House two hours later with an armload of application materials, she felt as if she were sinking beneath their weight. She had always made her own decisions, controlled her own life. Now she felt as if she controlled nothing. She couldn't even help her own husband. She knew they would never fill out those forms.

Every day when she went to work at the hospital on post, she had to pull out her military dependent ID to pass through the checkpoint at the gate. As she did, she was reminded of how small and powerless she had become. Riding the elevator to Labor and Delivery, she glanced up as a soldier got on. And she couldn't help it — she wondered why he wasn't over there instead of her husband. She knew it was selfish, but that was the feeling that came over her, unbidden, at the sight of anyone in uniform safely here at home.

As she changed into her nurse's uniform in the locker room, two other nurses talked about the war, about how it was a good thing. She felt like asking them, "What about the fact that we were lied to? Where are all those weapons of mass destruction that were supposed to be there? What about all the Iraqi children we've accidentally killed?" But she didn't have the nerve to disagree with them out loud, not in an Army hospital. She felt like enough of an outsider as it was.

During the months when Beth's and Marissa's husbands were deployed to Iraq, the number of military families who openly opposed the war was fairly small. So was the number of gung-ho war supporters who were not only well-informed enough to make a case for the war's original premise but were also willing to expend the energy to do so publicly at organized events. Most families with a loved one in a war zone have barely enough emotional and physical energy to get through everything they have to do each day. There isn't much left over for politics, beyond perhaps sticking a SUPPORT OUR TROOPS bumper sticker on the car. But that's less about politics than it is a plea for mercy.

Lynn Sinclair drove around Stem, North Carolina, in the car that she had covered in those kinds of stickers. Open her clothes closet during her husband Danny's deployment with the National Guard and you saw a lot of red, white, and blue. She wore pins, too, with slogans like I LOVE MY SOLDIER. And every day she clipped on a silver bracelet adorned with an American flag and the words PRAY FOR OUR TROOPS — OPERATION: IRAQI FREEDOM. Throughout the day, whenever she noticed it on her wrist, she was reminded to pray, whether she was driving down the road or in the middle of vacuuming or fixing dinner.

Lynn had learned to brace herself whenever Danny called; she never knew if he would be up or down. She tried not to let on if she was having a bad day herself. His was guaranteed to be worse, like the day he told her, "They said we'd be going through a bad area. They said we probably would run into trouble along the way." And they did, everybody bailing out the back of the transport truck and taking cover to return fire. He didn't tell her whether or not he hit anybody, and if he didn't say, she knew not to ask. He did tell her the man next to him was wounded. "It was like being in a movie, slow motion almost, very scary. I'm OK, though," he kept saying. "I'm OK."

She sometimes wore a T-shirt that proclaimed MY HUSBAND IS SERVING OUR COUNTRY AND I AM VERY PROUD OF HIM. Under that it said U.S. ARMY. She was wearing it in the grocery store when a young girl from the meat department paused nearby, squinted at Lynn's shirt, then said in a voice blistering with disapproval, "Oh, you support the war then."

At first Lynn thought, her mind racing, *What does supporting my husband have to do with supporting the war?* Then she thought about all the reasons she *did* support the war, like freeing the Iraqi people, but what good would it do to go into all that in the middle of the grocery store? So she just said, "Absolutely, I do."

The girl looked at her like she was dirt. "That figures," the girl said, and walked away.

Bring up the subject of today's peace movement, and many military spouses bring up the past — Vietnam. Their voices rise as they recall how war protestors seemed to hate the men sent to fight that war more than they hated the civilian leaders who sent them or even the war itself. They recount personal family stories of men with military haircuts being spat upon. A generation later, the military community's collective memory of those days is still painfully raw.

One of the youngest Hooah Wives identified with that old pain, and she hadn't even been born until ten years after the war was over. While Annie Cory's husband was deployed, she flew home to Washington State to visit her family. Driving up the highway from the Seattle airport to their small hometown, her parents told her there were antiwar protesters on the overpasses every Saturday. It was the main highway over the mountain pass from Canada, and it carried a ready-made audience of heavy traffic. Her parents said, "Annie, we just want to let you know this is happening so you don't get angry." She and her family had always been more conservative than most of their neighbors in town.

Sure enough, as they headed into the valley, there on the first overpass were the protesters, holding up their antiwar signs. Annie clenched her jaw. She could feel herself breathing faster. She had no words for how angry and hurt she felt, just that it was stupid; they were stupid; it was all so *stupid*. The valley had three or four overpasses and ten or fifteen protesters were up there on every one of them, all holding their stupid, stupid signs. She thought, *It's like Vietnam.*

She watched the last row of protesters whip overhead. *Fine,* she admonished herself grimly. *Fine. My husband's over there fighting for their right to do that.* There was no irony in her thoughts.

Most of the Hooah Wives didn't follow the news, so they didn't talk about the war much. Christine Perry, the wisecracking half-Korean woman, would throw pajama parties when her husband was off training and the wives would all burst in the door with their cigarettes and their cell phones and their pajamas.

Growing up in Chicago had given Christine's husky voice a nasal edge. She liked country music, which she sometimes forced Tiffany and Marissa to listen to, and she especially liked country songs dedicated to America's soldiers. The name of her soldier husband was tattooed on the small of her back. She tried to look at the wars in Afghanistan and Iraq the way he did, as a mission. "They need peace, too," he'd say. "These innocent civilians need peace and freedom, too."

Christine understood she couldn't know *exactly* what her friends were going through. Her husband hadn't deployed yet, in fact hadn't deployed in the five years they'd been married, but eventually he would. He'd been gone for most of the last year, training for a new assignment that in the future would frequently take him overseas. Christine had already learned how to go two months at a time without talking to him. She was already used to being a single parent to their three-year-old son. When she first moved to Fort Bragg, she'd watch the news alone at night and let herself cry. She'd see injured or dead soldiers on TV, and she knew that could be her friends' husbands, or soon her own husband. When the TV showed the widows and kids, she knew that could be her and her son one day, being handed a folded flag.

She'd tried to toughen her heart since then. When her husband finally did deploy, she guessed she'd cry the first week and then, like Marissa and most of her other friends, she'd get on with it. She had a strong jaw. She wore bright red lipstick. She told her husband, "Don't ever be afraid or sad in front of me because I'll lose it."

She liked telling the Hooah Wives what he'd been telling her for years: "I'm going to return home no matter what. If it means I've got my arms and legs in my pockets, I'm coming home. If I have to walk up on my nubs and knock on the door with my head, I'm coming home." How could she not believe him?

When Christine threw pajama parties, the Hooah Wives would sit around drinking margaritas and answering questions from her copy of *Questions for the Game of Life*, questions like, "If you could change one nonphysical thing about your spouse, what would it be?" They got a big laugh out of that one because a lot of people picked more than one thing.

They talked about the war only if it was something personal and specific, like if a Black Hawk went down that was attached to one husband's unit, or if there was a mortar attack on another husband's camp. They'd talk about it, and then they'd talk about something else. Then a cell phone would ring and it would be a husband, and the wife always went into the next room to talk and when the call was over, she came out crying because she missed him so much. They'd give her a hug and the unspoken reminder that she wasn't alone.

Christine never saw Marissa cry. Marissa said she was too busy to cry, and these days it was true. Eat, sleep, work, kid . . . it had all kind of blurred. If she hadn't been working with legal papers every day she wouldn't have known what date it was. She had no time to miss Charlie or think about their relationship, and that was how she liked it, better to just suck it up, because if she started crying now she'd never stop.

Whether Marissa was at a pajama party with the Hooah Wives, or at home on the Internet with them, she could type and laugh and bitch and moan. She could go on about what a wonderful day she'd had, or if she'd had a horrible day, she could spill her guts about how her kid was driving her crazy and she just wanted to lock herself in a closet. And the Hooah Wives would give her a hug, too, or if they were on the computer, a virtual one.

Marissa could call her best friend in Erie and talk about Charlie being in Iraq till she was blue in the face. But even though her best friend's husband was a former Marine, that was before she was married to him — she'd never been a military wife. Marissa began to realize that political discussions weren't the only kinds of conversations where a military spouse could find herself feeling like an alien. Her lifelong friend could listen, but she couldn't really know how Marissa felt. On the subject of getting through each day while her husband was in a war zone, it was easier for Marissa to talk to these women she'd just met than to her best and oldest friend.

With the Hooah Wives, she never had to explain or translate. A couple of words, and they understood the rest, because going to war, whether you're the one on the frontline or the homefront, is like going to Mars, and living there with the Martians, and hearing only Martianese being spoken. Still, you're an Earthling, a very adaptable species, and before long you're speaking the language and starting to feel at home in this place that at first had seemed so strange and otherworldly.

And then one day you go back to Earth, maybe just for a visit, maybe for good, and as you step off the spaceship, all around you in the spaceport you hear a Babel of voices, over the loudspeaker, passing you in the concourse, speaking in some strange foreign tongue, and all of a sudden, it hits you — that's the language you grew up speaking. In conversations, you sometimes find yourself searching for a word, a word you should know. Sometimes you dream in Martian. Your time on Mars has gifted you with a new way of speaking, a new way of looking at the world. And it has robbed you of the easy comfort you once felt in your mother tongue.

The Iraq War was only a few days old when my sister squeezed my arm and asked, hesitantly, "How are you doing?" as if I were sick. Now and then, as the weeks went on, she would ask the question again. She and I had always been close; her husband was like a brother. I had figured what better place to be during the war than with them, surrounded by twenty-four-hour love and understanding? But once I was there, as I watched their family go through their everyday routines, together, the way they'd always been, I suddenly realized I was the only person in that house for whom everything had changed. I stayed with them on and off for two months, and whenever my sister asked that question, "How are you doing?," I felt the need to reassure her and at the same time protect myself, and I would say, "Oh, fine, fine."

One time, she said, "I don't know what you do when you're alone, but when you're with us, you just seem so calm. I don't think I could be that calm."

I laughed. "Well, it beats being hysterical." And she laughed, too. I didn't mention that when I woke up that morning, as usual I turned on CNN to check the overnight news, then carried my anxiety into the shower where no one would hear me cry it out of my system so I could get on with my day. When I told Marissa that, we both shrieked with laughter. We had both thought we were the only one who'd discovered that secret trick. We agreed: What would be the point in announcing we were afraid our husbands were going to die and that this fear was with us every waking minute? Such an announcement would just undo our self-control, make us cry in the middle of the day, and ruin the rest of it.

It was Sunday morning and Marissa and Lexie were sleeping in.

As a child, Marissa had lived for a time with a foster family that was very religious, went to church three times a week. They were the ones who told Marissa she was demon-possessed and put her through weekly exorcisms. After that, she stayed away from churches for a long time.

But she had questions. Why did God allow injustice? Why did God allow people who didn't deserve it to get rich while good people were poor? Why would God let a little girl get hit on Christmas morning, her nose bloodied, just because she was two and excited and loud? And why would God later let her mother go to jail for a crime she didn't commit?

While Marissa was still in grade school, she started going to different churches with her friends, just to see if they were all as bad as that other one. In tenth-grade sociology, she did a report on religion that grew into an enormous study, tracing each faith through history, exploring how one morphed into another, and the more she researched, the more she realized they were all doing the same thing, trying to draw closer to God. They just had different ways of doing it. The more she researched, the more she realized that none of them appealed to her.

On her Vietnamese father's side, the members of her family were either Buddhist or Catholic. Her mother was a hippie; she wasn't anything. Charlie was raised Catholic and still wore a gold crucifix around his neck with his dog tags, still carried a medallion in his pocket of St. Michael the archangel, who led the war that cast Satan out of heaven. Across his back, he had tattooed the words: *Only God can judge.* As for Marissa, whenever anyone asked her what religion she was, she'd say, "Pagan," just to be done with it. During Charlie's deployment, she didn't have time for a spiritual crisis.

I did. The first time my husband went to war, I found time to question everything I believed. I'm Quaker. I'm a pacifist. I had always believed that with enough foresight and commitment to justice, all war could be prevented. But that first wartime deployment following September 11 put my beliefs to the test.

In the fall of 2001, Frank was scheduled to deploy with the Marines, participate in a couple of training exercises, maybe visit a few exotic ports of call. I had always wanted to travel around and see America, so I decided while he was off floating around the Mediterranean for six months, I'd drive across the country for six weeks.

A week before he was supposed to leave, September 11 happened. I thought maybe I should cancel my trip. It felt like maybe the whole country was under attack; I didn't even know if I'd be able to get gas. But by the time Frank deployed a week later, it was clear he wasn't going off to float around the Mediterranean. He was going to war.

I was frantic — I was grieving for the three thousand dead, I was afraid for Frank, and I was opposed to war. And yet when I drove past the smoking Pentagon in my hometown of Washington, D.C., and when I looked at the pictures of Ground Zero in Manhattan, I couldn't help feeling war was the right response. I couldn't help feeling that Frank was doing the right thing. This took everything I thought I believed in and turned it on its head. So I dealt with it like a grownup.

I ran away. I said goodbye to the man I loved, I put him on his ship, put my dog in my car, and hit the road, searching for some sort of peace. Ten thousand miles later, I had found it. I had always believed, as the Quakers say, "There is that of God in every person," and that this Inner Teacher will guide us in a still small voice if we'll just be quiet and listen. But I had never practiced that belief very much — my standard method for coping with stress or crisis was to get busy, too busy to feel, certainly too busy to listen to some wimpy little whisper in my soul.

My big, busy road trip should have been more of the same. But driving is like meditation; the white noise of the road allowed my mind to slip out of gear. Despite my best efforts to not deal with my crisis, something was at work inside me as I drove. I asked myself, more honestly than I ever had before, the same question many soldiers are asked when they apply for conscientious objector status: What would I do if someone broke into my house and threatened my nieces and nephews, the children I love? Could I kill that person? Others have told me they're not sure they could, even if their children were in danger.

I knew, without a doubt, that I could and I would.

Then I asked myself: Even if my leaders have made mistakes that led others to attack us, am I willing to stand by and watch my little nieces and nephews die for those mistakes? In all honesty, no. War is always a calamity, yet sometimes when all you have are bad options, war may be the best one of the bunch. I'm glad there are Marines, and soldiers, and sailors, and airmen who are willing to save us. But at the same time, I'm also glad there are people like the Quakers, who are willing to save us from our own worst selves.

As I drove, I began to come to terms with the fact that life is full of questions for which there are no clear answers. Why do we humans continue to unleash war on ourselves? Why do bad things happen to good people? For years, I had tried desperately to have a baby. I kept trying despite the fact that Frank didn't really want children, despite increasingly expensive and painful medical treatments, and at some point I started to wonder, *Why am I doing this to myself?* I thought maybe if I could figure out why I wanted a baby so badly, maybe then I could figure out how to let go. But in the end, I had to admit there really was no good reason why. The urge to make a baby is a very primal one. It's not an intellectual urge and can't be analyzed by the intellectual part of the brain.

Driving across America, I had a philosophical epiphany: We've been making war for about as long as we've been making babies. The urge to make war is probably as unstoppable as the urge to make babies. But my journey during that wartime deployment led me to more than just new intellectual destinations. As the miles rolled by, the Inner Teacher became real to me in a way it had never been before. My faith in God's ability to guide me — not provide clear answers, just guide me as I muddled my way through life — had grown and matured. I *believed.*

In the Center for Family Life and Religious Education on Fort Bragg, Chaplain Hartz sees wartime as a time of searching, of looking for someone to be on your side. "For people who've had a lifelong faith," he says, "when they're in trouble their instinct is to draw closer to God, and if they don't feel God there that can lead to a crisis." If they do feel God, it leads to a deepening of their faith.

Jody Tucker found God everywhere. She was a born-again Christian who supported the war, her husband gone with the National Guard, and yet sometimes she'd still wind up in the shower crying: "I can't do this, God, it's too hard, this isn't worth it, him being over there and the boys crying at night, this pain of being separated . . . it's not worth it." And then someone sent her an e-mail and below the message, down at the bottom in the electronic signature, were two Bible verses, including one from the Gospel of Matthew that read, *Come to me, all you that are weary and are carrying heavy burdens, and I will give you rest. . . . For my yoke is easy, and my burden is light.* Though she knew an ordinary human being had sent the e-mail, she believed God was behind it, and her faith grew. She honestly didn't know how someone without faith was able to get through a deployment. "If I wasn't sure my husband is in God's hands," she would sometimes say, "I'd go crazy."

Among spouses who have not had faith, Chaplain Hartz sees the same two categories as well: those who search for and find God, and those who don't. His job, as a chaplain, is to help members of the military community practice their First Amendment right to freedom of religion, whatever their faith background. Some chaplains are good at this. Some are not. Some suffer from compassion fatigue, while others are unable or unwilling to connect with people who don't believe the same way they do. I've heard more than a few spouses complain that talking to their chaplain was like talking to a wall.

Chaplain Hartz would counsel whoever walked through his door. He had been doing it for years. They would come in, sit down, and sometimes they were angry, sometimes at a loss. He would listen, and when they wanted to know why God felt so far away, he was the first to admit, "Well, there's no pat answer." He couldn't give them a one-size-fits-all solution, but he could tell them about his own walk, encourage them, offer to pray with them. He would suggest books and audio tapes. He always asked them, "Are you involved in a church?" He tried to hook them into a support group: younger moms with the mother's day out program, Catholics with the Catholic women's group, Protestants with the Protestant group. "The spiritual, physical, social, and emotional," he would tell them, "are all related."

At the chapel on post where Chaplain Hartz led Protestant services every week, a lot of wives had husbands away on deployment. Sunday mornings, when he looked out over the congregation, they were always there — they and their children always sat together, filling two whole rows, walking through each step of the deployment together.

Others were attending churches, synagogues, and mosques out in Fayetteville and other nearby towns. "If you're known there," says Chaplain Hartz, "and people come up to you on a weekly basis and ask how you are, you feel understood." Even though they're not military, their concern and your shared faith can help you feel like you're not in it alone.

Beth curled up on the couch with Danny, her fingers in his fur. She felt as if God had gone on vacation to the other side of the universe, and while He and Luigi were far away, she watched cop dramas, legal dramas, and medical examiner dramas. She'd seen them all. She still wanted to work in forensics. She wanted to do important work, work that would make the world a better place. Since she felt such a strong pull toward forensics and was good at it, she had thought that was what God wanted her to do.

It hadn't happened. Staring at the TV, her life felt pointless and empty. She never wanted to be a nurse. She never wanted to be married but have no husband. She didn't understand the trials God put people through. She hadn't been this pissed off at Him since she got divorced. Back in Florida, by the side of her pale blue pool, she used to read self-help books, books about spirituality. Now she read books about war and progressive social theory. *The People's History of the United States* sat among the bills and odds and ends on her kitchen table, a thick paperback with a bookmark halfway through it. She'd also been reading the Bible, trying to understand why things were the way they were.

Alone in the duplex with Danny, she yelled at God, wherever the hell He was: "What else do you want me to learn, for crying out loud?"

There are as many ways to cope as there are spouses.

Marissa Bootes held the phone to her ear and listened as Charlie's voice gave her the news she already knew: Another member of his unit had been killed.

Marissa called one of the Hooah Wives and said, "Let's go shopping." Marissa had grown up a window shopper, but between her fat salary and Charlie's extra deployment pay, for the first time in her life she could afford some retail therapy. She bought a TiVo, though she had no time to watch what she recorded on it. She bought a Web cam, so when they chatted with Charlie online, he could see them and they could see him. Two-way video links would eventually be available at a family facility on post, but this was more convenient. Seeing him, Marissa was struck all over again by how gorgeous he was, and also how tired and how dirty. Lexie got excited and yelled, "That's my daddy! What's he doing in a tent?" He'd been in a communications tent all along whenever he called, but she'd never imagined him that way. Marissa also bought silk flower arrangements, a futon for the guest room, cute outfits for herself and Lexie, a goldfish in a SpongeBob SquarePants aquarium, and a new answering machine.

She recorded the outgoing message without thinking: "Hey, this is Marissa. I'm not in, so leave me a message." When Charlie called and got the machine, he heard himself erased from her life. He hung up on it twice. When he finally got her on the cell phone, he demanded, "What, I don't live there anymore?" And Marissa laughed, "Well, technically, you don't!" But he was upset, she could tell, and the next time he got the machine he heard, "This is Marissa and Charlie and Lexie, we're not in . . ."

In the next state over, in Memphis, Michelle Nowak steered her SUV up to the gates of Graceland. She'd hit the road to see America, visit friends and family, and run away from the knowledge that every week her husband was dodging roadside bombs near Taji.

Across the country, just south of Seattle inside a big stone church, sunlight streamed through the stained glass and hundreds of people sat in silence, listening to Stacy Bannerman read out the names of the fallen. And the sound of her own voice, echoed by a bell after each name, cocooned her in a state of grace while her husband's mortar rounds boomed north of Baghdad.

In Alaska's winter dark, a new mother named Rachel Kair trudged through the snow to the gym, and as her husband parachuted into Afghanistan's remote villages, she huffed through Pilates and Powerflex, weight training, treadmills, and Spinning, until she was too exhausted to be anything but serene.

And back east in Pittsburgh, Pennsylvania, John Bugay tucked his five children into bed and then, with his wife in Iraq, convoying equipment for her weapons intelligence unit, he hunched in front of his computer and vented his fear and frustration through an online discussion board. He read all the news he could. He read the latest e-mail from the advocacy group Military Families Speak Out, or MFSO.

In Fayetteville, North Carolina, listlessly surfing the Internet, Beth

Pratt came across the MFSO Web site. She read the pages carefully. She considered for a minute. Then she sent an e-mail to the list: *I am the wife of a soldier that is deployed to Iraq . . . I have become deeply concerned about his welfare . . . He does not get sufficient time to eat and sleep . . . yet they need to be in top shape to survive . . . Are there other people out there that have heard the same thing? Is there anything we can do about it?* Over the next few days, Beth received more than eighty sympathetic e-mails from people just like her. They were just as far away, though, as the rest of her friends and family.

CHAPTER 10

Honorary Sisters

ROBERT FANNING KNEW Fayetteville. Fort Bragg had been his first duty station back in the seventies, and he'd returned often for special forces training. The posting that he and his wife, Donna, really wanted, however, was Germany. They pictured themselves over there doing their jobs during the week, and on the weekends hopping in the car with their daughter, Chieryssa, and touring the sights of Europe.

Robert had spent his entire career trying to get an assignment in Germany, with no success whatsoever. Donna, too; they were a dual military couple until the late eighties, when Robert decided to retire and stay home with Chieryssa. In the mid-nineties, Donna finally did receive orders to Germany, but then the orders were cancelled and changed to Korea. So she accepted an unaccompanied hardship tour and left Robert and Chieryssa behind for a year, in the belief that when she came back from Korea, she'd have her choice of assignments. Sure enough, a year later she flew back with orders for Germany — which were promptly changed again. The 82nd Airborne needed her at Fort Bragg.

Robert walked into the FRG meeting and took a seat, a tall, narrow man with a light beard and a tension in his posture that gave the impression he was always on his mark, ready to get set and go. In a roomful of women, he was the only man, the only person in the room with a wife in a war zone.

The Fannings hadn't given up on their goal of getting to Germany. In the fall of 2003, the Army finally packed them up and moved them to Germany, their dream duty station — and then promptly deployed Donna to Iraq.

Over the years, Robert and Donna had both deployed so many times they'd quit bothering to count. But this was their first wartime deployment, and it was Donna who had to go and Robert who stayed behind. He was forty-nine years old, married eighteen years, alone with his teenage daughter on a base in Germany. Knowing almost no one, he walked into the FRG meeting and sat down in the middle of a crowd of women.

Only 7 percent of active-duty military spouses were men, honorary sisters in the sisterhood of war. While their wives were not allowed to join units whose mission was frontline ground combat (such as tank, artillery, and frontline infantry units), women could and did serve throughout most of the Navy and Air Force, and in the combat support elements of the Army and Marine Corps — in the air wings, and in units as diverse as medical, intelligence, supply, and military police. Fifteen percent of active-duty forces and 17 percent of National Guard and Reserve forces were women.

But modern warfare is murky, and with no clear frontlines, the distinction between combat and support can become meaningless. In a firefight, the bullets don't care if you're a member of an infantry platoon on a combat mission or a military police squad on a public safety foot patrol; a roadside bomb will leave you just as dead whether you're convoying water for humanitarian relief or troops for an assault. In fact, in Iraq, convoying supplies was some of the most dangerous duty you could pull, whatever your gender or military occupational specialty.

In Germany, Robert became coleader of his FRG. He'd led an FRG before at Donna's last assignment and won awards for going above and beyond as a volunteer. He'd been involved in Army Family Team Building, as well. Working with an FRG had always come naturally, reminded him of his special forces units, which had been like families of eight to twelve individuals. The FRG had that same exclusive family feeling, only bigger. On Halloween, word spread fast that his coleader's husband had been wounded in Iraq, and when he heard Patricia's trembling voice on the phone, he helped her stay grounded with what he knew from his own years of soldiering. He told all the wives, "If anyone ever needs anything hauled, or furniture moved, or something repaired, call me." He knew to stay busy. He knew not to let himself imagine Donna in Iraq, the dangers that could befall her. Instead, he kept the picture in his head simple and generic: *This is just another mission that needs to be accomplished.*

It had thrown him off, though, when Donna deployed so abruptly. "Donna," he told his coleader, Patricia, "is my buddy. We get to Germany, we have all these plans, and within a matter of days, less than a week, my buddy's gone."

When Donna left, they hadn't even moved into quarters yet. He'd moved fifteen times as an adult, a lot more than that if you counted his Army brat years, so it wasn't the moving that threw him. It was setting up the household without her, in a place in which she'd never set foot. He unpacked everything but nothing felt settled, the placement of the couch and easy chairs, the arrangement of items in the kitchen cabinets — it was all *pending*. His interest in seeing the sights of Europe — gone dormant. Mornings, he'd wake up with his arm hanging over the side of the bed, his body squeezed onto the edge as if Donna, a major bed consumer, were still there. Even in his sleep, he was saving her place for her.

He got busy losing the thirty pounds he'd put on since he retired. Weights one day, high cardio the next. Biking and running through the German winter, he'd tell himself, *This is for Donna when she comes home. This is just another mission that needs to be accomplished.* But then he'd flip on the TV and see that more mortar rounds had been lobbed into Taji. So he'd send an e-mail. Nothing urgent. Just carefully, calmly: *Let me know when you can.* As soon as he saw her name on an incoming e-mail, he was happy again.

The company had one other husband, but what he did with himself, Robert had no idea. The man didn't get out a lot. Robert saw him at one event during the entire deployment. For Robert, the FRG was crucial; it kept him busy. His daughter kept him busy, too: sixteen years old and dealing with a new high school and her mother in a war zone. The FRG, though, wasn't as stressful. Talking to the mostly young women in the FRG whom he came to know well was like talking to younger sisters.

Still, he wondered if a few of them didn't have an issue with someone like him attending the wives' coffees, someone unusual, someone not like themselves. He had worried about how the men downrange would react, but they didn't seem to see him as a threat. It was among the women that a rumor briefly made the rounds about him and Patricia, his coleader. It was nothing all that interesting, just speculation, just someone's imagination run amok because he was a man and they were women.

The Hooah Wives didn't allow men.

I'm sitting with the group's managers, Jenn and Angela, at Jenn's kitchen table. "If anyone wanted a male in this group," says Jenn, "I would put my two cents in."

Angela agrees, "I wouldn't be comfortable with that."

In what Jenn calls her "previous life," her pre-Army life, she had mostly male friends because she generally got along better with men than women. "With guys it's more, 'Hey, let's go out,'" she says. "It's not all about feelings, 'I'm hurt and I'm upset.' I think when guys get into those emotional situations with women it makes it too hard to . . ." She lets the sentence trail off.

Official military family support groups like FRGs, with their strict guidelines, hierarchical phone trees, and businesslike meetings, are fairly well-equipped to set limits that prevent rumors and inappropriate behavior. Informal groups may not be so well equipped.

Before they founded the Hooah Wives, Jenn and Angela were involved in another online discussion board. Several men who applied to join actually stated in their application that they wanted to meet some military wives on the side. Jenn guesses it's because they know the woman's not going to leave her husband; she has children. "So she's just a little lay on the side," she says. "They know it's not going to go anywhere."

"And there are men who say they're a woman," adds Angela. Online, who can tell? Such men joined the other online discussion board and lurked. To prevent the same thing from happening in the new group, every applicant who wanted to join the Hooah Wives first had to meet with Jenn or Angela, face to face.

Whether or not they participate in any kind of support group, men with deployed wives face the same challenges as women with deployed husbands. The only difference is that they react like men.

Ken Meyer was on the phone with his wife, Angel, who was deployed to Iraq, when he heard a loud *kaboom* on the other end of the line, and Angel yelling, "*Oh shit!*"

Instantly, Ken's heart pounded in his ears. Blood rushed to the muscles that move the bones. His whole body tensed as if the caveman who lived at the base of his brain could actually hurl himself from his kitchen in Rolesville, North Carolina, all the way to Baghdad to shield his wife with his own body.

A few moments later, he heard a scuffling sound as Angel crawled out from whatever she'd ducked under, picked up the phone, and said, "I'm OK." Ken breathed heavily and got a grip on himself, just as he had the three or four times before when it had happened while they were on the phone like this. Rockets and mortars rained down on Angel's camp nightly, sometimes daily, too. He'd seen pictures of the big craters they left. The barracks next to hers had been hit. The fact was, over there a person could be vaporized at any moment, with no notice, just *kaboom*, and that would be it.

When Angel's North Carolina National Guard unit was activated with orders to go to Iraq, Ken went on a shopping spree, buying flashlights for her, Leatherman tools, a two-way radio, binoculars. As the date for her departure drew closer, it occurred to him that, in a way, he was entrusting the woman he loved to the care of another man. He had wanted to go look her first sergeant in the eye and say, "You take care of her!"

He managed to restrain himself, but apparently he wasn't the only one who had that thought. A couple of her friends in the unit made a point of promising him, as men, that they would look after his wife for him. Angel was a mechanic, the only woman in a platoon of mechanics, and the guys were like brothers to her. Once she was overseas, if they saw her talking to some guy they didn't know, they were right there wanting to know who was who and what was up.

Back in North Carolina, when Ken drove forty-five minutes to the National Guard armory in Oxford for the monthly FRG meetings, the wives of those men would greet him with hugs, which was nice because with Angel gone he wasn't getting a lot of hugs in any other area of his life. They hugged him because he was a strong, beefy man with a ring on his finger, a brother they could safely hang onto for a moment.

He knew that between meetings they were calling and e-mailing and confiding in each other and not him, but that was all right as far as he was concerned. They were mostly in their twenties with kids, and he was forty-three with two cats, two ferrets, and ten goldfish. They were women and he was a man. If someone had a problem, he wanted to solve it and they wanted to talk about it. He was glad to help out if they were home with something leaking or breaking, but he didn't necessarily want to get into how everybody felt about the leaking and the breaking.

Angel's day job was at a women's penitentiary. By law, when reservists or Guard members are called up, their civilian employers must save their jobs for them. But they still miss out on whatever promotions or pay increases they might have earned if they'd stayed. While they're gone, they receive military pay instead of their civilian paycheck. If the military pay is less, a few employers make up the difference. But for more than half of married Guard members and reservists, the switch to military pay means a cut in income. If they own a small business, it may be out of business by the time they return.

Spouses left behind who work outside the home may have to cut back or quit altogether so they can handle the increase in family responsibilities, further reducing the family's income — this is as true for regular active-duty families as it is for Guard and Reserve families.

Meanwhile, some expenses go up. Care packages, for instance, can eat up an amazing amount of cash for both supplies and postage.

"This must be an Angel shop night," said the checkout clerk.

Ken looked down at his grocery basket: canned grapefruit, beef jerky, and feminine hygiene products.

"Yep," he said. Rolesville was a small town. Every Friday night, he'd shop for Angel and box it up, and the next day when he took it to the post office, the postal clerk would ask if Ken had heard from his wife lately, which he always had because every third day or so Angel would pick up her rifle and trudge a mile through 120-degree heat in full battle gear to call or e-mail him.

Being enlisted, she was timed in everything she did — timed in the shower, timed on the computer, timed on the phone. Ten minutes into a call and in the background Ken would hear, "Time!" As the deployment went on, one of the private's wives told him at an FRG meeting that she had bought a Web cam for home because the camp had a Web cam on the other end, and it was so great to see her husband again. Ken ran out and bought a Web cam, too, and he and Angel watched each other wipe away tears. He held up the cats and the ferrets for her to see.

When he was boxing up care packages, sometimes he'd stick in a disk of one of the old-time radio shows they both loved: Jack Benny, Burns and Allen, *The Shadow*. Sometimes, he'd stick in a T-shirt he'd worn. Sometimes, she'd do the same in return. The T-shirts he received smelled like Angel but dustier, powdered with the fine talcum of Iraq. He held one to his face and suddenly he missed the way, whenever he was too overbearing, she would sling his guff right back at him with a flash of dimples in her tan face. He missed her when he opened the door to the house and tumbleweeds of cat fur went rolling across the wood floor, a reminder that now it was up to him to do something about the mess. He missed her in the silent middle of the night. But most of all, he missed her at dinnertime.

In the seven years they'd been together, at the end of a long day, they would always meet in the kitchen and create meals that were half improv theater, half science project. One time, they experimented with an Aztec grain of which they partook too much. It swelled in their stomachs and left them lying side by side on the living room floor, moaning and laughing at themselves.

Now, fixing dinner for himself alone, every once in a while Ken would hear himself sigh, "Oh, Angel." And then he'd have to stop what he was doing because he couldn't see for the tears.

"Hey, Ken, think your wife and her buddies could use some sunglasses?"

Ken was at a trade show. It wasn't long after Angel had deployed, and word had gotten around the exhibit hall that his wife was in Iraq. Pretty soon, everywhere he went in that big hall, people were loading him down with sunglasses and Nerf footballs and company calendars and other giveaways to send to Angel's unit in Iraq.

It got Ken thinking. Angel had mentioned that over there, mail equaled morale. Every generation of Ken's family had served in the military all the way back to the Civil War, with the exception of Ken. But though he hadn't served, as the manager of facilities and construction projects for a major retailer, he knew how to get things done.

He put a large collection box in his front yard and festooned it with red, white, and blue and a sign requesting donated items for care packages for the troops in Iraq. He talked Rolesville's hardware store and ice cream shop into putting out collection boxes, too. Then he contacted a snack food company in Raleigh and asked if they'd consider donating out-of-date snacks to go into care packages. "No way," said the man who answered the phone, "but we'd be glad to donate fresh snacks."

Then Ken got his FRG involved, and "Operation: A Bit of Home" became their project, too. Lynn Sinclair, the Guard wife who had adorned her car with bumper stickers in support of her husband, explained to her pastor that her Family Readiness Group at the Oxford armory needed donated items and postage money for Operation: A Bit of Home, and Pleasant Grove Baptist Church took up a collection. A couple of times, some of the wives took collection buckets out onto the street corner next to the armory and as cars went by, people would throw in a dollar or two.

Next thing Ken knew, up to 250 pounds of donated goods were avalanching into his house every week, his living room stacked floor to ceiling with snack food, sports equipment, magazines, sunscreen, hygiene products, socks, and donated boxes to ship it in. He'd take truckloads to the armory and the wives would help pack it up. Managing the flow kept him busy for three hours after work each day plus weekends; he was spending more on postage than food. So he started focusing on fundraising. Operation: A Bit of Home had turned into a project that would continue to consume Ken Meyer even after Angel came home.

After Donna Fanning came home, she and Robert and Chieryssa hit the road. They traveled all over Germany and to Italy, Austria, Switzer-land, Belgium, Poland, and England. "My buddy's back," Robert would say, looking at Donna. "My buddy's back." The night she came back was the hardest — the hardest night of the whole deployment. That was the night it was finally safe. All the fear and worry and sadness he'd locked away: It was finally safe to let it all out, his best friend back safe in his arms.

When the wife of a man named Butch came home from Iraq, the news cameras focused on him because his grin was so wide he looked like the happiest man in the crowd. But it was the painful, face-splitting grin of a man determined to smile his way to a happily ever after, even though he knew his soldier had cheated on him more than once while she was gone.

Butch was a Vietnam vet, a barrel-chested man with a neat white goa-tee who gave up a career in newspapers and radio to follow the woman he loved, first to Fort Hood in Killeen, Texas, then to Fort Polk, Louisi-ana, hard by the Texas border, which was where she'd left from fifteen months earlier. They'd both been married before and hadn't necessarily expected to find love again late in middle age, but on their first blind date they met at the Shoney's diner and discovered they had so much to say to each other, they shut the place down.

When she left for Iraq, Butch couldn't help thinking, *Who's going to take care of you?* For more than half a dozen years, he'd been getting up when she went off to work on post, fixed her coffee, walked her out to the car. *How you gonna eat? Who's gonna feed you?* That was what was going through his mind when she first left. *I should be going off to fight,* he thought, *not you.* For the first six or seven months, she ended every call and e-mail with *I love you.* They talked about how much they missed each other. They made plans for the future. They sent cassette tapes back and forth so they could hear each other's voices even when she couldn't call.

Butch rationed his news; anytime something happened, he wondered if it was her unit. He wondered which cable news operation he should trust — CNN seemed too negative, Fox spent too much time sugarcoat-ing everything. MSNBC seemed like it was somewhere in the middle, so that was the one he watched.

He stayed busy at the gym he managed on post. Mostly, he ran the place alone, so seven days a week he was the personal trainer, janitor, and counselor/father figure, all rolled into one. As the National Guard units came through Polk for training, on their way to Iraq, the kids would find their way to the gym to lift weights, play board games, listen to the stereo, watch TV, and talk to Butch. "Why are we going over there?" they'd ask. "Why are we going if there's no weapons of mass destruction there?" Some of the girls cried on his shoulder. The boys' voices were nervous and tight, their hands shaky. In Vietnam, Butch was in covert operations. He knew what fear looked like. He'd felt it himself.

One night, he was sitting at the computer in his home office, checking e-mail. He clicked on an e-mail from a friend of his and his wife's, and as he read, he realized it wasn't meant for him. *Be careful,* the friend had written to his wife. He read to the bottom, where he found the original e-mail that the friend was responding to. *There's a man over here that's interested in me,* his wife had written. *I know I'm married, but he's great. Don't let Butch know, OK?*

Be careful.

Why? Butch wanted to shout at his wife. Fear twisted in his gut. *Why?* He knew what fear felt like and knew it could make you do things you wouldn't ordinarily do. He had access to her e-mail account and he started spot-checking. He found e-mails between her and the man, who worked for a subcontractor in Iraq, and then later e-mails between her and another soldier. A member of her unit who came back early confirmed it for him over lunch at the Chinese buffet in town: "At first, all she could do was talk about you and how much she missed you, and then this guy shows up and they start talking a lot, spending time in his tent . . ." *Why?* he had wanted to shout, but he knew why. He knew fear could make anybody do things she wouldn't ordinarily do. Things maybe she could just leave over there when she came back home.

Butch would later estimate that among the 1,400 married soldiers in his wife's unit, about one third had had affairs with other soldiers while deployed, and about two hundred marriages split up when they all came back and he stood there grinning in the crowd of waiting families.

The soldiers marched in and stood in formation. At first, as his wife stood at attention among the other soldiers, she wouldn't look at him. Then, she'd just glance at him and his grin and look away. Butch swallowed hard and kept on grinning. When the soldiers were released, he hurried over, determined to hug her to him. She didn't hug him back. She just folded up; he could feel her shaking. In the car on the way home, she yelled as if she needed to be angry with him. That night, she slept on top of the covers, fully clothed.

The next morning, she said, "I want to separate and see if we can work it out that way."

"Work what out?" Butch said. She wouldn't admit there was anyone else, but still he said, "Look, I'm willing to put it behind us. Let's just move on."

A couple of days later, they attended a couples briefing. For Butch it was voluntary, but it was required for his wife, part of the standard reintegration process at Fort Polk for every married returning soldier. A chaplain introduced a civilian counselor, who instructed the roomful of two hundred people to sit facing their spouses. Those who were there without their spouses were simply paired up with each other. They practiced communication skills, saying things like, "I still love you," and "I understand." Butch's wife threatened to get up and walk out in the middle of it. They were given a questionnaire to fill out as a couple. Butch filled it out while she sat with her arms folded, staring into space. A week later, as the closed-circuit channel on post was running and rerunning shots of Butch grinning at his wife's homecoming as if his life depended on it, Butch's wife told him she wanted a divorce.

Butch was waiting for the divorce papers to arrive. They were due any day now at his new place in Killeen, Texas. His job at the gym on Fort Polk was a great second-income job, but he couldn't live on it. So he took the first job he could find, managing a Blockbuster video rental store back in Killeen, outside Fort Hood. He was still looking for gym work, though, preferably in some place like his hometown in Georgia, a place where he and his soon-to-be ex-wife had lived only briefly, where there were fewer memories.

He hadn't been to the movies since moving back to Killeen. When she was here at Fort Hood, they went to a movie every Friday night. He hadn't been to the Olive Garden where they often ate, or the Boston Market, or the best Chinese restaurant in town. Too many memories. His first night back, he drove over to the HEB supermarket because he'd always liked shopping there before. He walked in, and there among the bright mounds of produce and the clack of grocery carts and the aromas from the deli, waves of remembered peace and sudden loss washed over him. He spun on his heel and got out of there. He sat in his car in the parking lot, unable to drive, his big shoulders shaking, tears streaming down his face into his white goatee.

CHAPTER 11

Dreamland

IN ANCIENT GREECE, a blind poet named Homer told the story of Odysseus, who left home to fight the Trojan War. For twenty years, his wife, Penelope, waited for him to come home, fending off suitors, hoping he was still alive. When Odysseus finally returned, she opened her arms and welcomed him back, even though during his long journey home, he had cheated on his faithful wife more than once.

It goes both ways. When my stepfather came home from his second Vietnam tour, his then-wife asked for a divorce in the car on the way home from the airport. He said, "But I don't want a divorce." And then, because they lived in a state that granted divorces only in cases where there was cause, such as infidelity, she said, "You have cause."

In military towns then and now, there are photo albums with blank spaces where wedding photos used to be, amputated family group shots where an ex-spouse has been cut off the end of a row. In Fayetteville, in-side a beige duplex, on the coffee table, was a small photo album. On the cover of the album was a photograph of Beth and Luigi at his favorite surfing beach. They stood side by side, their heads tilted toward each other, he in a suit and tie, she in a short, pale green dress, holding a small bouquet. During his deployment to Iraq, that small wedding album had a permanent place on the coffee table.

Beth sat on the couch with the TV tuned to the usual medical exam-iner rerun. Camilla had invited her to lunch with some other wives. It seemed to Beth that whenever wives got together — not Camilla, but the others — they kept getting into that subtle little competition about how often their husbands called and Beth always felt like the loser. She hadn't heard from Luigi in a while. The silence was an ache inside her.

She picked up the wedding album and paged through photos of their south Florida friends eating wedding cake. She closed the album and the two people on the cover grinned up at her. They looked unnaturally happy. More than once, at work or at dinner with the wives, someone had said, *You know guys always cheat when they're over there.*

Among the friends pictured in the wedding album was a nurse named Debbie McKay. Her signature was on their marriage license as one of the witnesses. She called; she was going to be in Myrtle Beach for a few days. "That's only a couple hours from you," she said, making the argument to Beth. "Come hang out with me for the weekend."

It was gray and cold and a relief to be with a friend. They walked Danny on the beach. They lay around talking in the motel room, which was where they were when Beth's cell phone finally rang and she heard Luigi's voice say, "Hey, baby." She sighed with relief, "Hey, babe." And then *shhhhh-click*, the connection went dead.

In the minutes after the connection died, Beth unloaded to Debbie about how she was tired of it — she was tired of everything. She didn't know why she got married — it was like they weren't even married any- more. A few minutes later, when the phone rang again in the middle of it all, and she heard Luigi's relentlessly sunny voice from the other side of the world, she demanded, "Why don't you call me?"

"What do you mean?" he said.

She paced back and forth. "Everybody else's husband calls them. Every day, practically. It just makes me wonder if you don't love me anymore."

"Don't — what?" he said, and then his voice went supernova and Beth was so startled she stopped pacing. "I *work* all the time! I don't know what you think I'm doing over here, baby, but I work *all the time!* I barely get to sleep! When can I talk to you? When?" He couldn't believe she'd think he didn't love her. Even when he did find a minute to call her, he couldn't just pick up the phone. He had to stand in a long line and then after a few minutes, the phone would go dead. "You know I love you!" he yelled. "You're the person who keeps me sane!"

Beth was looking at the floor. She'd never heard him raise his voice like that before. She said softly, "I'm sorry." And then, quickly, before the line could go to hell again, she told him she loved him, too.

Afterward, she said to Debbie, "I'm glad he yelled at me. I needed to hear that. All I've been thinking about is the danger he's in when he's out on convoys. I didn't think about how hard he's working."

Debbie said, "I'm just glad you didn't mention you're lying around at the beach."

Beth laughed then, but after the fight with Luigi, she decided not to get together with other soldiers' wives anymore. The things they said just made her paranoid.

From then on, each day was like the same hammer: duplex, hospital, duplex, hospital, TV reruns on her nights off. She hadn't picked up her drumsticks since coming to Fayetteville. They just looked too heavy.

When Charlie called, he'd ask about Marissa's day and then he'd talk to Lexie if she wasn't asleep or at daycare, even though it always made him miss home even more. But he told Marissa it was even harder not to talk to them. He'd think about the things she and Lexie told him, the things they were doing, and that grounded him, that's what kept him going. They'd been together a quarter of their lives already.

Back in Erie, when they were living together in the trailer park, Charlie once picked Marissa up from work at his parents' garage on a Fourth of July weekend and announced that his sister was watching Lexie. "We're going to dinner," he said, "maybe shoot some pool or something." He turned left toward Travelport, which was a truck stop with great cheese fries that Marissa had had a special craving for when she was pregnant. But he drove right on past it. "So where are we going?" she asked.

He shrugged. "I just figure we'll go for a drive and go find a place."

"Oh," she said, "OK." They drove and drove. She started to get hungry. She asked again, "Honey? Where are we going?"

He shrugged again. "I thought we would go up to Niagara Falls and have dinner."

"Oh," she said, "cool." Then they spotted a go-cart place with a figure-eight double track, so they stopped and raced and played some video games. After a while, Charlie said, "So, uh, they have fireworks at the falls. You want to go up to the falls and have dinner up there?"

By the time they got there, the fireworks were about to start, so they just grabbed some food, ditched the car in a lot, and ran down to the falls as the first explosions flowered overhead. The falls were packed. They walked down along the river, squeezing in and out of the crowd, hanging on tight to keep from losing each other, until they were standing right next to the thundering white rush of water. The mist swirled around them, beading their skin and hair. The night sky boomed and sparkled.

Charlie turned to Marissa and lifted his hand. There on his pinky was a ring she'd seen in an antique store, the ring she'd wanted. Over the roar of the falls, she just barely heard him shout, "So, what's up, baby? Will you marry me?" And the fireworks exploded above them, and Marissa shouted yes and kissed him, and the people standing all around them burst into applause.

After their hurry-up wedding before he went in the Army, they drove back up to Niagara Falls for a weekend honeymoon. Marissa was wearing knee-high, high-heeled boots, and at one of the clubs she tripped and fell down the stairs. "Well," she said as Charlie helped her up, "that kind of sucked." But then they danced and the honeymoon improved after that, Marissa's body moving with Charlie's on the dance floor.

On the phone from Iraq, he said, "You need to get out. Go. Go have fun."

She said, "You really, really mean it?"

"Yeah, just go."

So she went out dancing at Broadstreet's with the Hooah Wives. Charlie could be very jealous, but not of other people. He was jealous of Marissa's books. Marissa would be lost in a book and Charlie would say, "Hello, pay attention to me!"

At Broadstreet's, the Hooah Wives policed each other. One night Tiffany saw a young Army wife she knew on the dance floor, drunk and kissing some guy. Tiffany marched out there, grabbed her by the hair, and dragged her off, snapping, "You are *married,* and that is not your *husband!*"

"Just remember," said Jenn, "he's coming home one day."

Some of the Hooah Wives had their husband's names tattooed into their skin, on the small of a back, an upper arm, a breast. The night the Hooah Wives were at Broadstreet's celebrating Christine's birthday, someone sitting at the pushed-together tables said, just loud enough to be heard through the music, "Oh my God, look who just came in." Someone else said, "Look who she came in *with.*"

Marissa turned to look. A woman named Nanette was leading a guy toward them through the crush. Marissa knew Nanette, and she knew Nanette's husband was deployed. Marissa's face soured like she'd just chomped the lime in her Corona. As they came closer, the commentary around the table cascaded lower: "She actually admitted it to me . . . Can't believe it . . . So brazen about it . . ." By the time they arrived, the table was silent.

Nanette shouted hi and handed a present to Christine. A few voices shouted hi back as if nothing were wrong, and Christine started pulling off the wrapping paper. Marissa smoked and watched the two of them make their way around the table to a couple of empty seats beside her. As they sat down she shouted over the music, "Look, if you're going to cheat on your husband while he's gone, that's your business. But get the hell away from me, 'cause guys talk, and I don't want anybody saying I'm hanging out with you."

Nanette's eyes widened, her mouth opened slightly. She got up and pulled the guy away with her into the dancing, sweating crowd.

Some of the other women exchanged the same wide-eyed looks with each other but nobody said anything till later, when they said, more in amazement than disapproval, "Oh my God, I can't believe Marissa did that!"

Christine just said, "Nanette made her own bed." Nanette had told Christine once that she was cheating, and Christine was surprised; she hadn't thought Nanette was like that. Nanette's husband had been deployed before. But he'd been home only two months before he'd had to deploy again.

As for Marissa, whenever the wives were at a bar, if a guy so much as asked directions, Marissa would bark, "We're married!" The other wives would tease her, "How do you know the guy's hitting on you if you don't even let him talk to you?"

Marissa didn't care. Because guys did talk. And what were the chances of a rumor starting? *Oh, I saw Marissa with so-and-so, and so-and-so is cheating on her husband,* and Marissa didn't want to be associated with that. She wanted Charlie to feel comfortable while he was gone; he had more important things to worry about, he had so much on his mind. And he trusted her.

Fayetteville's main drags are lined with bars and clubs and restaurants filled with young men sporting military haircuts and civilian clothes, and young women, some of them local, others newly arrived here with a soldier or soldiers themselves. When some people put their club gear on, they take their wedding bands off.

The dance is an old one. MP Hartz saw it twenty years ago and Chaplain Hartz sees the same thing today. "For some young deployed soldiers," he says, "just the fact that the wife's going to a bar doesn't sit well, the fact that she's out there where she's available. The wives say they only dance with each other, but there are guys there, right? He'll ask, 'Do you talk to them?' And she'll say no. But he's thinking, *But they're looking at you.* So you can see where this goes in his mind. It plants the seed of doubt."

Over in Womack's social work department, Lieutenant Colonel Pecko nods and sighs. "I was deployed nine months in the first Gulf War," he says gently. "After six or seven months, even I was having those thoughts, and my wife and I have a strong, long-term relationship. There was no rational reason. I was just feeling vulnerable."

Very young, newly married couples are the most vulnerable of all. The way Chaplain Hartz sees it, "When a young soldier rushes into marriage before a deployment, he's thinking, 'I may not come home. I want to experience this. I know she'll wait for me.' And she's seventeen. The basis of their marriage is sexual intimacy. Suddenly the sex is gone, and if that's what tied you together, then you could be in trouble." Combine that with moving to a new town where you can be anonymous, and the normal boundaries that keep you in line are no longer there.

Get a group of military wives together, and they'll say that as soon as your husband leaves on deployment, that's when everything breaks. They'll laugh and compare notes on the things they've had to fix by themselves — dead washing machines, broken windows, leaky roofs. For Joanne Perdok, it was the car, a shiny new red Volkswagen convertible that should have been lemon yellow.

It was 1965. Joanne's husband, Steve, was special forces, and he'd just left Fort Bragg for his first tour in Vietnam. He bought her the new VW so she wouldn't have any car trouble while he was away. But at the end of each work day, Joanne would walk out of the mini post exchange she managed at Simmons Army Airfield on Fort Bragg, hop in her cute little Bug, turn the key in the ignition, and as often as not, that lemon would just sit there going nowhere.

There was a nice married guy, Dave, a noncommissioned officer, or NCO, with the 82nd just back from Vietnam; sometimes he would help out. He'd stop and talk to her whenever he came into the mini PX, and he knew something about cars. Whenever he couldn't get the VW started for her, he'd work on it at her place — hitch it up to his car and tow it to her trailer in the Dreamland Trailer Court out in Fayetteville.

Joanne lived in town because, back then, if a soldier lived on post with his family, when that soldier went to war his family had to move out. Housing on post was for soldiers. There's an old saying: If the Army wanted you to have a wife, it would have issued you one. In those days, it was true. Families were like extra baggage that had to be stored somewhere else with the rest of a soldier's personal effects till he came back. Some wives went home to their parents. Some moved into dilapidated, unsafe neighborhoods near the post because that was all they could afford.

Joanne and Steve, knowing he would deploy, never bothered to move on post in the first place. They bought the trailer and rented a lot in Dreamland, one of the nicest trailer parks in town. When Steve deployed, their plan was for Joanne to take the trailer and their three-year-old son back home to Pittsburgh, where they were from, and stay there near their families till he came back.

But Joanne's in-laws told her to grow up. They came down to Fayetteville and sat in the living room of her new trailer with the fancy tip-out front and said, "You can't take this trailer up and down the highway every time he leaves. Are you still a little baby?" They wanted her to break loose from her close Italian family, though they didn't say it. In a way she did, too, but now that Steve was gone, she missed her parents and brothers and sisters and cousins. She missed having people to talk to who knew her as well as she knew herself. Still, one of the reasons she'd married Steve just as soon as she graduated from high school was to get out from under her father's heavy thumb.

So Joanne stayed in Fayetteville. It was 1965, she was twenty-three, and had never lived alone before in her life. As soon as Steve left and her in-laws went back home to Pittsburgh, things around the trailer started to break. Dave, the nice married NCO, was just helping her out.

He was from Oklahoma, outgoing and friendly. She'd never met a man who was so easy to talk to. Steve was more introverted, never much of a talker. The first conversation she had with Dave, he asked, "So, is your husband in the Army?"

"No," she said, "he's in special forces."

That made Dave laugh. "Last I heard, that was part of the United States Army."

She laughed, too, but that was how little she understood about the military. Special forces personnel and their families were so tightly knit that she thought they were a separate branch, like the Air Force, Navy, and Marines.

At the mini PX, a major saw her talking to Dave for a long time at the cash register, and after Dave left the major tried to do the same, plying her with compliments and sweet talk. Joanne was a stylish brunette with neutral lipstick and a chic bouffant, but she was also a good Catholic girl. She prayed her nightly personal prayers and her rosaries and attended the Mass every week. Back in school, the nuns' lessons had never included a course in pickup lines, so she didn't realize what the major was up to until he made some sly comment about Dave's frequent trips to the PX, and then it dawned on her: *He thinks I'm fooling around.* She was mortified, because Dave was just a friend, nothing more. Before she could catch her breath and explain, the major was inviting her to go off to the mountains with him for the weekend.

Joanne felt as if he'd stripped her naked right there in the PX. She felt dirty, that he would think of her like that. "I'm Catholic," she said. "I have a husband in Vietnam and a three-year-old son and I don't fool around." He gave her a look, as if to say, *Yeah, right,* and that was when she got mad.

I'll show you, she thought. She flashed him a smile. "You know what, I will go to the mountains with you." Then she added, "If we can go first to the Officers' Christmas Ball that's coming up. I would just love to attend that."

The major did what she expected him to do, sputtered excuses about just wanting to be alone with her. She knew good and well it was because too many people would know him at the military ball and word would get back to his wife, who was out of town. She watched him squirm, then cut him off. "I wouldn't go *anywhere* with you."

Instead, she went everywhere with her girlfriends, all of them, like her, married to deployed special forces soldiers. They'd take their children on picnics together, or take turns babysitting while the rest played cards or went out. Sometimes, they'd go to the NCO club on Pope Air Force Base, where "Good Vibrations" and "Strangers in the Night" blasted across the dance floor. They'd dance with the soldiers and laugh about one particular general's wife who was a fixture at the little bar downstairs in the officers' club — laughing that by the time her general came home from 'Nam, she was likely to have slept her way through half a battalion.

That was Joanne's world — soldiers and soldiers' wives. She had no local friends. Fayetteville's citizens had a love-hate relationship with Fort Bragg. They knew the post provided jobs and pumped large amounts of money into the economy, but the money came in many tiny, low-end increments from the poorly paid, junior enlisted soldiers who made up most of the tens of thousands of service members at Bragg. A significant portion of that money was spent by single soldiers in the bars that had mushroomed through downtown, and on the prostitutes who stood brazenly on the corners and called out to passing boys with military haircuts, "Hey, soldier, looking for a good time?" If the locals wanted to take their children shopping at the downtown department store, they had to wade through sleaze. They called it Combat Alley.

The pursed O's of the Pennsylvania accent in Joanne's voice marked her as an outsider, an Army wife. Once when she tried to shop at the Strawberry Barn, one of Fayetteville's nicer dress shops, the clerk followed her around with a scowl, as if she might steal something. She took the hint and left. Meanwhile, the antiwar protesters on the news were about Joanne's age, but that was all they had in common. The sight of them upset her — the husband she loved was over there, risking his life to do his job, and they were saying both he and his job were wrong. They seemed to blame the soldiers for the war.

Places like Dreamland and Trailer Town were full of women like Joanne: women far from home, with few friends, and without their husbands, who were all in Vietnam. And every day a staff car would come through Dreamland and the women would watch out their windows to see where it stopped. And if it stopped at the trailer of a friend, they would hurry over and they would hold her as she cried, because her husband wasn't coming home again. They were all the support they had.

Loneliness was the enemy.

For some, the sense of isolation from the wider world was unbearable. It was for the wife of Joanne's friend Dave. After he got home from his second Vietnam tour, she admitted to having met someone else while he was gone, another soldier. Dave wanted to stay together and start over, try again, but she wasn't interested. As his marriage crumbled, he confided in Joanne. One day in the mini PX he asked her, "What are you doing tonight?"

"My son and I are going to the drive-in," she said. "We're going to go see *Goldfinger.*"

"Would you mind company?" he asked. "My mother-in-law's visiting and I can't deal with her tonight."

Loneliness. The enemy. That night at the drive-in, after her son fell asleep, Dave kissed her.

One Sunday, Dave and his two sons joined Joanne and her son at the lake on post. They all seemed to be having a good time, but at some point Joanne looked up and there was Dave's oldest, looking at her. He was six, two years older than her own son, and his brows were drawn together over his dark brown eyes. He had the look of a child struggling with a math problem that wouldn't add up. Joanne was haunted by his eyes — something wasn't right and he knew it. She knew it, too. She was in love with two men and married to only one of them. Even if she hadn't loved her husband anymore, divorce was out. Her Roman Catholic religion wasn't a smorgasbord; you couldn't pick the parts you liked and leave the rest. She had to make her marriage work.

But Steve came back from Vietnam more silent than ever. Neither Dave nor Steve talked to Joanne about what they saw or did over there, but where Vietnam left Dave with nightmares, Steve shut down. He started to drink. He resumed his special forces training schedule, which was so demanding that even though he was technically home, he was with his family only about one week out of every four. Once he was back in Vietnam for his second tour and Joanne found out she was pregnant, she knew the baby was Dave's.

She told Steve when he came home again. Like Dave before him, Steve was desperate for them to stay together and start over, try again, and this time it was Joanne who wasn't interested. But Joanne was afraid of her church and her father, and she had fallen in love with Steve when she was fifteen — the man who now refused to believe the new baby boy wasn't his — so the marriage flailed on until first Dave, and then Steve, rotated back to Vietnam. Both men survived their third tours. The marriage did not.

Joanne's girlfriends gave her the name of the divorce lawyer they'd used. By the time Joanne walked into his office, so many Fort Bragg wives had been coming to him that he said, "Good God, what's going on over at Bragg?" Joanne choked out a laugh — it was that or cry. "Maybe you can give us a group rate," she said.

She sat her oldest son down in the living room, the Christmas tree blinking in the corner. He was seven years old. When she got to the word *divorce*, it scared him and he started to cry. She tried to be strong for him the way she always had and not let him see her cry. Crying was a personal thing, like praying the rosary, something she did in her bedroom with the door closed. She reminded herself and her son: For most of her marriage, Steve had been gone more than he'd been home. "Nothing's going to change," she told their son now. "It's always been me and you. It's going to continue to be me and you."

Thirty years later, in a Fayetteville development of big new homes, a wedding portrait on top of a TV in a great room captures a bride with long, dark hair, wearing a pale green, highwaisted chiffon gown, the groom in Army dress greens. The house around it is beautiful, the kind of place a young wife in a trailer court might have dreamed of. It looks professionally decorated, although Joanne did it all herself: the tasteful window treatments, the graceful arrangement of polished furniture, the displays of collected treasures. She started out working at a tiny PX. She had eventually become an account executive for a Fortune 400 cosmetics company, managing the military accounts in the southeastern United States and Panama. Dave had retired from the Army as a command sergeant major in the 82nd Airborne.

After Vietnam, as the Army shifted to an all-volunteer force, Joanne and Dave participated in the first family life symposium in Washington, D.C., an early effort to improve the Army's support for families. Joanne and the other spouses wanted a phone tree for each unit, so that spouses waiting out a deployment wouldn't be left in the dark anymore. They wanted training to educate spouses on the benefits available to them. And they wanted families living in military housing to be allowed to remain there when their soldiers deployed, *especially* when their soldiers deployed, because that was when the families most needed the support and security of the military community. By the eighties, those changes were underway.

When the person you love is far away for months on end, when his body is beyond your reach and you can't hold him and smell him and be reminded of his realness, when he blurs in your mind like a ghost, then each day you must dream him back to life. But each time you recreate him, you change him a little. You fill in the blank spots. Sometimes you fill in his outline with the details of his own best nature, the person he could be, his finer qualities taking up all the space his annoying habits and human failings used to inhabit. And you fall in love all over again.

Then again, sometimes you fill in his outline with the details of someone else's best nature, the person you *wish* he could be, a person who, unlike him, is within your reach. And in a time of war, when the rules no longer seem to apply — when young people may not grow old, and tomorrow may be worse than today, and love may not heal all wounds — you can dream yourself into a nightmare. Even if you're eventually able to turn it to something good, the pain remains. When Joanne thinks back on the special forces wives she knew from that time, she can't remember a single marriage that survived Dreamland.

Joanne divorced Steve and married Dave, and it was three years before her father finally allowed her into his house again. She was excommunicated from the Roman Catholic church, although she continued to attend the Mass and raised her sons in the Catholic faith. Steve remarried, too, but later died from the aftereffects of exposure to Agent Orange in Vietnam. Dave's ex-wife married her soldier and disappeared from Fayetteville, and Dave didn't see his three oldest children again until they grew up and came back to find him. And for years, if Joanne told the boys to go wake Dave from a nap, they'd say, "No, we don't want to." They were afraid of the way he'd thrash up out of his dreams, kicking and punching at some invisible enemy.

CHAPTER 12

Pigeons in the Desert

THROUGHOUT THE FALL and into the winter, nearly half of the pregnant women in Womack's labor and delivery rooms were there with their mothers or sisters or girlfriends. The husbands were all gone — gone to Iraq, Afghanistan, South Korea, South America, Africa . . . Beth was working the night that the wife of Luigi's commanding officer, or CO, went into labor and came in with her mother. Nine months after a unit returns home, there's usually a mini baby boom. In the case of Luigi's unit, by the time that date rolled around, the soldiers were back overseas again. Beth monitored the CO's wife, coached her, helped deliver her baby.

On another night in another labor and delivery room, the mother was nineteen and in labor with her second child. Down the hall, Beth took another young mother's history.

"How old are you?" she asked.

"Twenty-five," said the young mother. "This is our last child, our fifth."

Rarely did Beth see a patient her own age, and when once they had a patient who was thirty-three, the nurse taking care of her referred to her as *elderly*. It made Beth feel like she was going to be positively ancient by the time she had kids — assuming she was ever able to have kids, between Luigi deploying so much and the two of them requiring treatment.

In Minnesota, Luigi's sperm waited on ice. Though they had agreed that Beth would try artificial insemination while he was gone, now she hesitated. She knew she was getting older and had no time to waste, but the way the world was going, for as long as Luigi was in the Army he was probably going to be away at least half the time. The thought of having a baby without him there, like the CO's wife had done, scared her. She already felt so down these days. What if she had postpartum depression on top of it?

Beth flew home for Thanksgiving. She visited with her parents, her sisters and cousins, the friends she grew up with. One friend took her to a nondenominational church, and surrounded by singing, clapping people, people shouting, "Praise God!", Beth felt a little lighter, a little closer to God.

When she got back to Fayetteville, she opened up the phone book and called a nearby Methodist church. She grilled the pastor to see if it was Bible-believing, and then she visited one Sunday. From the two-lane road, looking across the big gravel parking lot, Cornerstone United Methodist Church looked more like a metal warehouse than a church. Inside, the walls were a soothing taupe color with white trim. High up, a row of small square windows cast squares of sunlight on the people below, about fifty of them, white, black, brown, in dressy dresses and jeans, some shaggy-haired, some with military haircuts. Sitting among them made Beth feel a little better, not much, but a little, and a good band led the hymns. She started going every other week on her Sundays off.

She decided she was ready to try artificial insemination, partly because she knew if it worked, Luigi would be home by the time the baby was born. She started by taking Clomid, which forced her ovaries to produce more eggs. She called for Luigi's sperm, which arrived on the front step of the duplex in two large, silver canisters of liquid nitrogen that were taller than Danny. She took a picture of the dog sitting between the two canisters and sent it to Luigi with the caption: *Here's Danny between his little brothers.* She gave herself an injection to trigger ovulation and an obstetrician she knew at Womack used a catheter with a long tube to inseminate her with Luigi's sperm. Then she waited.

While many of the pregnant women at Womack were huffing their way through each contraction without their husbands, many of the children on post and out in town were being tucked in by one parent fewer than they were used to.

The day five-year-old Lexie Bootes's father deployed, he was the one who woke her up. Marissa had already left for work. Outside Lexie's bedroom window, it started to rain, a dull drizzle. Charlie took her on post with him, and they spent the rainy morning together at his unit's headquarters. Before the buses left for Green Ramp, though, a friend came by, a soldier Lexie knew from playing with his kids. She started to wail as he gently pulled her away from her father. The soldier drove her, still wailing, over to the house of a friend of Marissa's.

Lexie whimpered in the woman's lap while the soldier crouched next to her, trying to talk to her about what she was feeling, until finally he had to get back to work on post. She was still crying when her mother hurried in late in the afternoon. Marissa held her close, murmuring, "Oh, peanut, I'm here." They talked about Lexie's daddy, while outside the rain fell.

Back home, Marissa started the water hissing for Lexie's shower. She reached to unclasp the necklace around Lexie's neck, and Lexie started to scream.

"What is your issue?" Marissa asked. Lexie had been taking it off every night since Charlie gave it to her the week before as an early Christmas present — DADDY'S LITTLE GIRL it said in gold letters. "You can put it back on after, just like always, just like I take all *my* jewelry off when I take a shower."

"No!" Lexie wailed. "I can't ever ever take it off! It's very important to me! Daddy gave it to me and I have to keep it on until he comes back!"

That brought Marissa up short. She folded Lexie into her arms and didn't say anything else about taking off the necklace. That night, when Lexie asked if she could sleep with her because she missed her daddy and didn't want to be by herself, when Lexie said maybe if they snuggled she would feel better, Marissa said gently, "Sure."

Marissa lay beside her little girl in the double bed, and she thought of Charlie, who was still in the air. For a moment, trying to imagine him flying farther and farther away from them every minute was like trying to imagine where someone goes when he dies. She snuggled closer to Lexie, felt her warm and real against her, felt the rhythm of her breathing, and she wondered who she was doing this for — Lexie? Or herself?

My husband Frank's Marine unit went to war with nearly everything it needed: M-16s, Mark-19s, .50-caliber machine guns, Humvees, amphibious assault vehicles, tents, welding and machining gear, field mess gear, medical supplies, high-tech communications equipment, and chickens.

Why chickens? Because the Marines had also packed sophisticated detection paraphernalia that, according to scientific experts, was supposed to sound a warning at the first sign of a chemical attack. However, burning oil wells could also set off the detectors, leaving the Marines to run around in gas masks for no good reason. So when it came to weapons of mass destruction, they relied on a no-tech, backup detection system: Chickens.

While the Marines sat in the Kuwaiti desert waiting to invade Iraq, the men were warned in no uncertain terms that the chickens were government property and were not to be liberated for barbecues of a private, unauthorized nature. The chickens soon took care of that themselves. They began to look peaked. Then they began to die. It was finally determined that the respiratory system of a domesticated First World chicken wasn't designed to withstand the heat and dust of a Third World desert environment.

"Well, sir," said one young enlisted country boy, "I coulda told you that."

So a backup to the backup was located — Kuwaiti pigeons. When the invasion began and miles of Humvees and amphibious personnel carriers rolled across the line into Iraq, several vehicles in each convoy carried one wire mesh cage equipped with one desert-tested feathered chemical agent detector: A pigeon. The desert version of a canary in a coal mine.

Back on the homefront, the pigeons are children. Children react to the stresses of a wartime deployment just like anyone else who gets left behind — and they're not as good at hiding it. Lexie was a smart, socially sophisticated little girl who had been potty-trained for years. But after her father left, as the same nameless fear that was overtaking her mother overtook her as well, now and then she would wet her pants.

At Fort Bragg's McNair Elementary School, a majority of the children tumbling into the classrooms were spending at least part of the school year with a missing parent; children of single soldiers were adjusting to a whole new caregiver. The students at McNair came from two military housing communities on post, and that fall and winter more than half were either saying goodbye to a parent, lonely for a parent, or welcoming a parent home.

The big bulletin board outside the front office was papered in beige-toned desert camouflage and bordered in yellow ribbon. Beneath the title OUR HEROES were rows of photographs of deployed parents in military uniform, a child's first name written below each one. Across the hall was a display of photos some of the parents had sent from Afghanistan: pictures of soldiers sitting on the ground eating flatbread with Afghan men, and more pictures of smiling Afghan children, the girls wearing colorful head scarves.

McNair was one of nine schools on Fort Bragg and Pope Air Force

Base operated by the Department of Defense for children living on post. On American military installations around the world, the DoD ran 222 schools attended by 100,000 children of active-duty military families. Whenever any of these children had a deployed parent, they were cared for by teachers, guidance counselors, social workers, and school nurses experienced with deployment-related issues.

"We watch," says Diana Ohman, the director of DoD Dependents Schools in Europe. "If a child's coming to school with red eyes and dark circles, or a child who's normally rowdy is suddenly quiet in the corner, or a quiet child is suddenly acting out, or grades are dropping, then we move in."

Ohman's school system of 112 schools on bases throughout Europe has developed an official Action Plan for Deployment Interventions. Schools pull together military family support services and community resources to make it easier to match needs with services. Principals meet with family readiness organizations and base and unit commanders to stay on top of deployments. Teachers moderate support groups for children going through deployment, and nurses lead walking clubs and healthy cooking classes for those who prefer doing something to talking.

On Fort Bragg, the support system is less formal but still extensive. Among the teachers trickling into McNair School every morning with their coffee cups and their armloads of graded papers are three Bragg Army veterans — Gary Wieland, Debra Joas, and Julia Foreman. I sit down with them around a table crammed into a small meeting room off the school's front office.

"Deployment is addressed here with the same frequency as bullying or any other typical behavior," says Mr. Wieland.

"If a parent deploys," says Mrs. Joas, "sometimes we'll let the child e-mail the parent from here."

Homefront parents network through the school. The guidance counselor teaches coping skills.

"The nurse knows them by first name," says Mrs. Foreman. "She knows them all." Across from the front office, next to the display of photos from Afghanistan, the green construction-paper sign on a glass door is cut in the shape of a cloverleaf. NURSE LAURA'S OFFICE, it says. Sometimes when children come through that door claiming to be sick, Nurse Laura figures out pretty quickly that the only thing wrong with them is a deployed parent. She gives them the Nurse Laura cure: plenty of hugs and one-on-one attention.

For children at McNair and other DoD schools, the support is good.

But only children whose families live on military installations are allowed to attend those schools, and there's only enough housing for about a third of all active-duty families. The rest live outside the gates, which means the vast majority of military children, 600,000, attend regular public schools. Another 100,000 are enrolled in private schools or are home-schooled. And that's just active duty. An additional half a million children of National Guard and Reserve families are also out there, scattered around the country, most of them in public schools.

Within three years of September 11, more than a million military men and women had left home to serve in Afghanistan and Iraq, with more leaving every month, including 300,000 Guard members and reservists. Since more than a third of them have children, and most of those children attend non-DoD schools, that's a lot of stressed-out kids sitting in the classrooms of civilian teachers who don't really know what they're dealing with.

This is not the fault of the teachers. For more than a generation now, there's been no need to draft vast numbers of citizens into the Army, so very few civilians know much about military life. Dr. Mary Keller didn't when she became area superintendent of schools in the Fort Hood, Texas, area, where more than half of the 30,000 kids in the school district came from military families.

Then one day, an Army general serving on her school board pointed out that military children move three times more often than their civilian classmates, living a life of constant transitions punctuated by the separations of deployment. "What," he asked, "does that mean to kids?"

Dr. Keller had to admit she had no idea. She had never thought through what it would be like to move every three years on average, to always be the new kid. She had never thought about how it must feel to be the only kid in class worrying about a parent far away in a war zone, because the average military child attends a school where most of the other children are not military — the military child population becomes barely noticeable when you spread it out across the whole country. For instance, less than an hour north of Fort Bragg in Raleigh, one homefront parent reported to Bragg's deployment and mobilization program that her child was the only one in his entire school with a deployed parent.

Dr. Keller went on to help found the nonprofit Military Child Education Coalition, or MCEC. As the executive director, her days are now spent connecting school districts around the country with the military installations in their communities, whether that's a small local armory or a major base like Fort Bragg. In the Fort Bragg area, Cumberland County schools, for instance, work closely with Bragg and have set up a military child task force complete with training in how to handle trauma and grief.

When principals, counselors, and teachers sit down for MCEC's training, most react as Dr. Keller did — surprised at their own lack of awareness. This is especially true in school districts that aren't home to a large military installation like Fort Bragg, and the vast majority of districts aren't. North Carolina and Virginia each have around 124,000 active-duty troops, reservists, and National Guard members, and Texas and California have even more, about 200,000 each. But thirty other states have fewer than 40,000.

"If you don't live in a military community," says Dr. Keller, "the war may seem like reality television. You see it, but you haven't been forced to think through its impact on military children."

On Fort Bragg, though, the three teachers I'm talking with at McNair School — Julia Foreman, Gary Wieland, and Debra Joas — have all been through deployments before, both as teachers and as soldiers and as parents themselves. They know that the stress starts during predeployment, as soon as the child finds out a parent is leaving. Though the teachers don't receive any kind of official list telling them which children are about to go through a deployment, they know.

"Some of the parents tell you," says Mrs. Foreman.

"The kids," says Mr. Wieland, "have their own way of telling you."

"You'll notice a behavior," says Mrs. Foreman.

"You'll see a lot of behaviors," Mrs. Joas agrees.

In Mrs. Joas's fourth grade classroom, a new girl, a child she didn't know very well, refused to do as she was told and threw herself down on the floor for a major kick-scream-holler-and-cry episode. Though Mrs. Joas was a physically fit, fifty-year-old retired sergeant major, a former military police officer with no apparent startle reflex, the fireworks caught even her off-guard. Not knowing if it was a psychiatric problem or just bratty behavior, she ignored it for about thirty minutes, at which point the other children began to complain: "Mrs. Joas, I can't concentrate."

"OK, let's go," said Mrs. Joas, taking the new girl by the hand. "We're going to the principal's office." Then Mrs. Joas got on the phone and left a message for the girl's parents: "Your daughter threw a temper tantrum today in class. What is going on at home? Is this normal behavior? We need to talk. Please come by and see me after school."

School let out, and there were the parents, waiting at the classroom door. Mrs. Joas described the girl's hysteria fit. And the mother just sighed, "Ohhhhhhh . . ."

The mother was about to deploy.

Before and during a deployment, children may react by trying to become Superchild and lose themselves in schoolwork or books. Or just the opposite: They may not want to go to school at all. They may become more irritable and harder to soothe; they may seem angry all the time and pick fights; they may suffer from insomnia, complain they have a stomachache, demand more attention. They may have difficulty concentrating, obsess about scary things, become either clingy or withdrawn and sad. They may cry a lot. A child stressed by deployment looks a lot like a child going through any kind of uncertainty.

"The manifestations of stress in children are similar, whatever may be going on at home," says MCEC's Dr. Keller. Divorce, death, deployment . . . "It's uncertainty that does it." But though the symptoms of a child whose parents are divorcing may look the same as those of a child whose parent is going to war, some of the cures are different, which is why Keller adds, "The teacher has to be able to connect the dots."

Schools can help teachers connect those dots by reminding parents, in newsletters and meetings, to let the school know as soon as they know a deployment's coming. Near major military installations, the local media usually give everyone a heads-up whenever a large deployment is planned, and when those headlines appear, a light bulb should go on over the heads of teachers and daycare providers. Schools can also ask local Guard and Reserve units to notify them whenever any members are activated. "Activation" means they've received the order to deploy but the deployment hasn't started yet.

Once a deployment does start, a child's home life inevitably changes. But in school, the bells still ring at the same time. Classroom routines, predictable and structured, anchor a child's day. In fact, the entire school can become a refuge when teachers and administrators put themselves in the shoes of a child whose parent is at war. Walk down the hall in those shoes and you'll be less likely to make a thoughtless remark about the war that will worry an already worried child. You'll turn off the TV news that runs in, say, the student lounge or the cafeteria, because it occurs to you that if your parent was in a combat zone, you wouldn't want to watch the latest bloody battle scene over lunch. You'll encourage a child who's been exposed to something upsetting to talk about it. And you'll encourage the parents, too.

As Mrs. Joas talked with the parents of the hysterical girl, she wished they had told her about the forthcoming deployment sooner, so she would have understood how to deal with the situation. Her husband had been a career MP in the same unit as she. Whenever the unit deployed, he went and she stayed behind, dealing with the rear detachment at work and her own children at home.

So Mrs. Joas knew what she was talking about when she told those parents, "You have to sit down and talk all this out with your child. You need to assure her that everything's going to run smoothly, that you're going to be able to stay in contact by e-mail and phone during the deployment. You need to be open and honest, put everything out on the line."

She ordered them to set up a routine now, and then lock that routine in place as the deployment began, because in a time of change and uncertainty, children crave the stability of routine. "Set a time for homework and reading," she said. "Set a time *limit* for TV and computer games. Once the deployment starts," she told the father, "dinner needs to stay the same as it is now. You don't need to be going out all the time and eating junk foods." She warned him not to keep his daughter home from school to keep him company or keep her up till all hours because he worked late and hadn't seen her all day. "Otherwise," Mrs. Joas said, "I'll see her trying to sleep in school the next day." Maintaining the routine, she knew, would also make it easier for the deploying mother to rejoin the family when she finally came home.

Mrs. Joas had a lot of parents who were getting ready to deploy. Some parents and children were exchanging mementos to remember each other by. Many were trying to build happy memories to sustain them during the time apart by doing special things together now on the weekends. But some parents were taking their kids out of school for weeks at a time to take special trips or to visit family, which made Mrs. Joas cringe, because she knew when those children came back they'd be struggling to catch up. She understood, though, what their parents were thinking: *If he doesn't come back, at least we had this time together.* So what could she say? No, don't go?

Outside on the playground, Mr. Wieland watched a boy standing off by himself during recess. Gary Wieland had spent thirty years mostly in special forces, teaching everything from demolitions to counter guerilla warfare in Central America, Southeast Asia, Africa, Germany, and Afghanistan back when today's bad guys were the good guys. Now, the tall, bluff man with a silver mustache was teaching lessons in math and English and no hitting to third graders. Normally, the boy standing off by himself was racing around the playground with the other children, but at the moment, he was rooted on the edge of the whirlwind, eyes on the ground. Mr. Wieland had already been told that his father was getting ready to deploy again, and he knew what needed to be done; in addition to a teaching degree, he had a degree in psychology. But he also had, as he liked to say, twenty other little souls demanding his attention.

So later, as he was moving his class through the halls, when he saw the school counselor coming the other way, Mr. Wieland put his arm around the boy's shoulders and steered him over. "His dad's going on back overseas," he told the counselor, "and he's taking it pretty hard. You got any time to visit with this rascal?" And the counselor said sure and put her arm around the boy in place of Mr. Wieland's.

Outside the gates of Fort Bragg, at a Cumberland County public high school, most of the civilian teachers had no military experience to draw on when it came to spotting military kids. Still, sometimes they would discover a student was struggling to cope with a parent's deployment and refer the child to counselor Thomas Johnson.

But Mr. Johnson didn't count on it. He'd become pretty good at picking them out of the crowd himself. Since military children move a lot, he kept an eye on students with transfers on their records. Then he watched for absences, or a call from a mother saying her child would be out sick for more than a few days. He pored over report card failure lists. When he spotted a red flag, he'd call that student down to his office during an elective class the kid could afford to miss.

Once Mr. Johnson pegged which students were going through a deployment, he made a point of spot-checking as the months went by. "How goes it?" he'd ask, just giving them a chance to vent, and if they needed more than that, referring them and their parents to services in the county or on post.

School counselors are only the most obvious resource for children during a deployment. Out in the civilian community, some mental health assessment centers and youth ministries offer support specifically for military children, as do Boys and Girls Clubs, Boy Scouts and Girl Scouts, and the National 4-H. The Military Child Education Coalition suggests even more creative referrals — for instance, the local bar association may be willing to provide no-cost legal assistance to military families that have children with special needs. And if there's a military installation nearby, teachers and counselors shouldn't assume that the homefront parent is aware of all the services available there, either.

"The goal is to create layers of support that are interconnected," says MCEC's Dr. Keller.

Back on Fort Bragg in the Center for Family Life and Religious Education, Chaplain Hartz, the former MP, is packing up his office and preparing to leave for a year in Korea without his family. In his first few years as a chaplain, Hartz had three major deployments. "In some ways," he says, "getting only one or two weeks' notice is a blessing, because you don't have time to think about it too much."

His family has had four months to prepare for this one. In those four months, he and his wife have watched their three good students stumble in school. The original, intact family is different from the family separated by deployment, when everybody's roles change. The three children can see the Deployment Family coming and they're tying themselves up in knots trying to figure out their place in it. Chaplain Hartz knows from past deployments that eventually his children will get back on their feet, but for now they've had time to stare out the window and wonder, *What do I want to say to him? How do I want to say goodbye?*

The predeployment period that leads up to goodbye can last anywhere from a few months to a few hours. Five hundred miles up the continent, where Montoursville, Pennsylvania, lay tucked into the folds of the Appalachians, the two Yocum girls and their older half-brother, Brent, had noticed their parents were doing more family stuff: driving them down the twisting roads into town for ice cream, playing cards together, throwing the Frisbee out on the grassy hillside that sloped down from the house, joining them while they watched TV.

One evening, their parents turned off the TV, and their father, a correctional officer at the federal prison, told them that it was possible he might deploy with his National Guard unit. But even if he did, he said, they shouldn't be scared. He brought out the big jug that held all the pennies they'd been collecting for years. He held up one penny and said, "This is me." He poured out a small pile of pennies and said, "This is the number of guys who are getting hurt while they're deployed." He pointed to all the pennies in the jug, which was quite a large jug and full of pennies. "This is the number of guys who come back just fine." And then he dropped his penny into the jug.

Though it didn't seem quite real, it did seem important and serious. Their father had built a brick patio out front with a spotlit flagpole where he flew three flags: the Stars and Stripes, the red and gold Marine Corps flag from his earlier days in the Corps, and the black MIA flag. Evenings, nine-year-old Allyson was in the habit of sitting out there with him to watch the sun slip down behind the mountains. Brent and their little sister, Jenny, started wandering out there, too, the three of them making bets with their father about which of the solar lights that lined the patio would come on first. Their mother would leave the dishes to sit with them.

Saturday nights, the three kids liked to roll out their sleeping bags and camp on the living room floor. Jenny was only six, but Brent was sixteen. He knew things. After their parents went to bed, they'd all whisper late into the night. "Dad said he doesn't have a definite date, right? Maybe he won't have to go after all." For several months, they whispered. "Did you see Mom crying during Mass? . . . Mom *always* cries during Mass . . . Well, I heard her crying in the bedroom the other day, I think they found out he's going for sure." Allyson's teacher seemed to be paying more attention to her. They whispered that maybe Mom had said something to him. They whispered about Brent's other dad giving up a lot of his weekend visits so Brent could spend more time with his stepdad. "I think Dad's really going," they whispered. "Yeah, he's really going." They had figured it out. They knew.

So when their parents sat them down and their father said, "You remember what I told you when I brought the pennies out —" Allyson started to cry before he could even finish. "You're going, aren't you?" she cried. And then she tried to be brave.

He was leaving in a week, headed all the way to North Carolina, to a place called Fort Bragg, to get ready to go overseas.

For teachers who are tuned into the process of deployment, it's a natural springboard into lessons in geography ("Let's look at the map to see where Jenny's dad is deployed"), math ("If Montoursville, Pennsylvania, is 6,079 miles from Baghdad, and a soldier is flying home from there on a plane that's traveling at a rate of 250 miles an hour . . ."), or civics ("Why did the Founding Fathers put civilians in charge of the military?"). In addition to teaching facts, lessons like these make civilian students more aware of what their military classmates are going through. Later, after the homecoming, some teachers invite returned parents to speak to their classes, so that while the other children learn, sons and daughters get a chance to be proud of their parents, a chance to feel as if maybe some of the sacrifice was worth it.

Jenny Yocum graduated from kindergarten while her father was gone.

At the graduation, her mother's video camera caught Jenny walking up to the front to accept a big package of cards and gift certificates and goodies to send over to the soldiers serving with her dad. She looked proud and pleased and just like her father, fair and tall for her age. What the camera didn't show was the way she kept sneaking peeks at the other fathers there. Because Jenny, Allyson, and Brent — they were all torn. They believed what their parents had told them: that there were bad people over there who had to be brought to justice and that their father was proud to do a small part to help. They wanted to be proud of him, too. But all the other children they knew had their fathers at home.

Down the mountains from Montoursville, Pennsylvania, almost to the Maryland border, seven-year-old Caleb Tucker and his little brother, Jairus, sat next to their mother in camping chairs as the hot rods rumbled through town. The last time the hot rods were here, they went with their father, a state trooper. But he had gotten on a bus at the same armory as the Yocums' father and he'd gone away, their mom explained, to help make sure other boys and girls could go to school and have electricity and water. At night, when it was time to say their prayers, four-year-old Jairus would pray, "And, Jesus, please make sure Daddy doesn't die."

Now Caleb watched his mother put on her best guy act. "Whoa," she said, and pointed at a passing hot rod, "look at those wheels."

Caleb shook his head. "It's just not the same without Dad, Mom," he said. No self-pity in his voice. Just a simple statement of fact. Nothing was the same since his father had ridden away on that bus, gone to Fort Bragg and then overseas.

On Fort Bragg at McNair School, Julia Foreman paged through the journals of her six- and seven-year-old students. Mrs. Foreman was originally from Jamaica and drove an Army truck for four years to pay off her college loans, including a year she spent deployed to Egypt. She married another soldier, got out, and now taught first grade.

Her students with deployed parents wrote in their journals about sad things. They wrote about bad things that could possibly happen. Or they said to her, "I miss my dad very much, he's lots of fun." They said it as if they had forgotten having said the same thing an hour before, and the hour before that.

They were not unusual in this. Researchers have found, during wartime, that while the children of civilians wrestle with issues of right and wrong, the children of those on active duty wrestle instead with fear, worry, and sadness. While Mrs. Foreman's own husband was in Iraq, her young son asked her, "If you die and Daddy's gone, who's going to take care of me?"

If you die. Julia Foreman almost cried. Her little boy, thinking through The Worst That Could Happen like any adult. She wanted to shield his eyes, his ears, his mind, but she knew that was impossible, so she answered him truthfully. If she died, she told him, this was the person who would take care of him at first, and this was the person who would transport him to whomever else was going to be the final caretaker.

Not far away in a house on post, fifteen-year-old Josh Groll put down his book and asked his mother, "Was Dad at that place when the bomb blew up?" Fear, worry, and sadness affect military children of all ages. Books took Josh's mind off it, the bigger the book the better — *Les Miserable,* for instance, and every hefty installment in the Harry Potter series.

His mother, Marena, answered him carefully. "Your dad is in a secure situation."

"Oh," said Josh, but he was still looking at her because that wasn't really what he was asking, and they both knew it. So Marena went on, "But if something should happen, well, that's a reality that could happen and people do pass away." And when she said that, it was as if she'd opened a door in Josh and all the questions he'd been holding inside spilled out, questions about what they would have to do if his father were killed.

Over in Germany, Chieryssa Fanning *didn't* want to talk about it.

Chieryssa and her father, Robert, had always been able to talk — he'd been her primary caregiver since before she even knew how to talk. And that fall they had plenty to talk about, with Chieryssa at a new high school and her mother in a war zone. But to Robert's frustration, their conversations, once so easy and energizing, had begun to short circuit.

About her grades, which were dropping, Chieryssa would say, "I'm just dealing with so much *drama* with my new friends." *So-called friends,* Robert would think, as he asked her what the drama was about. And then instead of talking about whatever was bothering her, like she used to, she would lose her temper, spin into an emotional meltdown, and slam her bedroom door.

Robert would keep her informed about her mother: where she was downrange, what she was doing. Chieryssa was hearing stories on the news and through the rumor mill anyway, and he didn't want her worrying over the wrong information. As long as he just talked nuts and bolts, it was fine. But dig a little deeper — emotional meltdown, *slam*. Robert felt like standing in front of that closed door and just banging his head against it.

And whenever the phone rang and Chieryssa heard her father call, "Hey, Chieryssa, Mom's on the phone," Chieryssa would act as if she didn't have time to talk. She always seemed to have some pressing business with her new friends. "So-called," deadpanned her father to her mother.

Yet Chieryssa's e-mails and letters to her mother in Iraq were full of sadness and worry and loneliness. *I love you, Mom,* she would write. But to say it, to actually talk to her mother, to hear her voice from so far away, in a place from which she might not come back, would have simply hurt too much.

Slam.

At Military 101 classes and predeployment briefings, the military hands out support items for children and advice for parents.

Deployed parents are advised to stay in touch. Period. Homefront parents are advised to talk every day about the parent who's gone. To help younger children grasp how long the deployment will last, they're told to create concrete ways to measure time: add it up day by day by adding links to a paper chain, or count down to homecoming with a basket of Hershey's Kisses. The child gets a "kiss" from Daddy or Mommy each night before bed. "If the return date changes," one pamphlet suggests dryly, "make adjustments when the child is not around."

Young children of deployed service members can put their crayons to work in coloring books with titles such as *Until Your Parent Comes Home Again,* which features a map for drawing a line between the child's home and wherever in the world the deployed parent has gone.

They can color pictures like the one of a boy, a girl, and a dog all crying with mom while their uniformed dad smiles down on them from a portrait on the wall.

They can open the green camouflage cover of an activity book entitled *Daddy's Days Away* and fill in the blanks that list each family member's extra jobs while dad's away.

They can pop *Your Buddy CJ* into the computer's CD-ROM drive and play emotional literacy games with a little bear in a red T-shirt, who tells them, "At first, I was upset that my parent had to leave, but then I was glad the troops were going to stop the bad people. And now I don't know what to think. I just know I'm really sad."

In the prefab house on the edge of Fort Bragg, Lexie Bootes walked up behind Marissa at the computer, which was playing a country music video about a little girl writing a letter to her father, who was a soldier. "My country needs you right now," the little girl's voice said, adding later, "Dear Daddy, come home to me soon. Your little girl needs you, too." And then as the piano played and the strings swelled, pictures of soldiers dissolved across the computer screen, soldiers in Humvees, helicopters, the desert. Then Lexie realized her mother was crying and her eyes started to burn. When Lexie suddenly climbed into her lap, crying too, Marissa looked startled. She hadn't realized Lexie was there.

"That's where my daddy's at?" Lexie asked in a small voice.

"Yeah." Marissa wiped the tears from both their faces.

"I really miss Daddy," Lexie said. "He'll be home, right?"

"That's what we want, isn't it?"

Lexie nodded. "Can I see it again?"

For a moment, Marissa hesitated. Then, *click,* "My country needs you . . ." Lexie watched closely: soldiers in the desert, soldiers in Humvees and helicopters, soldiers like her daddy. " . . . Your little girl needs you, too." And then it was another day and the soldier on the computer screen *was* her daddy. The Web cam brought them all together, Lexie on Marissa's lap in front of the computer in a corner of the dining room on the edge of Fort Bragg, Charlie in front of a computer in a communications tent in Iraq. The video image went both ways, but the audio went only one way, from them to him, so while they could talk, he had to type his half of the conversation.

"Why do you live in a tent?" Lexie asked him.

If Charlie had tried to type a complete explanation — that he didn't live in this tent, he actually lived a couple miles away in a barracks, but there were other guys in his unit who did have to live in tents because there weren't enough barracks anymore — before he was halfway finished, Lexie would have asked him fifty more questions. *We live in tents,* he typed, *because the bad guys blew up all the buildings.*

Lexie listened as Marissa read it out loud for her, and then Lexie asked, "Well, didn't you kill them all yet?"

Across six thousand miles, Charlie and Marissa stared at each other, both of them thinking, *Wow, where did she get* that *from?* She'd said it so lightly, as if killing people was like street sweeping — *Didn't you get that street swept yet?* They had never talked like that in their house, and no news of the war ever made it in past the front door either, no newspaper photos or television images of men dressed like her father in DCUs and actually firing weapons. Maybe she picked it up at the daycare, or maybe from some of the other military kids she played with.

Wherever she got it from, it bothered Marissa a lot. She'd grown up surrounded by inner-city violence, had been caught up in it herself more than once, and hearing a five-year-old talk about killing somebody like it was nothing, *her* five-year-old, gave her a sick, scared feeling.

She and Lexie had a long talk afterward. "Daddy's not killing any-body," Marissa said. "He's there to protect people, and that's the only rea-son he would ever shoot anybody, would be to protect himself or some-body else." Lexie listened and nodded.

She had asked a lot of questions when Charlie was getting ready to de-ploy. Marissa and Charlie had told her Daddy had a job to do that was very important, that Daddy was like a police officer. She understood po-lice officers and what they did, because her grandparents' garage in Erie was across the street from the state police barracks. Her grandparents' friends were cops; her grandfather worked on their cars, and cops were always hanging around the garage. Cops she understood. But she also understood guns, and she knew her father carried one. She wasn't stupid, and Marissa had to admit she wasn't wrong when she said, as she often did, "Daddy's in the desert fighting bad guys."

How much do you tell children? Colonel Stephen Cozza, chief of psychi-atry at Walter Reed Army Medical Center in Washington, D.C., regularly helps parents break the news to their children that their military parent has been wounded.

"No one way is the best or worst," he says. "It's unique to each family." But there are some guidelines.

Generally, if they're old enough to understand, they're old enough to be told. Most parents seem to get it right, but Colonel Cozza has worked with the occasional parent who chooses to keep children in the dark — for instance, the mother who tells her children that the reason their grandparents are coming to stay with them is she's going to a class re-union, when the truth is she's flying across the country to a military hos-pital where their father has been medevaced after his Humvee was hit by a roadside bomb in Iraq.

"The intentions are good," says Colonel Cozza. "You don't want to worry them. But children can guess when there's a crisis going on. They overhear a conversation or pick up on the emotions. If you don't tell them what it's about, their worries may be worse than the reality." And withholding information can undermine children's trust in their relationship with their parents. "If they find out the truth later, they start to wonder: What else are they not talking to me about?"

On the other hand, there is such a thing as too much information, as in the case of, say, a six-year-old, whose parents decide it would be good for her to look at the injured parent's amputated stump whether she wants to or not.

Colonel Cozza points out these are extreme and rare examples. "Just give children basic information," he advises. "Something like, his leg has been seriously injured and he will have to have surgery and be in the hospital for a while." Most of the time, children will tell you how much information they can handle by the kinds of questions they ask. A child who asks, "Does he still have a leg?" wants an answer along the lines of, "Well, they had to take off some of his leg to make him healthy."

Colonel Cozza's advice can be applied to any deployment-related questions a child may have. Basically, children need to feel secure, especially when their lives have been turned upside down by a deployment. One way to do that is to reduce the unknown. Answer their questions. Take a photograph — whether the picture shows an injured parent in a hospital bed or a healthy parent in a Humvee, children like to see where their parents are. And when the shutter clicks, try to smile.

We are all the storytellers of our own lives. Whenever parents, teachers, counselors, and daycare providers talk with children about deployment, they can help frame the way those children tell the story of their own deployment experience. "Poor little me" — that's one version of the story. "It was tough, but it taught me a lot and made me a better person" — that's another version, the one Dr. Mary Keller calls encouraging the courage of children. "It helps them grow up into resilient adults," she says.

But at the same, Dr. Keller points out that you have to pay attention to what's going on and know where to go if they need extra support.

Mrs. Joas had a crier. The good news was that the crying was a sign this child felt safe enough in Mrs. Joas's class to let her feelings show. The bad news was that this child had some very unhappy feelings. The little girl sat at her desk and cried and could not stop. Her father had just deployed, so Mrs. Joas took her to Nurse Laura, and Nurse Laura took her to the counselor, and after a couple of weeks the crying did stop. Then

Mrs. Joas noticed that this little girl, who had never hugged her in her life, had begun clinging to Mrs. Joas. And Mrs. Joas hugged her back and looked down at the top of her unbrushed head, and thought to herself, *She's being neglected at home.*

Like the adults who are left behind, the behavior of most children will change in some way when the deployment first begins, and then, within about six weeks, most will find a way to cope. But if the depression, crying, or acting out continue without letup for longer than six weeks, if the pigeons start keeling over in the desert, alarms should start to go off. If children hurt themselves or others, the alarms should ring even louder. Same if they stop bathing or brushing their hair, or start to look like they dressed in the dark; if they rapidly gain or lose a noticeable amount of weight; if they develop a drug or alcohol problem.

When the teachers at McNair saw a child struggling with a parent's deployment, they knew whomever he or she was living with was most likely struggling, too.

Mrs. Joas checked around. The clingy girl with the unbrushed hair had three brothers at home, all of them competing for the attention of an overwhelmed mother who was dealing with the deployment by partying hard. There were whispers that the mother was sleeping around.

So Mrs. Joas bought hair clips. She made time for hair fixing before class. And whenever that little girl wanted a hug, Mrs. Joas would hold her for as long as she hung on.

As far as her fellow teacher Gary Wieland is concerned, most homefront parents are overwhelmed. An overwhelmed state is the norm, in his opinion.

"It never gets easier," teacher and Army wife Julia Foreman says, speaking from experience.

"And the deployed parent," says Mr. Wieland, "he or she is off doing a wartime mission. That in and of itself encompasses every bit of energy and emotion that a soldier could possibly have."

Once, when Mrs. Joas assigned a homework project, two parents with deployed spouses called her. "I just can't work on it," each one told her. "No problem," said Mrs. Joas. She kept the children after school and did what their parents couldn't — bought the supplies and helped them complete the project.

"Sometimes they just don't have time to sit down with them," says Mrs. Joas. "I mean, you have to get the meal done, cut the grass, four kids."

"Might be a sibling in diapers, get to the commissary," says Mr. Wieland.

"It's nothing unusual for some of my parents to have, like, four or five kids," says Mrs. Joas. "And real young, I mean babies. I forgot how much time they took."

"Even a battalion commander's wife," Mr. Wieland says. "She has a college education, she may be more ready, but the fact of the matter is, she has the FRG to manage and that rear detachment infrastructure to interact with." When you're up to your neck in alligators, he says, it's hard to know you're there to drain the swamp.

Every night, Mr. Wieland and Mrs. Joas were on the phone, calling parents. They updated them on their children, then asked if they had any questions. Sometimes the parents had questions. More often they just needed to talk, especially during a deployment. Being a man, Mr. Wieland couldn't afford to let women with absent husbands get too personal.

But Mrs. Joas could, and she would listen to the litany of problems thinking, *Oh my, it's a good thing I got a counseling degree.* They cried. They told her more than she really wanted to know. But she understood from her years as a rear D noncommissioned officer, or NCO, that sometimes they just needed to vent to someone, and since they felt safe with her, she was that someone. So she listened.

Sometimes one of those struggling parents would recognize that her children were suffering, and she'd bring them to someone like Chaplain Hartz for help, who then had a chance to ask, "Well, how are *you* doing?" And she'd say, "Well . . ." and start crying. Chaplain Hartz would get her started with some pastoral counseling. He might refer her to parenting classes at Army Community Services, hook her up with a support group or a mother's day out program. If the situation seemed deeply serious, though, he'd refer her and the children to the social work department at Womack, where Lieutenant Colonel Pecko and his staff took over.

The lieutenant colonel spent most of his days managing the work of others, but for his own sanity he still occasionally broke away from the paperwork and the administrative meetings to do some hands-on counseling. By training and temperament, he was a child analyst and therapist, and here on Fort Bragg there was plenty of child therapy work to go around — child and spouse maltreatment made up a large part of the department's caseload. The parents came in on their own or were referred by chaplains like Hartz, as well as by teachers and doctors and neighbors and FRG leaders and NCOs in the rear Ds. Most of the family members who came in were there because they were having difficulty adjusting to deployment, and the number of deployed soldiers had quintupled since September 11. With a population of 45,000 soldiers and as many as 60,000 family members, the numbers of people needing help added up in a hurry.

When sixteen years of child homicide data were gathered in North Carolina, two counties stood out with more than double the rate of any other county: Onslow and Cumberland counties, home to the state's two biggest military installations, Camp Lejeune and Fort Bragg. Unfortunately, the numbers were too small to determine if the high rate of homicides around the bases went up during wartime deployments. Officials on Bragg began planning a child fatality review system, but the study has so far not been expanded across the country to see if the same numbers turned up around other major installations.

According to Lieutenant Colonel Pecko, on Fort Bragg child maltreatment cases usually involved spouses who were isolated, spouses whose coping skills had let them down. Their normal capacity to patiently nurture a child was gone. Or they were depressed. For someone who could hardly get out of bed, taking proper care of a child could become impossible.

Counseling these parents, Pecko tried to help them realize that under extremely difficult circumstances, "That could be any one of us." He'd sit all the way to one side of his chair, leaning hard on the chair's arm, one jump-booted foot on top of the other, as nonthreatening as a kid, and work with them to identify where things had broken down to cause them to rely on inappropriate behavior. He'd equip them with new coping and communication skills.

Some struggling homefront parents just need a break. The military services do try to offer regular opportunities for respite child care. On some Marine Corps bases, families who show up at Child Development Centers needing respite care cannot be turned away for any reason. The armed services also help provide child care when the military operational tempo causes a care emergency, such as the Air Force's Extended Duty Child Care program, round-the-clock care at some Navy installations, and extended hours at Child Development Centers on eighty-five Army posts. But as noted before, official military child-care programs still meet less than half of the overall child-care needs of the military families on active duty, including mobilized National Guard and Reserve families. Simple respite care for the spouse who's left behind can be hard to come by.

The Hooah Wives knew Marissa needed a break. She never fell apart in front of them, but she almost never made it to any of their get-togethers anymore. "Too busy," she said. She'd be on the phone with one of them, cussing about her day, and the Hooah Wife on the other end of the line would say, "You sound very stressed."

And Marissa would say, "I *so* need a break."

And the Hooah Wife might say, "Great! Let's get one of the girls to watch the kids and take a break, then."

But Marissa wasn't home with Lexie all day the way some of the stay-at-home Hooah Wives were with their children. Marissa didn't see Lexie enough as it was. It was rare she went anywhere without her.

When Marissa admitted, "I'm so tired," the other wives told her Lexie needed a structured bedtime. "Then I *really* would never see her," Marissa said. And so she pushed on, getting Lexie to bed when she could, finally falling into bed herself hours later.

In the morning, Marissa ran Lexie to the nearby daycare center. They'd finally had an opening a few weeks back, and just in time, because more than two months of caring for Lexie in addition to her own children had started to wear thin for Jenn Marner, the Hooah Wife manager who had volunteered to help during Marissa's child-care crisis early in the deployment.

After dawdling around her own house all morning, Lexie ran through the cold from the car into the daycare and down the hall to the big playroom, looking for her favorite teacher, Marie Michele Johnson. The room was equipped with toys and books and a low round table, where nearly a dozen small children were already seated. Most of them came from military families in the neighborhood — black, brown, and white, like a miniature United Nations. As Marissa turned to leave, Lexie ran back to the half door that separated the playroom from the front hall, yelling, "Mom! Mom!"

Marissa leaned back over the door so Lexie could whisper in her ear. Marissa couldn't understand a word she was whispering, but she didn't have time for a replay, so she just kissed her, said, "Bye, toots!" and blew out the door. Lexie blew back to her teacher looking as busy and intense as her mother, a girl on a mission. Marie Michele peeled off Lexie's coat as she passed within reach and steered her toward the table.

Marie Michele had moved in right across the street from Lexie a couple of months earlier, along with her husband, who was prior Army, and her two little daughters. She knew Lexie well — on the days Marissa called to say she couldn't get back before the daycare closed, Marie Michele took Lexie home with her, where Lexie would organize the Johnson girls in games of pretend until Marissa pulled up.

Marie Michele Johnson was an energetic woman with a big voice and an accent no one could ever peg because she grew up speaking first Haitian Creole, then Boston Southie. Ten percent of the children she helped care for at the center, which she also helped run, had at least one deployed parent that winter, and she could see it in each of them. One of the little girls had two deployed parents, which left her grumpy and hypersensitive. Lexie was a smart little girl, wound up tight, and had to be in charge of everything. *Maybe she was always like that,* thought Marie Michele, *and maybe she just wanted to control her friends if she couldn't control where her father went.* She'd seen the way Lexie would stare when her little friends' fathers came to pick them up. And sometimes Lexie would say, apropos of nothing, "I miss my dad."

That afternoon, when Marissa called to ask her to keep Lexie again till she could make it back to Fayetteville, Marie Michele wondered if maybe Lexie wasn't also missing her mom.

On post at McNair School, Mr. Wieland looked up from helping one eight-year-old with her reading to see that the desk of a boy named Christopher was empty again. He looked around and spotted Christopher bouncing around the children at the computers, his own work forgotten. Mr. Wieland rapped his knuckles on Christopher's desk. "Come on, Christopher, let's get back to work." Christopher was falling further and further behind every day. He was bright but unable to concentrate. His father was deployed. But that was only part of Christopher's problem.

On the days Mr. Wieland sent the class home with homework, he could count on his cell phone vibrating while he was in afterschool meetings — Christopher's mother, her voice strained and desperate, asking about the homework, "What do I do with this?" This was the rest of Christopher's problem. His mother was doing her best, but her best was limited — she was new to military life and overwhelmed by all her children, the Army, her husband being gone, the fear and grief of a war. She wanted her son to succeed. She just didn't have the resources to help him.

"This kid," says Mr. Wieland, "is in so many ways helpless. And mom is just as much of a victim as he is. When I look at this kid . . ." And then big, glib Mr. Wieland pauses, his eyes suddenly swimming with tears. He takes a deep breath. "When the father's downrange and I see the family back here suffering, then I go back and I think how many times I sent these guys . . ." He has to stop again.

As an NCO, Gary Wieland had been responsible for taking care of the soldiers he led, making sure they were combat ready. To him, that had meant making sure they were trained and equipped. Then, in his thirties he got married. With his wife, he had a baby. Gary Wieland looked down at the little girl in his arms and said to himself, *How stupid I was.* Until he had a child of his own, he didn't consider anything outside of the mission. "But after my daughter was born," he says quietly, "while I still believed I did the right thing, I realized that there was a whole lot more to it."

And meanwhile, over at Womack, up in Labor and Delivery, more children were being born. And as Beth Pratt helped them take their first breaths, as she waited to see if the artificial insemination would succeed in giving her a baby, too, she grieved that despite all her planning, a thousand things could still happen to prevent Luigi from being there for their child's arrival into the world. Each day seemed steeper than the one before as she struggled to make herself do ordinary things like walk Danny, do laundry, go to the commissary where, as she stood in line, she noticed the *Fayetteville Observer* in a stack beside the checkout.

> 82ND SOLDIER KILLED
> ROADSIDE BOMB TARGETS CONVOY
> By Laura King
> Los Angeles Times
> BAGHDAD, Iraq — A roadside bomb killed an 82nd Airborne Division soldier Sunday in the volatile Sunni Muslim town of Fallujah, 30 miles west of the nation's capital . . .
> Roadside bombs have become one of the most lethal threats to American troops in Iraq. The latest deaths bring to 325 the number of American combat deaths since the U.S.-led invasion in March . . .

A chill rushed over her, prickling her skin.

In the nearly four months since Luigi had gone to Iraq, more than a dozen Fort Bragg soldiers had been killed, yet Beth had never had a feeling like the one she had now, as if something dank and clawed were coming up fast behind her. Her scalp crawled. The checkout blurred. She struggled to keep the tears from spilling over until she got out into the parking lot.

Safe inside her car, she caught her breath and wiped her eyes. She wasn't a flighty kid. She was thirty-three. She should be rational about this. The name of the soldier from the 82nd hadn't been released yet, but there were thousands and thousands of paratroopers in Iraq — what were the chances? It didn't matter. She dug out her cell phone and dialed.

"Camilla," she said, trying to hold her voice steady, "tell me Luigi's all right, tell me nothing's happened to him, just tell me he's all right."

There was a pause on the other end. "He's all right, Beth," Camilla Maki said at last. And then she said, "It was Captain Blanco that was killed." And Beth's throat closed up.

The captain was Luigi's platoon leader. There were twenty-two men in that platoon.

Chaplain Christopher Dickey, who several times now had been one of those men in dress greens knocking at the door, boarded a plane in Fayetteville to fly back to his native Texas. In San Antonio, he followed the clip-clop of the horse-drawn caisson carrying Ernie Blanco's casket through the white grave markers of the Fort Sam Houston National Cemetery. He led the brief graveside service, offered whatever comfort he could to the family, the parents. Ernie had been single.

Afterward, Chaplain Dickey had several hours before his flight back. He sat in the airport alone. He read, uninterrupted — a rare thing on a normal day. He gazed out the window. It was a quiet time. The plane came and lifted him up into the air back to Fayetteville, where the *Observer* had reported that Captain Ernesto M. Blanco had been a proud Texas Aggie. He'd earned the Bronze Star in Afghanistan the year before. He wasn't smiling in the official photograph, but a man who had served with him there was quoted as saying he was always a happy guy. Always smiling.

Just like Luigi, Beth thought. She made a copy of the article for him, then tucked it away, out of sight. It was too easy to imagine Luigi's open, dimpled face in place of Captain Blanco's, smiling up at her from the newspaper.

Soon after that, Beth's body gave her the news: She wasn't pregnant.

CHAPTER 13

Hitting the Wall

MARISSA WAS BLEEDING.

Her period came and never left. She bled for twenty-eight days straight. "You have *got* to get that checked *out*," insisted Tiffany, her fellow Hooah Wife. Marissa dialed up doctors as she drove across whole counties, trying to find one who'd take an evening appointment so she wouldn't have to miss work. She became so anemic, she finally just left Lexie at Jenn's one evening and went over to the ER at Womack. She waited there for hours, only to have them tell her they couldn't find anything wrong with her. Then the bleeding just stopped.

Her days went on. Mornings, she'd race around yelling, "Come on, kiddo, get your shoes on!" She ran Razor outside, clipped him to his chain, and ran back in to forward the home phone to her cell phone, check her text pager and two cell phones — all charged — and throw them in her purse. She said to Lexie, who was dawdling in the middle of putting on her coat next to the back of the TV, running her finger through the dust on a ledge, "Remind me to go grocery shopping when I pick you up, peanut — outta milk again." Without Charlie here, Marissa never noticed when they were getting low. She pulled on her own coat, grabbed her briefcase and a Pepsi. Charlie was the milk drinker. She held the door for Lexie, then, high heels stomping, she slammed it behind her.

After dropping Lexie at the daycare center, having no one to share a morning smoke with anymore, Marissa would smoke alone as she got on the road. She spent her days in and out of government buildings, talking to clerks, jamming to music to keep herself awake at the wheel. She'd grab fast-food lunches, rotating restaurants because you can eat only so much of that stuff, but her favorite was an Arby's roast beef sandwich and cheese curly fries, which she ate only when the firm was paying, because it was expensive. Later, she'd pick up Lexie, microwave some mac 'n' cheese or cup o' soup for her, do some housework, then get Lexie to bed and work at the computer till midnight. She never saw anybody anymore, not even the Hooah Wives. She'd be thinking, *They don't even realize I'm not there hanging out.* Then the phone would ring, and it would be one of the wives, saying, "Hey, Marissa! You still alive? It's been two weeks!"

Sometimes her best friend from Erie would call, asking Marissa for advice about adopting a five-year-old child, a child who, like Marissa, had been through the system. When they were growing up, this friend had always been there for her, and Marissa was glad to be there for her now, no matter how tired she was, no matter how bad it made her feel to dig through all that crap from her own childhood.

Marissa was online doing FRG work, checking on a soldier's mother who'd been having some trouble. *How are you doing?* she typed.

Much better, the woman typed back. *But you have so much going on, I'm just wondering how* you're *doing.*

It was so weird for someone to ask her how she was doing that Marissa laughed out loud. *Honestly, I don't have time for a nervous breakdown!* she typed. She was only half joking. Most nights, by the time she crawled into bed beside Lexie, it was after two A.M.

The phone was ringing. It was early on a Friday morning. Marissa felt for the handset next to the bed and pulled it over to her ear without lifting her head. It was Charlie. She tried to follow what he was saying because it sounded important, but her eyes kept closing — dark bedroom, warm bed, Lexie's even breathing beside her. All of a sudden she heard: "What did I just say?"

"What?"

"If you're falling asleep," Charlie said, his voice sharp, "I'm going to go."

She was too tired to argue. "OK."

"Do you know how long I had to stand in line to talk to you?"

"Look, I'm really tired. I'll talk to you later. 'Bye."

It wasn't till she woke up a couple hours later that she had the energy to be mad at him for being mad at her.

She vented the next night at a party at Jenn's. "He didn't have any right to be mad at me," she fumed. "Four-thirty in the morning? That's not a reasonable time for anybody, it's an ungodly hour of the morning, no one in their right mind is awake at that hour, and I worked till two that night."

Eight faces frowned at her, Jenn and Christine and Tiffany and Angela and all their husbands, cocktails clinking in their hands. Tiffany's and Angela's husbands were both back from Afghanistan now, and Marissa was the only one at the party without a husband, which had never happened before. All the other times she'd gotten together with the Hooah Wives, there had always been at least one other wife there whose husband was gone, too, and all of a sudden the space between her, alone, and all these couples, together, suddenly seemed much wider than the space between their chairs.

The other women glanced at their husbands and Christine said, "You couldn't even wake up long enough to talk to him for a few minutes?"

"I have a very demanding career!" said Marissa. "He has no idea what I'm going through!"

"Hey, *he's* the one in danger," said Tiffany.

Which made Marissa snap, "He's not in danger, he's sitting around the freaking camp."

"Where they have mortar attacks," Jenn snapped back.

"Like a mile away!" Marissa's voice rose, cornered. "Look, I understand that he's in danger, but if he wants me to be understanding, he needs to be understanding. I just don't think he had any right to be mad."

The other women backed off then and turned to their husbands, who were giving each other looks that said, *What the heck?* And their wives told them that if they called home in the middle of the night, they'd be glad to talk to them. They were all stay-at-home moms. Marissa felt like saying if she sat around on her butt all day, she'd be glad to talk to Charlie in the middle of the night, too.

Charlie called the next day. It was Sunday, the middle of the day, and Marissa was wide awake. She yelled about how she worked sixty-plus hours a week and he yelled back about the two miles he had to walk to get to a phone. She yelled that on top of working at a job she was really starting to hate, getting spit on sometimes by strangers who were losing their homes, at the end of the day she had to come home and take care of Lexie and the dog and clean the house and do the laundry and pay the bills and keep up with her FRG work. By then he was just listening, and she said when she finally got to bed she needed those four hours and some days she felt like Superwoman but other days she just didn't know how much longer she could do it all, and then she started to cry. She told him about the cocktail party.

From across an ocean and a continent, his voice reached out to her. "That sucks."

She hugged the phone to her ear. Her voice quavered. "I just miss you so much."

The next time she was at Jenn's, Marissa said, "I didn't think about the fact that your husbands were all sitting there, too. That wasn't something that should have been brought up in front of them."

Jenn said, "We didn't think about you being the only one there without a husband. We weren't listening to you."

But in the end, Jenn's bottom line was still the same. "I was a single mom for a while after my first marriage. Granted, I didn't have to do it and worry about my husband getting killed, but I know what it's like trying to do it all, and yeah, you work hard, but he's over there getting shot at every day. He calls you in the middle of the night because he needs to hear your voice? Well, you just better suck it up and be there for him."

Suck it up. Tough it out. Soldier on. Over the course of her life, Marissa Bootes had learned a thing or two about soldiering on. You're not a victim, she would always say, unless you make yourself a victim. Sometimes, as she pushed herself through each day now, she would think, *I really am going to have a nervous breakdown.* Sometimes she'd tell herself, *You can't do this anymore.* But the next thought was automatic: *You're not a victim unless you make yourself one.* And she'd run up the next set of courthouse steps. But her husband was still in a war zone.

Luigi would listen to the phone ringing on the other side of the world, rubbing his forehead, his shoulders slumped, hoping to hear Beth's voice and at the same time dreading it. More and more often now, that voice he loved sounded lost and weak and it scared him.

When he first started hearing the despair in her voice early in the deployment, he couldn't figure it out. He'd be thinking, *Her concerns are nothing compared to mine — she's sleeping in a good bed and has good food, she has her normal routine, and us over here, we're in survival mode.* Convoying up from Kuwait, he hadn't been in Iraq for two hours before he heard explosions and his unit lost its first vehicle. Since then, he'd been driving on convoys to transport food, water, and ammo, going out on recovery missions at night when the medics needed a gun truck to go with them or special forces needed an escort. People were shooting at them all the time.

And then there were the nightly mortar attacks on the camp. It was as if they were on a schedule. If he was on the phone when the mortars started coming in, he'd say, his voice real loud and cheerful, "Gotta go, honey, time's up!" He always got off the phone before Beth figured out what the noise was because he hadn't told her any of this. She sounded down enough as it was. But about two months into it, the reality of the situation had slammed into him like an enormous wave — he could lose his life over here, easy. At the time, he was thinking she should be the strong one for him; she should be cheering *him* up. Instead, during every call he wound up having to put on his funny man act, trying to keep her from sinking when he felt like he was sinking himself.

Now she was on his mind all the time, while lying in his rack at night, standing guard duty, on convoys. He had long since gotten over that early resentment — something was wrong, he didn't know what, but something was seriously wrong. He was sure if he could just see her and hold her and tickle and tease her, he could get her smiling again, but stuck in the desert, he couldn't do much. He was a trained lifeguard, and he felt as if he were chained up on a dune and watching while the woman he loved drowned.

He heard her pick up. For a split second, he felt lighter, but as soon as he heard her voice, he knew that once again he had to take a deep breath and make his voice strong enough for both of them.

In Minnesota, Beth's mother was hearing the same thing. Chuck and Sandy Julian moved through their daily chores like people who had always relied on their bodies the way they relied on their farm implements and household appliances, as tools to be put to good use. They had never been big people and now, in their retirement, age had shrunk them a bit. Beth came late to their lives. By the time she was born, Chuck was forty-five years old; Sandy already had three girls by a previous marriage, and the youngest was nine. The three older girls would take little Beth outside and pull her around the yard in a box, their voices tinkling like bells, and the wind would catch that tinkling sound and carry it out past the barn and the windbreak of trees before losing it in the corn and alfalfa that stretched to the horizon.

Beth didn't get her own room till her two oldest sisters grew up and moved out. She painted it blue herself. It had a blue carpet. She liked blue. She and her last sister still had to share a bathroom, though, which was a problem, because back then Beth had big hair — two-hour big hair. She'd had it permed, and every morning she curled it and hot combed it and hair sprayed it.

When Beth flew home to her blue room for Thanksgiving, Chuck and Sandy watched as their beautiful youngest daughter recovered her smile, grinning easily every time the camera flashed, surrounded in the wood-paneled den by her grandparents, her aunts and uncles and cousins and sisters and brothers-in-law, her nieces and nephews. Then she got on the plane and disappeared back to Fayetteville.

Sandy called her most days, reaching out after her daughter, and over the weeks, as the year drew to a close, she heard Beth's hello gradually grow flatter. Sandy would tell the news from home, how much snow had fallen, who was doing what for Christmas. She'd ask if Beth had heard from Luigi and how the job at the hospital was going. She'd ask how Beth was feeling, and by the end of each call, Sandy could hang up and tell Chuck their daughter sounded as if she were feeling a little better. But the next time Beth said hello, she'd be flat again, and as the weeks went on, her bright voice wound down, slower and flatter, like a tape player running out of juice, until by the New Year, after working through Christmas at the hospital, her voice sounded dead.

Fayetteville, North Carolina, is a thousand miles from Hutchinson, Minnesota. For a mother and a father worried about their baby girl, it might as well be the moon. How do you help someone in trouble on the moon, if you're stuck here on Earth? So as the new year began, Chuck and Sandy Julian packed their car, closed up their house, and drove down the long driveway to the two-lane blacktop that led south through the snowy fields, south toward Fayetteville, determined not to come back until Luigi came home.

Chuck and Sandy moved into the spare room with the unused drum kit. Chuck sat on the couch with Danny curled up beside him and read books he pulled off Beth's bookshelves, which these days were filled with populist histories and political treatises. Sandy ordered home delivery of the *Fayetteville Observer* and watched the news. She went out shopping and discovered cozy coffee shops and nice places to eat out. She brought home groceries and cooked Beth's childhood favorites, beef stroganoff and lasagna.

For her mother's sake, Beth did her best to do more than just pick at the food and averted her eyes from the news coming into her home. It was a relief to have her parents around. She could let down her guard; she didn't have to try to be strong anymore. She agreed with her parents: Having them here with her was going to make all the difference.

To prove it, Beth joined a health club and started taking yoga classes. Every other Sunday, the Sundays she didn't work, she and Sandy and sometimes Chuck went to her new Methodist church, and she sang the hymns to the rhythm laid down by a drummer, three guitarists, a keyboardist, and a vocalist shaking a tambourine. Back home, Beth picked up her own drumsticks again.

She sat at the drum kit, body swaying, hands and feet in motion. She liked to lose herself in the rhythm of Incubus's "Drive." But she wasn't exactly making a joyful noise. She placed muffling pads on the percussive surfaces, so as not to bother the neighbors. She kept quiet at work, too. When she came upon conversations about the war, she'd hang back or walk away. She never heard anyone else say what she was thinking.

At home, she sat down at her computer to check her e-mail. Nothing from Luigi. Something though from Lou Plummer, a local peace activist and National Guard veteran she'd met through Quaker House. She clicked on it and read: *We're planning a peace march. It would be great if you'd be willing to speak.*

Beth's eyes widened. She had never spoken before a crowd. The biggest group she'd ever gotten up in front of was when she defended her thesis, and that was an audience of only about twenty people. Lou wrote that the organizers were expecting a thousand. Her heart beat faster at the thought of finally speaking up, maybe making a difference. But then it would probably be in the newspaper, maybe on TV.

"What if someone at the hospital saw it?" Beth wondered out loud, talking it over with Sandy. "I need my job." She knew they couldn't fire her for speaking her mind, but maybe they could make things hard enough for her that she'd just have to quit. Or maybe her patients might see her on TV and refuse her as their nurse. She wasn't sure she could take that kind of rejection right now.

Sandy asked, her voice matter-of-fact, "If you speak at this rally, what would happen to Luigi?"

Beth sat down at the computer. She typed back to Lou: *I have to think about it.*

Luigi called. "Hey, baby."

They exchanged the usual hurried *I-love-yous*. He told Beth silly stories about his day. She told him about the peace rally. "If I did speak at the rally," she asked, "would it bother you?"

She heard him laugh. "Far as I'm concerned, that's what I'm over here for, isn't it? Your freedom of speech?"

Beth Pratt had an opportunity to do something that was meaningful to her — speak at a peace rally. She had the support of her husband all the way from Iraq. She went to yoga. She went to church. She drummed. She ate the food her mother set before her. She was no longer isolated and alone. She should have felt happy, or if not happy, she should have at least felt the even-keeled buoyancy of a productive, well-ordered life.

She didn't. When she thought about the peace rally, she didn't know what to do. She wished someone would just tell her which choice was the right one. If Luigi had said don't do it, it would have been easy, she would have said no, but he didn't. Despair weighed her down. She hid in her room and cried. If Sandy knew she was crying, after a while she'd come in to make sure she was OK, and Beth would say she was, but she wasn't.

Most days, she'd come home from work and lie in bed, and she couldn't sleep. She felt as if she hadn't slept in years. She stared at the bedroom window, the dark curtains edged in daylight, and she tried to remember how Luigi walked, what he smelled like, but she couldn't remember anymore and it scared her. It was if he'd never had a scent or a way of walking, just an imaginary husband. She would add up the time and it always added up the same: She and Luigi had been apart now for as long as they'd been together. He'd be home in a few months, but the word was that then he was just going to leave again. Afghanistan this time, probably for a whole year, and she couldn't do anything about it. This was her life. All of a sudden, as if she had blinked and could suddenly see clearly, she wasn't sure such a lonely life was worth living.

It's a short step from helplessness to hopelessness. Once it's taken, some self-medicate with alcohol; many require antidepressants to keep the overwhelming feelings at bay. Among those who are left behind, suicide isn't common, but it's not unheard of either. In Beth's case, the arrival of her parents had the unfortunate effect of allowing her to let go of whatever last defenses she had.

Sandy was sitting at the kitchen table reading the newspaper when Beth walked in and said, "I don't think I can take this anymore." Sandy reached for her and Beth sank into her lap. She curled up in her mother's arms and cried like a little girl. Sandy rocked her. She didn't know what else to do. She and Chuck had come down to take care of their daughter, to make things better. But Beth only seemed to be getting worse.

Marissa was driving on post doing seventy in a fifty-five zone when the blue and red lights came on behind her, forcing her to stop. It was midnight. The MP asked, "Do you know what speed you were going?"

"I have to get to Womack," Marissa explained. "I was working at the computer and my daughter woke up screaming that her head hurt. She has a temperature of almost a hundred and four, she's burning up. I'm afraid she might have that viral infection that's been going around, that kids have been dying of."

The MP flicked his flashlight over Lexie slumped in her seatbelt. Her hair was wet with sweat, her cheeks flaming, the rest of her clammy and pale. He frowned, unconvinced. He was a kid himself. He said, "I hope you're not lying to me."

"Look at me," Marissa said. "I'm wearing sweats and I've got a sick kid in the back seat. Where else would I be going at seventy miles an hour in the middle of the night?"

He let her go, just asked her to do him a favor and slow down. The last time Charlie called home, he and Marissa had talked about the guy in his unit who'd been killed when a Black Hawk went down, and the tents in his camp that had burned after a mortar attack. He manned a gun on convoys. Now their kid was sick. She wasn't slowing down for anybody. She hit the accelerator and sped the rest of the way to Womack.

Five hours later, Lexie's temperature was headed back down, and they were dragging back home. Before she fell into bed, Marissa faxed the doctor's excuse to her supervisor, because if she tried to drive to her eight A.M. foreclosure hearings now, she might just wrap the company car around a tree. The firm could get someone else to cover those hearings.

At nine, her supervisor was on the phone with one clear message: If those hearings happened without her, she was fired.

Beyond the tree line at the back of the yard, artillery boomed in the distance. Marissa called the clerk of the court to find out if anyone had showed up at eight to make an offer on any of those foreclosed houses. "No," said the clerk, "no one." So Marissa dragged Lexie out of bed, took her to Jenn's, and raced to the courthouse to file the paperwork. "My dream job," she told Jenn, "and I hate it, I really hate it."

By the weekend, Lexie was still under the weather, so Marissa stretched out on the couch with her just to cuddle and watch cartoons. They'd been lying there a while when Lexie said, from out of the blue, "Mommy? Since Daddy's been gone, we don't get to snuggle and have fun anymore."

For a long, stunned moment, the only thing that moved was the animation on the TV screen. Then Marissa breathed, "You're right, kiddo." Before she got off the couch that day, she'd made a decision.

She cut back on her work. Over the next couple of weeks, her output dropped by a quarter. And then early one morning, her supervisor was on the phone telling her she needed to do more.

"I can't do more." Marissa was already smoking and typing and wearing the headset, trying to get ready for her hearings that day while she talked. "I can't go back to where I was. There's no more that I can give you."

Her supervisor said, "Well, what you're giving us now isn't enough. I'm going to have to let you go."

Marissa stopped typing. "No," she said. "I'm going to have to quit."

Marissa pulled off the headset. She stood up. She felt defeated and unsure of what to do next: the next hour, the next day, the next month. But when she thought of Lexie, still asleep in the double bed, she felt some relief. She lay down on the couch. All around her, the house was suddenly silent and still.

In an office inside one of the satellite health clinics on post, sat a social worker named Joanne Stanley. Before the tiny space had become her office, it had been the patient education room, and before that, it was an examination room. This meant that Joanne's desk was squeezed in between several large filing cabinets filled with patient education materials, and that the room had no window, though it did have a mirror and a sink. It also had a chair for her and a chair for a client. What it didn't have was very many people coming in to sit in that client chair.

The summer Charlie Bootes and Luigi Pratt were preparing to leave for Iraq, Joanne Stanley was getting over the end of a long relationship and looking to get the heck out of Dallas. She was a square woman with the corners gently rounded off — a soft lap, a quiet guffaw, and a boyish cap of hair the color of butter. She gave the impression that life would have a hard time tipping her over.

She wanted to go someplace green, but she didn't have the money to just pick up and move. She heard, though, that a military contractor was looking for licensed clinicians to fill some new behavioral health-care manager positions at Army posts around the country. It was part of a new program the Army was implementing to help soldiers and their families throughout the whole deployment cycle, from predeployment to deployment and on through reintegration during postdeployment. She decided to apply.

People who knew her wondered what on earth she thought she was doing. They knew she was not one to display a flag. But when she watched the news and saw the fighting in Iraq and Afghanistan, and she reflected on what the soldiers must be going through, she didn't see soldiers. She saw human beings in need. Her own personal counseling philosophy had always been that if there was a need, it didn't matter who she was helping. It was worthy just to help. By moving somewhere green and working with soldiers, she could meet their needs and her own needs at the same time.

Joanne pulled into Fayetteville about a month after Charlie and Luigi left. She got a condo and once all her boxes were hauled in, she walked out on the porch and saw big green trees and birds, and she was in heaven.

Her first day, she dug some clothes out of a box and drove to the post. At the gate, the guard scrutinized her driver's license, then told her to pull her PT Cruiser to the side, get out, and open the hood and all the doors and the back hatch. She'd never been on a military installation before. She was so nervous, she tried to get out of the car before she'd undone her seatbelt. Then she stood to the side feeling as if she had something to hide while he searched the car. She went through this routine for four days in a row before somebody thought to tell her how to get a Department of Defense employee sticker for her car.

The post was vast. Womack was enormous. She sat in on a video teleconference for all the new care managers. Joanne was in awe, because, my goodness, you could talk to posts all over the country. They were all briefed on the new Deployment Cycle Support program they were now a part of, helping soldiers and their families with deployment-related problems, which were growing due to the greater number of deployments. Joanne learned she was the first of five care managers planned for Fort Bragg — one at Womack, one at each of the three satellite health clinics on post, and one at the medical holding company where sick and injured soldiers were assigned until they recovered. Whenever soldiers or family members came into any of those facilities, from now on they were supposed to be asked, "Are you being seen for a deployment-related problem?" If they answered yes, that was supposed to trigger a referral to the care manager, who would then make an assessment to determine what services they needed and refer them accordingly. Though the new care managers were all experienced counselors, their role here was to be more referral- and crisis-oriented, get in and fix and go.

The care managers were told that another part of their job was to educate the rest of the post about the Deployment Cycle Support program — all the medical personnel, the service providers over at Army Community Services, the FRG leaders, and the commanding officers of each of the units.

Joanne spent a month educating herself first. She learned about the available services: mental health services, marriage and family therapy, confidential pastoral counseling, anger management counseling, substance abuse programs, domestic violence and child abuse intervention, parenting classes, social support groups, information databases, life skills training, employment readiness programs, financial literacy classes, private charitable agencies for those having trouble making ends meet, a clearinghouse of volunteer opportunities to help the isolated get out of the house — and that was just on post. There were more services out in town. She was amazed. The post was its own village.

It also had its own hierarchical structure — there was a very definite sequence in which things were done. Joanne spent her first months in daily fear of jumping the chain of command just by dialing the wrong person at the wrong point in the process. With the Deployment Cycle Support program being so new, the whole team needed to impress people, not mess up and have the leadership think they were idiots.

She pointed to the uniform of one of the first Army officers she met and said, "I want one of those." He said, "Yep, you can enlist." She laughed, but she wasn't kidding. She felt at a disadvantage without a uniform. She wished she could be like Lieutenant Colonel Pecko, who possessed a gentle quality plus a dissertation about the effect of professional support on female troops that impressed social workers like her, and a pair of silver oak leaves on his collar that impressed the military personnel. She felt she wasn't quite part of the family, as if she were somebody's stepchild. She couldn't point to anything specific that anyone did or said to make her feel that way, so she tried to own the issue of her discomfort. But she couldn't shake the feeling that she wasn't quite as sanctioned without a uniform.

Once Joanne started seeing clients, the toughest days were those when utilization in her program wasn't as high as ideally it could be. In other words, the days she saw no one. She'd wonder if word wasn't getting out or if people just didn't want or need help. After days like that, she'd go home and de-stress by playing video games, stupid, silly, addictive ones like Diamond Mine, where she could just sit there and mindlessly click.

At work, she rebriefed the doctors and nurse practitioners in the health clinic. She talked to the folks over at Army Community Services. It took longer to get herself worked into the command briefings for the unit commanders; she couldn't figure out how to get access to them at first. Her average daily client load went up to about three. The days she saw five people were big days for her. In the other places she had worked in her career, that wouldn't have been such a big day, but here, it was a great day.

A lot of the soldiers were gone, so mostly she saw spouses, and most of the spouses she saw were young, with maybe a high-school education. Her typical client would come into the Robinson Health Clinic where Joanne was assigned, see the doctor, the doctor would find her in distress and send her over to Joanne. Joanne would talk with her, console her, give her a listening ear. Typically, the young woman had no support in Fayetteville. She had recently moved here and then her soldier had deployed and she was completely alone. She was frantic. She suffered from severe anxiety and depression. She wasn't sleeping, she wasn't eating, and she may have been self-medicating with alcohol.

Joanne would listen and for the most part she felt sympathetic, though deep in her heart of hearts, she often thought, *Well, you kind of chose this life.* She'd tell the young woman about the availability of medication, substance abuse counseling, and support groups. She'd refer her to a therapist, or a chaplain, or a mother's day out group.

And then, typically, it would become clear the young woman wasn't interested in relieving her symptoms. She was so tired and overwhelmed that she was absolutely convinced the only thing that could make her better was for the Army to send her soldier home. She had already contacted the Red Cross.

The American Red Cross provides emergency communications between military service members and their families. If there's an emergency at home, the family contacts the Red Cross, the Red Cross verifies the emergency, and then transmits the message to the service member's unit in the field, where usually either the chaplain or the commanding officer delivers the message to the service member. Depending on the nature of the emergency, and whether or not the unit can accomplish its mission without the service member, and the availability of transportation to extract the service member from wherever the unit happens to be, the service member may or may not be allowed to go home.

Frantic young wives do not constitute an emergency. But Joanne hadn't yet acquired the necessary knowledge base to be absolutely sure of that, so she would just say, gently, "Well, my understanding is that we really have to keep the soldiers there because there's a need."

When these young women left the office, Joanne often felt she hadn't helped them a bit. Joanne would refer them to mental health, then call them to follow up, only to learn that one had given up and gone home to her parents. Or another had gone to see the psychiatrist as directed but just wanted the doctor to write a letter to the effect that her husband had to come home right now or the consequences would be devastating. Joanne would go home and attack the Diamond Mine.

She went to a briefing over at Army Community Services. The presenter was a woman named Sally Bean, an Army wife for more than two decades. She struck Joanne as very knowledgeable, so afterward she went up and told Sally about these young wives. "I feel badly because they're hurting and in pain, and what I'm offering to help ease that pain, they don't want." She wondered if there was something more that she could do or a different way that she should be going about it.

Sally Bean's take on it was that once the spouses got to that point, they were in major meltdown, and chances were they weren't going to be able to hear what Joanne was suggesting, particularly since the care managers were just focusing on a one-time referral. So the young women found their own solutions.

The social work credo is: "Start where the client is." Joanne walked away from that conversation realizing that her goal was different from the goals of those frantic young wives. She wanted to relieve their pain and suffering. They wanted their soldier home. Joanne couldn't give them that.

But she noticed they also seemed to want someone to really hear what they were saying, to have their experience acknowledged and validated. That, Joanne could give them. The military world these women lived in may have been foreign to Joanne — she was still having to constantly look up resources and research the community so she could be an avenue of information for them — but she was very familiar with the symptoms they were experiencing, the anxiety, depression, exhaustion, and occasional substance abuse.

Her goal became a simple one: to instill some hope that as bad as things were, there was a way to get through it. She'd tell them, "We'll find a way to deal with this," or "We'll see how we can make it better." She always said *we* so they'd start to think of it as a team effort. Her hope was that, by coming in and talking, they would at least realize they weren't alone.

As fall turned to winter, as the green leaves turned brown and drifted down, a surprising thing happened. Joanne got to the point where she was wishing she *had* enlisted when she was younger, or, rather, had accepted a commission as an officer specializing in social work. (She knew enough now to know that officers don't enlist, they're commissioned.)

The Army was starting to send officers who were mental health professionals out into combat zones with the soldiers, and the whole idea of going to other countries and helping people through war trauma struck her as important and exciting work, work that made a real difference. Unlike what she felt like she was doing back here on Fort Bragg.

And then one day, in the midst of all those young wives Joanne was seeing, in walked a woman whose husband had been in the Army twenty-two years. She was educated. She was very skilled. And she was a wreck.

She sat in the chair next to Joanne's desk and couldn't stop crying. She had all the same symptoms as those younger women: symptoms of depression, anxiety about her husband and his well being, the feeling of being overwhelmed by the demands of her job and her four children. And then the woman said, "This wartime deployment is just different from all the rest in peacetime."

In the evening, Joanne walked out into the cold air on the porch of her condo and looked up at the dark outline of the naked trees against the stars. If a spouse of twenty-two years was having that kind of difficulty, it really put in perspective all the young ones who'd been coming in. This wasn't typical. It wasn't normal. A wartime deployment was something very different.

She used to think, *You chose this life.* Now she realized that sentiment came from a place of ignorance. In the past few months, she had learned from the spouses what it was really like to live the military life. Those young women hadn't known what they were getting into any more than she had known before she came here. And they were so much younger and less sophisticated about the world than she was. Their soldiers were probably not much different.

She shivered and went back inside to do some diamond mining.

Joanne unlocked the door to her office/patient-education-room/exam-room at seven-thirty in the morning, her usual time. She turned on the computer to check her e-mail. She paged through some paperwork. These days she was also counseling clients. The perpetual shortage of resources meant that in addition to doing assessments and referrals, the care managers were having to do some individual counseling and set up support groups, which was fine with Joanne. She liked having her hands in counseling again.

The hardest days for her were still the days when she had these young spouses come in who had left their families many states away and were here in Fayetteville doing things on their own for the very first time, with no family or friends to fall back on, with no life experience to go on, in this wartime situation that was not normal. She'd never been very directive in her counseling, but one young woman who'd never lived away from home before had been so lost it was clear to Joanne that she needed to go back home while her husband was deployed. She just needed someone to give her permission. Joanne had told her, "This isn't a good way to feel by yourself. Go home."

Joanne knew there were dangers in going home. Her client would be leaving behind all the support resources Fort Bragg offered. And if her parents weren't supportive of the marriage in the first place, if they were thinking, *Our daughter was supposed to go to college, have a future of her own,* the marriage could be undermined. But for some people, for this person, going home was the right choice.

A good day was a day when Joanne Stanley was actually able to help people: be there for them and provide them with the resources and support *they* needed. Those were the days when she could believe she was making a difference. Here and there, she started having days like that.

Beth Pratt hunched on a chair in an anonymous, fluorescent-lit exam room at the Robinson Health Clinic. She picked at the skin around her fingernails.

The family nurse practitioner rustled through the door. "So what brings you in to us today?"

"Oh," said Beth, and stopped. Her voice was thin and scratchy. She started again. "I'm having a really hard time with my husband gone." Her eyes reddened. "I think I'm really depressed." Her thin voice wavered and she started to cry, which made her frown. "I cry like this all the time. And I just want it to stop."

The nurse practitioner nodded. She was older, with the same calm, comforting air of those women who've raised a whole brood of children and seen it all. She nudged Beth with the usual questions: Are you feeling any sense of hopelessness or helplessness? Have your sleeping habits changed? Have your eating habits changed? Have you lost weight? How about a change in sexual desire? Yes, Beth said to each question, struggling to get the word out, yes, yes, yes, and yes, adding to the last, "Actually I don't know, since my husband's not here." And her face crumpled again.

"Honey, have you had any suicidal thoughts?"

Beth didn't say anything. She just nodded.

"Do you have a plan? What are you thinking about?"

"I've been thinking," Beth said, "that if I had a gun, I'd shoot myself."

The nurse practitioner led her around the back way, down a long empty hallway where there was no one to see her red eyes and nose, her wet cheeks. The nurse had asked her, "If the social worker was available, would you talk with her?" And Beth had shrugged and said, "I guess." She followed the nurse practitioner to the open doorway of a small, window-less office crammed with filing cabinets and a sink.

"Mrs. Pratt," said the nurse practitioner, "this is Ms. Stanley."

Joanne Stanley, Lieutenant Colonel Pecko, the nurse practitioner all can rattle off the differences between clinical depression and just feeling down because a person is having a little trouble adjusting to a deploy-ment. In an adjustment reaction, military spouses may have difficulty sleeping or become very sad and withdrawn. But as time goes on, as they master the new routine and new responsibilities, they gain confidence and their outlook improves. In clinical depression, the sadness persists and the depressed spouse grows less and less able to cope with it. Over time, she'll develop significant symptoms, such as the ones the nurse practitioner asked Beth about. In the worst cases, some will have suicidal thoughts or stop functioning, unable to get out of bed.

A spouse suffering from an adjustment reaction usually either recovers on her own or with the help of friends, family, a support group, or maybe some counseling to help her learn more effective coping skills. Clinical depression, on the other hand, is a chemical disorder of the brain. The sufferer is not able to get better on her own and must have professional help to pull herself out of the hole she's in.

Beth Pratt was suffering from clinical depression. Within an hour of arriving at the clinic, she had received counseling from Joanne, a pre-scription for antidepressants, follow-up appointments with both Joanne and the nurse practitioner, and an appointment with a civilian psycholo-gist out in town. She hadn't known any of this help was available.

As the head of the social work department, Lieutenant Colonel Pecko supervises a staff of fifty, including Joanne and the four other behavioral health-care managers. The Deployment Cycle Support program that was just getting off the ground as Beth's husband was taking off for Iraq had been ten years in the making. It was actually developed at Fort Bragg be-fore going Army-wide.

In the early 1990s, a couple of things got the Army's attention. First, one out of every seven service members returning from the first Gulf War, according to Department of Defense data, either requested or required evaluation for Persian Gulf War syndrome, which involves a mysterious mass of symptoms from chronic fatigue to abdominal pain. And then came the summer of 2002.

That summer, there were five domestic murders connected to Fort Bragg. In three cases, soldiers just back from Afghanistan killed their wives; two of the soldiers then killed themselves. All the marriages apparently had been troubled beforehand, and none of the soldiers or their wives had reached out to any of the support programs the Army had available at the time.

There's no evidence that deployment was directly to blame. But an Army memo acknowledges that after a wartime deployment, service members and their families may also face "some degree of stress or trauma associated either with the nature of conflict or the disruption of their lives." In the short term, nearly one in five service members may also face major depression, anxiety, or post-traumatic stress disorder, according to a study of soldiers and Marines returning from Afghanistan and Iraq that was published in the *New England Journal of Medicine*. And most of those who need help won't seek it out, at least not right away. That puts stress on any marriage.

Before the murders, the Deployment Cycle Support program was still in development after nearly a decade. "The incidents gave us the impetus for getting this program off the ground," Lieutenant Colonel Pecko says. It rolled out within a year. In addition to the care managers and other improvements, the program required all returning soldiers to undergo physical and mental health screening to uncover possible trouble. Eventually, the program began to require a follow-up screening several months after their return, since trouble can take a while to develop. Plans were also underway to have soldiers fill out a similar survey before they deploy, to identify problems early on.

However, there are no mandatory mental health surveys for the families. Unlike soldiers, they can't be ordered to fill out surveys or attend predeployment briefings or any of those Military 101 programs that, among other things, educate spouses about the services available to them. As a result many, like Beth, literally don't know what they're missing.

The National Military Family Association reports that support providers have been very successful at reaching the families who live on military installations and getting information into their hands. "Many of the people I see," agrees Joanne Stanley, "live on post." On Fort Bragg, the housing authority's Community Life Program has a family support coordinator, and each community on post has a mayor as well as resident NCOs who have been assigned by their units to act as liaisons with their fellow residents. None of them rely solely on the flyers that the Community Life Program mails out. They literally go knocking on doors to determine if any families have unmet needs.

But most military families don't live on a post or base — and some, of course, live hours from the nearest installation — a fact that causes Joanne to sigh. "We're all aware of the need, and one of the things that frustrates us as caregivers is knowing the needs are out there and not being able to get to them. We talk about it and try to brainstorm ways of reaching out."

Joanne has given her presentation about the Deployment Cycle Support program to unit FRG meetings, and at pre- and postdeployment briefings. "But so few people show up to those briefings compared to the level of need," she says. "Not the soldiers, because the briefings are mandatory for them. But the family members."

Army Community Services reaches out when new soldiers first arrive on Fort Bragg. Part of the soldiers' orientation includes a visit to the ACS facility in the converted school, where they're asked if they have a spouse or child. They're also asked to provide an address. But when they first get there, their address may be some motel. At the time when Beth arrived in Fayetteville, the service providers at ACS were at the mercy of those overwhelmed new soldiers remembering to tell their spouses that ACS was out there.

That's because if the spouses don't live or shop on the military installation, the installation's official newspaper publications don't reach them. Neither do flyers posted at shopping areas on base, nor direct mailings to military housing areas. Sending information home with the service member is a dead end — verbal briefings are forgotten, and the vast majority of flyers handed out to service members to take home never make it out of the car and into the house, assuming they even make it into the car. In a survey asking spouses how they got most of their information from the military, handouts brought home by the service member were at the bottom of the list.

Even within the military, getting the word out can be a challenge. "At each post we're having to educate everyone that this is available," says Lieutenant Colonel Pecko. This is important because commanding officers, military medical personnel, military housing officials, and chaplains are sometimes the first point of contact, the first ones to catch a whiff that someone needs help.

But the real first responders are the spouse volunteers who lead the family support organizations. Spouses like Marissa Bootes and Camilla Maki, Beth's FRG key caller. Like them, many family readiness volunteers actively maintain contact with the families in their groups. But Joanne has counseled just as many spouses who tell her they haven't reached out to their FRG for help because they say no one has ever called them. When Joanne suggests they be proactive and make the first call themselves, they resist — without a clear welcome, they're very hesitant. "The FRGs," Joanne says, "need to reach out to every new family, because the unit itself, the FRG, may be the only point of contact."

So it comes down to the spouse volunteers, the family support organizations, to spread the word about the services that are available. But people rotate in and out of units all the time. When I became the Key Volunteer for my husband's company, I received a personnel roster listing spouses and phone numbers. I never once received an update and couldn't shake a new list out of the family readiness officer to save my life. I had to depend on my husband to notice when someone new showed up and then find out if a spouse was in the picture. Ferreting them out required time and detective skills. Plus, as has been noted before, some family support groups are well run, but others are virtually nonfunctioning. And somehow Beth didn't get the word, even though Camilla was concerned about her and reached out to her months before the medical professionals finally stumbled across her.

All those family support services that Joanne discovered during her training don't come cheap. The military invests in them because families have an impact on readiness. So why does the Pentagon spend so much money on these services, then rely on a haphazard patchwork of volunteers to spread the word?

"One, it doesn't cost them anything," says Sylvia Kidd from her office in the Association of the United States Army building just outside of Washington, D.C. After her years as an active-duty Army wife, she now runs AUSA's family programs. "No matter how hard we try, money is the big factor in everything. And two, because of tradition. Because that is the way it's always been. We've always relied very heavily on volunteers for our programs. The military," she says, "freely admits many of the programs wouldn't exist if it weren't for the volunteers working on them."

Besides being free, the volunteers have another advantage. They're not perceived as being part of the system. Spouses who need help are more likely to admit it to a fellow spouse, someone like Marissa.

After she hit the wall, Marissa had a lot more time to give to her FRG, dedicating a lot of effort to making it better.

After Beth hit the wall, she told Luigi and her parents she'd been to the doctor to get an antidepressant. She didn't tell them she'd been thinking about guns. She said to Luigi, "I feel like I should have been able to handle this. I feel like I failed."

She was crying. She still had bad days. She wondered sometimes if Luigi was sorry he had married her.

"Hey," he said, "I love you. Just because you're depressed doesn't mean I'm going to get rid of you. I'm stuck to you like a barnacle on the Deerfield Beach pier."

Marissa said the same thing to Charlie: *I feel like I failed.* She'd often just sit on the couch, slumped and defeated. She'd spent most of the deployment running away from her feelings. But in the end, she just couldn't run fast enough.

CHAPTER 14

Peace Also Takes Courage

MARISSA WAS CLEANING out the closets. The Hooah Wives were having a yard sale, and suddenly Marissa had hours to empty her life of junk. She had hours to snuggle in front of cartoons with Lexie and then run out in the backyard and jump on the trampoline with her, still trying to stay busy till Charlie came home. She had hours to teach Lexie to ride her two-wheeler. She told Charlie about it when he called, described Lexie wobbling off on her own for the first time, and he got quiet. Then he said, "Seems like you guys are going off someplace without me." She had hours to park herself out on the back deck and smoke and think about that.

Lexie was digging flowering weeds out of the yard and planting them in flowerpots. Marissa said, "We have to put some fertilizer and stuff in there."

"I know what I'm doing," Lexie insisted. "What about this?" She held up a dead stick in a pot.

"It might grow back." Marissa took a drag on her cigarette. She added dryly, "It needs a little water."

Sometimes Lexie scared her to death, she was so much like Marissa herself. Her grandmother had said to her when she was little, "Marissa, you're an old soul." Her earliest memory was from when she was two or three, a Christmas morning. Talking with her best friend back in Erie who was thinking about adopting, talking about the foster care system, had brought it all back, and now she had time to actually think about it.

This earliest memory was like all her old memories: her two older half-brothers fighting, and the oldest one saying to her, "Those presents came from the church, not from Santa. There is no such thing as Santa."

Marissa remembered crying, and their mother yelling at him because she was hurt — a church donated some of the presents, but she was working two jobs, cleaning houses and factories, working hard to buy the others, and it hurt her when her son said that. Marissa remembered getting a Betsy Wetsy doll that Christmas Day, like the one she'd seen on TV. Then her other brother grabbed Betsy and ripped her head off. She had bad luck with dolls. One of her cousins kidnapped another doll and cut off all its fingers and toes.

At the yard sale with the Hooah Wives, Marissa talked about finding a balance, about how money wasn't everything. "When the man you love is in a life or death situation," she mused aloud, "it makes you sit down and think about what really matters in your own life."

Beth told Joanne Stanley, "I wanted to do something important."

Each week, Beth sat in the straight-backed chair squeezed in next to Joanne's desk and gazed at the opposite wall as if it had a window with a view instead of a mirror with a reflection of Joanne's profile, her desk, her bookshelves. Beth felt a lot like this tiny office, once an exam room, transformed out of necessity into something it wasn't meant to be. "I never wanted to be a nurse, really. That's not why I got all that education."

"Maybe you should be thinking about what you'd like to do when you're feeling better," Joanne suggested.

The crowd of marchers came around the corner from Fayetteville's downtown. Before they appeared, you could hear them coming, soft at first, then louder, the beat of drums, the wordless buzz of a thousand voices. Then they appeared around the corner and marched down the hill to the park, wearing blue jeans and T-shirts, desert camouflage jackets, and gothic black. They pushed strollers, carried water bottles and signs and banners — BRING THEM HOME NOW — and an American flag. It was Fayetteville's largest peace rally since the Vietnam War.

The marchers streamed across the park toward the bandshell. A newsprint program listed speakers and performers: veterans, union members, Hip-Hop Against Racist War, a September 11th family member, and the fourth speaker on the list, "Beth Pratt — Military spouse from Fayetteville whose husband is in Iraq."

After the last big peace rally in Fayetteville, in 1972, someone firebombed Quaker House and burned it to the ground. Leading up to this rally, on the Internet a radical right-wing Web site had threatened violence. On a quiet side street outside Raleigh, a panel truck that was supposed to drive with the marchers had been vandalized, spray paint tangled across the crude mural on its side that depicted two soldiers in dress greens standing at the door of a woman who was collapsing with grief.

While all that had been happening, Beth had been at the little computer desk in her bedroom, printing out page after page of solid color. The thought of speaking at the rally still scared her. But she didn't feel she had much of a voice right now, and she was just as afraid that if she didn't take this chance she would beat herself up about it later. By the time the color print cartridge ran out, she had constructed a sign to carry at the march — red, white, and blue letters on a black background: PEACE ALSO TAKES COURAGE.

Peace and courage come in many forms. While Beth's journey led her outward, Marissa's had turned inward. At night, her best friend would call after her daughter, Izzy, was in bed in Erie and Lexie was in bed in Fayetteville. Night after night, they talked about Monica's plans to adopt and Marissa's memories of foster care.

"I'm going to classes and stuff," Monica said, "but they just tell you what they know."

"Which isn't shit!" Marissa laughed.

Talking with Monica was like getting back on a bike after years. She'd been talking everything over with her since fifth grade; she could do it without thinking. Together they crawled through Marissa's childhood, poking their heads into the darkest corners, the closets she never opened. No one but she and Monica knew everything that was hidden in there. In the picture of their fifth-grade class, the eleven-year-old version of Monica is wearing big glasses and short wavy hair. She looks like the good girl. Marissa's not in the picture at all. She moved a lot in those days, so she missed a lot of class pictures. Monica was the first person she ever trusted, the first person she ever loved until she met Charlie.

Marissa had trusted Charlie enough to marry him. But she still had never trusted him with the most hidden parts of her life. She'd never told him 90 percent of the things she went through before he knew her. He knew they were in there, and sometimes he'd press her to tell him, and she'd shove back and let him know he wasn't welcome in there. It was a painful, angry place.

Back when she was in junior high, everything made her angry. After she got into a fight with another girl at school, the judge put Marissa on regular probation for two years with a nine P.M. curfew, but she still partied in the woods and ran from the cops, and one night she stayed out till four A.M., drinking. She had to go to court in the morning. Her mother tried to ground her but she just got up and walked out, and she got away with it because her brothers had taken all the fight out of her mother. The judge put Marissa on intensive probation. She ran away to Philadelphia with a girlfriend until the cops picked them up and put them on a bus back to Erie, starved after not eating for two days. The judge put her on intensive specialized probation.

With Monica, Marissa could talk about anything — the fights, the partying, and also the deep, dark secret things she'd held inside all her life, the things she didn't tell anybody, not even the counselors she was sent to, the things she never ever whispered to anyone except her best friend.

Each time Monica said goodbye, Marissa would hang up the phone and sit there on the couch. Sometimes, she'd let herself cry for a few minutes. Then she'd get up and blow her nose and get on with whatever she wanted to get done before she went to bed.

A rhythmic squeak rose up from the backyard. Marissa was jumping with Lexie on the trampoline. When the Black Hawk helicopters raced along the tree line, they were so low and close Marissa couldn't hear anything but their thumping roar, and she could almost believe that if she pushed off just a little harder, she could jump up and touch one as they thundered overhead. Then they were gone, and the only sound was the wind in the pines, and the rhythmic squeak, and her daughter's voice, shouting, "Watch me!"

Charlie had gotten back from another convoy and called to let her know he was safe. Since he left in September, for six months now, every other day or so he would put on his helmet and his heavy body armor, pick up his weapon, and walk two miles, three miles to get to a phone. Sometimes he gave up sleep. Sometimes it was raining. It was always windy. They'd talk for a few minutes. Then he'd turn around and trudge back. Back and forth. Week after week. How many miles did that add up to? How much love? Marissa had always had trouble believing Charlie really loved her. Jumping in place with Lexie on the trampoline, the thought finally caught up to her: *He must really love me.*

"Watch me!" shouted Lexie. "Watch how high I can jump!"

How much love does it take, Marissa wondered, to be worthy of trust?

She didn't know the answer to that, but she did know she didn't want another paralegal job in real estate. She had become a paralegal only because she figured eventually she'd become a lawyer. "But I think I just realized," she said to Monica one night, "that dream of mine? Of becoming a lawyer? That was a kid's dream."

The dream of a kid who, when she was nine and living with her mother again after several years in foster care, was left alone with an eighteen-year-old babysitter. And the babysitter threw a party. The apartment was full of kids and they were drinking and Marissa was with them. The babysitter was sad, so she went in the bedroom, locked the door, and shot herself. Marissa's mother went to prison for two years, for providing alcohol to minors, or maybe it was for child endangerment. Marissa went back to living with relatives and strangers. And she knew, she just knew, if her mother had had a good lawyer she would never have been sent to prison. A good lawyer could have ridden in on a white horse, set her mother free, and restored her family — no, better than that — transformed her family into something it never was. In her dreams, a good lawyer would have saved little Marissa.

No lawyer did, though. The person who came the closest to saving her was a juvenile probation officer named Karen Permorsky. When Marissa was on intensive specialized probation and *still* getting in trouble, the judge was going to put her in a juvenile detention facility until she was eighteen, lock her up like a loser kid, a hopeless case. Karen talked to the judge. Marissa's oldest brother had managed to get his life together, for a few years anyway, and was living in a small town outside of Erie. Karen convinced the judge to let Marissa go live with her brother, start over away from the city and the criminal activity, learn how to be a kid again. Because of Karen, the judge gave Marissa one more chance.

Karen was the first adult who had ever believed in her. Marissa said, "I've thought about what it would be like to be a juvenile probation officer, to really make a difference in somebody's life."

"You'd be a really good one," Monica said.

Part of it was Marissa didn't want to be poor, and paralegals made a lot more money. "But also," she admitted to Monica, "I'm afraid I wouldn't be able to do it, just because the emotions would be too raw, seeing what the kids go through and being reminded of everything I went through." As Marissa talked with Monica, suddenly she wished the person on the other end of the phone was Charlie.

It was late when she hung up. She sat there on the couch and wished Charlie was here with her to hold her, and listen to her while she told him all the things she'd never told him, as if they were as close and intimate as she was with Monica, because tonight, as she was talking to her friend, for the first time ever she had felt as if she were cheating on her husband, emotionally cheating. She sat there on the couch and let herself cry about it for a minute. Then she got up, took a shower to let it all out, and got ready for bed.

A few days after Beth finished making her sign, that crowd of nearly a thousand people marched up a quiet downtown street toward the park. The only people who saw the peace march, besides the marchers themselves, were some startled motorists, a few dozen reporters and camera crews, one hundred police officers, and about a hundred and fifty counterprotesters.

At the sight of the marchers, the knot of counterprotesters waiting across the street from the park pressed together and shaded their eyes against the sun to see. They held up their own signs: PROUD ARMY WIFE and WHO DIED FOR YOUR FREEDOM OF SPEECH? They sang "God Bless America." From among them, a voice shouted, "Traitors!"

As Beth entered the park, carrying her sign and walking alongside Marena Groll, the Army wife who had first referred her to Quaker House, Beth glanced up at the bandshell. She looked as if she wished she hadn't eaten breakfast, which suddenly wasn't sitting too well. "Can I do this?" she asked.

Marena rubbed her arm. "Yes, you can!"

The bandshell was a vast shaded space littered with sound speakers and microphone stands and drums. Below it, a thousand people spread across the grass in the sun. Beth walked across the stage and stopped in front of one of the microphones, silhouetted against the crowd. She gripped the pages of her speech as if they were a ballet barre that could steady her. She leaned forward.

"My name is Beth Pratt. I'm a nurse and I grew up in Minnesota."

Her voice boomed over the crowd. She told them it had taken all the courage she had to stand up there and speak for those few minutes. "As far as supporting the troops," she read, "I support my husband one hundred percent, along with all of the other soldiers that are making sacrifices for us. Ending this war and bringing them all home safely would be the best form of support that I can see."

She spoke for just three minutes. When she turned away from the mike, her heartbeat faded out of her ears and the crowd's roar faded in.

Out on the southwestern end of town, Marissa was much too far away to hear even a whisper of the protest. No newspaper or TV news brought word of it into her house. As she laughed with Lexie and the Hooah

Wives, she had no idea it was even happening and she preferred it that way. When I mentioned it to her later, all the laughter went out of her.

"I think it's bullshit," she snapped. "It kills morale, it makes life harder for the soldiers and their families." She may not have heard about the protest, but she sure had been thinking about the issues surrounding it, because the words were pouring out. "Charlie's coming home soon," she said, her voice rising, "but he could be going back in less than a year and I don't even want to *think* about that, but we can't bring them all home now, it's stupid. Our soldiers are over there risking their lives, they're building schools, and those protesters are saying it's for nothing. And it's *not*."

In the *News & Observer* in Raleigh, North Carolina, there was this:

BRAGG DEMONSTRATORS DISAGREE PEACEFULLY
By Dan Kane
Staff Writer

FAYETTEVILLE — They are two women with loved ones serving in Iraq, and their voices waver with the constant fear that at any minute they could receive the worst possible news from overseas.

But they stood on opposite sides of the police line as the biggest anti-war protest to hit Fayetteville since the Vietnam War took to the streets Saturday.

Beth Pratt, 34, whose husband was dispatched to drive a truck for the Army, spoke of an unjustified war and occupation that has already killed one member of his platoon.

"I would like the people who are making the decisions in this war to leave their families, go halfway around the world and have little communication with them for several months and then come back for a few months just to turn around and have to go back again," she said to hundreds of protesters who marched to Rowan Park.

Across the street from the park, Jennifer Gaines, 24, joined about 125 opponents of the rally, waving flags and reciting the pledge of allegiance. She fought back tears as she spoke of her fiancé, a military policeman who is a week away from returning home.

She disagreed with the protesters who said they could support the troops while opposing the war. Doing so, she said, was putting those troops at risk.

"You support them, you support what they do," said
Gaines, a former surgical technician for the Army . . .

Jennifer Gaines had enlisted at eighteen; her father was retired Army.
When her four-year enlistment was up, she got out and went back home
to Fayetteville, got a job as a surgical tech at the hospital downtown. She
bounced with energy. She had punky red streaks in her hair and a silver
stud in her tongue.

She worked with a woman named Rebeccah who wanted to introduce
her to a soldier named Rick. Rebeccah had a drink waiting for her when
she got to the bar, and Jennifer said, "Now, that's a friend right there!"
Then she got her first peek at Rick, who looked a lot like James Dean, and
she thought to herself, *I have found my rebel*, because she had posters of
James Dean all over her apartment.

She teased him, "What's a rebel like you doing in the Army, man?"

And he just said, "Oh, please, in the Army all of them are rebels." He'd
been in almost ten years and he was starting to believe he was never going to meet a girl, so he was thinking about getting out.

"Halfway to retirement?" Jennifer exclaimed. "That would be stupid."

They had been dating six months when he deployed to Iraq in April
2003. Jennifer was scared for him, but he just said, "Pfff . . . whatever."
He'd done it so many times before, including a deployment to Afghanistan that he'd just returned from. He was going to be gone a year, so he
got out of his lease, put his life in storage, and moved in with Jennifer for
the last two weeks.

Those last two weeks seemed unreal, like a fairytale. "Gushy" was how
Jennifer described it. They'd be sitting on the couch being gushy and
Rick would say with a big sigh, "Let's go for a walk and talk." And Jennifer would think, *Oh my God, this is it, he's going to ask me to marry
him!* While Rick, though gushy, was thinking, *You make me take out the
trash, you can come with me — that's a long walk.*

After he left, Jennifer binged on the news. She watched Fox News every
morning. She programmed the TV to turn on when it was time for her to
get up, her new alarm clock. She read the *Fayetteville Observer* every day.
Every night, she would come home from work and lie on the couch, dis-
tracting herself with her regimen of shows, starting with the Cash Cow —
Call in now! Win a thousand dollars! — but during the three months she
lay on the couch every night she never won. She ate a lot of McChicken

sandwiches, because they were comforting and delicious and only a dollar. She put on weight. She tried yoga until she got stuck: She was in a back bend during class and her back locked up and the instructor had to come over and unstick her.

One day, Jennifer was at KFC with Rebeccah and some friends, and across the street the Greek Orthodox Church was raising money with a car wash. Jennifer's car needed washing, so she and her friends went over and ran into one of the doctors she worked with. He asked, "How's your boyfriend doing?" Next thing she knew, she was just boohooing. A Jewish rabbi was standing nearby. "Hey," he suggested, "let's say a prayer for him." The rabbi got them all in a circle and prayed a little prayer for Rick and another little prayer for Jennifer.

She was depressed for about three months and then she just decided, *I can't keep doing this for a whole year. It hurts my stomach.*

She didn't hang out with the wives in Rick's unit much. Of the thirty guys in his platoon, only two were married, and in the rest of the company most of the wives had been through the Afghanistan deployment and were good friends already. Jennifer wasn't a wife, in any case. So she'd get the call: "We're having an FRG meeting." But as far as social events, she was left out. She wasn't too bothered, though. She had her own friends, and her mother. She'd hang out with her mom every weekend. Her father had deployed to the first Gulf War, so her mother knew what she was going through.

One workday in December, she got out of surgery and there on her cell phone was a voicemail from Rick, saying he was coming home for two weeks over Christmas. She jumped on the nearest doctor. She shook him, squealing, "He's coming home! He's coming home!" She pinged off the walls, made everyone in the break room listen to his voicemail. "Listen! Listen!"

When he came in, she drove all the way up to Baltimore to get him. R&R back to the States was doled out by lottery, with the lucky winners flown back at Pentagon expense to a gateway airport such as Baltimore-Washington International, but from there they had to make their own way home. The Baltimore terminal was pretty empty at six-thirty in the morning, and when Jennifer finally found him in all that emptiness, he took one look at her and suddenly had a big grin on his face because, well, she was wearing what she would call a "boobie shirt" — it showed off her assets.

A contingent of local veterans and their wives had come out and they were clapping and cheering, passing out flags and cookies, and as Rick and Jennifer were holding each other, two of the veterans wives asked them to kiss again so they could get a picture, so they did, and they kept on kissing, and one of the wives said to the other, "I don't think they're doing that for us." But while Jennifer was kissing Rick and smiling and crying, she was smelling him, too — hygiene can be a challenge on the frontlines — and the first thing she said to him was, "Oh God, you really stink."

Rick asked her to marry him that night.

Driving back to Fayetteville, he told her, "It's strange. It's good to see you, but it's weird because things are still rolling in Iraq, there are hairy situations." The day he left, he wasn't sure he was going to get out because he was surrounded by a five-thousand-man uprising, and he was thinking, *Man, I'm going to miss my plane.* But at the same time, there was talk it might take another week and a half to get the trouble under control, and he was so worried about his guys he couldn't relax. All his soldiers were still over there, and they were young, and he had left them behind.

What about me? Jennifer thought. *What about me?* But then Rick explained that in all his deployments, he had always brought home all his guys. "If something happened while I was gone," he said, "that would mess with me bad." So Jennifer started worrying, too, thinking, *God, I don't want anything to happen to his guys, that would just make it worse on him.*

When the two weeks were up, it was harder to say goodbye than when he left the first time. Then Jennifer had that long drive home from Baltimore all by herself. She cussed and yelled in bumper-to-bumper traffic around D.C. and cried the whole way back to North Carolina.

When it got closer to the time for him to come home for good, the early morning news reported a rocket attack in the exact place where she knew for a fact that he was, and she sat up in bed and cried, "Rick!" She called Rebeccah, who she knew would be awake, and Rebeccah told her, "Calm down, calm down, turn the TV off, get off the phone and get ready for work, I'll see you in a few minutes."

By the time Jennifer got to work at the hospital, she could sniffle through her tears, "I don't think it's him, I think he's OK."

Rebeccah just held her, murmuring, "It's OK, it's OK, he's coming home in a couple weeks." But all Jennifer could think was, *There are guys who died just before coming home.*

Her mother knew a woman whose husband had died recently in a helicopter crash in Korea. Her mom went over to babysit the kids, and she said to Jennifer, "Be thankful, Jennifer, be thankful. And be good to Rick. You better treat him good."

The next time Rick called, Jennifer laughed and said, "My mom loves you more than she loves me!" But in her heart she knew: You don't know how valuable a life is until you've got your loved one over there, and you're worrying, because that was the worst part of it all, the worrying, not knowing what he might be in the middle of. For instance, not knowing until much later that what he was in the middle of was a road. He was riding down a road in a Humvee with his soldiers, watching a rocket-propelled grenade whip past the windshield, then looking out the side window and seeing another one coming straight at them. "Oh, fuck!" he shouted, and then it hit the side with a flash and a percussive boom, rocking the Humvee, shaking up Rick and the others inside, but not killing them — not even injuring them. The Humvee was armored, one of the few at the time that was. Not knowing any of that while it was going on was the worst part.

With one week to go, an Army wife Jennifer knew told her about a counterprotest that was going to be held across the street from Rowan Park. Jennifer said, "Hey, I've never been to a protest." She wasn't a political person until the war. In her family that was taboo. They didn't talk about politics or religion, and if Rick hadn't been over there, she knew she wouldn't have paid much attention to the war at all. But since he'd deployed, she had become very political. She wanted to know what was going on — that was why she watched the news so much. She wanted to know more about why he was over there and if he was going to have to go *back* over there. Her father was in the first Gulf War, and she would say, "We have to finish it this time."

So when she heard about the counterprotest, she didn't have anything else better to do that day, and it seemed like something fun she could do that would make her feel better. She stood across from the park with a couple of Army wives and all the other counterprotesters, and a reporter from the *News & Observer* came up and interviewed her. A radio reporter did, too. And so did I.

As the marchers appeared around the corner from downtown, I walked up to the small cluster of counterprotesters and I asked, "Is anyone here an Army wife?"

"We are!" sang out a trio of women. Jennifer added, "Well, I'm a fiancée, actually."

I asked them, "So what do you think of this peace protest?"

Jennifer spoke up first. "They have the right to say what they want."

That wasn't what I was expecting. "Then why did you come out here?"

"Because we support the troops!" she exclaimed, with an unspoken *duh!* on the end.

"The peace marchers say they support the troops, too," I said. I asked her if she thought it was possible to support the troops but oppose the war.

No, she did not. "Because that's their job," she said. "If you don't support what they're doing, how can you say you support them?"

A man standing nearby pointed at the oncoming marchers. "Look, they're carrying signs that say 'No more soldiers, no more war.' They're saying they want to get rid of her fiancé. What kind of support is that?"

The next time I met with Jennifer, it was in the quiet of her apartment. She told me she felt good that she was there at the counterprotest. "It got me hot, though," she said, "seeing some of those people out there. But the one that got me real hot, that I wanted to just go across and just slap her face, was this girl, this young girl carrying a baby doll covered in blood. It was like, we're baby killers? That got me hot."

"Because she was carrying that bloody doll?"

"Yeah. It was like, this is not Vietnam, and that's what they were trying to do. They were trying to do a whole 'nother Vietnam. And it was just so frustrating. I think it's really important that we were out there to stop that, to show our support. Because we don't need these soldiers coming home to what our Vietnam vets had to deal with."

Then Jennifer tells me about another peace protester she can't forget, a man in his forties or fifties. Her voice drops as she describes how, as he walked past her, he said, "I hope your husband dies."

After Beth turned away from the microphone and made her way through the speakers and tables back offstage, a reporter from the *New York Times* was waiting at the edge of the bandshell. "Could I take a couple minutes of your time?" the reporter asked.

Beth blinked and looked around. "Oh. Sure." As the speeches boomed on behind her, she began to talk, and now and then someone walking by would touch her on the arm, murmur, "Thank you for what you said," and continue on. A passing Vietnam-era veteran with a long gray ponytail pressed his palms together and bowed slightly in her direction. Beth spoke to reporters from local newspapers, and small magazines, and a pudgy man with a cell phone on his hip.

He shook Beth's hand and introduced himself. "I'm a producer with NBC." His crew had had some technical difficulties while she was speaking. He wanted her to come over to the camera and tell the rest of the country what she'd just said up there.

Beth frowned and hunched her shoulders. "You mean national TV?" Suddenly, she looked smaller. She glanced around for a familiar face. "Television. I don't know. I don't know if I should do that."

"What you had to say was very powerful," the producer said, cupping his hands in front of him as if offering a gift. "It's a great opportunity to get your message out there."

She hesitated. "I'm sorry, I'm just worried about my job. And my husband . . ." As the producer pressed on, she mumbled, "I have to think about it, I don't know." The other reporters exchanged glances. The producer said, "It's right over there, it won't take long." And then Lou Plummer, one of the rally's organizers, shouldered his way into the middle.

"Back off," he barked. A veteran of the National Guard, Lou looked more like a bouncer than a peace activist. "You don't have to live in this town, but she does. I live here, I know what it's like." As the producer argued with him, another newspaper reporter moved in and asked Beth another question.

From the *New York Times* on Sunday morning, March 21, 2004:

FROM MIDTOWN TO MADRID, TENS OF THOUSANDS PEACEFULLY PROTEST WAR
By Alan Feuer

Marking the one-year anniversary of the invasion of Iraq, crowds of sign-waving, slogan-chanting demonstrators marched through Midtown Manhattan and scores of cities . . .

At a park in Fayetteville, about five miles from Fort Bragg, where the Army's 82nd Airborne Division is based, some 700 demonstrators dotted a grassy slope under the pines.

"You can feel very isolated and alone," opposing the war in a military town, said Beth Pratt, whose husband drives a truck for the military in Iraq . . .

That same morning Beth's parents loaded up the car and headed back to Minnesota. Luigi was coming home in three weeks.

His voice crackled over the phone, "I wish I was there already so I could have heard you! I am so proud of you!"

Beth told the civilian psychologist she was seeing that she liked the feeling she got at the rally. She wanted to touch people's lives in a mean-ingful way. She asked, "I wonder what I can do? I wonder what I'm sup-posed to do with my life?" She wondered what people at the hospital were going to say.

They didn't say anything, at least not to Beth. She heard that one coworker said to another, "I hope her husband doesn't think he's going to stay in the Army." But that was all. Beth floated through the week, and then, while she was tidying up a delivery room, a phone call came in for her at the nurses' station.

She frowned. She never got calls at work unless it was Luigi, but no, they said it wasn't her husband. She went up the hall to the nurses' sta-tion and picked up the phone. "Hello?"

"Is this Beth Pratt?" asked an unfamiliar male voice.

"Yes."

"Is this Beth Pratt, RN?"

"Yes. Who is this?"

"This is Sergeant Brown. I just want to thank you for everything you're doing for the soldiers."

"What do you mean?" Beth asked, confused.

"The organizing you're doing for the soldiers," he said.

"I think you may have the wrong person. I'm not organizing any-thing."

"Didn't you help with the rally?"

"Oh, right. OK."

"Right," he said. "So which outfit is your husband with?"

She told him. Then she asked, "What unit are you with?"

He mumbled a unit number and something she couldn't hear. "What was that?" she asked.

And he said, very fast, "Military intelligence."

Her heart was suddenly loud in her ears. "I have to get back to work now." She hung up. The other nurses bustled around her, oblivious. She felt alone and scared, turning one way, then another, not sure which way to go at first. She escaped back to the delivery room she'd been tidying, closed the door, and burst into tears.

She got a friend to check the roster. There was no Sergeant Brown with that unit of military intelligence.

That night, Beth went to bed worried.

She woke up annoyed. She called Chuck Fager, the director of Quaker House, and Lou Plummer, the rally organizer who had told the TV producer to back off, but they didn't know what to make of it. A couple she'd met at the rally, the founders of Military Families Speak Out who were the parents of a deployed Marine, ran it past a military vet activist they knew. He e-mailed them back: *Trust no one!*

When Beth read that, she laughed. That night, the kitchen door of the beige duplex opened and a small rectangle of light spilled into the dark backyard. Danny trotted out, and then Beth, and when Danny raced away as if he were herding sheep, she marched after him into the darkness, alone and seemingly unafraid.

Up the highway, on the edge of Fort Bragg, Marissa hung up from another phone call with Monica.

Her emotions hadn't gotten away from her this time. She didn't even feel like crying now that she was off the phone. *Maybe,* she thought, *maybe I'm getting to the point that I could handle working with kids like me.*

It takes a four-year bachelor's degree to become a juvenile probation officer. Marissa's degree was a two-year associate's degree, so she drove over to Fayetteville Tech and registered for the fall. And the times when Charlie called home sounding angry and hollow and tired of being in the desert, she tried to hold him up. "You are providing security," she told him. "If we pulled out now a lot more people would die, it would be chaos. You guys are over there risking your lives and it's not for nothing." She poured herself across six thousand miles. "And I am proud of you."

In an e-mail, she wrote: *We've been together so long that we needed to be apart for a while. We needed a break from each other to appreciate each other and miss each other. And truly sit back and look at our lives and see what we have, because we were taking it for granted. A lot of things we took for granted.*

On the phone, Charlie said, "You've changed."

He meant she wasn't pissed off all the time anymore. But Marissa thought it was something more. "While he's been gone," she told Monica, "without him being in my face all the time, I think I've opened up my heart again to him." She thought about that. Then she said, "And now when he comes home, I know that I'll be able to really trust him."

When he came home, she was going to tell him everything.

Beth is in a car that's driving too fast down the road. The car spins out of control and she is thrown out. She goes flying through the air. Then she really is flying, smiling into the wind, banking past rows of houses. After a long while, she lands in a full baseball slide, arms out. She examines her wounds — forearms scraped up, a bone sticking out of her elbow, but nothing lethal.

Then the dream was over and she woke up.

PART III

COMING HOME

CHAPTER 15

Back to Green Ramp

I N THE SUMMER OF 2003, around the time when Charlie and Luigi were getting the word that they'd be deploying to Iraq, I was waiting for Frank to come home from there. *Bring the dog,* he wrote in his last letter. So I was gripping Rosie's leash in the same Camp Lejeune parking lot where earlier I, along with only a handful of other families, had said goodbye. Once again, it was midnight, but this time I was standing on the edge of a crowd of wives and children and aging parents, all of us listening for the deep rumble of diesel bus engines.

Finally, I heard it. Everyone heard it, every head turning, the sound growing louder and louder before the first bus emerged around the barracks: white glaring headlights, festive amber running lights, and a long row of lighted windows. From beneath a nearby tent, a DJ's speakers blasted "God Bless the USA" as the towering buses roared in one after the other. They pulled up in a line in front of us, stopped with a hiss, and a mass of men in desert camouflaged uniforms spilled out into the crowd.

The last time Frank deployed, he came home in the daylight. His Marine battalion had been among the first into Afghanistan after September 11. So a satellite television truck joined us in the hot, sunny parking lot where we families waited, beaming out to the rest of America close-ups of Marines hugging their girlfriends and wives and hoisting their toddlers. This is what people outside the military community see when the troops come home. Then the cameras switch off and to the outside world the homecoming appears to be over. In reality, the homecomings go on for months. In some ways, they go on for the rest of our lives.

The night Frank came home from Iraq, there I was, surrounded by a crowd of overjoyed people, just as I was when he came home from Afghanistan, and when he came home from the Persian Gulf before that. I felt the same joy this time, too. I also felt alone. Because while whole armies go to war, it's the individual war-fighter who comes home. In a few minutes, it would be just him and me, trying to muddle our way through the very personal consequences of our nation's huge impersonal policies.

As a chaplain, Frank briefs the sailors and Marines as they near home, preparing them for the stresses of homecoming. His advice: Have no expectations and put your spouse's needs first. If you both do that, you can avoid most of the disappointments and fights.

Easier said than done. The first time Frank left for a major deployment was the fall of 1999. He spent six months in the Persian Gulf aboard a ship packed with more than five hundred men and women. I celebrated Christmas and the new millennium without him. I discovered I liked the freedom to come and go as I pleased, eating when I felt like it, letting the dishes pile up in a sink full of water. It was like being single without the stress of dating. By the time that massive gray ship overshadowed the pier, sailors lining the rails, a brass band thumping, the tugboat in the harbor fountaining water, I had schooled myself to expect the worst: We might have grown into strangers, I might find I was happier when he was gone.

Instead, we had a two-month honeymoon. Our time apart had given us the breathing space we hadn't even known we'd needed, time enough to kick the bickery habits that can emaciate a relationship, time enough to remember why we loved each other. So I was looking forward to another honeymoon after his second long deployment, the one that took him to Afghanistan in the wake of September 11. After seven months, he came home in the spring of 2002. In the weeks that followed, people would wink and ask me how this second homecoming was going. They'd look surprised when I admitted, "A little rocky." Even that was an understatement.

Within days of his return, I was crying in the kitchen, reciting all the times he'd hurt me most in the nearly seventeen years we'd been married — not the most romantic exercise. He leaned against the counter, as far away from me as possible, shouting, "Well, maybe it's over! Maybe we should just call a lawyer!"

"Don't be stupid!" I shouted back. He's a chaplain, but that doesn't mean either of us is a saint. We had good days, but even they were booby-trapped — at any moment, a fiery rage could ignite us both. I remember thinking, *If we're having this much trouble, knowing what we know, married as long as we've been married, no children to add to the pressure, how on earth are those young couples with babies and money problems surviving?* We fought at home. We fought driving down the highway. I threw a Styrofoam cup in lieu of slugging him. He threw it back.

Fortunately, time is a wonderful healer. About nine months later, we were pretty much back to normal. Then he left again, this time for the Iraq War. Now, after four months in a war zone, he was flying home.

Back in Vietnam, when troops first began flying straight home from war zones, they discovered the abrupt change from machine guns to McDonald's could be destabilizing.

When Frank came home from Afghanistan, he came slowly, by ship. His deployment had been long but for him had included only one month in-country in Afghanistan, one experience of coming under fire with no casualties, and several months to decompress during the voyage home, albeit with a difficult roommate. "We didn't do anything," he said of that deployment. "They shot, we shot, we came home."

In Iraq, by contrast, I knew his battalion had lost two men in the battle of An Nasiriyah. I knew from his letters that he himself passed through there as the fighting continued the next day. In the aftermath of other firefights, he'd seen the dead and the dying. If Afghanistan left him so brittle, what must he be like now that he'd been through something so much worse? As his homecoming drew near, I tried not to have any expectations. But still, I was expecting the worst. I was expecting to welcome home a stranger. I thought in some ways he might be as unrecognizable to me as the men in a photo he sent home from his last deployment: a band of brothers lined up in two rows in front of a tent, a typical wartime keepsake photo in every way but one — they all had the same freakish black insect heads. They were all wearing gas masks.

At midnight, the buses rounded the barracks, and the wives and girlfriends screamed and pointed, and a mother from Ohio held a welcome home sign high over her head. And the mass of men in desert tan uniforms stepped off and the crowd enfolded them.

Every time my husband came home, I thought I knew what to expect. Every time, I was wrong. Near the end of any deployment, the excitement and relief that the one you love is almost home leads to high expectations, whether you're aware of them or not. After the emotional crucible of a wartime deployment, the expectations tend to be even higher. Same for the fear — fear of the unknown, fear that you may no longer be loved, fear that the violence of war may have wounded the one you love in ways not visible to the eye. And for those already in an unhappy or abusive relationship, the unknown is not what they fear.

My handbook for Marine Corps spouses labels this emotional phase "Anticipation of Homecoming" and predicts that in addition to all the feelings listed above, we spouses will "start changing patterns back to the way they were before your Marine left."

Six months into the deployment, Charlie Bootes and the rest of his unit began to make their way back to Kuwait to prepare themselves and their vehicles and equipment for the long trip home. A month later, Luigi Pratt's unit followed. They were part of the largest redeployment of troops back home to Fort Bragg since World War II. As the convoys moved south, Beth feared the loss of love. Marissa feared the invisible wounds.

She'd been on the phone with Charlie when artillery had thumped on the other side of the trees, on Fort Bragg. The windows gave a tinny shiver. Charlie could hear it over the phone, and Marissa said half jokingly, "I'm afraid you're going to come home and hear that and jump up and put on your Kevlar."

Charlie didn't say anything. Marissa didn't expect him to. She already knew he didn't talk about his own invisible wounds, wounds like her own, the ones she had decided she was ready to show him.

And then there was the time right after Marissa left the law firm, when she was telling Charlie about the root canal she had to have, which cost two hundred dollars. She said, "I've never had to pay a dentist so much in my life!"

"Well, you're not paying for it," Charlie grumbled. "You don't have a job."

Marissa hung up. She stared at the phone in surprise. She'd never done that before.

A few minutes later, it rang again. "Don't hang up on me!" Charlie yelled. "Do you know how many freaking numbers I have to dial to call you every time?"

"Then don't yell at me like it's my fault!" she yelled back.

The next time he called, he asked about some of the other bills.

Marissa went down to the Quick Pack and Ship, where she used to go every weekend to overnight big packages of legal documents, and asked about a job. Not because of Charlie, but because she could see for herself they couldn't live on what he made, and also because she was bored.

Marissa thrived on pressure — the more she had to do the more she got done — which meant that these days she was getting nothing done and even the house had gone all to hell. The job paid only $6.50 an hour, but it was part-time and she could get time off whenever she needed it. The woman who ran the place was married to an active-duty soldier, too. She understood that when Charlie came home, the Pack and Ship wouldn't be seeing much of Marissa Bootes for a while.

The phone rang, Charlie calling from Kuwait. Again, he questioned her about the bills, as if after six months all of a sudden he no longer trusted her. He used to say things like, "Whatever you do is fine with me," or "I know it's rough on you." Now he would say, "*You're* not getting shot at!" And Marissa would fire back, "How dare you?"

But she continued to frown after she said it, because Charlie wasn't like that. He had never cared about money, even when they were dirt poor, living in a trailer and hardly able to buy milk. And here he was yelling about money? It didn't make sense.

"What's going on, Charlie?" she finally demanded. "Because degrading me and putting me down is not going to make you feel better. Tell me what's really wrong, because I know I'm doing a damn good job. Others are cheating, they're becoming alcoholics, and I'm not doing that, I'm taking care of Lexie, I'm paying the bills. So what is going on?"

The other end of the line was silent.

"Charlie?"

When he spoke again, she could tell from the smallness of his voice that he was crying. "Your lives are going on and I'm stuck over here. I just want to get out of this place so bad. Home is all I ever think about anymore."

And Marissa realized that with his face finally turning toward home at last, he was reaching back across the miles, trying to reinsert himself back into her world. Once upon a time, it seemed like forever ago now, paying the bills was *his* job.

Marissa hurried out the door of the Quick Pack and Ship. With the redeployment home getting close, she had put together a reunion briefing for the twenty wives in her FRG who lived in town, calling them and sending announcement e-mails. She stopped off to pick up food for a spread, then hurried on post for the briefing.

The battalion FRG leader arrived, an experienced Army spouse who had been through homecomings before. A representative from the rear detachment was on tap to answer practical where-and-when questions.

The chaplain came to address relationship issues. And two women from an Army Community Services program called Operation Ready brought along a slide show on how to have a successful reunion, which would back up their talk on the importance of realistic expectations and good communication.

Not a single wife showed up for the briefing. Marissa and the speakers enjoyed the food and went home. She was philosophical about it. As much as she felt the wives would have been better off if they'd been there, she figured some of them were just too busy. Some, with their soldier about to come home, were rushing around trying to finish all the projects they had planned to get done while he was gone. Others had been through so much and had had so little control over anything during the deployment that, at this point, they didn't want to be told what to do or how they were going to feel about anything. Their soldier was coming home and they wanted to deal with *this* at least on their own terms.

Those who attend reunion briefings, both service members and their spouses, receive advice and warnings like this from Navy chaplains Bryan Weaver and Richard Saul, quoted in a handbook for Marine spouses:

I. Thou shalt expect your homecoming to be stressful.
. . . Both of us are idealizing our return and reunion. Out of our hardships and separation come our dreams. On one hand, we dream about our houses, home-cooked meals, hobbies, driving our cars or trucks, spending time with our children, and intimacy. On the other hand, our wives may be dreaming about help around the house, time away from the kids, support and encouragement and spending quality time together . . .

II. Thou shalt enjoy being an invited guest in your own home.
. . . Please try to remember that personal growth has probably taken place and things are not the same. When you first return, allow the family to continue functioning as they have for the past six months . . .

III. Thou shalt not criticize your spouse upon your return.
. . . She needs your encouragement, praise, and thanks . . . She is the glue that has held the family together . . .

IV. Thou shalt change.
Change in life is inevitable . . . When you see changes, remember Commandments I through III.

V. Thou shalt spend quality time with your children.
Children equate love with time spent with them. Period.

VI. Thou shalt not treat your wife like a one-night stand.
. . . Kindness and respect go a long way toward kindling the spark of romance . . .

VII. Thou shalt compromise your social activities for the first few weeks.
. . . Resist the urge to pack the first couple of weeks after a reunion with a full social calendar that leaves both of you exhausted . . .

VIII. Thou shalt watch your finances.
The best liberty port is where your family resides, making it tempting to go out and celebrate with spending sprees . . .

IX. Thou shalt confess to a chaplain and not to a spouse.
While honesty is always the best policy, timing and discretion are essential . . . If something is weighing heavy on your heart or mind, see a chaplain, civilian clergy, or a counselor.

X. Thou shalt give your time, talents, and treasures to your family.
Often during deployments, many households have separate accounts to manage the finances during the long months of separation . . . make a conscientious effort to integrate available funds toward the needs of the household . . .

On the subject of homecoming day itself, the handbook also provides perky answers to such burning questions as "Should I cook or should we eat out?" Answer: "Eating out is easier; but if you cook try to make it something that can easily be reheated, because standing at the stove for an hour isn't very romantic. (Unless you're naked!)"

The Sunday before Easter, I knocked at the beige duplex, smiling and dressed for church, but when Beth opened the door, I dropped the smile. She was wearing her cell phone headset and her eyes were red from crying. She gave me a thin-lipped smile through her tears and waved me in. Luigi was on the phone from Kuwait, telling her his return date had been delayed again.

In the military, nothing's certain until it happens. Delays are common. Two days, a week — to some people this is no big deal. For others, with expectations so high, the constantly shifting target is unbearable. As Beth dressed for church, she asked me, "Was it like this when your husband came back?"

"When he came back by plane?" I said, "Oh, yeah. Every time he gave me a date I was like, yeah, yeah, whatever, I'll believe it when you get here. Hell, Beth, I didn't let myself believe he was really coming back, much less that he would come back on a particular *day*."

She considered that. "I respect women who can do this," she said at last. "I'm just not cut out for it. I don't like the separation. I don't like all this not knowing."

At the church, when Beth went up for communion, she stopped at the Lenten cross and like a few others, got down on her knees. She knelt there for a long time, her head bowed.

Driving home, she said darkly, "I don't feel like I'm married. I don't care if I see him again. Did you ever feel like you didn't want to be married anymore?"

"All the time," I said, and we both laughed.

The laughter faded and she drove on in silence.

She was afraid. One year ago yesterday, she and Luigi had said their vows to each other on a Florida beach. Since then, they had spent most of their first year apart. She was looking ahead to when he came home, and she was afraid she would still feel the way she felt in this moment, and maybe he would feel this way, too.

She went home, changed into a set of old scrubs, put Sarah McLachlan on the CD player, and stripped the peeling wallpaper off the bathroom walls. Then she painted them pale blue.

Not long before, on a steeply wooded street nearby, another Fort Bragg wife got a call telling her that her husband was coming home early. The ringing phone interrupted *American Idol*. Teresa Metzdorf pulled herself away from the escape of other people's off-key dreams and disappointments, reached across the bed, and picked up the receiver. "Hello?"

"Hey, baby," said a voice that sounded vaguely like her husband with a mouth full of cotton.

"Hey," she said. "What's wrong with you?"

"I lost my leg," said the voice. And then the phone went dead.

Teresa's husband, Staff Sergeant Daniel Metzdorf, was a paratrooper, an airborne infantryman who had spent six months in Egypt and then eight months in Afghanistan. Half a year after getting back from Afghanistan, he left for Iraq. He'd been there ten days.

Teresa stared at the dead phone, thinking, *Someone needs to call me!* The petty concerns of wannabe pop stars were muted and forgotten. As if her thoughts had power, the phone rang again. It was a nurse in Baghdad. "How do I get to him?" Teresa demanded.

She had to make more calls, to Fort Bragg, to her family, to her mother-in-law, her breath coming short and fast. She felt the bedroom narrowing. Oh God, she prayed, please let me not pass out. Her family had lived in Fayetteville for six generations; her mother lived only a few blocks away. By the time her mother got to her, Teresa was sitting on the floor next to the couch, trying to take slow, deep breaths, trying to keep from passing out.

Daniel and his squad had been patrolling the main supply route between Kuwait and Baghdad when they spotted a pile of trash that looked suspicious. They got out to check — it was definitely suspicious. The Humvees were armored, they were safe, or at least safer than being on foot, and Daniel ordered everyone to get in. They turned back toward the Humvees. And whoever was watching them hit the remote control and the pile of trash blew up.

The explosion killed three men instantly. It riddled another man with shrapnel, left him bloody and unrecognizable and screaming, "My face, my face!" It hurled Daniel fifty feet. He lay in the road, blood oozing from shrapnel wounds in his upper left arm and pooling around his right leg. He could feel the spreading wetness beneath his leg, but he didn't look, didn't want to see that most of his leg was gone between the shin and the thigh, probably taken out by the old artillery shell used to make the improvised explosive device that had been hidden beneath that suspicious pile of trash. So he didn't look as he lay there on his back, just set aside his weapon and concentrated on taking off his Kevlar vest and his uniform blouse while the blood spread out farther and farther from his leg. Then another soldier was kneeling over him, a friend who tied off his thigh with a tourniquet and saved his life.

The squad rushed to load him up with the others. When they ran out of room in the Humvees, they carried the soldier who'd been hit in the face with shrapnel on the hood all the way back to the fire base. Daniel was medevaced to Baghdad. He lost so much blood so fast there wasn't enough on hand to replace it all. The doctors and nurses rolled up their sleeves and hurried to transfuse him with enough of their own blood to keep him alive as they amputated his leg above the knee. The next day, he was placed in the belly of a plane filled with other wounded men and women, strapped into litters and stacked in rows, on their way to the Army's medical center in Landstuhl, Germany. From there, he would be flown to Walter Reed Army Medical Center in Washington, D.C. "You can meet him at Walter Reed," Teresa was told. She headed for the airport.

By then, it had been four days since the phone had rung. Four days of nothing but waiting and not knowing — the worst part of deployment, the thing she hated most: the not knowing, now magnified till not knowing was all she could think about. It was one of the reasons why she always volunteered to be a key caller for her FRG during a deployment. The key callers got the information first, they got the scoop.

Teresa was tall and leggy, and with her infectious smile and long red hair she looked like the girl next door. But she was actually a forty-year-old woman. She dealt with trouble, like these deployments she hated, by taking charge of anything that could be taken charge of. In the first ten days of this deployment, before the phone rang, she had already redecorated the whole house, made plans to take a cruise with her mother and her best friend, and started assembling her weekly care packages for Daniel. But in the four days since that call, there wasn't enough spending money in the world to distract her from her inability to take charge of what was happening to her husband now. During those days, her mother tried to get her to eat while she wondered who was with Daniel, who was holding his hand. She pictured him alone and in pain, and she cried.

Now Teresa was standing in the security line at the airport in Fayetteville, on the cell phone with Daniel in Germany, who was telling her he was about to be placed aboard a plane, too. He started to sound short of breath. He hung up. Soon, a nurse called Teresa back to explain that Daniel had just suffered a pulmonary embolism, a blood clot shutting down the flow of blood to his lungs, which could kill him. Suddenly, Daniel was too sick to put on a plane. But Teresa, still standing there in the Fayetteville airport, was told to go on to Washington and wait for him there.

As her plane was taking off, a florist's delivery van stopped in front of her house. When it pulled away, a big colorful bouquet of tulips sat by the front door. They were for Teresa, from her husband, on the occasion of their third wedding anniversary. He'd ordered them four days earlier, only hours before the explosion.

The first time Teresa met Daniel Metzdorf, she thought he was a little stuck up. He was six-foot-two and movie-star handsome, like Ben Affleck. What she really liked about him was the way he made her laugh. He'd grown up with eight brothers, could give as good as he got, and his big, buoyant personality could lighten up everyone within range of his voice. The first time they met, he told her he'd call. *Yeah, right,* she said to herself, *classic blow off.* A day later, her phone rang. He'd been making her laugh ever since.

Eight miles north of the White House, in a dense, rough-and-tumble neighborhood of northwest Washington, behind high fences and armed guards, stand the red brick and concrete buildings of Walter Reed Army Medical Center. After the war began in Iraq, a whole new prosthetics department was established here. The facilities for physical and occupational therapy doubled in size, additional civilian contract workers were hired, and reservists called up. Three times a week, the flights from Germany brought in a steady stream of patients. Within two years, by early 2005, the medical staff had treated around four thousand men and women fresh from the wars in Iraq and Afghanistan.

Only a quarter of those patients were suffering from what could be called war wounds, the kind inflicted by hostile action and honored with Purple Hearts. In all wars, the majority of the casualties are the result of illnesses and accidents, not hostile action, such as the Marine on the frontlines who's taken out by the flu, or the soldier on the supply line who's run over by a forklift.

By the time the staff at Walter Reed wheeled in the one-thousandth patient wounded in action, more than 11,000 Americans had been wounded by hostile action in Iraq. In Vietnam, 25 percent of the wounded had died of their injuries. In Iraq and Afghanistan, only 10 percent of the wounded were dying. That was partly because their body armor was now tougher — the Kevlar helmets and vests with those ceramic plates did a better job of protecting their vital organs.

But in addition, the latest high-tech medicine made it possible to save more of the wounded. Every infantryman in Iraq carried tourniquets and special bandages designed to quickly clot blood, which saved the wounded from bleeding to death in the first minutes. Portable mini-hospitals were positioned close to the action, so that within a few more minutes the less seriously wounded could start getting patched up, eventually going back to their units, while those with major injuries could be in the hands of a surgeon, who would stabilize them just enough to fly them on to the next step. Within twenty-four hours, they could be in fully equipped American military hospitals in Landstuhl, Germany, or Rota, Spain. Within a few days, they could be back in the United States.

Most of those who'd been burned went to Brooke Army Medical Center in Texas, which specialized in treating burn injuries. Others whose faces had been torn up went to the Air Force's Wilford Hall Medical Center, which was also in Texas and specialized in facial reconstruction. Marines and sailors usually went to the National Naval Medical Center in Bethesda, Maryland, just outside of Washington, D.C. But more than half of all the evacuated wounded went to Walter Reed Army Medical Center, most of them soldiers, but some of them Marines, because Walter

Reed, with its specialized orthopedics department, was where most of the amputees went.

Teresa Metzdorf flew to Washington to wait at Walter Reed. She waited for two days. When she finally saw her husband, lying on a hospital bed in the x-ray department, she couldn't really *see* her husband. An oxygen mask covered half his face. His buoyancy was gone, pinned down by pain. He mumbled, his voice muffled and pinched by the mask, "Don't touch the bed, it hurts so bad." That's all he would say. "Don't touch the bed . . . It hurts so bad . . ."

When she finally saw what was left of his right thigh, she couldn't really see a thigh. She saw a Christmas turkey swaddled in Saran Wrap, a ten-inch stump swollen to twice its normal size and rigged with pumps to draw off the accumulating fluid.

Blast wounds are messy. Explosions can shake and damage the brain, rupture eardrums, pierce eyes, shatter bones, break backs, mangle arms and legs, and, when a rocket-propelled grenade is involved, char skin and flesh. The propulsive force of an explosion drives the bombs' metal scrap into the body. It also drives in bits of the garbage the bomb was hidden under, bone splinters from the guy standing next to you, fabric and buttons from your own uniform, as well as gravel, dirt, and most especially, bacteria. *Acinetobacter baumannii,* to be exact, a species of bacteria that thrives in the soil of Iraq. It's not much danger to healthy people, but if you're wounded, it can kill living tissue; it can cause pneumonia, high fever, or blood and wound infections; it can eventually leave you dead. Get hit with a blast wound, and survival depends on staying ahead of the infection that constantly seeks to race from the wound through the rest of the body.

To prevent that from happening, Daniel Metzdorf was on massive doses of antibiotics. The raw, hypersensitive wound at the end of his thigh would be left open and unsutured for the first two or three weeks so it could be regularly "debrided," the dead flesh and foreign debris washed out and away, which is such a painful process that he was knocked out each time. The dressing was changed three times a day. Even so, overnight, a small pimple on the back of his hand ballooned into an infection so severe the hand had to be surgically split open on both sides to relieve the pressure.

Daniel was wheeled away to surgery twelve times in twenty days. He had a morphine button he could push as often as every eight minutes. And every eight minutes, he pushed it. Days, as he drifted in his own timeless world, Teresa stayed by his bed in the intermediate intensive care unit. At night, she told the staff, "Whenever he wakes up and wants to see me, call me."

Then she'd make her way back to Mologne House, the medical center's 285-room hotel with a lobby of soaring pillars and rooms like a very nice Holiday Inn. It was built in the late nineties for visiting DoD personnel and service members and their families, active duty or retired, on official business or just a family vacation in the nation's capital; they paid about half what they would have at a similar hotel anywhere else in D.C. During the Iraq War, however, there was no room at the inn for mere vacationers. Mologne House was completely booked up with wounded outpatients and the families of wounded inpatients.

Alone in her room, Teresa would fall into bed and sleep hard . . . until the phone shrilled next to her head. Daniel was awake and asking for her. She'd run a brush through her hair, pull on her coat, and crunch through the bright, snowy night back to the ICU, her breath puffing white.

Her take-charge self was back. She tapped out daily e-mail updates for a hundred worried friends and relatives. Whenever Daniel needed something, she spoke up. She spoke up for the fiancée of the soldier who'd been riddled with shrapnel in the same blast and was now just down the hall. His fiancée had no official standing, so Teresa organized things for her. The nurses encouraged Teresa to help with Daniel's care, too — for most family members, pitching in is better than being a helpless bystander. So she helped him drink his meals, a liquid diet of Ensure that just couldn't keep up with all the calories his body needed to heal; fifty pounds melted off his frame. She helped change his bandages. She didn't think about the flat place in the bed where his leg should be. She was too busy hoping he wasn't going to die.

After twelve days, Daniel stabilized and was transferred to Ward 57. Officially, it's the orthopedics ward. But everyone calls it the amputee ward.

Teresa followed Daniel's bed as the orderly rolled it through the corridors, which are laid out in a big H around the nurses' station. Visit Ward 57 when there's a war on, and you'll see the same types of patients Teresa did. The muscled man wearing shorts and a fierce expression, leaning on a cane and walking like a toddler, one leg hairy, the other smooth and plastic. The pretty young woman humming past in an electric wheelchair and a gray T-shirt that said ARMY, one leg smooth and plastic and the other simply missing. Through an open door, a friendly young man sitting up in an easy chair, one leg caged in an external fixator, a network of metal rings and rods that disappeared into his skin to hold the crumbled bones inside in place.

Teresa tried not to stare. The news reports always rattled off so many killed and wounded, but they never said what *kind* of wounds. She realized she'd been picturing neat little bullet-hole wounds, like in the movies, not body-parts-blown-off wounds. As she walked those corridors, she felt as if her eyes were opening for the first time and all she could see were missing hands, missing arms, missing legs. She wondered, *Why doesn't the world know about this?*

The body armor and the medical advances mean more people are surviving with major injuries. A small number are paralyzed, usually after being shot. Most injuries these days, though, are caused by blasts, not gunshots — nearly 90 percent of the wounded at Walter Reed were there with blast wounds, most commonly multiple shrapnel wounds. Many also had crippling head injuries. Two percent had lost limbs, or part of one. This was double the rate of the Vietnam War, because back then, if your legs were blown off, you usually ended up dead, not wounded.

Now, more amputees were surviving. And once you're an amputee, or married to an amputee, you're in the amputee club. You form a bond. You treat each other's losses like badges of honor. You stare at each other in physical therapy. Your husband, who's sitting at a row of machines hand-cranking a wheel, may have lost a leg; you may be used to seeing his jagged scar line, the one that looks like a smiling whale. But across the large, open, brightly lit room, that guy over there, the one hooked up to an IV and lifting weights, has lost an arm and it looks completely different. You compare wounds. You ask each other, "If you could choose, would you rather lose an arm or a leg?"

Daniel never had to think about it. "An arm."

"But you need your hands for everything," Teresa would protest.

And Daniel would say, "But you have to walk everywhere."

Legs are how you carry yourself out into the world. Legs are how you stand tall. Without legs, you feel as if you have no power.

"I'm only half a man," Daniel had mumbled to his father on the phone while he was still in Germany. "What's Teresa going to think?"

"Who is this?" his father had scolded. "Whoever this is, you hang up the phone, and when Daniel comes back, you tell him to call me. I didn't raise a son to think like that."

At Walter Reed, Teresa had a front-row seat on depression. She watched tired young wives, girls really, as they in turn watched their mangled young husbands now and then stare off into space like men who had traded one endless desert for another. Those young wives were going to have to trudge that desert with them, and they knew it, and often with small children hanging onto them the whole way, weighing them down. Some marriages didn't survive the trek; some were limping along for other reasons before it even began.

An Army psychiatrist tells the story of the husband coming back with a serious head injury, the consultation liaison team meeting with him and his wife in his hospital room, talking with them as a couple, and they're nodding. And then, out in the hallway, she grabs the psychiatrist and whispers, "Doc, I was thinking of leaving him when he came home. What do I do now?"

From her front-row seat, Teresa herself watched five wives leave their soldiers there on Ward 57.

Teresa was lucky and she knew it. She was starting out with a marriage that was on solid ground. She had no small children who needed her — her kids were grown — so she could focus all her energy on Daniel. And in the long run, Daniel proved to be genetically incapable of depression. He found himself in a desert, he couldn't help searching the wavering horizon for an oasis. After that phone call with his father, after he arrived on the amputee ward, he seemed to right himself. He named his stump "Junior," as in, "Junior's feeling pretty good today." He gave the credit to Teresa. "You coming every morning with a smile on your face," he said, "makeup and hair done."

But Teresa knew she was able to be upbeat like that only because he wasn't bringing her down. She'd hear some of the other wives and girl-friends say, "Oh, I *got* to get back to my job." When Teresa left Fayette-ville, she, too, had left behind a full-time job, as a graphic designer and operations manager at a printing company. For the time being, however, Daniel was her full-time job. But this new job didn't come with a pay-check, just a stipend from the Pentagon, and their income dropped. Even so, whenever she saw other women heading back home after only a short visit, saying they had a job to get back to, she knew most of the time it wasn't really the money — it was the sight of the desert ahead. If it hadn't been for Daniel floating himself above that inner wasteland and pulling her up with him, she couldn't say for sure she wouldn't have done the same.

Meanwhile, Daniel was rogering up for cheer-up duty on the ward, rolling around in his wheelchair making everybody else feel better. He mimicked the politicians who regularly showed up on Ward 57 looking for intact hands to shake. He laughed at all the celebrities eager to visit the wounded, even as he laughed with them: the entire New England Patriots football team, a Miss America, the country singer Clint Black, Dale Earnhardt, Jr., and David Letterman. With Jon Stewart, he traded dueling one-liners.

Daniel wasn't the only one. His friend who'd survived being riddled with shrapnel, who now had a metal plate in place of a cheekbone, watched all the celebrities making a beeline for the guys and gals in the wheelchairs and quipped, "Man, everybody wants to be an amputee these days." At a weekly dinner for the wounded, the wife of one amputee asked another amputee, "Is that your leg over there?" They both burst out laughing, and then the amputee allowed as how the lonely prosthesis leaning against a nearby wall was indeed his leg, and as they discussed the pros and cons of its design, they paid no attention to the television crew that moved slowly among the dining tables, the camera staring from the videographer's shoulder, the light mounted on top sweeping across the wounded and their families like a spotlight on a stage.

While depression usually descended quickly on the quadriplegics and paraplegics, the close bonds among the amputees, plus all the media attention, tended to keep depression at bay for a while. Teresa looked around Ward 57, took a deep breath, and told herself, *OK, other people are dealing with this. We can deal with this, too.*

Still, sometimes when Teresa was alone, anger would overtake her. "Why did it have to happen to Daniel?" she'd rage to herself, to her mother, to her best friend. "Why? Why? Why?" She couldn't understand why they had all been sent over there. And then her anger would wear itself out and let her go and she'd be left alone with sorrow. "We had the perfect life," she'd weep. Close enough to perfect, anyway. And now things would never be the same. She wished everyone in America could walk the halls of Ward 57.

She wept, too, on the other side of the Potomac River as she walked behind a caisson clip-clopping through Arlington's white headstones, feeling guilty. Inside the casket on that caisson was one of the soldiers who'd been killed by the same roadside bomb that blew off Daniel's leg. What was a leg compared to a life? What right did she have to grieve over a lost *leg?*

In the ICU at Walter Reed, Major Teresa Duquette-Frame knew exactly what Teresa Metzdorf was going through. The major's husband was a soldier, too. He'd been shot in Iraq, lost the use of his hand, and hadn't had a pain-free day since. Major Duquette-Frame, blond and athletic, had deployed five times herself and was now a senior staff nurse in the busy ICU. Surrounded by the hissing, humming, and beeping of modern medicine and the bustling conversations of teams of specialists in lab coats and scrubs, she had come to believe that, medically, the injuries could be dealt with. It was the psychological part that took more time to get a handle on, both for the wounded and their families, because like the families of the dead, the families of the wounded go through the same classic stages of grief: denial, anger, bargaining, depression, and finally acceptance.

From the psychiatry department, Colonel Stephen Cozza dispatched consultation liaison teams of psychiatrists, psychologists, and social workers to all the new patients' bedsides as soon as they were admitted. The liaison teams didn't wait to be called in for a consult, which might leave injured service members feeling as if something were "wrong" with them. Instead, right from the start, the liaison teams served as part of the hospital trauma team, helping all the wounded in their journey back from an injury. The liaison teams would also treat any immediate problems, such as depression, then help the patients and their families look ahead to the possibility that they may have been psychologically wounded by combat exposure as well, in ways they couldn't yet see. The team would describe the warning signs to watch for once they got home, assure them that the team would follow up in the months to come.

In the meantime, on Ward 57, head nurse Lieutenant Colonel Regina Tellitocci would notice the circles under one wife's eyes, see another step out of a room to pace the corridor and wipe away tears. She'd hear a woman's voice flash with anger. Usually by then, they'd already put in a couple weeks as the wife, the mother, the go-between, the go-fer, the go-get-'em cheerleader, the decision-maker, the rock, and it was starting to wear them down. Lieutenant Colonel Tellitocci was a hummingbird in BDUs and combat boots, nipping in close to say, firmly, cheerfully, "You gotta take care of yourself to take care of your service member." She'd give them permission: "Sleep in tomorrow," she'd say. "Go down to the National Mall between the Capitol and the Lincoln Memorial and walk on the grass, get some fresh air."

The nurses who saw the families every day made sure they knew the bus schedules, the location of the commissary, the places they could stay. At Mologne House, when the staff saw a wife at the front desk looking lost, they steered her toward Army Emergency Relief, the Walter Reed Society, the American Red Cross, the United Service Organizations (more commonly known as the USO), and the hospital's new Medical Family Assistance Center, or MedFAC. MedFAC was created as the wounded began to stream back from Iraq and bewildered family members began to stream in from around the country.

In MedFAC's outer office, several soldiers and civilian staffers sat at desks taking calls and flipping through paperwork while family members steadily trickled in the door: young wives in tight jeans, a mother in loose-fitting comfort clothes, someone's stocky brother who clutched a folder and shifted as if his suit and tie were an itchy skin he'd like to shed. They settled into couches draped with quilts and afghans, or swirled in and out the door and then back in again. Among them came a tall, distinguished-looking man in a long black overcoat. Mike Wagner, a retired colonel from the Army Reserve medical service corps and the director of MedFAC, had a fatherly, Germanic face and a patient voice.

Mike would tell his staff, "We are servants." He and his staff would serve these waiting family members, arranging everything from taxis to massages. They gave the families anything they needed from the tons of donations that poured into the American Red Cross station at Walter Reed, rooms piled high with teetering stacks of clothing, boom boxes, handmade American flag quilts, toiletries, toys, snack foods, suitcases, and files overflowing with prepaid phone cards.

But most of all, the MedFAC staff gave them time. When a wife came into Mike's office and burst into tears because she had been living for months in a hotel room at Mologne House with two small children and a husband who lost a leg in Iraq and was now an outpatient, Mike listened, and nodded, and felt weary, and also blessed. Sometimes he would go up to ICU, to the bedside of a chaplain whose head had been caved in by a roadside bomb, who now lay silent and still, hooked up to machines that gurgled and breathed. Mike would talk to this chaplain and trust that he listened the way God did.

Later Mike tells me that he believes everyone comes back wounded. "The wounds of the soul run deeper than the physical wounds," he says. "And we generally only focus on treating the individual, but the families need treatment, as well. They're casualties, too." He sighs. "They pay an awfully high price." After a year of caring for families at Walter Reed, he wants to see more holistic treatment that extends beyond individuals to the family and outward to the whole community, at all levels — medical, psychological, spiritual, and ceremonial. "When a soldier gets wounded," he says, "the family gets wounded. Their community gets wounded. The nation gets wounded."

Daniel Metzdorf still had two legs. One was solid enough to see and touch. The other one wasn't — but though hands passed right through it, Daniel could feel exactly where it was, as if his brain had outlined it with a dotted line.

As Daniel recovered on Ward 57, Teresa asked him, "So where's your leg at today?"

He winced painfully. "Pointing straight up in the air."

The pain of a major injury such as a severed limb puts the whole body on high alert, making it ultrasensitive to any additional pain. This ultrasensitivity, called "windup," is a natural response that helps the body protect itself from further injury. At the same time, when nerves are severed, they send a tidal wave of signals to the brain, which starts remaking its map of the body. The theory is that windup gets mixed into the map-making process, and chronic pain from a limb that no longer exists gets hardwired into the brain.

To reduce the phantom pain in his phantom leg, Daniel was taking an epilepsy drug, one of many drugs he was on. Blood-thinning drugs helped prevent any more potentially fatal clots — a hazard when you break a thighbone. Just in case a clot did go gunning for his lungs again, a filter was inserted into his chest. And the antibiotics, always the antibiotics. Some of the drugs he was on bloated him till he looked six months' pregnant.

He graduated from the wheelchair to crutches.

"When you were lying there in the road," Teresa asked in a tender moment, "did you think about me?" She heard about that sort of thing all the time, guys calling for their sweethearts as their lives flashed before their eyes.

"Hell, no," Daniel laughed, "that shit hurt!" All he could think about was the pain.

Teresa went with him to physical therapy. Lying in bed had quickly drained away his strength, strength he was going to need to haul around the dead weight of a metal and plastic leg. She went with him to occupational therapy, where he wobbled on his one leg while he bent over to pick up trays from the floor, then straightened, getting the feel for his new center of gravity, then bent over to do it again. Get-well cards poured in. Teresa taped them to the wall of the hospital room, 137 and counting. The guys would call from Iraq. Five women from Teresa's FRG came all the way up from Fort Bragg and brought Daniel gift mugs, candy, an afghan, and a red thong Speedo because the guys had called them from Iraq, too, and somehow convinced them he needed it for physical therapy. Teresa found the nearest Target store and bought him T-shirts that said things like I DO ALL MY OWN STUNTS and QUIT STARING OR I MIGHT DO A TRICK.

He graduated from the crutches to a prosthesis and a cane.

"Where's your leg now?" Teresa asked.

"It's getting shorter," he said. "The foot's right about here —" and he held his hand in the empty space next to his left knee, the visible one.

After four to six weeks on Ward 57, most amputees are discharged to continue rehabilitation as outpatients. In the big occupational therapy room, the sign over one door reads FORT INDEPENDENCE. The door opens to reveal a model apartment where the newly disabled relearn how to get out of bed, how to go to the bathroom, how to button a shirt and launder it. In the model kitchen, two therapists work with a slight kid barely out of his teens, his face speckled with reddish marks that should be from acne but are more likely the result of shrapnel. He's struggling to crack an egg. By the time he's done, bits of eggshell float in the bowl and yolk smears both his hand and his new hook. Embarrassment and brain damage dance him around the kitchen, gasping and goofy with laughter.

It may take a few months, it may take a year, but eventually this boy will leave here and get on with the rest of his life. "Some are still trying to find out what it is they want to do," says Colonel William Doukas, chairman of the Department of Orthopedics and Rehabilitation. Better prosthetics have made it possible for more amputees to remain on active duty, and the military appears to have had no trouble finding jobs for those who do, especially as it struggles to fill its ranks during a war and an improving economy. "But only a few return to their duty station," says Colonel Doukas. "Most take medical retirement and go home."

The colonel is an orthopedic surgeon who parachuted into Panama with a Ranger battalion during the 1989 invasion. He's cut from the same cloth as his patients, who are used to doing jobs that require exceptional physical abilities.

Once they're disabled, however, they have to find a less physical way to make a living. A man who has always been happiest when he's in motion may not find much satisfaction in a more sedentary job. For his wife, it can be hard to live with a person who's frustrated and unhappy, and she may not have the coping skills necessary to deal with it. She may not have the job skills necessary to support them both, either, even with his disability benefits.

At the same time, this is when depression over the injury may begin to emerge, along with symptoms of combat trauma. Colonel Cozza, chief of psychiatry at Walter Reed, has noted that the rates of depression and post-traumatic stress disorder do go up after discharge, which is why his consultation liaison teams follow up for three to six months or longer.

Meanwhile, severely disabled soldiers and their families receive personal, ongoing support from the Army's Disabled Soldier Support System, or DS3. And those who require long-term nursing care are transferred to a VA facility.

However, reservists and members of the National Guard who are not severely disabled get shuffled into a second-tier system. In the early days of the Iraq War, that system was overwhelmed. Hundreds of sick and injured soldiers returned to Fort Stewart, Georgia, where they waited on "medical hold" while Army personnel decided whether they were disabled and, if so, what benefits they should receive. They waited in hot, dark, cinder-block barracks with no air conditioning and no bathrooms — the squalid latrine was in a separate building. They waited weeks, sometimes months for proper medical treatment; there were similar wait-times at other posts where returning reservists and Guard members languished on medical hold. Many were then told that problems that had surfaced while on deployment were nevertheless pre-existing conditions from before their military service. Then they were discharged.

Efforts were made to improve the situation. But a year and a half later, the Government Accountability Office sampled the records of nearly nine hundred Army reservists and Guard members and found that a third were still having trouble getting medical care. Either they weren't receiving appropriate care, or they were on waiting lists for months, sometimes until their orders expired, at which point they were no longer on active duty and therefore no longer eligible to receive medical care. During the months it took them to get back into the system, they received no pay or benefits, and some of their families couldn't pay the bills.

Veterans who need treatment and counseling in the years to come may not fare much better. The Veterans Administration is currently underfunded by billions of dollars.

Seven months after Teresa Metzdorf flew to Washington to welcome home her husband, she brought him all the way home to Fayetteville.

Some things were the same — they were still best friends. Other things had changed — they were closer now than ever before. There were also new accelerator pedals on the left side of the brake pedals in their car and their pickup. They had traded chores, Teresa hauling the garbage can up to the top of the driveway each week while Daniel folded the laundry. She didn't jump on his back anymore and go for piggyback rides. He dressed more slowly than he used to. And every six months, he now had to go in for an HIV test, because the hurried transfusions that had saved his life in Baghdad had, of necessity, come from untested blood donors.

They both went back to work. Teresa's boss had held her job for her. And Daniel was still in the Army, the first above-the-knee amputee to be allowed to reenlist in the 82nd Airborne. For the time being, he was a career counselor, convincing other soldiers to reenlist, too. He traveled around speaking to civic groups. Now more than ever, he could make everyone within reach of his voice feel a little less weighed down. He told Teresa he felt as if his life had a purpose it didn't have before, like he was making a difference. They went skiing together, and when he flew past her on the slope, she shouted after him, laughing, "I hate you so bad!" They were planning a tandem parachute jump. He had never been a self-conscious person and he still wasn't. He wore shorts everywhere. It didn't seem to bother him when people stared.

It bothered Teresa though. She wished he could just wear a shirt emblazoned with the story of what had happened so strangers could stare at his leg, stare at his shirt, satisfy their curiosity, and be done with it. She'd see them staring and she'd think, *He's such a handsome man and they're looking at his* leg.

And though Daniel no longer needed the cane, it was still a challenge to walk with the prosthetic leg strapped onto Junior. An amputated limb changes shape quite a bit the first year and the prosthesis has to be constantly adapted to fit. Daniel would come home from Bragg and take off his leg, because by the end of the day Junior was pretty sore. He'd swing around the house on crutches, which was quick and easy and took the pressure off Junior, but also made it impossible to do something as simple as carry a coffee cup.

The Jacuzzi bubbled in the darkened room off the master bedroom. In the moonlit shadows was a bookshelf filled with souvenir ballcaps, gifts from the athletes and celebrities who had visited Ward 57 while Daniel was there. On the wall hung framed photo ops of those celebrity visits, and some of the get-well cards, and a letter from the president congratulating Daniel for completing the New York City Marathon on a handcrank bike nine months after he lost his leg.

Teresa sat next to Daniel in the bubbling water, his arm around her shoulders. Beyond the wall of windows, the moon's reflection sparkled in the spillway that rushed down the wooded slope below.

"Do you still have phantom-limb pain?" she asked. He was off all the drugs now.

"Yeah," he admitted.

At Christmastime, when they were laughing and putting up the tree together, Teresa had said, "Can you imagine me doing this by myself?" It was a thought that ticked regularly through her mind, like a way to mark time — how close she had come to The Worst That Could Happen, to a life without Daniel to make her laugh. Now she looked down at the bubbles, at the space occupied by his phantom leg. "Do you think about it much?"

He answered her quietly, "Every second of my life."

Back in April, when Teresa Metzdorf was still up at Walter Reed watching her husband learn to walk again, the rear detachment had contacted Marissa Bootes with the official word: After seven months, *her* husband's unit was finally heading home.

They were coming on flights spread out over several days. Marissa got on the phone and began passing the word: "Hi, this is Marissa Bootes with the FRG and I'm calling to let you know your husband will be arriving Tuesday morning, around ten." She rushed Charlie's car to the garage to get some work done on it that he'd asked her to take care of while he was gone. She took her FRG notebook with her, talking on her headset the whole way over there: "Hi, this is Marissa Bootes and I'm calling to let you know your husband will be arriving on Tuesday around seven P.M. . . ." She lit a cigarette as she drove. "Your husband will be arriving Wednesday morning sometime after four . . ." She caught a ride with me and I took her to work. "Wednesday around three in the afternoon . . ." At work her cell phone rang. "Yeah, Wednesday at eight P.M. . . ."

Reunions are stressful for children, too. Mostly it's good stress, but it's still stress. Sometimes they expect everything to be exactly like it was before, which is why Marissa talked everything through with Lexie ahead of time, explaining that it might take some time for everyone to get used to each other again. And since special preparations can help kids get ready and make the upcoming reunion seem more real, Marissa bought poster-board. Tiffany, her fellow Hooah Wife of tube sock fame, came over with a Tupperware container of markers, glitter, and glue. I came with the camera.

Tiffany and Marissa discussed the best way to spray paint "Happy Birthday and Welcome Home" on a sheet and hang it on the front porch. Together, they helped Lexie decorate a poster with "Welcome Home Daddy!" Marissa sketched out the words. Lexie smeared glue on each letter.

"Good job, kiddo," Marissa said, only half her mind on what she was saying and doing. "I'm nervous," she admitted to me, standing back with a cigarette.

Tiffany sat at the table holding out a palmful of glitter. Lexie sprinkled pinches of it across the glue.

"It's been so long," Marissa said. "We've changed." She took a long, thoughtful drag.

Lexie spotted Charlie first.

Back at the house, Marissa and Lexie and Charlie's mother had been on their way out the door when Lexie said, "Wait!" and charged back to her room, ponytail swinging.

"Hurry!" Marissa yelled after her. They were running late for Green Ramp because Marissa had been coordinating soldiers' families all day, and the day before. And meanwhile, Charlie had been kneeling in a row of soldiers in the Kuwaiti desert, hands behind his back, mouth open, another soldier walking down the row dropping a sleeping pill on each tongue. He'd been climbing the steps up into the plane and then surfing down the aisle on a food tray because he was going home at last and on his twenty-third birthday. He'd been dropping into sleep as the plane took off for the long flight home.

Lexie had charged back into the living room clutching her binoculars.

Now, on the edge of a crowd of cheering families outside at Green Ramp, Lexie pointed at one soldier in the rows of soldiers wearing identical tan-colored DCUs and maroon berets as they marched across the open tarmac from the plane. "There's my Daddy!" she shouted.

Charlie and the rest of the soldiers marched into the building, ruck-sacks on their backs, M-16s hanging muzzle-down from their shoulders, and the wave of families carried Lexie, Marissa, and her mother-in-law in after them. Inside, the soldiers stood in formation while the band played, and officers made speeches. If you just glanced at the soldiers, their faces all looked the same, serious and professional and fixed straight ahead. But if you looked closely, you saw a mouth pursed against a grin, you saw a lip trembling, you saw a pair of eyes sliding to the side — Charlie, trying to look at his family without turning his head.

Inside Marissa, it felt as if something was winding tighter and tighter. Then the soldiers shouted, "Hoo-*ah!*" and broke formation and Charlie rushed over and grabbed up Lexie in one arm, the other around Marissa. The hug felt kind of stiff, as if he was holding back, and it hit Marissa: *He's as scared as I am.* And so they remained, awkward and unsure, until Charlie's mother put her arms around them all, a family sandwich. And then Marissa never wanted to let go.

In that cinder block building on the edge of the tarmac, Lexie was perched in the crook of Charlie's arm, sitting sidesaddle on the M-16 slung across his body, and she was asking, "Can I take my daddy home to play now?"

That same day, in a tent in Kuwait, Luigi was dialing a phone, and when Beth answered, he gave her another return date. The next day her key caller Camilla confirmed it: Luigi would be home Saturday, the day before Easter. Beth danced around the duplex. She gave Danny a bath. She hung a new blue shower curtain in her newly blue-painted bathroom.

It was early April, the beginning of what would soon be, for the Americans, the bloodiest month of fighting in Iraq since the beginning of the war. On the way to work, during a break in the music on the car radio, Beth heard a report: With the sudden increase in fighting, some of the soldiers who were supposed to redeploy home were going to have their tours extended. Then someone at the hospital said they'd heard that as many as half the soldiers of the 82nd who were still over there were going to be held back. "If that's true," Beth said with a feverish laugh, "I really am going to go crazy, I will flip out, I'll have to check myself in."

Friday morning, Camilla called. Luigi's flight had been canceled.

Beth tried to understand why things were the way they were. She didn't believe life was random. She'd gotten over being mad at God because in the end, she concluded, God was all she had. Her husband couldn't be there for her. Her friends were far away and couldn't be there for her. It was just her and God.

That night Camilla called again. Luigi's flight was back on.

Beth quit trying to understand anything. She went to the mall and bought new underwear, a matching set in periwinkle blue.

The next day, Beth and I stood next to the military band inside the building at Green Ramp. The soldier musicians were playing the Austin Powers theme, and in the middle they all lowered their instruments to shout, "Groovy, baby!" in unison before rocking on to the grand finale. Beth bounced to the music, happier than I'd ever seen her. The plane carrying Luigi had just landed. In a few minutes, his unit would march in through the big sunbright doorway across from where we were standing.

We'd been waiting for a couple of hours. I was surprised when she asked me to come with her. Whenever Frank came back, I always wanted it to be just him and me. "You're sure you don't want to be alone?" I asked, but she looked at me as if I were crazy. "OK, OK," I laughed, "I'll be there." We came over to Green Ramp early and of course the plane was late. We waited on the stacked-up bleachers inside the shed, killing time. I asked her, "When you look back over this deployment, would you say it was a good experience or a bad one?"

She thought about that a while. Then she said, "Good."

"Really? With everything you've been through?"

"Well, if it wasn't for the deployment I wouldn't have met you or Camilla or the people at Quaker House," she said. It also forced her to think about war, in a way that watching from the sidelines never had. "You know," she said, "when you first asked me if I was changing, I didn't think so. Now I think I've changed a lot. One month ago even, I still didn't consider myself a pacifist."

"You do now?"

She nodded. "War is so destructive," she said. "Both sides are convinced they're right. I was always against this war, but I still used to think sometimes war could be a good thing. I don't think so now."

A few nights ago, she was surfing the Internet. She surfed to Doctors Without Borders, an international medical charity that serves people without access to medical care, primarily in the Third World. She thought it might be the significant work she'd been looking for since speaking at the peace rally. "They have a six-month commitment," she said. "Whenever it is that Luigi deploys to Afghanistan, I'm thinking I might go overseas, too."

In the end, she would go no farther than downtown to join the occasional peace vigil. What she wanted was a family with Luigi. She knew it was going to be hard enough to make that happen without her being gone, too.

Now Beth bobbed her head to the rhythm of the band. And on this day, the same scene played out at Green Ramp that has played out here for decades. The band plays. The phalanx of soldiers marches into the hangar in desert camouflage, rucksacks on, black automatic rifles slung from their shoulders. An officer makes a speech. Then the soldiers are dismissed and the families rush forward and neat rows of desert tan dissolve into the crowd of blue jeans and miniskirts and strollers with babies. When Frank came home, I couldn't find him in the stream of dusty uniforms. But Beth spots her husband immediately. She runs to him. He wraps her in his arms. She touches his face, his ears, the back of his neck, his arms, his face again, as if she cannot believe he is real. And then she kisses him, her arms around his neck, her hands dangling, lost in him.

I turn away, so I can cry.

The War at Home

L EXIE WOULDN'T LEAVE Charlie's side until she finally fell asleep that night.

Later, Marissa lay beside him in bed. Outside in the darkness, the firing range boomed. She had expected Charlie to be jumpy, but he lay quietly. In many ways, it was as if he'd never left.

He said, "Artillery sounds louder. Are they closer than they used to be?"

Marissa shook her head on the pillow. "I don't think so."

"Are they going to do that all night?"

She laughed. "Yeah."

"When the mortars fell on us at night, we'd just roll out of our racks, put on our Kevlar, and go back to sleep."

The darkness boomed.

"Artillery," he said, "sounds different than mortars."

From that handbook for Marine spouses, on the typical reactions of spouses during the phase after their Marine comes home:

Renegotiation of the Marriage Contract

a) May feel a loss of independence
b) Start being a "married" spouse again
c) Share roles, responsibilities, and decisions
d) A feeling of too much togetherness
e) Hesitation towards intimate relations
f) Falling in love again!

*   *   *

Generally, the first week or two that a unit is home, its members report for duty each day and work a light schedule. It gives them some stability and lets them ease back into home life. Then they get anywhere from two to four weeks of leave.

That first week, Marissa decided to wait to talk with Charlie about her childhood till they went on leave and things quieted down. Charlie left for the post early every morning, and at the end of each day, he had taken over picking up Lexie from daycare. Even if he hadn't, Lexie's daycare teacher Marie Michele Johnson could have guessed he was home. Lexie had seemed lighter after Marissa quit her job with the lawyers. *Now with her daddy home too,* Marie Michele said to herself, *that little girl is like a balloon.*

When Luigi got home each evening, he and Beth would walk with Danny, then curl up on the couch together. Despite having e-mailed and talked on the phone during the months they were apart, Beth still felt she had so much to say she didn't know where to start. A week later, they headed south to Florida to spend a week with Luigi's family and their friends, while Charlie and Marissa and Lexie headed the other way, driving north to Erie. On the way there and back, as the miles rolled by beneath their wheels, Charlie and Marissa talked about Iraq. They talked about the law firm. They talked about the future. They fantasized about what they'd do if they ever won the lottery.

They hadn't done that since Charlie went in the Army. It had been as if learning to make war was so caustic it had stripped him of his imagination. But the reality of war itself seemed to have nurtured it back into existence, and as the miles rolled by, he and Marissa created an alternative universe together, one in which they won the lottery and moved to New Orleans, where they lived in an old plantation mansion and opened a club of their own, a spectacular club down in the French Quarter with a five-star restaurant, three levels, and a soaring lobby with one-way glass floors so you could see down but not up.

Beth and Luigi flew north to Minnesota, where most of Beth's family finally met Luigi for the first time, and now Marissa and Charlie went south. They took Lexie down to Florida, first to Disney World and then Daytona Beach, where they lay on the white sand and ran with her down into the crashing waves. Marissa had dreamed of a family time like this when she was Lexie's age. Those years whispered through her mind, but she couldn't mention them out loud, not with Lexie around. And once she was asleep and Marissa was finally alone with Charlie, that sadness was the last thing she wanted to bring up.

*　　*　　*

Back in Fayetteville, life returned to the way it had been before the deployment, or almost the way it had been. Whenever Beth and Luigi were together, they were usually touching, a hand on an arm, an instep against an ankle. Riding in the car with Luigi at night, heading down to Wilmington after work for a weekend of surfing, Beth noticed that he drove more slowly than he used to, that he crowded the center line, that whenever an overpass loomed in the headlights, eerie and overexposed in the darkness, he would duck as he drove under.

She asked him about it. Luigi hadn't been fully aware of what he was doing, but when Beth pointed it out, he admitted that in Iraq he had gotten in the habit of driving down the middle of the road to avoid improvised explosive devices, what everyone over there called IEDs, hidden on the roadside. And he drove slowly to give himself enough time to avoid any scattered bits of trash in the road, which could also be concealing IEDs. The ducking? Attacks sometimes came from overpasses.

As they got in the car, now and then he'd joke and tell her she had to look out, because in Iraq that was always the job of the person in the passenger seat, to be the look out, and he'd laugh as he said it. But once, she overheard him talking on the phone with another soldier. "Sometimes," she heard him say, "when I'm driving and I see something in the road that looks like an IED, I have flashbacks. I feel it all over again."

Late one evening, Beth was at the computer, Luigi across the room asleep in bed. Suddenly, he sat up and started talking. She couldn't quite make out what he was saying, just that it had something to do with the Army. He seemed worried, his voice urgent and ragged. "What are you talking about?" she asked, before she realized he wasn't talking to her. She leaned toward him — he was talking to his Army buddies, dreaming, eyes open. Then he lay down again and closed his eyes. In the morning she asked about it, but he didn't remember anything. He said, "Wake me up if it happens again."

It did happen again, and Beth tried to wake him, but he wouldn't come out of it. From then on, whenever he sat up and talked in that anxious voice, she let him alone.

She woke him from a nap. Still in the fog of a dream, he asked wearily, "Do I have to go back to the hangar now?"

Immediately following a traumatic event, it's perfectly normal to experience aftereffects like uncontrollable shaking or, later, nightmares. That's the body's natural way of processing stress and releasing it. Some people, though, experience so much stress they're psychologically injured by it, and that causes a severe reaction; many of them will need professional help to heal. The difference between "normal" and "severe" lies in how long the reaction goes on and how intense it is. For instance, it's normal to be jumpy for days or even weeks after returning from combat — after all, the heightened responsiveness can protect you on the battlefield. But if the jumpiness is pronounced and goes on for months, that's a severe reaction, and the service member may need help.

Some people fill up with stress faster than others, depending on their personality type and what they've been through in life. People who fill up faster are more likely to suffer psychological injury and a severe reaction. People who are exposed to combat for long periods of time without a break are also more likely to suffer. During World War I, the British discovered that frequent breaks of a few days just behind the frontlines were more helpful than long, infrequent breaks far away from the fighting. During World War II, the intense fighting endured by the Marines in the Pacific for months on end produced just as many psychologically wounded casualties as physically wounded casualties.

As Marines and soldiers began returning from Iraq and Afghanistan in 2003, among those who had been in more than five firefights, nearly 20 percent reported symptoms of major depression, anxiety, and post-traumatic stress disorder, according to a report in the *New England Journal of Medicine.* That's compared to just over 9 percent after one or two firefights, and 4.5 percent among those who experienced no firefights, about the same as the general population. Among Vietnam veterans, close to a third were wounded psychologically, and experts suspect that eventually the toll may be similar for today's combat vets, since there are always some who take longer to realize or admit they're injured.

Technology is also to blame for the suffering. Armies used to need daylight to stage a battle. As a result, soldiers had time to sit around the campfire at night, compare stories, try to make sense of what had happened to them that day. But with the technological advances of the last hundred years, war has become an industrialized, twenty-four-hour-a-day business. There is no built-in downtime for what is now called "Critical Incident Stress Debriefing" — and even with chaplains and a growing number of psychologists making the rounds of the frontlines drawing out those who need to talk, it's not always possible to find the time.

So, sometimes the stress of combat exposure gets tucked away. It festers. Eventually, it may boil over into headaches, nausea, guilt, depression, nightmares, memory problems, emotional outbursts. Or it may manifest itself in something as small as an increased startle reflex. In the

First World War, they called it "shell shock," in the Second, "battle fatigue." Now it goes by the less poetic name of "combat trauma." Not
everybody suffers from it, and some experience just a mild case. Others
may experience a variety of short- and long-term mental disorders, from
depression and substance abuse to other anxiety and adjustment disorders. The more extreme and prolonged cases are classified as post-traumatic stress disorder, also known as PTSD. Simple PTSD sufferers are
unable to turn off the hyperalert survival skills they learned in combat;
they're constantly mobilized for danger. Same for complex PTSD sufferers, who've also been robbed of their ability to trust anyone, even those
who love them.

Of the thousands of casualties medevaced from Iraq and Afghanistan
to Walter Reed Army Medical Center, about one in ten were psychiatric casualties — because sometimes trouble rears up before the fighting
stops. Sometimes it takes a couple of months to surface.

And sometimes it takes years. In 1994, officials at the Veterans of
Foreign Wars noticed a sharp increase in the number of World War II
veterans claiming to suffer from PTSD. It was no coincidence — 1994 was
the fiftieth anniversary of D-Day. The ceremonies and media coverage
brought back the nightmares those men thought they'd left behind half a
century before. Suddenly, they were flailing at their elderly wives in their
sleep and hiding guns under the bed. There are even indications that
combat veterans who suffer from dementia later in life may be more
likely to behave violently as their deteriorating brains unleash old memories, more so than people who were never exposed to war. And while the
majority of combat veterans live normal, productive lives, a significant
minority have been linked to higher incidences of drug and alcohol
abuse, domestic violence, depression, and unemployment.

You don't have to kill anyone to suffer from combat stress. War ex-
poses you to extreme fear, uncertainty, exhaustion, noise, and horrific
sights, over and over again. When Frank's unit moved through An
Nasiriyah during the last stages of the fighting there, the Marines in the
convoy rolled past the dead, including one body in the middle of the
road that had been driven over so many times the only thing left of it was
a mushy lump leading to a pair of feet. Some of the men, like Frank, dealt
with such sights by silently analyzing them: That's a rib, those must be
the intestines. They kept it at arm's length. Others took it right in and
were shaken by it. "I'll never be able to watch war movies the same way
again," one officer admitted grimly. That particular body made such an
impression that long after the Marines returned home, if you mentioned

Pancake Man, everyone in the unit knew exactly what you were talking about.

Fighting in Iraq usually meant fighting in places like An Nasiriyah, or in Fallujah, Mosul, or Baghdad — in other words, in urban areas. Twenty-five hundred years ago, the Chinese military theorist Sun Tzu wrote, "The worst policy is to attack cities," and most modern-day military commanders would agree with him. But by 2010, that's where three out of every four people in the world will probably live. It's also the only battlefield where America's outgunned enemies can hope to avoid being wiped out. So going to war is more and more likely to mean going to war in cities, especially Third World cities.

This is unfortunate, because cities — where paramilitaries can hide among the civilian population and needle a conventional army with frustrating hit-and-run ambushes — are uniquely suited to screw up the people who must fight in them. The National Vietnam Veterans Readjustment Study found that a good way to bring on PTSD is to put war-fighters in a situation where they have no control and nothing has any meaning. Urban warfare tends to bog down and drag on, making it easy to lose sight of who you're fighting and why. It lacks a clear frontline, increasing the chance that you'll accidentally kill your friends instead of your enemies, which adds to the sense of meaninglessness.

According to the study, a slightly better way to bring on PTSD is to expose war-fighters to frequent combat. The intensity of urban warfare does just that, with attacks that can come from anyone, anywhere, at any time. Whether you're on a spooky, bombed-out street or in a seemingly friendly crowd in a marketplace, your body is constantly flooded with adrenaline, you never feel safe, increasing the likelihood you'll burn out. Across Iraq, attacks sometimes topped one hundred a day.

Even more effective: deprive war-fighters of sleep, water, food, ammunition, the chance to get clean or warm or cool or away from insects, snakes, or rats. The intensity of urban warfare uses up supplies at a much faster rate than other forms of warfare, straining supply lines and leading to shortages of everything.

The best way of all to bring on PTSD is to expose war-fighters to abusive violence. Since urban warfare produces higher casualties, you're forced to watch more and more of your buddies suffer and die at the hands of an elusive enemy you rarely see, tempting you to give in to frustration and rage and possibly engage in abusive violence.

That temptation can be held in check by a strong sense of ethical purpose, capable leadership, and strict rules of engagement. Yet a 1997 Marine Corps assessment points out that in urban warfare "Even clear rules of engagement . . . are sometimes difficult to enforce, especially in the face of mounting losses among the security forces." You listen to your buddies scream in agony, you career from fight to fight without a chance to grieve properly, and you may start to misuse or modify your equipment to make it more lethal. You may stop worrying about civilian casualties and just blast away. But if you do, there's a price to be paid.

An Army manual for combat stress control warns, "Seeing and perhaps accidentally inflicting casualties on civilians (especially if they are women and children) increases battle fatigue, especially if the civilians are perceived as friendly." In that case, the soldier is essentially blameless yet still suffers. Imagine then how much greater the cost to the soul if the violence is inflicted deliberately, in a rage.

Even if you're like most and don't intend to hurt war's innocent bystanders, when you fight a battle on a heavily populated battlefield, the sheer numbers of bystanders make it hard to avoid them all, especially if you use the weapons that are most effective in an urban environment: machine guns, artillery, and cluster bombs. And no matter how many precautions you take, "Noncombatants cannot be counted upon to behave sensibly," as the Marine Corps assessment put it. Which may be true, but may not make you feel much better when, faced with a split-second decision, you blow away that vanload of women and children whose driver inexplicably ignored your warning shots and raced toward your checkpoint.

This, then, is the nature of the fighting in Iraq and in all the other morally messy, asymmetrical conflicts into which we are sending more and more American men and women, from Iraq to Afghanistan to the Philippines. In addition, there's the more general issue of killing, which is integral to any kind of warfare. Normal human beings have a natural resistance to killing, but modern U.S. military training uses sophisticated conditioning techniques to overcome that resistance. Even without their superior weaponry, trained American troops would still be the most effective, most lethal fighting force in the world. And yet, any sort of killing in combat can take a toll, though it varies. Pilots and artillerymen, who sometimes kill large numbers at long range, rarely express regret, while an infantryman who kills one person at close range may well be traumatized.

If you tinker with a human being's natural programming you have to expect there will be consequences, not just for the warrior and the warrior's family, but for the larger society as well. Lieutenant Colonel (Retired) Dave Grossman, a psychologist and former Army Ranger, writes in his groundbreaking book, *On Killing*, ". . . the American soldier in Vietnam was first psychologically enabled to kill to a far greater degree than any other soldier in history, then denied the psychologically essential purification ritual that exists in every warrior society, and finally condemned and accused by his own society. . . ."

Today's warriors may not be getting all the help they need, either, to cope with what their nation asks of them. Within the first two years of the Iraq War, tens of thousands of combat veterans had already applied for disability benefits, both for physical and psychological wounds. A few had begun to trickle into homeless shelters. More were dying in high-speed car crashes that seemed like a death wish. The suicide rate among Marines reached its highest level in five years — still lower than the rate among their civilian peers, but in wartime, military suicides usually go down. The actual numbers were small, but the trends were ominous.

At the same time, the military had already begun to change policies that had added to the suffering of Vietnam veterans, and hired experts like Lieutenant Colonel Grossman to help. The best way to prevent combat trauma and psychological injury is to prevent war. But when war becomes necessary, the next best way to prevent crippling psychological injury is through unit cohesion, leadership, and training. Create cohesive units of buddies who stick together throughout their deployment; who are led with integrity by capable, trustworthy leaders; and who receive training in ethics to equip them with the moral toughness necessary to handle the life-and-death challenges of war. The military services have come a long way but still have a way to go. When it comes to killing, even Army paperwork betrays a certain squeamishness. The questionnaire Charlie Bootes and Luigi Pratt filled out before returning home asked if they saw anyone wounded, killed, or dead; if they engaged in direct combat in which they discharged their weapon; or if they ever felt they were in danger of being killed — but it did not ask if they themselves killed anyone.

What does all this mean to the individual soldier? While Luigi was in Iraq, he never fired a shot, except in training. Though he experienced more attacks than he could count, whenever a firefight erupted, his job as the driver was to keep his hands on the wheel and his foot on the gas. Yet he was in the same constantly hyperalert state as everyone else, and his job transporting supplies and soldiers sometimes required him to pick up dead soldiers as well. It would be nearly a year before he let himself open up about that to Beth — about the National Guard unit, for instance, blown apart by a roadside bomb, the horror and sorrow of picking up what was left of their bodies, seeing and smelling up close what explosions do to human bodies, then driving them back to the base.

Charlie experienced many attacks as well, and found himself in situations that required him to fire his weapon, though as far as he knew he never hit anything.

Based on the frequency of the firefights both of them went through, both are at increased risk for long-term depression, anxiety, or PTSD. But so far, both men seem to be among the estimated 80 to 85 percent who, in the short term at least, appear to be coming through the wars in Southwest Asia changed, certainly, but with their mental and emotional health mostly intact.

Just like before, Charlie and Marissa snuggled with Lexie in front of the big TV, all three of them together on the couch as if there had been no interlude of war. Marissa went back to making sit-down dinners. Charlie took back his old job of washing the dishes, just like before.

But he suggested Marissa continue handling the bills. "You got it under control," he said, "and I'm just going to be gone again soon." Lexie would be sitting at the table and Charlie would pass behind her and his hand would rest briefly on her head.

Marissa was in the bedroom when she heard the vacuum start roaring out in the living room. She peered around the corner and saw something she'd rarely seen before: Charlie, running the vacuum around the house, unasked. She stood there watching him and marveled, *Who is this man?* He wasn't the same Charlie she'd fallen in love with all those years ago in eleventh-grade history. He was older, but he was also looser, and graver, like a person with nothing to prove. Like a man. He wasn't a boy anymore. She was falling in love with him all over again.

They went to a marriage enrichment class on post where they were asked to rate their marriage before and after the deployment on a scale of one to ten. Marissa gave it a four before, and after — a ten. Charlie gave it a nine because he figured there was always room for improvement, and Marissa thought he had a point.

Starla Smith, the wife of the commander of one of the other brigades, says, "I think they need to have *re*-reintegration briefs about four months after they get home," just to reinforce the information the couples were probably too distracted to hear when they were preparing for the homecoming. The marriage class may have served that purpose for Marissa and Charlie.

They went to Family Day at Charlie's unit, Marissa tagging along while Lexie went to work with Charlie, a little girl in pastel play clothes with her battle-dressed father, sitting in a Humvee, in a missile launcher, standing close beside his legs while the company stood in formation.

They invited the Hooah Wives over for a barbecue. While they were getting ready, Charlie stood to one side of the dining room as Marissa struggled to pull open the table leaves by herself. He watched for a moment, a small smile playing across his mouth, before he finally asked, "You want some help with that?"

Marissa straightened, looked at the table, looked at him, and laughed. "I keep forgetting I don't have to do it all by myself anymore!"

Cars began to park up and down the street, women carrying in platters of deviled eggs and salad and brownies, some alone, some trailing children, and some husbands, too. Three of the husbands leaned against the kitchen counters close to the cold beer, talking military shop. Out on the deck, Charlie manned the grill, spatula in one hand, cigarette in the other, a couple of the wives who were smokers keeping him company. In the living room, Marissa rolled an animated movie on the big TV and the couches filled up with kids and a couple of the adults.

Angela, the Hooah Wives comanager, was one of the last to arrive. Reggie had gotten back from Afghanistan five months before. She had listened to the other girls — "gells" was how she said it in her British accent — whose husbands were back, listened to them talk about how much more independent they were now. Angela didn't feel that way at all. She was glad to hand the decision-making back over to Reggie. Before he came into her life, she'd been a single mum for years, and she didn't miss it. It felt good to be held again, to feel safe.

The day Reggie came home, ten-year-old Chanelle had run straight to him. Regan hung back, a bit shy, sneaking glances. But he was just three, and that was normal for little ones. Eventually Reggie asked, "Could I have a cuddle?" and Regan grinned and ran to his dad.

Now Angela was five months' pregnant with a homecoming baby and she was alone again with Chanelle and Regan. Reggie was out on a two-month training mission. Angela took a seat in the circle around the TV. But whenever Reggie was gone, she'd always found it hard to sit through gatherings if the other hubbies, as she called them, were there. Around the corner in the kitchen, the men's voices rumbled. Through the sliding glass door, Charlie wielded the spatula in a cloud of hamburger smoke. Angela hurried back out the front door in tears.

One of the other Hooah Wives followed her. "It's OK," Angela quavered, blowing her nose. "I'm just having a moment. I just miss him."

When they went back inside, Tiffany was showing off her new look, her hair short and sleek. She'd gone to the beauty parlor for a haircut, and on impulse told her hairdresser to cut it all off, all her long curls, gone. "What does Andre think?" someone asked. "Oh, he *likes* it," Tiffany giggled. "He says it's like being with another *woman!*"

Andre wasn't there that day, but he was home. He'd been home for a number of months. Before that he'd been in Afghanistan with his special forces unit. It was his second homecoming from a wartime deployment to Afghanistan, and this one had been better than the first one. But then, it couldn't have been much worse.

That first time he had called her when he got as far as Germany. "Baby," he said, "I'm on my way home."

He'd been gone five months. Tiffany was so excited that she filled the ruffly living room of their shotgun rental with balloons. She sprinkled rose petals from the front door to the bedroom and hung welcome home banners. She baked quiches, dipped strawberries in chocolate, lit candles, and put a magnum of Dom Perignon on ice. She expected fireworks. She expected sex out of this world. She pictured herself running into his arms at Green Ramp with her welcome home sign and the music playing and people cheering. Neither one of them had received much if anything in the way of a reunion briefing.

The next time she heard from Andre he said, "Come pick me up, I'm at Fayetteville Regional Airport." Tiffany hadn't realized special forces often came and went like that, no warning, no fanfare, flying on commercial airlines.

Her two younger boys were with her ex, so it was just her and her oldest, Gabriel, rushing to the airport that night. She had gotten her hair done, makeup to the nines; she had on leather pants and a little leather blazer, her stiletto heels on. She was ready for him. But when she got there, she didn't know where to go, couldn't find him anywhere, till finally, down in baggage claim, she turned around and there he was, walking toward her in jeans and a shirt like anybody else.

"*Baby!*" she cried, and ran up to him screaming, "*Aaaaaaaah!*"

And he said, "Glad to see you, you look great, but, baby, not now, I got some missing equipment I got to take care of." He picked Gabriel up, though, and gave him a great big hug. Tiffany wanted to hug that man, too, she wanted to hold him, and all he could say was, "Baby, not now." He was an NCO; taking care of his men and their equipment was his job. He hurried off to deal with the equipment.

Tiffany and Gabriel waited three hours. Things improved once she got Andre in the car, where he finally gave her her own great big hug and a kiss. And when he walked in the door of the house and saw everything she had done for him, he was awestruck. "Oh my God," he said. That first night was *great*. Until she woke up and found him asleep on the floor. The bed was too soft, he explained, he could not sleep in the bed.

Within a few months, he called her a whore and she found herself on the ground in front of their house with his hands around her neck.

The first recorded case of PTSD was described by Homer. Odysseus came home from the Trojan War and went on a murderous rampage. Some months before Tiffany's husband attacked her, those three other Fort Bragg wives were attacked and killed by husbands just back from Afghanistan.

Most warriors who come home suffering from combat exposure don't display such dramatic symptoms. Some simply withdraw. "The service members may not even be aware that they're withdrawing," says psychiatrist Colonel Stephen Cozza. "And the spouses may not recognize that it's the result of combat exposure. So they think it's them and take it personally."

In general, chaplains and social workers report that after a deployment, most couples pick up where they left off, good or bad . . . except now with the added stresses that come with any deployment. The first marriages of combat veterans are 62 percent more likely to fail than the first marriages of civilians, according to a study coauthored by William Ruger, a Liberty Fund fellow and Cato Institute research fellow. If the service member or spouse has found the deployment particularly stressful, whether due to their experiences or their personality type, even strong, stable, long-term relationships can take a hit.

When Andre left for Afghanistan, his relationship with Tiffany was brand new and vulnerable.

They had met not long after September 11. Tiffany was twenty-five and bartending, working to get over a long and unhappy relationship. She'd left her three boys with her mother in the Carolina sand hills, country so rural it made Fayetteville look like the big city. Andre walked in, heard her let out a laugh as generous as her body, found out she was Catholic, too, probably the only Catholic girl in there, and it was all over.

Eight months after they moved in together, it was Tiffany who bought a diamond ring for Andre, who was seven years older, and asked him to marry her. They were married in the summer of 2002. Five days later, he left for Afghanistan.

For three months, Tiffany barely got out of bed. Her mother moved in to take care of the boys, and she would plead, "Tiff, get out of bed." Tiffany would say, "Mommy, I don't want to get out of bed. If I sleep, I don't see the time and the days will go by quicker and he'll be home quicker."

Another Army wife finally talked her into going camping. Soon after that, she was online reading about a bombing in Afghanistan. She saw something about the wives and how they were coping with it. That was how she found the online group that eventually became the Hooah Wives. She spent the rest of that deployment with them, sharing cigarettes and long conversations at their houses or at Broadstreet's on Nickel Night. She could get wasted for thirty cents. "Hey," she'd say, "we're *military* wives! We like a good *deal!*" She made new male friends, too. She'd always had male friends before she met Andre, and her new best buddy was a single soldier named Cisco.

Some nights, Tiffany got wasted, plastered drunk, and this was one of those nights. Cisco stopped Tiffany's car in front of the shotgun rental. She and Cisco had spent hours talking about old school rap, old school R&B, life, and Andre — especially how worried she was about Andre. Cisco got her out of the passenger seat and across the yard. At the door, he said, "Look, Tiffany, I'm just going to kick you inside the house and after that, you want to roll to the couch, you on your own." He unlocked the door and gave her a little push. "I'm going to throw the keys in behind you and lock the door handle and I'll be gone."

"You're my best buddy, Cisco," Tiffany said.

"Good night, Tiffany."

"Good night," she said, and then the door closed and she was alone.

Going out with the Hooah Wives, or with Cisco and other friends, took her mind off Andre when she wasn't talking about him. She dropped onto the couch. She wasn't just afraid for his safety; she was afraid for *him*. He'd call home talking about the Afghani children he saw, how hard they had it. "Looking at them," he'd say to Tiffany, "all I see are our boys." Once, after a shell exploded, he saw a wounded child and he felt like he was looking at Gabriel. He picked up the child and tried to get medical help for him. "And, Tiff," he said, "it wasn't allowed, they turned that child away." He got quiet. "I just want to be with my family. Oh, baby, I just want to come home."

Tiffany didn't know what to do besides what she'd been doing, sending him a care package every week and a letter every day, sealing each one with kisses. Whenever the guys in Afghanistan saw a package come through covered in lip prints they'd shout, "Hey, Andre, your wife sent you another package!" But they weren't enough. By the end he was warning her, "I've seen too much over here, I'm not the same man."

Tiffany listened. And then she said, "Well, baby, you know I'm a little different, too, I'm *used* to doing things on my own now."

Soon after he got home, the nightmares started, and the night sweats. Tiffany's ex-husband became a problem. He hadn't been a problem before. Tiffany and Andre would make love and sit together in the bed, which was where they always did their best conversing, and Andre would say he didn't want that man calling his house anymore. He didn't even want him coming by to drop off the boys. Cisco was a problem, too. Andre *said* he wasn't a problem. But he was.

Andre told her a story, the Afghani children again. Once, he gave a group of them each a pencil. After that, whenever they saw him they remembered him, as if he'd given them the greatest gift on earth. The story, it seemed to Tiffany, was like a snapshot, a single snapshot pulled from a whole album he kept out of sight.

Money became a problem. Before Andre left, he'd paid all the bills. Tiffany always had access to everything, but she never spent any money without asking. She would say, "I need to go to the grocery store, do you think it's OK for me to get fifty dollars out?" But as soon as he left, all his creditors began calling and she didn't know jack. So she paid them all off. The night she was going over the Christmas list and he told her she had wasted his deployment money, she got so pissed off she gave him back the checkbook and ATM cards. "I don't *need* this," she said.

Andre told the story about the time a live bomb was found behind his tent. He told the story of stepping on a land mine. He stepped on it, heard the tiny sound it made as it armed, and he froze. He stood there with his foot on it until explosive ordinance disposal, EOD, could get there. The guy from EOD said, "OK, on the count of five, after I put my foot here, you run like hell." Stories like these Andre told her. But he never told her what he actually did over there.

Tiffany would say, "Babe, we have *got* to talk to somebody, you've got issues that you're dealing with from Afghanistan, you're waking up with night sweats, you're fighting in your sleep! You need to go talk to the chaplain or somebody." But Andre would just shake his head. He didn't think it would look good to the guys in his unit or his chain of command. Besides, he didn't think he needed any help.

He wasn't alone, according to the study in the *New England Journal of Medicine*. Among soldiers and Marines returning from Afghanistan and Iraq who were suffering from various forms of combat trauma, the majority believed that if they sought help, they'd be seen as weak. They believed the leaders of their unit would treat them differently and their buddies in the unit would have less confidence in them. Half believed it would harm their career.

In most cases, the fear is unfounded. Their fellow Marines and soldiers who weren't suffering symptoms were half as likely to believe any of those things.

Yet the stigma remains. Some of the stigma is built into military life. To survive, the job requires you to be tough, strong, and lucky. Anything that makes you seem soft, weak, or unlucky is not a good thing. But the stigma is also built into the language. Take the term *post-traumatic stress disorder,* for instance. Jonathan Shay, a Veterans Administration psychiatrist who works with Vietnam vets and is the author of *Odysseus in America: Combat Trauma and the Trials of Homecoming,* writes, "The American Psychiatric Association has saddled us with the jargon 'Post-Traumatic Stress *Disorder*' (PTSD) — which sounds like an ailment — even though it is evident from the definition that what we are dealing with is an *injury:* 'The person experienced, witnessed or was confronted with an event or events that involved actual or threatened death or serious injury, or a threat to the physical integrity of self or others.' We do not refer to a veteran who has had an arm blown off by a grenade as suffering from 'Missing Arm Disorder.'"

The stigma could be reduced if every war-fighter received a thorough and ongoing education in combat stress management *ahead of time,* starting in basic training and continuing through deployment. That would make managing combat stress an integral and natural part of the job of fighting a war, just another eventuality to plan for, like up-armoring Humvees to protect against roadside bombs. In 2002, the Marine Corps developed a Warrior Transition program. Near the end of each deployment, while still in-theater, chaplains meet with groups of twenty-five to fifty Marines and sailors for an hour of discussion about their combat experiences, their reactions to it, and their imminent return home. It's a start, but it starts too late. By then you're already playing catch-up.

If a combat veteran begins showing symptoms of combat trauma or, worse, develops a full-blown case of PTSD, the spouse is going to need help, too. As a psychologist and trauma specialist, Aphrodite Matsakis has spent years working with the wives of Vietnam veterans suffering from PTSD. In her book *Vietnam Wives: Facing the Challenges of Life with Veterans Suffering Post-Traumatic Stress,* Dr. Matsakis writes that in addition to dodging the husband's flashbacks and outbursts while supporting the family if he can't hold down a job, the wife ". . . often assumes major multiple caretaking functions with respect to her vet. She may . . . serve as a buffer between him and the world." According to Dr. Matsakis, if their husbands don't get help, these women often wind up harvesting the same bitter fruit as the men they love — emotions that are frozen and numb, anger that seethes underground, unreasonable guilt, alienation from friends and family, isolation, and depression.

"And if they have children, this affects more than just the couple," says Colonel Cozza. In addition to running the psychiatry department at Walter Reed Army Medical Center, he's also the associate director of the Center for the Study of Traumatic Stress at the Uniformed Services University of the Health Sciences. "PTSD, depression, and the substance abuse that may result from it can all impact a person's ability to parent a child. We understand there's stigma, but you're doing yourself and your kids a favor when you seek help. PTSD, depression, and other mental disorders are diagnosable and treatable."

Some days Tiffany would look at Andre and she would wonder aloud, "Who *are* you? I don't know you."

And he would say, "I don't know you either." He would say, "Maybe we just got married too quick. There's a lot of stuff about me you don't know, and there's a lot about you I don't know."

Tiffany laughed at that. "No, honey, there's *nothing* about me you don't know, because I already told you everything. But you don't tell *me* everything."

He said, "You don't know."

"You're right," said Tiffany. "I don't."

Tiffany got back in the habit of going out with the Hooah Wives. "Why don't you come with us?" she'd ask Andre. He would just shrug. Her friends took her out for her birthday and she came home happily drunk.

The whole next week, when they were watching TV, if she reached out to cuddle against his chest, he said, "Baby, no." If she leaned in to give him a kiss, he said, "Baby, can you just, please . . ." turning his head.

At the end of the week, a heated discussion turned into a shouting match.

The next evening, her godsister drove up and Tiffany went outside barefoot to talk to her. Andre said her bare feet looked cheap. "Why don't you just go with your whore friend!" he shouted. "And stay with her!" He threw her shoes into the yard. "I don't want you in my house!" Tiffany decided that house was as much hers as his, and she was going back in it. Andre took a swing at her but he must not have wanted to connect because he missed. Tiffany took a swing back but she missed, too. Then they were tussling on the ground and Tiffany's godsister broke them up. She put Tiffany and her shoes in her car. "Come to my house," she said. "Y'all cool off."

When Tiffany and her godsister came back in the morning, Andre was putting a padlock on the front door. Tiffany tried to push inside. He pushed back. This time, when they swung at each other, the swings connected. Tiffany heard her dress rip, then she was on the ground and she couldn't breathe, Andre's hands around her throat. She was bigger than him, she flailed at him, but he was too strong, she couldn't breathe. Then a neighbor from next door ran over, knocked him in the side of the head, and hauled him up off of her.

Someone called the police, who handcuffed Andre. Tiffany stumbled up into the house, bruised and dusty, holding her dress together. As the handcuffs went on, Andre shouted after her, "Now you're going to take my *career* away from me?"

Inside, Tiffany turned to the police officer. "You know what? I'll just leave."

The officer shook his head. "Ma'am, you are all bruised up. We are taking him to jail."

Tiffany swore she would refuse to press charges. "Please," she begged, "*please* don't take him to jail. He's a good man, he just messed up. I pushed his buttons and he pushed mine. He has worked so hard," she said, "and now his career will be ended."

The fear that a domestic violence incident is an automatic career-ender is common in the military community. But like the fear surrounding combat trauma and PTSD, this fear, too, is mostly unfounded. "We have people who come through our treatment program every day," says Fort Bragg social work chief Lieutenant Colonel Pecko, "and they move on and go about their career and do very well."

While combat vets have a somewhat higher chance of being involved in domestic violence, there's no hard evidence that military families overall are any more violent than civilian families. However, they do have a higher rate of treatment. In the civilian world, families often don't receive help until things get so bad the police are at the door. In the military, if a commanding officer suspects trouble at home, the CO can order a service member to get help early on — the military system is focused on treatment rather than punishment.

The staff of the Family Advocacy Programs on military installations investigates cases of child and spouse abuse, and provides intervention and treatment. They also try to prevent it from happening through seminars and classes on everything from new-father skills to conflict resolution.

Lieutenant Colonel Pecko's social workers help provide treatment. The treatment approach is controversial among some civilian domestic violence experts, who disagree about whether treatment alone even works. They also rightly point out that it provides no protection to the spouse who is on the receiving end of a battering or the losing end of a mutual fight. But they assume as well that the civilian world they know is the same as the military world.

It's not. "The bulk of our cases," Lieutenant Colonel Pecko explains, "are young, impulsive, immature, fairly newlywed couples. They're just learning how to live together, and so they haven't established these longstanding patterns of power and control." Those patterns, well entrenched, are what you tend to find in civilian cases by the time they get help. In contrast, less than 5 percent of Fort Bragg's spouse maltreatment cases are estimated to involve couples with a long history of battering, a behavior that is very hard to change once it becomes ingrained. In those cases, Lieutenant Colonel Pecko says they might recommend that the batterer be considered for separation from the Army. Discharge. Goodbye.

That is what men like Andre are afraid of. And their wives, too, if they're dependent on their husband's military paycheck and benefits. And so they keep quiet. They don't realize that, odds are, they're one of the 95 percent of troubled couples that the military is focused on saving.

In Tiffany's case, however, she wasn't afraid of losing her husband's income and benefits because in that moment she assumed she'd already lost them. She assumed her marriage was over, that she was going to be back on her own again. So her fear was for Andre. She continued to insist she would not press charges. Eventually the police officer went back outside, gave Andre a withering lecture, and took off the handcuffs.

The situation would not have gone away so easily if they had been living on post. There, the law enforcement officers who came to the house would have been military police and Andre and Tiffany would have become the subject of a Family Advocacy Program, or FAP, investigation, which becomes part of a service member's record.

But Tiffany and Andre didn't live on post. So Andre was lectured and Tiffany was allowed to gather up a few things and leave.

Then the informal system took over. The Hooah Wives began posting online, *Where's Tiffany at? We haven't heard from Tiffany in two days! What the heck is going on?* Tiffany heard about it, so she posted, *Look, ladies, I'm having some personal problems, I won't be online for a couple of weeks. I'll see you when I see you.*

The Hooah Wives ignored that. The phone at Tiffany's godsister's house began ringing — "Tiffany, you want to come stay with me? Tiffany, you want me to send Bert to go talk to him?" By then, Tiffany was having second thoughts about leaving, and she told them what she was telling herself. "He messed up," she said. "We all mess up. *I* need to talk to my husband."

She called. She wrote a letter. Andre wouldn't answer. A soldier friend who had rushed over to help the morning they'd fought, a man who had also been in Afghanistan, told Andre he had screwed up and gotten less punishment than he'd deserved. "You weren't in the house hearing her beg that man not to take you to jail," he said. "That's a good woman and she loves you and she wants to make it work, but you've got to hurry up and get your ass off your shoulders and talk to her."

When Andre finally came over to Tiffany's godsister's house, everyone cleared out. The two of them sat in the living room in silence. After a while, Tiffany said, "We both have got major problems. And you've got a lot of problems from over there."

"Yeah," he said, "I've got a lot of issues with that, I admit that."

They were silent again.

"Come home," he said at last. "Come home."

Andre went to his health clinic on post and enrolled in anger management classes. He started seeing the anger management specialist. He told his chain of command that he had something going on that he had to take care of so he could continue to take care of his soldiers. He said, "I have an appointment every Thursday at the clinic at three that I have to go to, so I won't be at formation." He sat down with the chaplain, too, and she turned out to be someone with whom he found it easy to talk.

Many service members and their families prefer to talk with a chaplain because they believe they'll have a little more privacy. Discussions with military social workers, therapists, psychologists, and psychiatrists become part of the service member's medical record, which can be reviewed by his or her commanding officers. Discussions with chaplains, on the other hand, are considered confidential — in other words, the chaplain cannot tell anyone what was said without the permission of the person who came in for counseling. But there are some requirements and exceptions, and these vary slightly from service to service, even from chaplain to chaplain, so people who are concerned about privacy are advised to ask the chaplain about it right at the start. In Andre's case, in the quiet of his chaplain's office, he expected and received the privacy he needed to talk about whatever was troubling him.

As for going to see a social worker or psychologist, Lieutenant Colonel Pecko believes, "The people whose careers would actually be impacted by receiving mental health services on post would be a real small minority." That minority might include soldiers whose commanders still believe if you need help you're weak, or soldiers with other blemishes on their record, or those with top secret clearances, like Andre, who was special forces. But even Andre was able to get confidential help from a chaplain. He also could have called Military OneSource to get a confidential referral to a civilian mental health provider. The military would have paid for the counseling, but any record of the therapy would have remained outside the military system; his chain of command would never have known. In any case, talking with his chaplain and attending anger management classes on post didn't prevent him from later being promoted.

The Hooah Wives were Tiffany's counseling. When she and Andre disagreed about something, usually money, she would go to the wives for a few hours. She told Cisco she couldn't see him anymore. "In this house," she told him, "male friends cause too much confusion."

Tiffany and Andre went back to getting to know each other. He slept on the couch; she slept upstairs. Tiffany would ask, "Would you like dinner, Andre?" And he would say, "Yeah, Tiffany, if you don't mind." She'd ask if she could use the car, if she could have twenty dollars to go get groceries. Then one Sunday night, family night, the night when they all sat around the TV and watched Disney movies, the boys were on the floor and Tiffany and Andre were sitting on the couch. She was sitting close to him.

"You cold?" he asked.

"Yeah," she said. "I'll go get a blanket."

She got a blanket. He spread it over both of them.

As the nights went on, he stopped sleeping on the couch. And once when they were arguing, Andre's hands went up and Tiffany flinched. She flinched even as she realized he was throwing his hands up in frustration, not because he wanted to hit her. He saw her flinch and tears welled in his eyes. "Oh my God," he said softly. "What the hell have I done?"

Less than half a year after coming home, Andre was ordered back to Afghanistan. He had two weeks to get ready. Part of Tiffany cried, *Oh no, he can't go, we're working on saving our marriage, we're working on becoming a family again.* But this time around, another part of Tiffany knew the score. "OK," she said, "I know your orders can't be changed. Let's deal with it."

She focused on the positives. They'd be able to get a little ahead on the money while he was gone. Her time, once again, was her own. She wouldn't be tripping over his smelly boots for a while. She cried when he left, but she didn't take to her bed. From Afghanistan, Andre, too, sounded better than last time. Tiffany would get online with the Hooah Wives: *Hey, girls, let's go out!!!* She'd meet them at Broadstreet's, blowing off steam with cigarettes and nickel drinks.

Annie Cory would be there, too, though she had to wear a black Broadstreet's T-shirt that identified her as underage, because she was one of the youngest Hooah Wives. When Tiffany first met her, Annie was tall and slim. Her hair was dyed bright red, and she was wearing a punk rock T-shirt and what looked like a spiked leather dog collar on her wrist.

Annie had changed since then. Under the influence of the Hooah Wives, she had shed the punk wardrobe and let her hair go back to its natural dark color. Jenn Marner, the tough comanager, had told her, "There are other ways to get noticed without drawing negative attention." Annie also wasn't slim anymore. Her husband, Will, had deployed a few months after Tiffany's husband, around the same time as Marissa's husband, and since then Annie had been putting on the pounds.

Tiffany got the feeling Annie was here at Broadstreet's a lot. She was posting online at three A.M., sleeping all day, always drunk at parties and wildly, desperately cheerful, as if trying to convince herself she actually was. She wasn't like that before Will left.

Days, Annie Cory stayed busy. She volunteered at Womack because she was interested in studying medicine. She volunteered to coach a soccer team of three-year-olds. She was the volunteer mayor of her community on post and a volunteer key caller for the FRG.

Nights, Annie would go to bed and she'd just lie there. Without Will's body next to her to hold and touch, it was as if he were a ghost, as if there was no such thing as Will anymore. It was an eerie feeling. She stopped sleeping.

She spent time with the Hooah Wives. One of the other younger wives lived over at the barracks, and Annie got to know a lot of single soldiers there. About once a week, her ghostly husband would become flesh again and call her. She could see him in her mind then, with his blondish brown hair and cleft chin. They'd known each other since first grade, when they would climb on top of Annie's bunk bed and pretend they were plankton, and then a big whale would come along and eat them and they'd fall off the bunk bed. Sometimes, they had pretended they were chipmunks. Thirteen years later, when Will was in the Army, he went back home to Washington State to marry his Annie.

For the ten minutes Will was allowed to talk on the phone from Iraq, his voice often sounded flat and tired. Once when he called, he told her he'd been injured a few days before. He didn't make a special call. He was just telling her now that he happened to have the chance. He didn't want her to worry, he said.

There'd been a firefight. In the middle of it all, he saw some Iraqis trying to hide behind a pole, and when he ran over to confront any fighters among them, he saw that not only were they unarmed but they also had children with them. He was waving them out of the way to safety when a rocket-propelled grenade exploded against the wall beside him. Shrapnel from the explosion hit him near his ear, and the blast had affected his hearing. But there was another guy in his unit who was shot twice in the abdomen and kept on firing back till he passed out. "Compared to him," Will's disembodied voice told her, "I don't deserve a Purple Heart." Then the call was over and the real live Will evaporated back into the world of Annie's nightmares.

The single soldiers at the barracks threw awesome parties. Those guys partied all the time, which was good because more and more Annie had to avoid being alone if she didn't want to be haunted. They'd say, "Just drink a fifth and it'll be OK," and she discovered they were right, because then the haunting pain went away, and eventually she'd pass out and get some sleep at last.

Will was on a convoy when a sudden flash and boom blasted the road ahead. A couple of Humvees further up the line of vehicles, a roadside bomb had just killed his staff sergeant.

Annie was seeing a lot more of the soldiers than she was of Tiffany and the other Hooah Wives, who were mostly older, in their mid- to late twenties, and didn't party as hard. With the wives, Annie would just get online and post, *I like to drink, hahahahaha!* They'd post motherly cautions back. They'd warn her about the people she was hanging out with. Jenn told her, "It's guilt by association." Which was why they were starting to keep her at arm's length as much as she did them; it was mutual.

"We're going on missions for a couple of weeks," Will's voice told her over the phone, only not that directly. Like most couples, they had worked out a code. He said, "I might not be able to call you for a while."

Annie was drinking a fifth and a half of liquor every night. Sometimes she was drunk when he called, and she knew he'd worry if he knew, but she could fake sobriety for ten minutes. The other wives in the FRG never saw the drunk, crazy Annie either — she didn't want to do anything that would hurt Will's career so she was all business with them, too. On long, rambling calls, though, like the ones she made across the country to her parents every night that she wasn't partying, there was no point trying to hide it. She'd cry to them about her friends who were wasting their lives away drinking. Her parents told her, "Annie, we're praying for you." And then between themselves, they nervously started trying to figure out how to come up with the money to fly her home and put her in rehab.

Sometimes when Will called, they'd fight over something small. He'd snap, "I didn't get a letter from you this week." And she'd snap back, "Well, I'm sorry that this week the mail truck blew up, but there's not much I can do about IEDs, now is there?"

Marissa called. "Hey, I'm cooking some steaks, you want to come over?"

"Well," Annie said, "I don't know." She knew exactly what Marissa was doing. She didn't like the way it made her feel, like she might need someone's help to get her out of a situation she had put herself into.

Christine was more pushy, caught her online and as they instant-messaged back and forth, got her to admit she wasn't doing so well. *If you ever need anything,* Christine IMed her, *you know you can call me.* But Annie didn't call. She'd just sit alone and listen to depressing, bad punk music and think about Will in Fallujah, and his dead staff sergeant, and his friend with two bullets in his abdomen. She was watching her weight go up and up, and not going to school like she'd planned, not on her way to becoming an EMT or a doctor, and she looked at herself drinking another fifth and it just made her drink even more.

Gradually, the husbands of the women Annie had been partying with for months began to come home. The single soldiers she had been hanging out with were deploying. She was alone with her thoughts more often now. Then, on the phone one day, Will's voice said he was fairly sure he would be home within the next couple of months. And she said to herself, *OK, Annie. You have to clean up your act.*

Two months after Will Cory got back, Annie threw a full bottle of Gatorade at him. He came right back at her, grabbed her and threw her on the couch. "Don't you ever do that to me again!" he shouted, and he went on shouting, getting down in her face. She was crying and gasping for air, his face in hers, and all of a sudden she felt as if an iron band had clamped around her chest. Her eyes widened in panic as she struggled to get a breath, her heart racing, grabbing onto Will to help her.

When the panic attack was over and she could breathe again, Will was holding her. "Wow," he whispered. "This is nuts." As she took a deep breath, he said, "I don't want to see you like that again."

Their homecoming hadn't started out like that. At Green Ramp, Annie had thrown herself into his arms and he'd hugged her tight and kissed her and everyone took pictures. A couple of days later, though, they started bickering over something small and somehow it exploded into a shouting match of escalating putdowns. By the time the smoke cleared, they couldn't remember what had started it all.

They'd been known to push each around back in high school. Will had seen that kind of thing happen at home, and both he and Annie had tempers. They both had to have the last word. But they had cut all that out before they got married, and nothing ugly had happened during the six months he was home after Afghanistan — Iraq was actually his second wartime deployment, but Annie had spent the first one, the one when he was in Afghanistan, living at home with her parents.

Iraq was different. Will was coming home after a long string of firefights and Annie was coming off eight months of depression, anxiety, and heavy drinking. They had both changed a lot. And this time, they also had housemates.

Their half of their small duplex wasn't meant to house two families.

But a shortage of housing units on post, and a lack of decent, affordable housing alternatives out in the surrounding civilian community, is a problem at every military installation. Annie and Will had a soldier friend who was waiting for housing for his wife and two-year-old, so when Will got back they offered to let him and his family move in temporarily. The first day was fine. But when the two-year-old got out of bed the second night and ran screaming through the house, Annie and Will lay in their bed and looked at each other, eyes wide.

Combat stress, family history, inner demons, the aftereffects of anticipatory grief, a lousy living situation, a young marriage — these are the poisonous ingredients for a toxic stew. The needling and shouting turned into pushing and shoving, which became clawing and punching, which ended in Annie's panic attack on the couch.

Will called his unit chaplain and set up a time to go in and talk. But when the day came, things were hectic and his commanding officer wouldn't let him go. Will set up another appointment, but it happened again, and after that he didn't hear from the chaplain anymore. So Annie called the chaplain. He gave her the number for Fort Bragg's Center for Family Life and Religious Education, but when she called over there and left a message, no one ever called her back. She felt as if nobody cared.

One of the Hooah Wives gave her another chaplain's phone number. Will actually made it to that appointment and even liked this chaplain better than the first. But then Will's unit left for a month of training in the field.

Veterans may have trouble gaining access to services, too. They may live far from Veterans Administration hospitals and outpatient clinics. Once they get there, they may find that underfunding has left the staff and services overbooked. In the past, as many as a quarter of the vets who asked for help were forced to wait months to get it. Now in a time of budget cuts, ongoing wars, and increasing numbers of combat veterans, that situation is likely to only get worse.

As for Annie, she decided she needed help, too. She called Tricare, the medical insurance program for military families, and said, "I think I need a mental evaluation 'cause I'm nuts."

"OK," said the woman on the other end of the line. To Annie's surprise that was all she said, "OK." She referred Annie to a civilian therapist; it was that easy. The therapist put Annie on an antidepressant and started her on an anger management program. Once Will got back from the field, Annie made a point of scheduling all her therapy appointments at five in the afternoon, so that on the chance his CO let him leave work on time, he could go with her. Four months after his return from Iraq, that was all the counseling Will was getting.

Along the way, Annie had also become very close to the other women in her FRG. It was as if the Iraq deployment had bonded them together the same way it had bonded their husbands. This was an important part of Annie's recovery, because as VA psychiatrist Jonathan Shay points out, "Recovery happens only in community." Two people, whether they're a husband and wife or a therapist and a patient, are not a community. This is as true for the spouses as it is for the vets.

Will could have used a community of his own, but the fact that Annie had one seemed to help them both. And then, with four days' notice, Will was sent back to Afghanistan.

A year earlier, the night the Hooah Wives launched themselves at Broadstreet's, someone took a photograph, capturing two rows of about a dozen young women, some in jeans, some dressed to impress. Annie's in the back row, labeled "too young" in her black Broadstreet's T-shirt. Her head is tipped to one side, her round face complicated and vulnerable. She looks as if she's trying to smile and just can't.

Jenn Marner's in the front row, all aglitter in black, her blond hair tousled, her smile wide open. She has tucked her legs neatly beneath her and planted her hands firmly on her knees.

Behind Jenn sits Angela, in a little black dress and what looks like pearls, her hair upswept, her smile gentle. Both she and Jenn face the camera straight on.

Marissa kneels on the end, one forearm resting on a drawn-up knee, her smile practiced from her modeling days. The smile puts you at ease — it's meant to — but look a little closer and you realize her face is guarded, slightly turned away, lips together. It's like her posture, which seems relaxed but with that drawn-up knee, she could be on her feet in a second, ready to fight or flee.

More recently, at that Hooah Wives barbecue, Marissa had told me Lexie was going up to Erie by herself soon, to spend a couple of weeks with her grandparents. She said, "I'll probably tell Charlie everything then."

CHAPTER 17

The Real News

L EXIE WENT TO ERIE. Lexie came home. I called Marissa. "How'd the talk go?"

She sighed. "The times we've been alone have been so nice, I didn't want to ruin it. I mean, when is it a good time to say, 'Hey, I was raped and beaten, want to hear all about it?'"

I was raped. This was the first time Marissa had ever come out and said it to me. She had hinted before, but only indirectly. Now when she finally said it, she tossed it out there almost casually, though I was sure it wasn't. With Marissa, I got the feeling she always knew exactly what she was doing, and for that matter, that she knew exactly what I was doing, and maybe even what I was about to do. *I was raped.* That's all she said. Over the years, that was all she'd ever said to Charlie.

"He wants to know," she said. "He knows it happened, he's known that all along, and sometimes he presses me to talk about it, and I'm like, 'Why do you need to know?'"

It was three in the morning, every window in the Bootes's house dark except for a pale glow through the living room curtains.

Marissa sat on the rug in a pool of light, next to an open plastic storage bin full of old photographs, clippings, and drawings. The artifacts of her childhood. All around her, the house was still. She couldn't sleep. She leafed through a scrapbook she had put together in junior high, full of clippings she'd read that had touched her. On one page was an article she had torn from a magazine in a doctor's office entitled "Words to Live By: 12 Secrets of a Happy Life." It quoted people like John Lennon and

Katharine Hepburn. And this from the classical guitarist David Russell: "The hardest thing in life is to know which bridge to cross and which to burn."

It was a warm evening late in July, and I was on the phone with Marissa. She and Charlie were well into what my Marine Corps handbook for spouses calls the "Reintegration & Stabilization" phase — he had been back for nearly four months, though he wasn't home at the moment. Marissa and I were talking about her mother, and somehow the conversation turned to the years when Marissa was on probation.

"I was out a little bit after curfew," she said. "I was supposed to be in by nine P.M. And I knew if my mother realized I'd broken curfew, she would call my probation officer."

Marissa was thirteen, and she and a friend were out with their boyfriends. Marissa told them she had to get home; it was past her curfew. Their boyfriends said they'd walk them both home, but their plan was to walk Marissa's friend home first, then Marissa, and she said, "No, I have to get home. I'll just go myself, it's only two blocks." She set off in a hurry. She was a block from home when a stranger, a man she'd never seen before, dragged her into an alley.

He raped her. He beat her. He took the jacket she was wearing, a starter jacket with sports logos on it that she had borrowed from her friend.

When he finally let her go, she ran. She didn't feel the cold. She ran the last block and vomited in the phone booth outside her building. Then she pounded down the stairwell into her mother's apartment, locked herself in the bathroom, and started filling the tub. Clouds of steam rose up from the rushing water. Her mother tried to talk to her through the door, but Marissa couldn't make out what she was saying over the blast from the faucets and her own sobs, and then she submerged herself in the scalding water. Somehow, her mother broke into the bathroom, yelling at Marissa for being out late, assuming she was late for the usual stupid reasons, and Marissa shouted it at her: "*I was raped!*"

Her mother called the police. Her mother made her go to the hospital. And because she'd been out after curfew, her mother called Karen, Marissa's probation officer. Karen insisted Marissa go to counseling but Marissa didn't want to, and it didn't do any good anyway. It hurt that night, and after that she put it away, determined never to be a victim. She lived her life without regrets, because regret, she believed, would get her nowhere. "There's no point in crying about it," she insisted to me on the phone that evening. "In my life, there's so much that if I start crying like the world's going to end, then it will end."

We were on the phone again the next morning, talking about her FRG work, when Marissa said, "Since I met you, I've started writing about my life, and there's a lot, I had no idea there was so much! I started with my earliest memories at three and so far I'm only up to five and there's already a lot. Charlie said, 'What are you writing, a book?' And I'm like, 'You can read it as I go or you can wait and read it all at once when I'm done.'"

A light goes on inside my head. "Is this how you're going to tell him?"

"Yeah," she says, "because when I try to talk about it with him, I get too emotional."

I bite my lip. "Marissa, don't let me push you into anything."

"You're not pushing me into anything. Last night I told you things I haven't told him yet."

"I had that feeling," I said.

"Yeah, and it didn't bother me, so that told me if I could tell you and be OK with it, I'm ready to tell him."

She was ready — not just to tell Charlie how a man had once assaulted a young girl. She was ready for Charlie, her husband, to know her more completely than anyone else ever had.

The house was dark, Lexie asleep in her room at one end, and at the other, Marissa and Charlie lying next to each other, when she told him everything.

He didn't know what to say. There was nothing to say. All he could do was hold her. "You know," she said, "I don't regret anything that happened to me, I don't. It made me stronger. It made me the person I am." His arms tightened around her. "I feel blessed with all the knowledge I've gained. I have to use it to help other people."

"But if you could go back and change it," he asked, "would you?"

"No."

"No?" He was surprised. "Not even the bad things?"

She looked at him. "To take away the bad things that happened would take away some of who I am. If I'd made different choices, maybe I wouldn't be here with you now. Maybe I wouldn't have this beautiful little girl. When I was little, I used to wish I had a normal family, but I never thought I would. And now I do. I have you and Lexie. That dream came true."

* * *

Beth and Luigi dreamed of a little girl, or a little boy.

One day, not long after Luigi returned, Beth learned she was unexpectedly, miraculously, pregnant.

The weeks went by. Then she was lying on the examination table with Luigi beside her and the heartbeat that had been there before was gone.

A week later, she miscarried.

More weeks went by. Luigi said, "I'm thinking I might get a weapon to keep here at the house, so I can go out to the range and practice."

"I don't want to have a gun in the house," said Beth.

"Why not?" he asked. "You grew up on a farm, you grew up around weapons, what's the problem? It might be a good idea in this neighborhood anyway."

And Beth said again, "I don't want a gun in the house." And then she told him why: that while he was gone, if there had been a gun in the house, she might have used it on herself.

Luigi went still. His eyes widened and he made a sound, *hoooo*, a high, scared, shocked sound, as if he'd glimpsed a vision of how different a life he might have come home to. He blinked back tears. He didn't get a gun.

Ever since Beth spoke at the peace rally, she had been praying for God to show her what she was supposed to do with her life. She hadn't been able to find a job in forensics, and nursing was something she was good at, so she wondered if maybe God was trying to tell her something. Maybe she was *supposed* to be a nurse. Maybe she just needed to find the right place for herself — the Labor and Delivery department of an Army hospital wasn't it. She took a job with the Public Health department, helping ensure that poor children received the health care they needed. The hours were more regular, enabling her to be home at the same time as Luigi.

A month after she miscarried, she was pregnant again. They talked about money, about how much time she could afford to take off after the baby came. Beth discovered, to her amazement, that if she quit her job to stay home with the baby and they were living on Luigi's pay, they would qualify for the Women, Infants, and Children welfare program, or WIC.

Marissa and Charlie were going over their budget, and Marissa was thinking they could really use a lottery win right about now — there was no way they could afford for her to go back to school. They were behind on their bills as it was. Charlie's income was back down to what it was before he deployed, and at the Pack and Ship Marissa was making less than a third of what she'd been making at the law firm. That firm had been based in Charlotte, and Charlie understood that she didn't want to do the kind of unsatisfying, low-paying paralegal work she could get in Fayetteville, but he asked, "So what do you want to do?"

"I don't know," Marissa said.

It frustrated him when she said that. "Why the hell did we pay all that money for you to go to school then?"

All she knew was that she wanted to do something important, something that would make a difference. She put in applications, but the available jobs weren't good for much except marking time. She wished her work for her FRG was the paying kind, because it was work she liked doing and was good at — she had recently been given an award for all her organizing efforts while Charlie was in Iraq. Since he'd been back, she'd finally had the time to complete FRG leader training and had spent days in class over at Army Community Services, working her way through Army Family Team Building. She would eventually be selected for one of the military's most prestigious honors for volunteers, the Dr. Mary E. Walker Award. Meanwhile, the bills were piling up.

There came a morning when Marissa woke up and looked at the clock. She jumped out of bed, hours late getting Lexie to school.

"What the hell is wrong with you?" Charlie asked when he found out. She lay on the couch, pointing the remote at the TV. The house was dirty, the bills were piled up on the computer desk; she didn't care. Half the time she couldn't remember when she was supposed to be at the Pack and Ship or what she was supposed to do. He'd ask, "What is going on with you?"

And she'd say, "I don't know."

"What do you mean, you don't know?" he'd demand. The only other time he'd ever seen her like this was when she had post-partum depression after Lexie was born, and seeing her that way again was unsettling.

"I'm down, I'm in a funk, I don't know."

He started calling from work to make sure she was up and taking Lexie to school.

Marissa heard the Army was finally creating new paid positions for support staff to help the overworked FRG volunteers. It sounded like exactly what she was looking for. She put in an application. She put in an application, too, at the local headquarters of a fast-food chain, pushing paper in the human resources department.

When the phone rang, it was the fast-food chain. She was hired.

* * *

About a year after Charlie and Luigi began their first deployment, both men got the word: Their units would probably be deploying again the following spring, this time to Afghanistan, this time for a year.

That evening, Luigi gave Beth the news.

"It's unfair," she cried. "Why do they keep sending the same guys?" She was so angry she didn't even want to be near him. She went into the bedroom, closed the door, and called me.

Her voice was rough with tears. "He's going to miss the whole first year of this baby's life. I'll have to quit my job and go home to my parents — how's that for one big regression, huh? But I can't stay here." She cast about desperately for some strategy that might keep him from being deployed. But after a few minutes, her voice became resigned. "I know it's not his fault." And then, "At least he'll be here for the baby's birth."

Luigi looked up from the couch when Beth came out of the bedroom. She curled up next to him and he held her close. Part of him hoped this deployment wouldn't be as hard on her because now she had her church, and some friends in town, and a new job she liked, and after Iraq he felt he was better prepared emotionally to deal with the stresses he knew he'd be facing, too. But these days, part of him was much more aware of Beth's emotional status, on the alert at all times, and that part of him looked ahead at the deployment looming on the horizon and was afraid.

Marissa lay beside Charlie in bed, awake in the dark. She had taken in the news quietly, but once inside her, it had weighed down on her heart. Now, several nights later, as she lay there blinking into the lonely darkness, her heart felt as if it were being crushed. Tears slipped out of the corners of her eyes and onto the pillow. She chewed her lip, but still the tears came, and then her body began to convulse with sobs.

Charlie moved beside her. "Marissa?" he mumbled. He sat up, awake now. "Marissa?" He looked at her helplessly. "What's going on?"

The curse of being a strong woman, Marissa thought. *Other people don't know what to do when you show a moment of weakness.* She choked out the words: She was afraid. Of another deployment. Of the loneliness. Of losing him.

Charlie put a hand on her shoulder. "I don't know what to do," he said hesitantly, "or what to say." He took her in his arms. "But if you need to cry, go ahead." So she did. *Even strong women,* she thought, *need to lose their minds every now and again.*

After a while, he murmured, "I don't understand why you're crying now about stuff you won't have to worry about till later."

"Because later," she said, "later I'll have to be strong and suck it up. I won't have the luxury of your strong arms to keep me sane."

When she had no more tears to cry, she left him to go clear her head in the shower. Then she lay down beside him again, felt him warm and breathing against her, and slept a long, deep sleep.

In our democratic society, the men and women who defend us give up the right to say no when our elected leaders tell them to go to war. They give up nights spent holding the one they love. They give up seeing their child take her first steps, or wobble away on a two-wheeler for the first time. They give up Saturday afternoons spent working on their trucks and drinking beer in front of a football game. Sometimes they give up their lives.

Does this make them especially noble? Or all the more disposable? There is a growing gap between those who serve and those who don't. These days very few of us, and very few of our leaders, have experienced the day-to-day reality of military life. And since the earliest years of our republic, the fewer the number of veterans among our leaders, the more likely we have been to go to war.

In my sister's warm, shady backyard, I spread a sheet out on the grass. Then my nephew and two nieces crouched over it with cans of red and gold spray paint. In a few weeks, Frank would be home. WELCOME HOME UNCLE FRANK the children sprayed across the sheet, then added a scimitar, a flower, and a blob. The scimitar represented Iraq, according to the nine-year-old. The flower represented what the seven-year-old was sure Frank was missing most while in the desert. The blob, my five-year-old nephew explained, was a gun.

"Except Uncle Frank doesn't carry a gun," I reminded him.

"I know," he said impatiently, "but he's in *war*."

When we go to war today, do we send people we see as noble? Or disposable? How our nation answers that question will give us a hint of our future. The kids and I left the red- and gold-painted sheet to dry on the grass, and while they ran off to play on the swing set, I got back to the books I was reading on the history of the Roman army. If history is any guide, a democracy, which values the worth of each individual, will fight its wars with citizen soldiers, while an empire, which exploits the many to benefit the few, fights its wars with people it thinks it can afford to lose.

Empires are an ominous development for the individuals living in them. Reading these books, I had been struck by the ways in which an army reflects the society it defends. Before the Roman Empire was an empire, it was a democratic Republic. Rome rose to power with an army of noble citizen-soldiers — farmers, business owners, and aristocrats, every male Roman with enough money to equip himself with armor and weapons. They deployed for a single campaign, or a year, and then went home to their everyday civilian lives. Though they were draftees, they willingly gave up most of their rights as citizens during their training and deployment and submitted themselves to the Roman army's extreme discipline — they could be flogged on a commander's whim, executed for falling asleep while on guard duty. They submitted to all this because they identified closely with their government; the Roman Republic's battles were *their* battles. Military service was a duty each man of property believed he owed to his community.

As a result, Rome's citizen militias were highly disciplined. They were so successful that they defeated the massive trading empire of Carthage. They acquired provinces a thousand miles from their homes, and the native populations of those provinces then paid taxes and provided markets and materials that made Rome rich. Of course, those faraway provinces had to be defended — or kept in line, depending on your point of view — which required the Romans to build permanent garrisons and staff them with troops deployed for long tours of duty.

But if you send a farmer off to occupy a province for ten years, when he comes home, he probably won't have a farm anymore. So Rome made the transition from a broad-based, conscripted army of citizen soldiers to a mostly volunteer, professional military. Most of the new recruits came from the poorer classes or the foreign provinces, men with few opportunities. They were treated as if they were disposable — they had to be willing to give the Roman army twenty-five years of their lives, most of it spent far from home. For all that time, they were subject to the same harsh discipline the drafted militias had been. Unless they were officers, they weren't allowed to marry, though many of them set up housekeeping and raised families anyway with women they considered their wives. In return, they were paid, their basic needs met. They were given membership in the greatest military organization the world had ever seen. They were given a purpose in life. And when their service was complete, assuming they lived that long, they were given Roman citizenship, or if they were already citizens, special legal status as veterans.

The Roman Republic was still a democracy, but with its occupied provinces, it was starting to look an awful lot like an empire. Within another hundred years or so, it was one, ruled by a dictator who took on the title of Caesar. From there, Roman society decayed into despotism and exploitation, the very rich ruling the very poor.

Out in the backyard, it was twilight, birds chattering and settling into the trees. As I folded up the welcome home sheet for Frank, I wondered what our military revealed about American society. I didn't think America was Rome, not yet. But we do have our foreign "provinces," and we do have economic relationships with them that have made us rich. We have our permanent overseas garrisons. Do we also consider our military service members to be disposable? Even unconsciously, do we see them as a mass of two million identical uniforms, of which the loss of one, or a thousand, hardly matters? Are the casualty reports just a headline we skim past, or do we stop and see each name as an individual, a precious, irreplaceable human being who is loved by a mother, a father, a sister, a boyfriend? A wife?

I was checking into a motel in Fayetteville when my eye fell on the local newspaper stacked at the front desk. 3 FROM BRAGG KILLED, shouted the headline. ROADSIDE BOMB EXPLODES. Beneath the headline was a small close-up of a man with a high-and-tight haircut, a handsome man, softly smiling. "Ferrin," read the caption. The slight smile was what caught my attention. Usually in these official photographs, they're not smiling.

A couple days later, that small, smiling photo was in the paper again, next to FRIENDS HONOR GI AT MEMORIAL RITES. Below this headline was a picture of two women hugging near a table that displayed a framed portrait of a man, a woman, and two children, and a painted plaque, FAMILIES ARE FOREVER. I looked closely. The woman facing the camera was the widow, her eyes closed, her pale, fine-boned face half-hidden in her friend's hair, her own dark hair tucked neatly behind her ear. Her name was Melinda Ferrin. I looked at that photo for a long time. I felt as if I owed her the time. Then I filed the newspaper away with the rest of my research. That was as close to widowhood as I wanted to get.

Months later, when I finally had to admit to myself that the book I was working on needed a section about that knock at the door we were all afraid of (even on the page, I didn't want to go there), I thought of Melinda Ferrin. It took a long time to work up the courage to pick up the phone. Each day, I'd put it on my list of things to do, *call widow,* and each day I'd find twenty other things I needed to do first. Finally, after weeks of diligent procrastination, my nervous hands cold and sweaty, I dialed the number for the only Ferrin listed in the Fort Bragg area.

It was disconnected.

Within a few days, I had tracked her to Utah, but by then I'd sworn off cold-calling widows. I knew I wouldn't want to get a call like that from out of the blue anymore than I wanted to make one. So I wrote a letter. More weeks passed, during which I met Trish Rierson and Michelle Hellermann, who'd also lost their husbands, and I concluded that in her silence Melinda Ferrin had given me her answer, and that was OK.

Three months later, I opened my e-mail and there it was, a message from someone named Melinda Ferrin. *Hello Kristin,* said the subject line. In an instant, she was transformed from a half-hidden face in a photograph, a generic widow, into a living, breathing human being. *I am sorry for my tardiness in responding,* she wrote. *I'm just feeling like I'm getting back into life after losing Clint.*

In a small town a few minutes south of Fort Bragg, in a sandy development of vinyl-sided little houses tucked in tight rows where the pines used to be, Melinda Ferrin used to look out the window as her husband, Clint, got out of his car in the driveway. A staff sergeant, he would walk in the door dressed for war and six-year-old Zack and three-year-old Maddie would jump on him, crying, "Daddy's home! Daddy's home!" Melinda knew he was exhausted, but an hour with Zack and Maddie and he looked like a man who had just drawn a deep breath of fresh air.

The day Clint left for Iraq, he and Melinda were driving onto Fort Bragg when he said, "Now, remember what we've talked about."

"What exactly are you referring to?" she asked.

"I just want you to remember that I want to be buried in a pine box. And I want you to remarry and be happy."

"Stop talking like that," she said gently. In the nine years they'd been married, she had relied on their Mormon faith during his previous deployments to Bosnia, Sierra Leone, Kosovo, and Afghanistan. She and Clint had been sealed in a special ceremony in the temple two years after they were married, to ensure that if they lived righteous lives, they and all the children born to them would be together forever, even after death: an eternal family. She had faith that everything happened for a reason, and if it were Clint's time to go, the Lord would take him, whether he was asleep in his bed or in the middle of a war. And if instead he was meant to come home again, and hoot and groan with Zack in front of a video game, and run his fingers through little Maddie's hair while he cuddled with her, his face dreamy, she trusted that he would.

In his daily letters and e-mails from Iraq, Clint often admitted he was scared. On the phone, he said, "Well, we're back from another mission, and any mission you come back from alive is a good one."

In another call, he said, "You know what I miss the most? Having you tickle my back. That's one of the things I miss the most." It was Friday night in North Carolina, Saturday morning in Iraq; her day ending, his just getting underway. "Goodbye, I love you, talk to you again soon." They hung up.

Eighteen hours later, the doorbell rang. Melinda opened her eyes and looked at the clock beside the bed. 6:10. She grabbed her robe and hurried to the door trying to figure out what day of the week it was, trying to remember if she had daycare kids coming this early. She looked out the peephole and saw three men in dress greens.

"No," she cried, even as she opened the door, "no, no, no . . ."

The roadside bomb that exploded as Saturday drew to a close in southern Baghdad sent shrapnel tearing through a Humvee on its way to seek out and destroy an enemy position that had been firing rockets. The explosion killed three of the men inside, and Melinda Ferrin was no longer a wife.

Before Clint Ferrin deployed, sometimes he would call Melinda and pretend to be someone else, both of them knowing it was him. "Hello? Melinda Ferrin?" he said one time in his best wheeler-dealer voice. "My name's Brock Danger, model scout, and I've been hearing a lot about how beautiful you are, so I'm going to sign you up as a model. Oh no," he'd say as she giggled, "I won't take no for an answer."

For the first six months, Melinda had days when she raged inside: *My life is gone, all my plans, my hopes, my dreams for the rest of my life, gone.* Other days, she was so heavy with grief and loneliness, all she could do was cry. At first, she stayed busy just trying to get through each minute. Then through each hour. Then each day. She started to have more good days than bad. She told herself, *One day I'll be with Clint forever.* She tried to be happy, like Clint would want her to be. She was glad to be back home in Utah, surrounded by the people and the starkly beautiful land she knew.

Three-year-old Maddie talked about Clint all the time. "My Daddy likes games, my Daddy is so strong, my Daddy is so big." And then she'd add, "But he's dead." Yet one day in the store, she saw something her father liked. "Let's get it and give it to Daddy," she said, "when he comes back."

For three months, six-year-old Zack wouldn't talk much about his father. And then it was Father's Day, and Zack began to cry.

"Come on," Melinda said. "Let's all go pick a big bunch of flowers for Daddy."

They took the flowers over to the cemetery and placed them on the grave. There beneath the vast, blue Utah sky, Zack finally started to talk. He and Maddie and Melinda talked about riding bikes with Daddy, and where he was now and when they would see him again. And then they all talked *to* him.

After that, sometimes Zack would come to Melinda and cuddle beside her.

"I miss my daddy," he'd whisper.

"I know," she'd whisper back. "Me, too."

And now, near the salt-rimed edge of the Great Salt Lake, Melinda Ferrin is dreaming. Clint walks in the door. "You're alive?" she asks in joyous disbelief. "Oh, yes," he assures her. "It was all a mistake." A great weight lifts away from her body and she feels lighter than she's felt in months. What a terrible mistake, but her Clint! He's alive, he's standing right in front of her, with his soft, familiar smile . . .

And then Melinda Ferrin wakes up and she's alone in the bed and the sun is rising over the folds of the Wassatch Mountains. She has woken up from this dream so many times before. And she has cried, so many times before, her face salty with tears, because it can't be. How can he really be gone? And out on the desert plain, the salt water glints and stretches to the horizon.

Back to the east, beyond the mountains, back in North Carolina where the sun is already high in the sky over a beige duplex, Beth Pratt is practicing her drums. She sits at the kit, her belly swelling with the baby inside, her body swaying, hands and feet in motion, losing herself in the rhythm. The pads are still on the drums.

Standing next to her, you can hear the noise she's making just fine. But outside, all you hear is a muffled beat. Walking away down the row of beige and tan duplexes, you don't hear anything at all.

Keep going all the way to Fort Bragg, and in an office there you'll see a tall, slender, silver-haired woman going through a stack of job applications. She sits with the relaxed ease of a woman who has seen a lot of water flow under the bridge, which she has — her husband just retired from the Army after thirty years. Her name is Sally Bean, and she's helping get a new program off the ground that's designed to support the FRGs. The program got its start when a four-star general who'd been making the rounds of Army installations kept hearing that the constant deployments were stressing the families and burning out the FRG volunteers.

In the old days, Sally thinks, your husband might deploy once or twice in his entire career. But these days, with the current operational tempo, spouses know their soldier will deploy frequently and can be gone for a year with only a few months turnaround before going again. Sally tells the young spouses she meets, "This 'suck it up and don't complain' is for the birds — if you're not angry when he goes away for the third time, I'd be worried about you." She's known for a long time that many families have trouble connecting with the help that's already out there. The new program will place paid professionals in every brigade-sized unit, and their job will be to help the volunteer FRG leaders help the families.

Sally reads the applications one by one. She's looking for someone who's knowledgeable about the military and FRGs or, better yet, some-one who has *volunteered* in an FRG, someone who has proved through his or her volunteer work that military families are a personal priority. She's looking for someone who has organized activities and knows how to get things done, someone who's enthusiastic and upbeat even under stress, someone who can relate to the volunteer FRG leaders, find out what they need, and give it to them.

She flips to the next application and reads the name: Marissa Bootes.

The concrete block buildings at Green Ramp look exactly the same as they did when Charlie left, the same way they'll look if he leaves again — big, workmanlike, impersonal. Inside, Marissa's setting up a table and unpacking boxes. She lays out cookies, sodas, and pamphlets about mission readiness, Army Family Team Building, Army Emergency Relief, and Army Community Services. She empties the boxes quickly. She's done this many times already. She'll do it many times again.

Soldiers huddle with each other and with their families. They're scat-tered around the big empty terminal, soldiers wearing tan DCUs and carrying black automatic rifles, surrounded by mostly women and chil-dren. The unit leaving this time is a small one. Marissa is content to stand next to her table; she knows better than to force herself on anybody today. As an FRG Assistant, she can be making herself available here at Green Ramp one day, briefing commanders the next. Meanwhile, she's tracking down new spouses and putting their FRGs in touch with them. If a family's in crisis, she's helping the FRG leaders cut through the red tape.

A senior enlisted wife comes over to Marissa's table. She nibbles a cookie and talks about a reunion briefing she and Marissa will be attending tomorrow night, for a battalion that's coming home. A couple of younger wives stop by, then the lieutenant colonel, his wife, the chaplain.

A shouted order echoes around the concrete walls. The soldiers hug their families and hurry into formation over by one of the garage doors. It's open to the tarmac, where a chartered passenger jet waits in the sun. The soldiers march out into the bright light, their families trailing after them.

Marissa stands next to her table, watching. Slowly, the families trail back through the terminal. They're wiping their eyes now. Marissa watches, knowing one day soon that could be her again. When the last family leaves, she packs up and loads the boxes into her car. She lights a cigarette and for a few minutes, she just sits.

Here on Fort Bragg, people constantly say goodbye — but then, most of the time, they get to say welcome home. Not long after I meet with Lieutenant Colonel Joseph Pecko in the social work department at Womack, he himself is deployed to Iraq. In Chaplain James Hartz's office, half-packed as he prepares to leave his family behind for a year in Korea, there are a couple of institutional office chairs, a box of tissues. A lot of people have sat within the painted cinderblock walls of this office and cried.

"You'd like to be able to wave a magic wand," he says, and then his eyes well up. He looks down for a long moment and clenches his jaw. At last he says quietly, "It makes me grateful for my own relationship."

Chaplain Hartz has had to leave his family before. "There are benefits," he says. "If the soldier handles it right, his spouse's growth as a person is phenomenal. If the relationship is solid and he's not threatened and he can accept that, and say wow, she's more of a woman, she's stronger, she's a better person, and we're a better team . . ." He leans forward. "The real news is, most of us make it."

CHAPTER 18

The Terrible Relief

A ND SO, ONE NIGHT in the summer of 2003, I was waiting for Frank to come home from the war in Iraq. I was gripping Rosie's leash, on the edge of a crowd in a Camp Lejeune parking lot. Across the way, the painted sheet hung from the barracks' second-floor catwalk, WELCOME HOME UNCLE FRANK one of a long row of colorfully painted sheets.

We wives had been given a little trifold brochure. It told us: "Returning home can be every bit as stressful and confusing as leaving." Our Marine or sailor might have changed, might feel claustrophobic, might feel awkward about closeness, or overwhelmed by the everyday noise of home life. Go slowly in making changes, we were told, make time for our spouses and remind them they were still needed. "Be patient in rebuilding your relationship."

I pictured myself a quilt on a clothesline, moving with the wind, giving way when pushed, wrapping myself around him when he fell down, exhausted, to sleep. I wondered how long I'd be able to keep it up.

Then, at midnight, the buses rounded the barracks, and the wives and girlfriends screamed and pointed, and a mother from Ohio held a welcome home sign high over her head. And the mass of men in desert tan uniforms stepped off and the crowd enfolded them.

Now it was one A.M. The first thing I wanted to do was make sure Frank was OK. "I'm fine," he reassured me. "We didn't do anything. All I did was sleep in the dirt and ride several hundred miles in a Humvee."

The first thing Frank wanted to do? Go to McDonald's. After months of eating out of foil pouches, he wanted a large order of fries and a chocolate shake. Driving him home, I stopped by the late night drive-through. We were following the advice he himself gave to Marines. "Don't drive," he told them. Not for a few days, anyway. The accident rate among returning service members is always higher. They haven't slept properly in months, or driven civilian vehicles according to civilian rules of the road. Alcohol is always a problem, too — after the mandatory teetotaling of a deployment, their tolerance may be lower than they remember.

The second thing he wanted to do was soak in the tub. Actually, we both wanted him to do this. Back in the parking lot, before we hoisted all his gear into the car, we manhandled it into oversized trash bags to contain the dust and the smell of sweat, and dirt, and something like the murk at the bottom of a trash can. Frank himself was only slightly cleaner. We drove home with the windows down. When he climbed out of the tub, the water was brown with the dust of Iraq.

The third thing he wanted was me.

In the morning, he stared out the window. "I forgot."

"Forgot what?" I asked.

"How green it is here. It's so green."

He'd lost twenty pounds; I saw that right away in the newly sharp line of his jaw, the bag of his uniform.

He was browner, a farmer's tan from the hot days of T-shirts after they were finally allowed to shed their head-to-toe chemical and biological suits.

And he kept turning down the A/C thermostat. Our apartment felt like winter. He said apologetically, "It was just so hot over there." What could I say? I dug out my fleece vest.

But the next day, I didn't have my fleece in the truck. The battalion had been given four days of liberty and we were driving up from Camp Lejeune to Richmond to see family. We were having one of those little unspoken battles over the interior temperature. He twisted the control knob colder, into the blue. A few minutes later, I twisted it into the red. Blue . . . Red . . .

All of a sudden, he gasped, "Heat! Dust! It's closing in, it's so hot — flashback! Flashback!"

We both burst out laughing, but for me, it ended the battle. I twisted the knob back to blue. And shivered.

In Richmond, my sisters had baked a red, white, and blue cake and the brothers-in-law were out back grilling yabba-dabba-doo-sized steaks.

The nieces and nephew came running. They hugged Frank, then rebounded, staring up at him from a distance and giggling, bouncing on their toes, unsure what to do.

"I know why you have no hair!" our little nephew finally blurted. "'Cause it was dirty!"

That was another change — he was bald. At some point, he had shaved off what little hair he had left because it was easier to keep clean. I couldn't decide if he looked like an assassin or a cancer patient.

Later, I came up behind him when he was sitting on the couch, put a hand on his shoulder. He startled like a rabbit. But that wasn't a new change. He had startled easily for a while after Afghanistan, too. For too long he was listening to booms and crackles, automatically cataloging each one: threat, nonthreat, threat, nonthreat. "Even when it was quiet," he said, "you were listening for it."

One day it rained, and he walked outside and lowered his head, let the downpour beat against the back of his smooth skull. "Rain," he murmured. "I love rain."

I huddled just inside the door. I was sick of rain. "It's been raining the whole time you've been gone."

His shirt and his shorts darkened. "In Iraq, if we saw clouds coming it was almost always a dust storm. When it did rain, which wasn't often, there was so much dust in the air it rained mud." He tipped his face up into the downpour, his body relaxed. "I love this rain." Yes, he had changed. He was balder, thinner, tanner, more averse to heat. But the biggest change of all — he was mellow.

Mellow was not a word I ever would have used to describe my husband before. He was intense about details, a stick-it-out-to-the-bitter-end kind of guy. He was still that way. Just softer somehow.

The four-day liberty was over and he was back at work, back in his office on Camp Lejeune every day, and I was borrowing his truck to run an errand. Before going into the store, I removed one of his electronic gadgets from the windshield, a global positioning satellite device, so it wouldn't get stolen. It was a pain in the neck, pulling off the suction cups.

At the end of the day when I picked him up from his office, he looked at the blank spot where the GPS was supposed to be. "I'm going to have to show you how to take it off the windshield," he said. "You don't have to remove the suction cups."

"Oops," I mumbled, "sorry." I steeled myself, because he was particular about his gadgets. I was waiting for the lecture on the Correct Procedure

for the Removal of the GPS. I was reminding myself that he had just returned from a war. I should let him vent without venting back. *Quilt*, I
was thinking, teeth gritted, *be a quilt.*

After a minute, he pointed at the blank spot. "That would have annoyed me before." He sounded a little surprised.

I looked at him, surprised myself.

"But after all the death I've seen, it's no big deal."

I didn't know what to say. I was pleasantly surprised at the change in
him, yet painfully aware that this mildly happy moment in my life was
due to the unspeakable suffering of others.

That evening, I sat with Rosie on a nearby beach. It was misty from the
surf and nearly empty this late in the day. I watched Frank wade into the
white-crested waves and just stand there, gazing out at the ocean as if he
were gazing all the way back to Iraq.

In Iraq, his was a support unit, supposedly in the rear with the gear.
But the enemy attack on part of the Army's 507th maintenance company,
Private Jessica Lynch's unit, proved there really is no rear anymore.
Frank's battalion roared north out of An Nasiriyah in the wake of the
fighting, past scattered bodies, a blasted minivan, its windshield wipers
still ticking back and forth. I told him it was OK with me if he wanted to
talk about it, and it was OK with me if he didn't. He talked about it, a little at a time. A near miss from friendly fire. A dead girl next to a burned-
out bus. A dying man squatting nearby, in shock and staring into space.
Pancake Man. It's common for soldiers to take pictures of death, but
these images were not among the snapshots Frank brought home.

The tide was coming in, crashing around Frank's legs. He stood out
there in the waves a long time. I could see him breathing deeply. I waded
out to join him, Rosie behind me.

"I feel like I don't deserve to be here enjoying this," he said, "not when
other people still have to endure all that misery. There are Americans
over there who won't be home for a long time. And the Iraqis can never
get away."

I was expecting Frank to be busy. He was busy last year after Afghanistan,
responding to suicide threats, domestic disturbances, Marines getting
into fights in town. Back then, the emergency calls for help averaged
about one a week in his battalion. That was in addition to the steady
stream of people who came knocking on his door.

It's Frank's job to help his Marines and sailors cope with coming home
and, if they come apart, to get them the help they need to put the pieces

back together. It's all confidential. He has never told me anything specific. But after Afghanistan, he worked late, came home tired, and at midnight the phone would ring. He'd climb out of bed, pull on his uniform, and drive back to the barracks or the hospital. Meanwhile, he was trying to cope with his own rocky homecoming. He knew exactly what they were going through.

This time around, none of that seemed to be happening. It was the third week since he'd been back, and our days and nights had been peaceful. The rest of the battalion seemed peaceful, too, everyone settling into familiar routines: Marines servicing amphibious assault vehicles, sailors conducting physicals at the clinic. I was starting to wonder why this homecoming was so easy when the last one was so hard.

I asked around for a statistical study on homecomings, some data to compare why some go well and some don't. But both Frank and the social workers at the base shook their heads. As far as they knew, no such study existed. All they knew was what experience had taught them, that couples tend to pick up where they leave off, that if they had trouble before, they'll have trouble after.

But Frank and I didn't have trouble before Afghanistan.

We were crammed into the bass-thumping bar at the officers' club, all the battalion's officers and staff NCOs and their wives. We were getting half-lit on empty stomachs while we waited to be let into the dining room for the Wife Appreciation Dining In — since this was a combat unit, the spouses were all wives. The dress was casual but the men still looked as if they were in uniform, a whole company of belted khakis, neatly ironed shirts, little white triangles of T-shirts, and hair shaved high and tight.

I stooped to shout to the tiny dark-haired schoolteacher beside me. "So how's it going, Sylvia?" Our husbands drove across Iraq together; her husband was a staff sergeant.

"It's just so wonderful to have Paol home again!" she shouted back.

"Has he changed?"

"Yes! He's thinner!"

"Frank, too!"

"And much more relaxed!"

"You're kidding! So's Frank! I wasn't expecting that!"

"Me either!"

We sipped our drinks.

"Why do you think that is?" I asked.

"Maybe seeing how people lived over there just puts things in perspective?" She frowned. "He keeps saying people here in America are so lucky."

Frank had said the same thing: *Americans don't appreciate how good they have it.*

"A little ice," said Sylvia, "a little air conditioning, and he's happy."

After dinner, I ran into Jennifer Lewton, the wife of the operations officer, who had been my connection with the battalion during the deployment. We'd never met face to face before — she was fit and tan and looked younger than she was, a mother of three, a Marine officer's wife for fourteen years. This was their third deployment, too. She reported her husband also hadn't changed as much as she expected. "A little more patient maybe," she said.

The following week, when I stopped by the small base house of one of Frank's young Marines, his wife agreed. "Maybe he's a little more mature," Michelle said. Her husband was a corporal. "But he was mature before he left. I changed more."

Personally, I didn't feel like I'd changed at all.

Michelle had been married less than a year. She was twenty years old, cute and blond. A week after her husband left for Iraq, she gave birth to their first child. "When John was home, I never did the bills, never went out alone. So I did all that stuff. I had to be more strong, for him and for me, and the baby. And now it's kind of hard, too, because you've done everything by yourself, and then here comes someone just stepping in."

As we talked, John passed through the living room with the baby in his arms. He told me his son was awesome. Michelle looked happy. "I love being able to hand the baby off to him now," she said. "It's nice. I get to sleep in a little bit."

While John was in Iraq, he came upon a dead woman who had been blown in half — enemy fighters had used her as a human shield. She was still clutching her dead baby. He looked at her, and he saw his own wife and the son he had yet to hold. And now when he looked at Michelle, and held his son, he thought of that woman and her baby in Iraq, and the unknown man who loved them.

A few streets away from Michelle and John, I knocked at the back door of Frank's assistant's tiny house. Tony's gear from Iraq was still piled on the porch.

"It's too stanky to keep inside," said his wife, Heather, young and coltish as she waved me in. She added, "At least till he cleans it." Frank had been cleaning his, too, climbing into the shower each night with another piece of gear to wash it down.

Tony was an enlisted sailor from the hills of North Carolina. He looked like he could have carried Frank over his shoulder without any trouble. In Iraq, Tony's job was to protect Frank, since Frank wasn't allowed to carry a weapon. Frank liked to tell the story of how Tony would bellow, "Sir! Get your ass down!" and then crouch over Frank with his M-16 pointed in the direction of danger.

Tony saw what Frank saw. He was only twenty-one. I asked Heather, "Are you and Tony all right?" Before he left, I knew, they were fighting, that common, subconscious way of coping with the sadness of separation — pick a fight so you're glad to say goodbye.

"We're closer than ever," she said. "Now it's like — if he's in the bathroom, I'm in the bathroom."

"Really?" My eyebrows went up.

"I wasn't expecting it to be like this." Heather shrugged, as mystified as me. "He lost a bunch of weight. But he just seems like the same old Tony to me."

Like Michelle, Heather claimed she was the one who had changed the most during this, their first deployment. Looking back, I guess I changed the most during our first deployment, too. And I also changed during our second deployment right after September 11, which shook up my whole view of the world. Maybe Frank wasn't the only one who was brittle for that homecoming.

While Tony was in Iraq, Heather bought new furniture, the first major purchase she'd ever made by herself. In the four years since she and Tony met in high school, she had grown six inches. In the four months since he went to war, she had started to grow up. "He's noticed that," she told me. "He's a little more aggressive, a lot more protective over me. He's like, 'You're supposed to be off at eleven, it takes thirty minutes to get home, why aren't you home?' It's weird. I'm used to not being home till one, two, three o'clock in the morning from work. I figure if I'm getting paid for it, what does it matter? I guess he's trying to control me." She laughed. "But it's not working!"

Heather, Michelle, Jennifer, Sylvia — they were all so different from me, their husbands were different, and yet, talking to them I didn't feel alone in this anymore. We were all going through the same thing, more or less.

Pushing a grocery cart through the commissary with Frank, I asked, "Why does this homecoming seem to be so much better than the last one? For everyone?"

He shrugged. "It's a different battalion, for one thing."

The mission of this battalion was to move infantry from point A to point B in amphibious assault vehicles that could swim out the back of a ship, then rumble up onto the beach and across the land on tracks like tanks. The Marines called them "amtracs." Every Marine is a rifleman, but most of this amtrac battalion had never had to fire a shot off the firing range. They were mechanics and drivers and clerks.

The battalion Frank went to Afghanistan with was different. That was an infantry battalion, special operations capable, trained in reconnaissance, assaults, and defensive maneuvers, intensively drilled in the months leading up to deployment. An infantry battalion attracts people who are already gung ho, and then the training and the deployment wind them even tighter.

So this amtrac battalion was different. Still, I didn't entirely trust the apparent tranquility. I was waiting for the other shoe to drop.

Frank let his hair grow back, which for him meant a patch of stubble on top of his head. It was the Fourth of July and his battalion had been given another four days of liberty. We drove home to D.C. this time, shuffled through the metal detectors onto the Capitol lawn, and stretched out to listen to Dolly Parton. She sang "When Johnny Comes Marching Home" while old newsreel footage played on the big screens flanking the stage: soldiers coming home from the World Wars, a POW stepping off a plane from Vietnam and kneeling to kiss the ground, and more recent footage of soldiers, Marines, and sailors running to hug their families.

Looking up at the screens, I sensed that I was part of a long history of sacrifice, part of something noble and bigger than my small self, and yet also tragically repetitive. It made me cry.

Frank patted my hand. He seemed melancholy, too. "You OK?" I asked.

He shrugged. "I love my country. But . . ." He shrugged again, looked at the people on the grass around us, civilians mostly. "All the patriotism feels a little bit alienating, coming from people who did nothing but wave a flag." He didn't resent them. He was just experiencing that Different Planets feeling I had sometimes felt around people with no one in the fight. He went on, "We weren't patriotic over there. We never knew what was going on, it was just one big slog. We wanted to get it over with and get out. We weren't allowed to wave flags anyway."

Neither of us was in the mood to stay for the fireworks.

We were curled together on the couch, watching *Gangs of New York*. A Navy ship was shelling the nineteenth-century slums of New York City.

Wounded characters staggered through the chaos of smoke and dust, flickering flames, blackened buildings. Frank was tired when the movie started. I had expected him to be asleep by now. Instead, he was wide-awake and staring at the TV.

"This scene reminds me of the aftermath of that firefight north of An Nasiriyah," he said. He rolled the tape back. He pointed to one character, so covered in soot and dust you couldn't distinguish blood from sweat, saying, "That's what that dying guy sitting in shock near the burned-out bus looked like."

He talked for the next hour, inside in the living room, outside as we walked the dog. He talked through details I hadn't heard before. He wished he had offered the dying Iraqi water, though they were under orders not to stop. He wished he could have helped the civilian he saw gathering bodies by a bus, arranging them with stoop-shouldered care. He wished he'd done more for his Marines, though what more he could have done he didn't know. He wished he could go back to Iraq so he'd have an opportunity to redeem himself in his own eyes. He's always good in a crisis. But this time there were no crises. Just low-grade fear and horror.

I began to realize that as relaxed as he had seemed, part of him had been on guard against himself. Now, more than a month home, he was finally feeling safe enough to open up and look inside.

Frank's workdays were getting longer. Each morning another Marine or sailor stuck his head in Frank's office. *Hey, Chaps, you got a minute?* Longer-term symptoms of combat trauma were finally starting to surface in the battalion.

They would continue to do so. Within six months, Tony and Heather's marriage would break apart, her newfound independence applying only to him as she headed back home to her parents. In a year, another of these young men would send Frank an e-mail after they had both gone on to new assignments. He'd reach out to Frank for help because, while sitting on his couch watching the movie *The Legend of Bagger Vance*, a battle scene burst onto the screen, and as the camera focused on the dead bodies, he was overcome with nausea and threw up. *Since then,* he wrote in an e-mail, *every time a movie is on and it shows that type of crap I feel uncomfortable, which I think is bullshit. I've been home since last year, why all of the sudden would this happen? Since we were in the shit together, have you had any crap like this happen to you, and if so is this maybe normal, delayed, maybe alcohol-induced, reaction shit? I don't know but I don't like it.*

Frank wrote him back: *Things sometimes overwhelm me too . . .* On a practice field, olive-drab bayonet dummies look for a moment like burnt, bloated bodies; midnight thunderstorms turn into nightmare artillery and his shouting wakes me up. Frank explained to this young man that talking about it could help inoculate him against the power of such memories and reactions.

But for now, still at Camp Lejeune with symptoms just starting to surface, we were standing at the window in the dark before going to bed, watching a mountain range of storm clouds that lined the horizon to the west and north. The plane that brought Frank home came in from the north after flying over the Atlantic, and over Europe and the Middle East before that. Frank was on that plane for twenty hours.

"Who were you sitting next to all that time?" I asked.

He named an officer I didn't know. He didn't know him well either. I asked what he was like.

"Didn't matter," he said. "By the time they put us on the plane we'd already been awake twenty-four hours. We slept half the trip. It was heaven compared to the last deployment." He shook his head. "Tom."

All he said was the name, but suddenly, I remembered. And I understood. Tom was one of his roommates on the ship that took them to Afghanistan and then brought them home. Officers work out of their tiny staterooms, so Frank spent the better part of each day with only inches between himself and Tom. Tom read Frank's computer screen over his shoulder. Tom inserted himself into Frank's private conversations with his assistant. Tom nattered at him from his bunk at night. There was no downtime from Tom. Frank spent six months living on a ship with Tom and one month living away from him in a tent in Afghanistan. To this day, he looks back on Afghanistan not as a time of fear, and dirt, and discomfort, but as a vacation from Tom.

The storm clouds lit up from within. "Compare the stresses of this deployment with the last one," I said.

Frank didn't even hesitate. "The biggest difference was Tom."

Apparently, for Frank, a bad roommate was more stressful than getting shot at.

When we finally climbed into bed, we lay there, his hand on mine, and watched the distant storm flickering on the walls.

Jennifer, the ops officer's wife, once said to me, "I think people in the civilian world can never imagine how extreme the feeling of relief is when he comes back." That was all she said, but suddenly we were both shiny-eyed with tears. That was all she had to say. We both knew exactly the relief she was talking about, and more — we knew every moment that led up to it, no explanation required.

When the war started, now and then a vague, monstrous cloud of worry would descend on me and I'd have trouble breathing — anticipatory grief, though I had no name for it at the time. The only way to get a deep breath was to imagine The Worst That Could Happen, walk myself through every detail, make it real, and ordinary, and manageable. I imagined the knock at the door. I imagined the sober faces of the chaplain and the casualty assistance calls officer as the CACO announced the news that my husband was dead. Then I worked through the logistics — I'd need to call Frank's brother, so he could go tell their mother in person. I'd need to get out the funeral plans Frank had left behind, contact his church, and the morning of the funeral, have a good cry by myself before I had to sit through a public service, ride behind the hearse to Arlington, and listen to a bugler play "Taps." Imagining The Worst That Could Happen was like taking practical action, like scrubbing clean a festering wound. It helped keep me calm and strong. I clutched The Worst That Could Happen to my heart, where its weight kept me grounded when the ups and downs of the daily news threatened to spin me head over heels.

Once most of the combat was supposedly over, I was still careful not to let giddy relief unbalance me. Relief makes you weak. I noted the ongoing fatalities — the snipers, the Humvees overturned in traffic accidents, the plane that crashed full of Spanish soldiers headed for home from Afghanistan. I was determined not to let myself feel relieved until Frank was actually in my arms.

That night he came home, there I was, standing on the edge of the crowd in the dimly lit parking lot. Rosie was hiding behind my legs, tired of being petted by strangers. A woman pushed a stroller past us, wearing a red, white, and blue miniskirt. Children lunged at each other, wielding tiny American flags like swords. Then the DJ interrupted the music: "Your men have touched down at Cherry Point!"

Your men have touched down at Cherry Point.

The crowd screamed. For a moment I felt overstretched with emotion, as if I might pop, my eyes pricking with tears. But even now that Frank's plane had landed safely, I reminded myself that he still had to get from Cherry Point Marine Air Station to Camp Lejeune, over forty miles down the North Carolina coast. At any moment, a bus could blow a tire and slam into an embankment, or run off a bridge and sink straight to the bottom of a river.

Over the next three and a half hours, the DJ announced the slow progress of our husbands and sons and brothers and fathers toward us through the night. *Your men are on the buses and pulling out of Cherry Point!* The crowd cheered, then cheered again as the buses rolled through a nearby town, *They've made it to Swansboro,* cheered when they passed the guard gate at the edge of the base, *They're on board Camp Lejeune,* closer and closer, *They're at the armory.* They were just a few blocks away now, filing off the buses to turn in their weapons, filing back on.

Then I heard it. Everyone heard it, the deep rumbling hum of diesel engines. The headlights rounded the barracks and the DJ's speakers blasted a soundtrack as the towering buses roared in. It was nearly midnight; I'd been on my feet in that parking lot for four hours; I'd been rushing around for days, up at dawn getting the apartment ready because we'd been warned they might be gone a year, and yet here they were coming home after only four months. I should have felt exhausted, but I didn't. I felt as if I could run up a mountain. The buses pulled up in a line in front of us, stopped with a hiss, and a mass of men in desert tan uniforms spilled out into the crowd.

They all looked the same. I tried to make out faces coming off the buses, but I couldn't seem to see past the uniforms. After a few minutes, I spotted a face I knew — Tony, tall and searching over the heads of the crowd — and I saw Heather rushing to him, then stopping, suddenly shy. I hung back with Rosie and hoped Frank could find us. I watched one Marine after another bow into the arms that loved them.

Behind me, Rosie exploded into a fury of barking, the deep throaty bark she reserved for strangers. I turned to shush her, and there was a Marine, wearing a backpack and carrying a pair of heavy-duty cases, woofing at her, egging her on. And I was thinking, *If this guy's going to act like an idiot, I'm not going to call her off.* Then he dropped the cases and bent over, crossing his arms over his chest the way Frank and I do when we want her to jump up and greet us, and he said in a high, baby voice, "Rosie, come here, girl."

At the sound of Frank's voice, Rosie stopped barking, and I was so overwhelmed I was numb. Rosie strained toward him, trying to catch his scent. Automatically, I unhooked her leash. She leaped for him. He dropped to his knees. She licked his face then zinged around him, whimpering and yelping.

Frank reached for my hand to help him up, but I was already on my way down, on my knees with him, my arms around his neck. I buried my face in his shoulder and cried.

For millennia, men have been leaving home to go to war: More than two thousand years ago, fifty-nine thousand men left their homes in Carthage to go to war with Rome. Seven hundred years ago, forty thousand men left their homes in Japan to go to war with Mongol and Chinese invaders. Two hundred years ago, hundreds of thousands of men left their homes in France to go to war with the rest of Europe. For the past six months, more than one hundred thousand men, and women, too, had been leaving their homes in America to go to war with Iraq. And then, war after war, the survivors come home, and those of us who love them hold them in our arms and cry with terrible relief.

And when the day comes and we wake up and feel him warm beside us again, we raise up on one elbow, careful not to wake him, and look down at every feature of his sleeping face. And we whisper to ourselves in joyous disbelief: This is my *husband*.

SELECTED SOURCES

SELECTED SOURCES

The stories in this book are true. Some I observed firsthand. Some of the events and conversations were related to me by those who experienced them. Where possible, these remembered stories and my retelling of them have been corroborated. In addition, about half of the military and civilian DoD personnel I interviewed were allowed to speak with me without a public-affairs officer present. All the military spouses but one shared their stories without a military minder.

The people in these true stories are all real people; those who provided me with information are listed below. In a few instances, mental health professionals who discussed specific cases have changed some of the personal characteristics to ensure that the patients cannot be identified. But there are no composite or fictional characters. Most of the people named in this book have chosen to use their real names, or some form of their real names; a few have chosen to use pseudonyms to protect their privacy. The following names, listed in order of appearance in the book, are pseudonyms: Frank, David, Tiffany, Denise, Luis, Nanette, Butch, Christopher, Andre, Gabriel, Heather.

I also relied on books, news reports, and Web sites; I've included a representative list for those who may be interested in further reading. **The Web sites in bold print are especially good resources for military families in all service branches and civilians who want to support them by taking action.** These and other resources are available at www.kristinhenderson.com.

INTERVIEWS

Angela, military spouse; **Peter Anderson**, general manager, Mologne House, Walter Reed Army Medical Center; **Della Austin**, military parent; **Patricia Bahl**, military spouse; Lieutenant Colonel **Anthony Baker**, chief of Family Programs, National Guard Bureau; **Stacy Bannerman**, military spouse; **Stefani Barner**, military spouse; **Sally Ann Bean**, FRG cocoordinator, XVIII Airborne Corps, military spouse; **Anna Beck**, military spouse; **Becky**, military spouse; **Aster Black**, station manager, American Red Cross, Walter Reed Army Medical Center, military spouse; Specialist **Charlie Bootes**, U.S. Army; **Marissa Bootes**, military spouse; **Susan Born**, military spouse; **Martha Brown**, manager, Deployment and Mobilization Program, Army Community Services, XVIII Airborne Corps and Fort Bragg, military spouse; **John Bugay**, military spouse; **"Butch,"** military spouse, former technical sergeant, USAF; **Susan Byerly**, Ed.S, executive director, student services, chairman, military child task force, Cumberland County Schools, North Carolina; Lieutenant Colonel **Lillie Cannon**, USAF, retired, military spouse; **Ashley Chapman**, military spouse; **Catherine Chosewood**, military spouse; **Jean Claffey**, M.Ed., LPC, manager, Marine Corps Family Team Building, MCRD Parris Island, military spouse; **Jamie Cline**, military spouse; Staff Sergeant **Edward Collins**, U.S. Army; **Annie Cory**, military spouse; Colonel **Stephen Cozza**, chief of psychiatry, Walter Reed Army Medical Center; **"Denise,"** military spouse; Chaplain (Captain) **Christopher Dickey**, U.S. Army; Colonel **William Doukas**, chairman, Department of Orthopedics and Rehabilitation, Walter Reed Army Medical Center; Major **Teresa Duquette-Frame**, senior staff nurse, ICU, Walter Reed Army Medical Center, military spouse; **Vanessa Espinosa**, military spouse; **Chuck Fager**, director, Quaker House; Sergeant First Class **Robert Fanning**, U.S. Army, retired, military spouse; **Melinda Ferrin**, military spouse; **Christy Fessey**, military spouse; **Julia Foreman**, teacher, military spouse, former sergeant, U.S. Army; **Anna Fox**, military spouse; **Betsey Gonzales**, military spouse; **Marena Groll**, military spouse; **Hannah**, military fiancée; Chaplain (Major) **James Hartz**, U.S. Army; **Trish Head**, military spouse; **"Heather,"** military spouse; **Pam Heitz**, military fiancée; **Michelle Hellermann**, military spouse; **Marcia Herman-Giddens**, PA, Dr.PH, senior fellow, North Carolina Child Advocacy Institute; **Kimberly Huff**, military spouse; Sergeant Major **Debra Joas**, M.Ed., U.S. Army, retired, teacher, military spouse; **Marie Michele Johnson**, daycare provider; Senior Master Sergeant **Thomas Johnson**, MA Counseling, MAHRD, USAF, retired, school counselor; **Chuck Julian**, military parent, former sergeant, U.S. Army; **Sandy Julian**, military parent; **Rachel Kair**, military spouse; **Mary Keller**, D.Ed., executive director, Military Child Education Coalition; **Sylvia Kidd**, director, Family Programs, Association of the U.S. Army, military spouse; **Marcie Lewis**, military spouse; **Jennifer Lewton**, military spouse; **Jana Lord**, coordinator, Army Family Team Building and Army Family Action Plan programs in Europe, military spouse; **Camilla Maki**, military spouse; **Jennifer Marner**, military spouse; Sergeant First Class **William McKay**, U.S. Army, retired, coordinator, Community Life Program, Fort Bragg; **Teresa Metzdorf**, military spouse; **Ken Meyer**, military spouse; **Michelle**, military spouse; **Kevin Miller**, former sergeant, U.S. Army; **Nicki Miller**, military spouse; **Michelle Nowak**, military spouse; **Diana Ohman**, director, DoD Dependents Schools in Europe; **Rebecca Paden**, military spouse; **Pam**, military spouse; **Dorothy Parent**, military spouse; Lieutenant Colonel **Joseph Pecko**, chief, Department of Social Work, Womack Army Medical Center; **Joanne Perdok**, military spouse; **Christine Perry**, military spouse; **Lori Pittari**, military spouse; **Beth Pratt**, military spouse; Private E-2 **Luigi Pratt**, U.S. Army; **Joyce Wessel Raezer**, director, Government Relations, National Military Family Association, military spouse; **Trish Rierson**, military spouse; **Jennifer Gaines Riley**, military spouse, former specialist, U.S. Army; **Debbie Roath**, military spouse; **Candance Robison**, military spouse; **Carolina Rodriguez**, staff, Deployment and Mobilization Program, Army Community Services, XVIII Airborne Corps and Fort Bragg, military spouse; **Victoria Rogers**, military spouse; **Jessica Salamon**, military spouse; **Samantha**, military spouse; Captain **Matthew Scherer**, assistant chief, Amputee Physical Therapy Section, Walter Reed Army Medical Center; **Daysha Scruggs**, military spouse; **Alex Shirley**, military spouse; **Lynn Sinclair**, military spouse; **Starla Smith**, military spouse; **Brad Snyder**, CEO, Armed Forces Services Corporation; Colonel **Dennis Spiegel**, U.S. Army, retired, deputy director, Army Emergency Relief; **Joanne Stanley**, LMSW-ACP, behavioral health care manager, Department of Social Work, Womack Army Medical Center; **Joanne Steen**, military spouse; **Catherine Stokoe**, director, Navy Fleet and Family Support Program, Commander, Navy Installation Command, military spouse; **Sylvia Tadeo**, military spouse; Lieutenant Colonel **Regina Tellitocci**, head nurse, Orthopedics Ward, Walter Reed Army Medical Center; "Tiffany," military spouse; Colonel **Mary Torgersen**, director, U.S. Army Casualty and Memorial Affairs; **Anna Torres**, military spouse; **Jody Tucker**, military spouse, former master sergeant, Air National Guard; Private First Class **Erin Ukleja**, U.S. Army, military spouse; Colonel **Michael Wagner**, Ph.D., U.S. Army, retired, director, Medical Family Assistance Center, Walter Reed Army Medical Center; Chaplain (Major) **Jeffrey Watters**, U.S. Army; **Melinda Whitney**, military spouse; Sergeant Major **Gary Wieland**, M.Ed., U.S. Army, retired, teacher; **Rebecca Wilkins**, military spouse; **Clara Wright**, military spouse and parent; **Julie Yocum**, military spouse.

BOOKS AND REPORTS

Achilles in Vietnam: Combat Trauma and the Undoing of Character and *Odysseus in America: Combat Trauma and the Trials of Homecoming,* Jonathan Shay, M.D., Ph.D., Scribner, 1994. A VA psychiatrist uses the *Iliad* and the *Odyssey,* the ancient poems about the Trojan War and its aftermath, to explain how war affects today's warriors. These two books describe the causes of post-traumatic stress disorder, how it affects war-fighters and their families, how it can be treated, and, better yet, how to prevent it. These are intense books written in everyday language for professionals and laypeople alike. Combat veterans should use caution when considering whether to read these two books.

Acts of War: The Behavior of Men in Battle, Richard Holmes, The Free Press, 1985. A soldier's-eye view of what it's like to engage in combat; reveals why veterans can look back and say going to war was both the best and worst experience of their lives.

Black Hawk Down, Mark Bowden, Grove/Atlantic, 1999. The definitive account of the battle of Mogadishu, which Trish Rierson's husband survived only to die two days later in a random shelling.

The Book of War: Sun-Tzu, *The Art of Warfare,* and Karl von Clausewitz, *On War,* Modern Library, 2000. Analysis of warcraft from the two most influential military theorists in the East and West. While Sun-Tzu is an easy read, Clausewitz's tome is often heavy sledding.

Invisible Women: Junior Enlisted Army Wives, Margaret C. Harrell, Rand, 2001. Pioneering look at a group that had been mostly overlooked prior to this report. The women's stories are presented in a series of case studies, in their own words.

Military Allowances and Federal and State Safety Net Programs, National Military Family Association, March 2004. The financial impact of deployment on military families, especially those with disabled children.

Military Compensation in the Age of Two-Income Households, E. Casey Wardynski, Rand, 2000. Analysis of the military spouse income gap — women married to military men tend to earn much less than women married to civilians.

A New Social Compact: A Reciprocal Partnership Between the Department of Defense, Service Members, and Families, Military Family Resource Center, Department of Defense, March 2002. A review of the relationship between DoD and military families.

On Death and Dying: What the Dying Have to Teach Doctors, Nurses, Clergy, and Their Own Families, Elisabeth Kübler-Ross, M.D., Scribner, 1969. The groundbreaking book on the five stages of death: denial and isolation, anger, bargaining, depression, and acceptance.

On Killing: The Psychological Cost of Learning to Kill in War and Society, Lieutenant Colonel Dave Grossman, Little Brown and Company, 1995. An unflinching examination of a subject our society prefers to avoid, and the negative impact this avoidance has on the people we ask to kill for us.

The Pity of War, Niall Ferguson, The Penguin Press, 1998. Provocative analysis of the causes of World War I and its effects on the nations and soldiers who fought it. That war still has lessons to teach us today.

Reducing Collateral Damage on the Homefront: Child Abuse Homicides Within Military Families and Communities in North Carolina: Facts and Recommendations, North Carolina Child Advocacy Institute, September 2004. An analysis of sixteen years of child homicide data in North Carolina.

The Roman Army: 31 B.C.–A.D. 33, A Sourcebook, Brian Campbell, Routledge, 1994. A collection of original, ancient source material that reveals everyday details about the Roman military and the lives of the people who served in it.

Serving the Homefront: An Analysis of Military Family Support from September 11, 2001, through March 31, 2004, National Military Family Association, July 2004. Study of military families during deployment, describing the greatest needs, best practices, and recommendations in the areas of communications, training, partnerships, and community support.

Soldiers and Civilians: The Civil-Military Gap and American National Security, Peter D. Feaver and Richard H. Kohn, editors, MIT Press, 2001. An exhaustive study of the growing gap between the military community and civilian society and the implications for American democracy and national security. Should be required reading for every citizen.

Surviving Deployment: A Guide for Military Families, Karen M. Pavlicin, Elva

Resa Publishing, 2003. An encyclopedic reference book full of carefully researched facts and tips from a military wife with extensive experience at getting through deployments.

Vietnam Wives: Facing the Challenges of Life with Veterans Suffering Post-Traumatic Stress, Aphrodite Matsakis, Ph.D., The Sidran Press, 1996. Nuts and bolts guidance for anyone living with a veteran from any war who's suffering from PTSD, the most severe form of combat trauma.

We Were Soldiers Once . . . and Young: Ia Drang—The Battle That Changed the War in Vietnam, Lt. Gen. Harold G. Moore (Ret.) and Joseph L. Galloway, Random House, 1992. Written by the husband of Julia Compton Moore, who was instrumental in changing the Army's casualty notification procedures. Includes a description of how the old notification system, suddenly overwhelmed with casualties, relied on taxi drivers to deliver death notices.

Working Around the Military: Challenges to Military Spouse Employment and Education, Margaret C. Harrell, Nelson Lim, Laura Werber Castaneda, and Daniela Golinelli, Rand National Defense Research Institute, 2004. Research and analysis that challenges assumptions about why military spouses earn less than their civilian counterparts.

NEWSPAPER ARTICLES AND MEDIA REPORTS

"Army Pushes a Sweeping Overhaul of Basic Training," Thom Shanker, *New York Times*, August 4, 2004. The lack of a clear frontline in Iraq and how that's affecting Army training.

"As Ranks Dwindle in a Reserve Unit, Army's Woes Mount," Greg Jaffe, *Wall Street Journal*, August 5, 2004. The challenges faced by activated Guard members, reservists, and their families.

"Battlefield Aid for Soldiers' Battered Psyches," Steven Lee Myers, *New York Times*, June 21, 2003. The Army's efforts to improve treatment for soldiers suffering from combat trauma.

"Body Armor Saves Lives in Iraq," Vernon Loeb and Theola Labbé, *Washington Post*, December 4, 2003. The latest Interceptor vests and the shortage of them early in the war.

"Civilians Vital to DoD Mission," Staff Sgt. Kathleen T. Rhem, U.S. Army, American Forces Press Service, June 5, 2000. The kinds of work performed by civilians employed by the military.

"Clogged VA Delays Iraq Vets' Care," Gregg Krupa, *Detroit News*, November 8, 2004. More than a year and a half into the war, a growing backlog holds up treatment and disability claims for as long as six months.

"Coast Guard Tabs Ships, Crews for Deployment," Gerry J. Gilmore, American Forces Press Service, February 26, 2003. Though it's not widely known, the Coast Guard, too, deploys to the Persian Gulf.

"Combat Duty in Iraq and Afghanistan, Mental Health Problems, and Barriers to Care," Charles W. Hoge, M.D., Carl A. Castro, Ph.D., Stephen C. Messer, Ph.D.,

Dennis McGurk, Ph.D., Dave I. Cotting, Ph.D., and Robert L. Koffman, M.D., M.P.H., *New England Journal of Medicine*, July 1, 2004. Revealing report on a survey of the mental health and attitudes of soldiers and Marines returning from combat zones.

"Coming Home Means Counseling for Troops," Estes Thompson, Associated Press, March 15, 2004. Fort Bragg chaplains and counselors conduct briefings for returning soldiers.

"Demonstrators Mobilize for Anti-war Rally," Greg Barnes, *Fayetteville Observer*, March 11, 2003. Interviews with rally organizers and groups opposed to the rally.

"The Emotional Cycle of Deployment," Kathleen Vestal Logan, *Proceedings*, February 1987. The emotional stages homefront spouses experience during deployment.

"Essex Jct. Woman Struggles While Husband Serves," John Briggs, *Burlington Free Press*, January 31, 2004. A National Guard spouse deals with uncertainty during deployment.

"A Father Transformed by Anguish," David Finkel, *Washington Post*, January 15, 2005. Followup story about the father who set himself on fire after being notified that his son had been killed in Iraq.

"Final Six Months of 2004 Deadliest Ever for U.S. Forces in Iraq," *Agence France Presse*, January 1, 2005. U.S. general declares attacks in Iraq sometimes topped 100 per day.

"A Flood of Troubled Soldiers Is in the Offing, Experts Predict," Scott Shane, *New York Times*, December 16, 2004. Historical trends and current surveys indicate combat veterans will need help adjusting.

"Fort Bragg Killings Raise Alarm About Stress," Barbara Starr, CNN, July 27, 2002. Over the course of six weeks, four soldiers, three just back from Afghanistan, killed their wives; a brief summary.

"Guard, Reserve Service Takes High Financial Toll," Howard Berkes and Marisa Penaloza, NPR, *Morning Edition*, March 15, 2005. Family income drops for many mobilized Guard members and reservists.

"Homeless Iraq Vets Showing Up at Shelters," Mark Benjamin, United Press International, December 7, 2004. Advocates fear they are the leading edge of a new generation of homeless vets.

"Insurance Policy: Troops Freezing Sperm," Frank Buckley, CNN, January 30, 2003. Gulf War veteran advises younger soldier to store sperm before deploying.

"Iraq War Is Affecting Small State in a Big Way," Jonathan Finer, *Washington Post*, February 9, 2005. Rural Vermont and multiethnic Hawaii have highest National Guard mobilization rates.

"IRR Call-up Puts Lives in Disarray," Donna Leinwand, *USA Today*, August 5, 2004. The disruption that results when inactive reservists are called up.

"Is Anyone Ever Truly Prepared to Kill?" Jane Lampman, *Christian Science Monitor*, September 29, 2004. The experience of killing in combat.

"Medical Evacuations in Iraq War Hit 18,000," Mark Benjamin, United Press International, March 31, 2004. A report to Congress on the medical care received by wounded soldiers declares some of it very good, some of it bad.

"Memories of War Strain Families," Malcolm Garcia, *Kansas City Star*, August 23, 2004. Another battle awaits veterans at home as many are wary of counseling.

"Military, Civilians Follow Different Callings," Rudi Williams, American Forces Press Service, May 30, 2000. Civilian perceptions of military service members don't always match reality.

"Military Families Share Pain and Joy," Sandra Pedicini, *Orlando Sentinel*, July 18, 2003. The concerns of homefront spouses at Fort Stewart, Georgia.

"Military in State Pays a Big Dividend," Al Greenwood, *Fayetteville Observer*, February 12, 2004. Statistics on the economic impact of military bases in North Carolina.

"Military Mirrors Working-Class America," David M. Halbfinger and Steven A. Holmes, *New York Times*, March 30, 2003. Demographic information on who joins the military.

"Military's Response to Rapes, Domestic Abuse Falls Short," Amy Herdy and Miles Moffeit, *Denver Post*, November 18, 2003. Investigation into violence within the military.

"Military Wife Rebuked for E-Mail," Christian Davenport, *Washington Post*, July 27, 2003. Worried spouse sends a speculative e-mail to her FRG list and the group's leaders respond.

"On the Prowl!" Paul Fain, *Military Money*, Summer 2004. Payday lenders charge young cash-strapped service members high interest rates.

"The Painful Truth," Steve Silberman, *Wired*, 2005. The pain caused by physical injuries on the battlefield and the medical advances that are helping to control it.

"The Permanent Scars of Iraq," Sara Corbett, *New York Times Magazine*, February 15, 2004. Wounded veterans struggle to reintegrate into civilian life.

"The Price of Valor," Dan Baum, *The New Yorker*, July 12 & 19, 2004. The effects of combat on soldiers coming home from Iraq; also looks back at earlier wars.

"Reservists, Guard Troops Find Military Benefits Lacking," Vicky O'Hara, NPR, *All Things Considered*, March 3, 2005. Despite improvements, many wounded Guard members and reservists still enduring long waits for care and benefits.

"Reservists May Face Longer Tours of Duty," Bradley Graham, *Washington Post*, January 6, 2005. The reasons behind the increases in call-ups.

"Returning Home: Warrior Transition Program," Mary D. Karcher, *Leatherneck*, July 2004. The Marine Corps' program to help Marines return from combat zones to normal lives.

"Service Members Urged to Attend Legal Affairs Long Before Deployment," Gerry J. Gilmore, American Forces Press Service, August 18, 2003. Military attorneys provide free services that help service members with their legal readiness before deployment.

"Sick, Wounded Troops Held in Squalor," Mark Benjamin, United Press International, October 17, 2003. The conditions in which some soldiers lived while in "medical hold."

"Soldiers Facing Extended Tours," Josh White, *Washington Post*, June 3, 2004. The Pentagon's stop-loss policy, which some call a draft by another name.

"Soldier's Sperm Offers Biological Insurance Policy," Arthur Caplain, Ph.D.,

MSNBC, November 24, 2003. The ethical issues of sperm donation by service members.

"Spouses Learn to Deal with Grief," Kevin Maurer, *Fayetteville Observer*, December 13, 2003. The 82nd Airborne chaplains conduct a seminar about anticipatory grief.

"Steady Drop in Black Army Recruits," Josh White, *Washington Post*, March 8, 2005. Blacks and women proving harder to recruit as Iraq War continues.

"Stress Levels High Among Service Members, Some Red Flags Raised," Donna Miles, American Forces Press Service, March 9, 2004. In a confidential survey of service members, one-third report feeling stressed-out by their work.

"Suicides in Iraq, Questions at Home," Theola Labbé, *Washington Post*, February 19, 2004. Examines a rise in suicides among deployed service members.

"Troops Make Stop at Sperm Bank," Vicky Eckenrode, *Augusta Chronicle*, January 31, 2003. Soldiers in Georgia store sperm before deploying.

"Tiny Corner of Louisiana Mourns Six Soldiers," Manuel Roig-Franzia, *Washington Post*, January 10, 2005. The impact of relying on National Guard troops to fight our wars, especially when a single unit from one area sustains multiple casualties.

"Trauma of Iraq War Haunting Thousands Returning Home," William M. Welch, *USA Today*, February 28, 2005. Service members who are psychologically injured after combat exposure.

"U.S. Marines Suffer Most Suicides in Five Years," Reuters, December 21, 2004. Statistics on unusually high number of suicides among Marines in a time of war.

"Vermont Leads Nation in Iraq War Casualties," Wilson Ring, Associated Press, January 29, 2005. Across the nation, rural areas send a high percentage of their population to the armed forces and as a result experience a higher number of casualties per capita.

"Vets Say Dubya Ignores Their Needs," Ann McFeatters, *Pittsburgh Post-Gazette*, February 24, 2005. Budget shortfalls at the VA limit the care veterans receive.

"War on TV Affects Students of Deployed Parents, Parents, Teachers," Sergeant First Class Doug Sample, U.S. Army, American Forces Press Service, March 31, 2003. Statistics and guidance on how to help military children deal with media reports on the war.

"Where Talk of War Includes 'Mom' or 'Dad,'" Sara Rimer, *New York Times*, February 14, 2003. The effect of deployment on children.

"Women in Combat Draw Little Comment," Matt Kelley, Associated Press, January 4, 2004. Report on the new role of female service members in the Iraq War.

SELECTED WEB SITES

www.fatherhood.org/deployeddads.asp
"10 Ways to Stay Involved with Your Children During Deployment." Advice from the National Fatherhood Initiative.
www. ausa.org

"Association of the United States Army." The latest in Army-related news, legislation, and family programs.

www.defenselink.mil/specials/outreachpublic/barriers.html

"Barriers Between Civilian, Military Need Breaking." Report on the growing gap between the military and civilian worlds from the American Forces Press Service.

www.objector.org/girights

"Conscientious Objection." Overview of the process service members go through when applying for conscientious objector status. Also, info on the Delayed Entry Program.

www.dmdc.osd.mil/ids/archive/vietnam/body.htm

"Comparison of Service Populations of the Vietnam Conflict and the Persian Gulf War." Demographic information.

www.usuhs.mil/psy/courage.html

"Courage to Care." Fact sheets and health information for professionals serving the military community and for military families, from the Uniformed Services University of the Health Sciences.

www.defendamerica.mil

"Defend America." Suggestions and resources to help civilians support the troops.

www.usarec.army.mil/im/formpub/REC_PUBS/r601_95.pdf

"Delayed Entry Program." Handbook for recruiters.

www.us-army-info.com/pages/dep.html

"Delayed Entry Program." Overview of the program for recruits.

www.dodea.edu

"Department of Defense Education Activity." Facts about DoDEA, the military school system and support for teachers and parents.

www.deploymentconnections.org

"Deployment Resources." Deployment resources for families, military members, and reservists from the Department of Defense, with links to private support and advocacy organizations.

www.vnh.org/FM22-51/07FM2251.html

"Field Manual No. 22-51: Leaders' Manual for Combat Stress Control, Chapter 7: Stress Issues in Army Operations." An introduction to the challenges of modern warfare, including urban warfare, and how to prevent combat trauma.

www.goldstarwives.org

"Goldstar Wives." Information and support for military widows.

www.guardfamily.org

"Guard Family Support." Family support info for all geographically dispersed military families, including Guard members, reservists, and active-duty.

www.gulfweb.org/bigdoc/selfhelp.cfm

"Gulf War Syndrome." Information from the National Gulf War Resource Center; more resources at www.ngwrc.org.

www.militarychild.org

"Military Child Education Coalition." Resources for teachers and military parents, including info on children and deployment. Additional resources from the DoD at www.militarystudent.org.

www.mfso.org

"Military Families Speak Out." An organization created by military families for the purpose of opposing the Iraq War.

www.mfrc.dod.mil/stat.cfm

"Military Family Resource Center." 2003 demographic data on military service members and their families.

www.mfri.purdue.edu

"Military Family Research Institute." A variety of helpful reports and resources for and about military families.

www.militaryonesource.com

"Military OneSource." Information hotline available 24/7 for military members and their families. Provides answers to anything, from how to boil water to how to find childcare providers in your area. Also, offers referrals for free confidential counseling with a civilian therapist outside the military system — online or 1-800-342-9647.

www.globalsecurity.org/military/ops/mout.htm

"Military Operations in Urban Terrain." An overview of urban warfare.

usmilitary.about.com/cs/generalpay/a/retirementpay.htm

"Military Pay." An overview of retirement pay.

usmilitary.about.com/library/milinfo/pay/blenlistedsalary.htm

"Military Pay." Income data from 2003.

www.militarywives.com

"Military Wives." Support for wives and husbands of military personnel in all services, including the Reserves; includes forums for connecting with other spouses.

www.ncptsd.va.gov

"National Center for PTSD." Information on post-traumatic stress disorder from the Department of Veterans Affairs; includes info for military spouses and children.

www.arng.army.mil/history

"National Guard History." How the Guard evolved from state militias.

www.nmfa.org

"National Military Family Association." Support and advocacy for military families.

www.army.mil/organization/unitdiagram.html

"Operational Unit Diagram." Introduction to how the Army is organized.

www.psych.org/public_info/ptsd.cfm

"Post-traumatic Stress Disorder." Information from the American Psychiatric Association.

www.quakerhouse.org

"Quaker House." Information and assistance for service members who believe they've been discriminated against or need help seeking a legal discharge.

www.defenselink.mil/specials/insignias/enlisted.html

"Rank and Insignia." A complete chart.

www.military.com/Resources/ResourceFileView?file=Reserve_Ready.htm

"The Ready Reserve." Explains the structure of the National Guard and Reserves.

www.bt.cdc.gov/agent/smallpox/vaccination

"Smallpox Vaccination." Information from the Centers for Disease Control and Prevention.

www.defenselink.mil/news/Feb2003/d20030225sofa.pdf

"Status of Forces Survey." Reveals the state of military morale.

www.geocities.com/Pentagon/6453/lessonsintro.html

"Urban Warfare Quick Look: Lessons Learned from Russian, Israeli and British Operations." Real life case studies and what war-fighters can learn from them.

www.taps.org

"Tragedy Assistance Program for Survivors." Support and information for surviving military family members.

www.defenselink.mil/specials/outreachpublic/index.htm

"Why We Need a Military." Information from the Pentagon that attempts to narrow the gap between the military and civilian society.